FIONNUALA NÍ AOLÁIN was born in Dublin in 1967 and moved to Connemara in 1971. She was educated in Galway and is a native Irish speaker. In 1985 she won an Irish national scholarship to attend Lester B. Pearson College in Vancouver, Canada. In 1987 she undertook an LL.B. at Queen's University Belfast, and further gained a Ph.D. there in 1997. In Belfast she was a member of the Committee on the Administration of Justice (CAJ), and was on its executive board from 1990 to 1993. In 1991 she was awarded the Civil Liberties Trust Studentship at Queen's, was a Fulbright Scholar in 1993–4, was a visiting scholar at Harvard Law School, 1993–4, and a Van Leer Fellow at the Van Leer Institute in Jerusalem, 1997–8. She was an Assistant Professor of Law at the Hebrew University, Israel, 1997–2000, and is currently a visiting professor at Columbia University, New York, and Professor of Law at the University of Ulster.

D1610844

The POLITICS OF FORCE

Conflict Management and State Violence in Northern Ireland

Fionnuala Ní Aoláin

Foreword by John Wadham

THE
BLACKSTAFF
PRESS

BELFAST

First published in 2000 by
The Blackstaff Press Limited
Blackstaff House, Wildflower Way, Apollo Road,
Belfast BT12 6TA, Northern Ireland

This book has received support from the
Cultural Diversity Programme of the Community Relations Council,
which aims to encourage acceptance and understanding of cultural diversity.
The views expressed do not necessarily reflect those of the
NI Community Relations Council.

Typeset by Techniset Typesetters, Newton-le-Willows, Merseyside

Printed in Ireland by the Leinster Leader Limited

A CIP catalogue record for this book
is available from the British Library

ISBN 0-85640-668-6

www.blackstaffpress.com

for
Pamela

Contents

Foreword

Liberty (the National Council for Civil Liberties) welcomes the publication of *The Politics of Force*. The Civil Liberties Trust, Liberty's sister organisation, had a tradition of providing financial assistance to postgraduate students at Queen's University Belfast who were working in the areas of human rights and civil liberties. Fionnuala Ní Aoláin was one of the most able of these and this book is the result of many years of hard work. The results are impressive and Liberty and the Civil Liberties Trust are very happy to be associated with it.

The use of lethal force by the state goes to the very heart of human rights. The frequency and circumstances of the use of such force are key issues in the assessment of the degree of compliance with, for instance, Article 2 of the European Convention on Human Rights. Perhaps as important as how the death occurred is the systems that are in place to investigate and inquire into deaths at the hands of state actors. Without adequate and robust systems unnecessary deaths will reoccur, without adequate sanctions law-enforcement officials have impunity.

Northern Ireland has seen too many people killed during the conflict. Each death is a tragedy no matter what the politics or intentions of the person killed. Thousands were killed by killers from both sides of the divide. Many of those killed were soldiers, police officers and others connected to law-enforcement agencies. Some of the relatives and friends of those killed will be unhappy with the principle of human rights which asserts that we must respect the rights of those who were doing the killing. This book starts from the premise that everyone has a right to life and questions whether all those killed at the hands of the security forces needed to die. The conclusion is that they did not.

Anyone with even a passing interest in the conflict in Northern Ireland will know that there have been many controversial deaths involving the police and the army. So intense has the conflict been that merely to raise questions about some of these deaths has been controversial itself. Even those who, like John Stalker, were asked to investigate collusion between the security services and paramilitary groups have had problems. Too often questions about controversial deaths have been ignored because it has been assumed that those who raised the questions were doing so for ideological reasons. In many cases it is assumed the questions have been asked because they themselves supported violence or one side in the conflict. The space for the objective analysis of human rights compliance was squeezed out by the conflicting ideologies of nationalists and loyalists.

Of course some of the controversial deaths were investigated in great detail, although not always with sufficient independence. It is heartening to see a new inquiry into those who died on Bloody Sunday. It was also important that the European Court of Human Rights analysed the death of the PIRA members in Gibraltar. However, this is the only book to look at all the deaths that involved police officers and the army in Northern Ireland.

Some of those who were killed in such circumstances were killers themselves. Often they were killed to prevent them inflicting violence on others. However, what emerges from this study is a systemic failure by the state to protect their rights. Of course, to extend a positive right to life to those who are intent on killing others is not easy but it is in these circumstances that the principles of human rights are at most risk and must therefore be most jealously guarded. Those who have responsibility for upholding this most fundamental right have a duty to make sure it is respected, even by police officers who are confronting those who wish to kill them.

Unfortunately this book demonstrates that there has been a failure to uphold this most precious right. It is apparent that many deaths were unnecessary. Unfortunately the analysis of these deaths must go further and raises very controversial issues. It seems that during at least some periods some deaths were part of a clear strategy on behalf of the authorities. This strategy appears to have accepted that the use of lethal force could be used as a tactic and that certain deaths were intended at the outset. Finally this appears to have been a strategy accepted, if not promoted, by those fairly high up the chain of command.

The analysis of the different phases of the use of lethal force and the connection between these and other patterns, particularly the use of emergency powers, is fascinating and at the same time troubling. This book will undoubtedly be used by those who see conspiracies everywhere but its thesis is more sophisticated. There is no doubt that there were conspiracies on the part of those in the law-enforcement agencies to ensure that terrorists and others were killed but the truth is that the extent of 'leeway' allowed or 'set-piece' ambushes encouraged was part of a bigger pattern. This is what makes this book so fascinating.

Even where in the fewer cases the death could not have been avoided the procedures designed to investigate deaths have been woefully inadequate. Even simple rules on securing the scene of the death and collecting up the crucial forensic evidence were ignored. Delays and systemic failures in the inquest system have ensured that there has been no authoritative and independent assessment of the deaths of these people. The complaints systems and the civil courts have also been inadequate.

The system of adjudication before the European Court of Human Rights has also failed. It has failed partly for domestic reasons. Lawyers have been unsure of how to use the system, cases have run into the sand because of problems in domestic proceedings and funding for cases has not been available. The system has also failed because of delays. However, the political and controversial nature of these deaths has made it very difficult for the court to be truly objective. The controversial nature of these cases was demonstrated by the threat of the then UK government to remove itself from the court mechanisms completely following the decision in *McCann* which involved the shooting by the SAS of the three PIRA members in Gibraltar. The court in these and in other terrorist cases have leaned too far towards the respondent state. Finally, the court system has yet to develop a way of dealing properly with systemic abuse of rights. The use of lethal force in Northern Ireland seems to demonstrate a clear need to develop ways of dealing with patterns of state violations and the need to go beyond the instant case to look at the processes and procedures. Nevertheless, the final decision in *McCann* was a brave one for the court and it has gained in stature as a result.

Peace in Northern Ireland is an important prize and support for those fighting for peace is crucial. This book is a valuable contribution to our understanding of the conflict in Northern Ireland, the role of the law-enforcement agencies, and the need to respect the human rights of all. I hope that we have seen the end of killings by all sides and that the right to life for everyone in Northern Ireland will be respected more carefully in the future.

JOHN WADHAM
Director, Liberty
London

Preface and acknowledgements

Methodology

Northern Ireland is a society facing the arduous task of transition from conflict to coexistence. In that process a dual challenge is presented to its multiple communities. The first is imagining and implementing new structures and institutions of governance. The second is coming to terms with its history and more particularly acknowledging the reality and depth of the experience of conflict itself. It is the latter portion of this challenge which defines the scope of this book's examination. Part of the narrative of any internal conflict is a disclosure of the state's role in facilitating, combating and managing conflict. This book seeks to examine in detail the manner in which the United Kingdom has sought to contain and control an internal conflict occurring within its recognised international borders between 1969 and 1994. As a liberal western democracy operating within the rule of law, the reality of internal conflict has exposed particular stresses and weaknesses for the dominant state experiencing the Northern Ireland conflict. This study of the conflict reveals the mechanisms of conflict control which become particularly significant to a generally democratic state experiencing internal crisis. These can be broadly categorised as first, the use of legal mechanisms to limit conflict; second, the use of force to quell internal dissent. Thus, this book is concerned with the use, transformation and manipulation of law in its interface with exigency. It is also concentrated upon the use of force by agents of the state.

The analysis of the use of force contained in this book is wholly new, and based upon extensive empirical research. Much of the discussion on the use of lethal force in Northern Ireland is replete with unsupported political and legal generalisations. This book seeks to give unequivocal authority to the discussion of the use of lethal force in the jurisdiction by firm grounding in empirical authority. Given the controversy associated with many of these deaths, this methodology section seeks to make clear from the outset the method of investigation and analysis which underpins all empirical assertions contained in this work.

The empirical analysis is based on a complete census of all lethal force deaths that occurred in the jurisdiction between 1969 and 1994. It should also be noted that this category includes all lethal force killings which relate directly to the Northern Ireland conflict, hence, for example, the inclusion of the deaths of Mairead Farrell, Daniel McCann and Sean Savage in Gibraltar during March 1988. It is important to note that the study is not based on a random dataset of the target study group. The requirement for inclusion in the study was that the victim's fatality had to be caused by an agent of the state who was on duty,[1] or acting in pursuit of duty obligations to the state when force was exercised against a citizen. 'Agent of the state' implies a law-enforcer who was recognised (by uniform, licence or confirmation) as a member of a state institution,[2] whose function is the maintenance of law and order on behalf of the state. Not all deaths included on the dataset are strictly conflict related. Citizens killed by agents of the state while engaged in (or suspected of) ordinary criminal activity are also included. This is because any comprehensive study of the use of force by a democratic state must take account of those deaths which occur as part of the ordinary law-enforcement activities of state actors. These fatalities also provide a valuable source of comparison to those deaths which are directly conflict related. Also included in the study are deaths of security force personnel (soldiers and policemen) killed while on duty by other state agents acting in a (generally mistaken) law-enforcement capacity. Again, these deaths provide a valuable source of comparative analysis to the deaths of civilians and others killed by state use of force.

Certain deaths are completely excluded from this analysis. Thus, for example, this study does not examine controversial deaths which observers suggest resulted from collusion or complicity on the part of state agents with members of paramilitary organisations. Also excluded from the dataset are all vehicular deaths caused by agents of the state while on duty. A number of these deaths are extremely controversial, and raise many similar issues of legal accountability identified as relevant to the cases included and analysed from the dataset.[3] However, it was felt that legal categorisation in these cases was imprecise and causality difficult to determine, and thus all such cases were entirely excluded from analysis. Deaths caused by the use of force by security force personnel acting off duty are excluded from this study (and specifically criminal acts of violence by state agents). Such actions do not generally leave agents of the state open to argue in any criminal investigation or proceedings that they were acting in pursuit of a law-enforcement purpose, facilitating an array of legal justifications for the use of force to come into play.

It is acknowledged that many of these deaths are controversial and any categorisation will be subject to stringent review. Thus, fatalities where causality was uncertain or significantly disputed were excluded from this study.[4] Nonetheless, it remains certain that inclusion or exclusion from such a study will remain contested for a certain number of cases, which inevitably arises in a study which pertains to sensitive and unresolved deaths in a situation of conflict. It should also be acknowledged that in the time frame examined, over three thousand persons lost their lives as a result of the conflict in Northern Ireland. Of that number, this study is focused on what appears to be a small subset of 350 persons.

Identifying the individuals who were victims of the use of force was relatively unproblematic. Court records, newspaper clippings, access to existing databases, such as that held by the Irish Information Partnership and the much appreciated use of the inquest records of the Belfast City Coroner, were the starting point. The more difficult information to obtain was detailed breakdown of the relevant facts in each case. In particular, identifying the causal aspects of fatality and the legal and investigatory procedures which followed death was much more troublesome. Here the sources were varied. The study followed a network approach. Family members were interviewed when identified and willing to talk about the loss of a family member. Members of the clergy who had maintained records and details of incidents which occurred in their communities gave valuable amplification to particular deaths. Solicitors who had represented family members in legal proceedings after a fatality were also interviewed. A number of grassroots organisations, whose genesis was a particular death or series of deaths, provided information which is not generally in the public domain. These included the Cullyhanna Justice Group, Relatives for Justice, the Campaign Against Plastic

Bullets, and the Bloody Sunday Justice Campaign. The bibliography to this book also lists the various academic and journalistic sources which were used to glean information about particular incidents.

It should be pointed out that there is some disparity in the amount of information available on each individual fatality. Deaths during the critical militarisation phase, 1969–74, proved particularly difficult to source. This was due both to diminishing memory for family members and others, and also to the high number of fatalities in that phase, which meant that scant details were recorded publicly when multiple deaths took place. The limited information in the public domain regarding certain deaths will affect the categorisation of these fatalities. Were full and independent investigation to occur classification of these deaths on this database could undoubtedly be subject to revision.

The core of the work is the survey of individual deaths placed on a database format. Each individual death constitutes a case file in the database. Thus, even where the use of force resulted in multiple casualties, each individual fatality is uniquely registered. The information in each case file was then minutely broken down to discrete subcategories. A total of thirty-five descriptive subcategories attached to each solitary case file. The framework of these categories have three broad themes. First, personal descriptive information directly related to each victim. This included age, gender, religious affiliation and organisational or institutional membership. Second, data relating to the actual incident or context in which life was lost. Included here, for example, were the geographical location of death, the institutional affiliation of the agent who exercised force, whether eyewitnesses were identified, and a classification of the context of death. Third was the examination of the legal processes which followed fatal use of force. Relevant here were inquest proceedings and outcomes, referral of cases to the Director of Public Prosecutions, criminal proceedings if any, civil liability claims against the state, and international legal process concerning the death.

Cross-referencing of variables was the source of the factual information for the study. The categorisation process has both elements of objective and subjective assessment. Implying certain facts from incomplete data was only undertaken where a high degree of accuracy was potentially attainable. Thus, where a person's religious affiliation was unclear, conclusions could be drawn from name, home address and organisational affiliation (for example, PIRA, UVF). Analysis of fatalities in a conflict situation is invariably contentious. Nonetheless, it is important to stress that many of the categories included in this study are legal in nature, and thus precise and identifiable criteria attach to the process of consigning a particular fatality to a defined status. It is conceded that parallel research emerging from different fields of study could reach varying conclusions over the status and classifications of some of these deaths. This work is a legal study and draws upon the standards of domestic and international law to contextualise and place the deaths under examination. It is those standards which inform the study and within which any critique of the categorisation process should be contextualised.

The core classification, that which is most politically and legally significant, lies in the assessment of the context of death and the status of the deceased. Fatality categories have three broad subdivisions. First, deaths in public order situations. Second, deaths in security-related contexts. Finally, a miscellaneous category. Public order situations refer to a variety of situations in which fatality was premised on public confrontation (or a perception of public confrontation), between the state and a group of citizens. Both violent and nonviolent confrontations are included in this category. The complexity of such situations is wide ranging. They include riot (or dispute over riot), rally, curfew, affray, public altercation, robbery and hijack situations. It is evident that some activities such as robbery and hijackings might also fall into the category of security-related deaths, where state agents would have perceived a paramilitary nexus to the activities of the deceased. Given that the information available on these fatalities reveals that the majority are correctly placed in the public order classification, I note that in a small percentage of the situations reviewed there was a security element to the contextualisation of the use of force which is insignificant to the overall analysis. Fatalities which occurred proximate to a situation of confused public order also fall under this broad banner.

Security-related deaths are those which occur in contexts where the perceived threat (from the viewpoint of the security forces) is to the stability of the state from paramilitary organisations or activity. Included are gun battles, checkpoint deaths (both personal and vehicular), refusal to halt, and set-piece deaths. Set-piece deaths have become the most controversial of all lethal force deaths in Northern Ireland. The following markers identify such deaths: the deployment of specialist police or military units, evidence of foreplanning in the confrontation (usually informer information), little apparent attempt to arrest rather than to kill, and massive use of firepower against the deceased.

The miscellaneous 'other' category covers an amalgam of fatality contexts. It includes accidental discharge of a weapon, and situations where the information available does not allow a specific category to be ascribed. This is a catch-all category, intended to subsume all deaths which do not fall into the specifically enumerated situations.

The second critical classification is of the status of each individual victim. The legal standards of international humanitarian law are fundamental to the analysis of this portion of the database material. Where the deceased was clearly identified as a member of an illegal organisation, there was no difficulty in imputing organisational affiliation. In some cases, more controversial conclusions were drawn from the circumstances of death or a particular political context which precluded official statements by paramilitary organisations claiming membership or association with the deceased. These political contexts were primarily agreed ceasefire commitments, which might have been undermined by an admission of active service activity, causal in the individual's death.

Problematic legal issues arise in respect of identifying paramilitary membership in two specific cases. First, where the circumstances indicate that organisational affiliation had no causal effect on the fatality. For example, a member of a paramilitary organisation, watching television in his home, is killed by a stray bullet that enters through the sitting room window. Second (a variation of the first), a member of a paramilitary organisation is killed while 'off duty', that is, he is killed with forethought and the assumption can be made that he was 'acting as a civilian' from the known facts of the incident. That is to say, the security forces would have known that he was a member of a paramilitary organisation, but that at the moment of lethal discharge he was not armed and not directly engaged in paramilitary activity. In this study, paramilitary membership, whether active or not at the time of death, has been used to significantly determine the victim's status on variation two but not variation one.

Paramilitary status aside, the other singularly important category is that of civilian. 'Civilian' has a particular legal definition in the context of international humanitarian law, and this is the context which is imported to this study. The term 'civilian' advances the idea that those who are not combatants, not involved in armed conflict, should always be treated humanely and should not be made the object of military attack. The term connotes a protected class of persons and presumes that those who fall under its title are outside the causal framework of conflict. However, the expansive use of the term was felt to be too far-reaching and insufficiently precise for the purposes of this study. Thus, the broad category was reconstructed with an emphasis on an intricate understanding of the potential nuances of the classification. The first substratum is that of 'uninvolved civilian', meaning that the individual is not related to (by presence, action or omission) the context in which fatality occurs. The second substratum is that of 'civilian'. Lack of qualification is not intended to imply pejorative assumptions about the deceased's motives or actions, but indicates that he or she may have consentingly or otherwise agreed to be present (or remain) in a situational context which was a causal factor in the loss of life. The other civilian categories include armed criminal civilians, criminal civilians armed with replica weapons, possibly armed criminal civilians, and unarmed criminal civilians. It is acknowledged that categorisation may contain elements of subjective judgement, particularly in controversial cases where facts are disputed.

The use of the term 'lethal force' requires qualification. For the purposes of this study the term has an interrelational meaning, implying the legal status of the individual who exercises force, the actual physical results on the body of the person experiencing that force, and finally, the classification of the mechanism used to cause harm or injury. Serious nonfatal injury to the body has been a phenomenon associated with the use of lethal force from the beginning of the conflict. These classes of injury have been excluded from the empirical study for methodological reasons. As many of these injuries were never documented officially, or recorded publicly by the media, and lacked official or legal investigation, it proved a difficult task to establish with accuracy what exact numbers and scope of injuries were at issue. Nonetheless, it should be pointed out that what information is available points to horrific permanent injuries caused to citizens, many of them children. According to the Northern Ireland Office, 55,367 plastic bullets were fired between 1 January 1973 and 31 December 1990. Described by the state as nonlethal weapons, plastic baton rounds alone have been responsible for seventeen deaths between 1969 and 1994. Significantly, and outside the scope of this study, are the hundreds who have been extensively and life-changingly injured by blindness, brain damage, paralysis and disfigurement.

The initial statistical collation was carried out on a Macintosh Statistical package, and analysis was undertaken using Minitab and BMDP statistical software. Dr John Newell of the Department of Statistics, Glasgow University, acted as consultant for all the statistical analysis presented.

Acknowledgements

In completing this project, I must first acknowledge the patience and good humour of my friend and doctoral supervisor Professor Colm Campbell. This book has had a long birth and he has been consistently encouraging and supportive throughout. A large debt is also due to John Wadham of the National Council for Civil Liberties who never quite gave up on this book seeing the light of day. His patience is, I hope, ultimately rewarded.

I spent the first three years of research at Queen's University Belfast and debts are owed to many there who listened, encouraged and read early drafts of my writing. They include Professor Tom Hadden, Professor Brice Dickson and Professor Stephen Livingstone. At Harvard Law School I was given a quiet space in which to gather my thoughts in the 1993–4 academic year. My thanks are owed to Professor Henry Steiner and the community based at the Human Rights Program for opening up new horizons and thoughts on my research. From 1994 to 1997 the Law School at Columbia University was my academic home and my work has grown significantly from the friendship and intellectual rigour of Professor Louis Henkin.

Both during my time in Belfast and since I have left, the Committee on the Administration of Justice, and particularly Martin O'Brien, have made their resources, time and expertise freely available. Dr John Newell gave untiring assistance with the statistical analysis, in addition to his excellent taste in good Irish music at critical junctures. Jane Winter gave extensive and useful comments on an earlier draft of the book.

I am grateful for the access given to me by HM Coroner for Greater Belfast, John Leckey, to large volumes of inquest reports, and the resources of his office during the periods I was researching at the Crumlin Road Courthouse. My research would not have been possible without the support of the Civil Liberties Trust Studentship, the Lawlor Foundation, and the Fulbright Commission. My thanks to Blackstaff

Press for its professionalism in dealing with, and enthusiasm for, the contents of this book, but especially to Hilary Bell, whose stellar editing guided and improved my writing throughout. Special thanks are also due to Carina Rourke of Blackstaff Press for her unending patience and diligence in ensuring that all the details were right.

As with all Herculean tasks, a heavy toll is taken on friends and family by protracted research. My thanks are due to my family in Na Forbacha, Limerick and New York for retaining a healthy perspective on how much time writing should occupy in one's life. Claire Archbold gave good Antrim advice throughout, and the occasional walk in the Mournes to clear my head. Oren Gross inherited this book with me, and we will both be grateful for the quietness in our lives without it. Finally, and most importantly, I wish to thank my friend Julie Harrison, without whom this would never have been done.

FIONNUALA NÍ AOLÁIN
New York
January 2000

Introduction

In April 1998 a new politics gained a precarious foothold in Northern Ireland. The politics of accommodation and compromise were given voice in the Good Friday Agreement, followed by a referendum in which a distinct majority in both nationalist and unionist communities endorsed change to the long-standing political order.[1] This reconstruction of the political landscape was not simply about brokering a deal among the relevant political parties; it also sought to recontract the basis upon which two distinct communities share a narrow geographical space with one another. The agreement is not just about tinkering with the structures of political life, rather, it is about reformulating those structures and creating new ones to accommodate diversity and difference. It seeks to create new configurations that will channel the conflicts of identity and generate spaces of participation for all segments of Northern Ireland's communities. Inclusiveness has become the means to circumvent the historic exclusions of the state. Change in Northern Ireland is palpable. Change is also undoubtedly difficult.

While making the leap towards mutual accommodation, both communities are still firmly rooted in competing versions of past and identity. The past is never far away in Northern Ireland: the new political landscape is dotted with reminders of the need to acknowledge and come to terms with recent and long-standing histories. In the process of rebuilding a fractured society each mini-negotiation about the various components of regenerated political life reverts into a more formidable conversation about conflicting truths concerning the nature of the conflict itself. Transcending this circularity, as much as initiating a new politics, is one of the challenges of the new order. This book argues that, notwithstanding the need to move purposefully beyond history, the past needs and demands definition. The Northern Ireland peace process effectively harnessed constructive ambiguity as a necessary element of achieving compromise, but such ambiguity cannot be sustained indefinitely.

Like many other societies experiencing conflict transition, there is need to affirm truths: in part to preserve an accurate historical account of conflict, thereby preventing the causality of its recurrence; and in part to restore a measure of lost civility in torn civic life, thereby allowing for some measure of communal reconciliation.[2] This is not a simple task. Assuming the authenticity of any single narrative of the conflict may serve to alienate one side from the other in the process of remaking and reconciling. Trying to confirm the veracity of any single conflict narrative produces it own practical problems. These include the obvious question of which institution or social process has sufficient impartiality to undertake this enterprise – the courts, the politicians or the academic? Moreover, as students of history observe, histories of internal societal conflict are rarely linear. A 'thin' telling of any conflict's narrative avoids examining the broader society and cultures from which the causalities of conflict emerge, and entirely obscures competing perceptions of victimhood. To create a deeper history of the conflict, multiple narratives are necessary.

This book evaluates one particular facet of Northern Ireland's conflict history, namely the use of lethal force by agents of the state. By examining this microcosm of state activity during the modern phase of the conflict, we gain an understanding of the macrocosm of state response to a situation of prolonged internal strife. More particularly, we gain new insights on the status and definition of the experience of conflict itself under domestic and international law. In short, we attain a further narrative on the conflict and its mutations – both political and legal.

This work was commenced at a juncture when political resolution was a vague hope on a distant horizon. Nonetheless, the use of lethal force has been and remains a crucial element of Northern Ireland's political and legal landscape and requires examination and understanding. Violence, both by and against the state, has been a defining feature of Northern Ireland's self-definition since it emerged as a distinct political entity in 1921. Understanding the shape, scope and rationale of the use of force by any state, and in this specific context, that of the United Kingdom, is an indispensable prerequisite to understanding the state itself, and crucial in establishing accountability where the state has failed to protect the lives of its citizens.

Within certain communities in Northern Ireland the use of lethal force by agents of the state has created a profound consciousness of distance from and rejection of the authority of the state. It has sharpened issues of state accountability and transparency, and held up a mirror to the United Kingdom's rhetoric of democracy and rule of law. The use of force has created national and international headlines, being a testing point for the state's commitment to its own domestic law and its international human rights treaty obligations. This is undoubtedly linked to the pre-eminent status of the right to life in international law as the foremost human right, from which all other rights' protections sequentially follow.

As the experiences of other jurisdictions surmounting internal conflict show, accountability for past human rights violations may be a necessary element of broader societal reconstruction, not only by providing a mechanism that enables victims and their families to channel their grievances towards peaceful dispute settlement, but because functional legal process may affirm faith with the rule of law generally and heal wider societal wounds.[3] Guatemala, Chile, Cambodia, South Africa and Bosnia have all sought to create mechanisms whereby accountability for past violation of rights can occur in the process of societal restructuring.[4] In these contexts, legitimisation has been given for stating that human rights violations are an intricate part of the conflict's narrative. Indeed, human rights are affirmed to be at the heart of the conflict and at the core of its resolution. In the process of political reconciliation the significance of accounting for past grievances (perceived or real) is a crucial aspect of negotiating a future. To assume that past human rights violations will simply cease to be pertinent to the transitioning political situation is myopic and potentially foolhardy.

The star role in this modern morality play is given to the state. The state's first soliloquy should be the acknowledgement that it has not been a neutral nor passive actor in the experience and management of societal conflict. As this book will illustrate, states play a decisive and considered role in the management of low-intensity conflicts, and Northern Ireland is no exception to the rule. In that context, the state must also bear responsibility for its transgression of generally accepted human rights norms.[5]

Accountability in this expanded sense does not only imply state culpability. It mandates that all those who have ordered, carried out, or by other means facilitated violations of human rights disclose and acknowledge such transgressions. Hence, it must be fully acknowledged that the use of lethal force by agents of the state in Northern Ireland has not occurred in a vacuum. Between the start of the conflict in 1969 and republican and loyalist ceasefires in 1994, the use of indiscriminate and deadly violence by paramilitary organisations in Northern Ireland caused immeasurable loss of life, untold suffering to communities and families, and purposeless destruction of the collective fabric of Northern Ireland's society. Republican and loyalist paramilitaries killed almost three thousand people in this time period, many of them simply ordinary citizens going about their familial and working lives, unwittingly caught up in the maelstrom of prejudice and sectarianism manifested in random violence. No society can comfortably absorb such extensive loss without traumatic consequences for its own sense of identity and resilience. Equally, families and communities who have lost loved ones at the hands of paramilitary organisations hold a deep reservoir of hurt that can rarely be overcome no matter how strong their fortitude and determination. Acknowledging this wider community of loss is an integral part of this political and legal analysis.

Nonetheless, this book is focused on a smaller subset of loss arising from the conflict – the 350 deaths caused by agents of the state between 1969 and 1994, determined as outlined in the preceding methodology chapter. Thus far there has been no comprehensive analysis of state resort to lethal force as a discrete subcategory of loss of life or injury arising from the conflict in Northern Ireland. Nor has there been significant statistical or systematic analysis of the patterns discernible in the manner, distribution and responsibility for deaths caused by agents of the state. This work is intended to redress that empirical gap. It does so on the basis of a full and complete census of all lethal force deaths that occurred in the jurisdiction between 1969 and 1994. It is critical to note that the study is not based on a random sample of the target study group. Thus, the empirical conclusions avoid the unsupported political and legal generalisations that have characterised the discussion on lethal force within and outside the jurisdiction.

However, the significance of analysing lethal force deaths is not exclusively limited to understanding the individual contexts in which citizens have lost their lives. The use of lethal force by agents of the state is, I argue, significantly linked to an evaluation of security policy, emergency regulation and the political management of the crisis in Northern Ireland since 1969. Lethal force is but one response on a continuum available to any state confronting a situation of internal crisis. The manner in which it has been utilised in Northern Ireland gives an extraordinary insight into the manner in which the United Kingdom, operating in a democratic/ rule of law framework, has defined and controlled exigency. This work demonstrates that lethal force is not an isolated aspect of state practice, explained only as 'spur-of-the-moment' decisions by law-enforcers. Rather, the use of lethal force operates through broader policy determinations designed to control conflict, having a sophisticated interplay with law and legal process that has been obscured in contemporary public discourse.

So this is also a book about law, and more concretely about how situations of internal conflict provoke and maintain contradictions and ambiguities in legal process and institutions. Northern Ireland's legal infrastructure constitutes a bundle of paradoxes. These paradoxes are in large part derived from competing narratives about the nature and status of the conflict itself. Law has both defined and processed the components of the conflict. It has done so in a no-man's-land of legal language, because neither domestic nor international law has developed an uncontested formula for the control and definition of situations of internal conflict that prolong over many years. Thus, it is no exaggeration to argue that Northern Ireland has functioned in a state of legal limbo since the start of the conflict in 1969.

An examination of the use of force by the state is a means to develop a more refined understanding of the operation of law in a situation of internal conflict. By tracing and revealing the tortuous interplay of force with legal accountability, we not only learn more about the deficiencies of law in individual cases but we expose its inherent contradictions. These contradictions are rooted in the attempt to use ordinary, 'normal' legal procedures in tandem with, or modified by, extraordinary legal and extralegal norms designed to cope with societal crisis. As this book illustrates, ordinary law has been bent out of shape and beyond all recognition in Northern Ireland. Its surgical remoulding has been both responsive to the conflict and defining of it. This tells us that legality is not a neutral actor in a situation of conflict. Law defines and takes sides and it has done so in Northern Ireland.

What this analysis also reveals is that situations of internal conflict are not one-dimensional. Equally, neither is the response of law and its institutional structures consistent and unchanging throughout any particular conflict. In confirming that internal conflict is not uni-experiential, Northern Ireland conforms to a general pattern mirrored in other jurisdictions by manifesting distinct cycles in its conflict history. This book defines three distinct phases of conflict in the jurisdiction. First, the militarisation phase between 1969 and 1974. This phase is characterised by the deployment of the army. The military was tasked with both regular civilian responsibilities and the restoration of order occasioned by the loss of control by, and confidence in, local civilian authorities. The militarisation phase is also defined by spiralling violence, and the extensive use of emergency and extraordinary common law legal powers by the state. These also provide the ingredients which would theoretically satisfy international legal requirements for internal armed conflict status in the jurisdiction. The second cycle is the 'normalisation' phase between 1975 and 1980. In this phase the conflict is prolonging beyond its envisaged duration and the state seeks to demilitarise by ostensibly handing control back from the military to local law-enforcers. This phase is also characterised by the entrenchment of emergency powers and the particular emphasis on employing a modified legal system to control the conflict itself. The scale of overall violence diminishes in this phase of the conflict and the applicability of armed conflict status under international law becomes more problematic. Finally, the third phase, 1981–94, is termed the active counter-insurgency phase. Here the state has internally acknowledged the limits of legal process in controlling extended exigency. Thus, the emphasis of the state is two-fold. First, active counter-insurgency is a key component of the state's arsenal in confronting persistent paramilitary violence, dependent on the deployment of specialised forces (both police and military). Second, law remains a pivotal, if secondary, means of countering internal conflict. Hence the modification of legal process and the use of wide-ranging emergency powers remains a key part of the state's strategy throughout this phase. In terms of international law (as chapter 5 will discuss in detail) this book argues that the prolonged extension of conflict in tandem with certain military characteristics tend to suggest that Northern Ireland falls within the regulatory regime of low-intensity internal armed conflict under international humanitarian law standards in this period.

Situations of internal conflict are messy, from the point of view of both law and politics. Modern practice shows convincingly that such conflicts invariably arise from incompatible claims over territory and state legitimacy. This is the metanarrative of such conflicts. In the Northern Ireland context, the metanarrative was surgically sliced from the rhetoric of the state in its acknowledged conflict management strategies between 1969 and 1994, but invariably reasserted itself in the actual practices of conflict management. This is what becomes evident in the microscopic examination of the use of force and the application of legal processes during the same period. This book reveals that disjunction and the long-term obstacles that it may create for the healing of a divided society.

1

A brief historical overview

The use of lethal force in Northern Ireland is not an isolated example of institutional or individual behaviour. Between 1969 and 1994 the use of force was intimately and inexorably linked with prevailing political policies of managing strife. It was also responsive to the progression of conflict in Northern Ireland. In most democratic societies the state has a monopoly on the methods and means of violent coercion. In societies experiencing internal strife the state has an array of methods available to it to control and manage disorder. The use of force is one such method. Understanding how lethal force fits into the broader picture of conflict control strategies is critical to understanding its significance both to the state and the communities who experienced its use.

Figure 1 Lethal force deaths, 1969–94

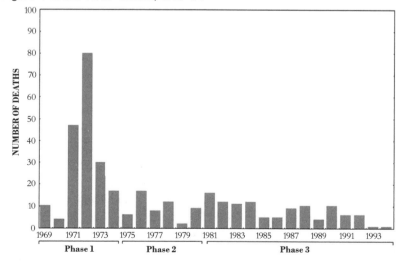

Equally, the use of force is not static in a conflict situation. It is responsive both to changes in the progression of conflict and the state's perception of its own vulnerability. In order to chart progressions and patterns in the use of force in Northern Ireland, it is necessary to place force in the context of the modern history of the jurisdiction. The use of force requires contextualisation in the framework of the wider strategies employed by the state to confront low-intensity armed conflict over the twenty-five-year period under review in this book.

I
The emergence of a substate

The six-county Northern Ireland substate came into existence in 1921, a year before the independence of the twenty-six-county Irish Free State.[1] The division of Ireland resulted from an initial attempt to give some form of limited autonomy to Ireland as a whole. This political move was ideologically and militarily opposed by the Protestant majority in the north of Ireland. This majority, a by-product of colonial settlements in Ulster[2] by Britain in the seventeenth century, viewed itself as British, culturally and politically. The political independence of the Irish and Catholic state was perceived as undermining the identity by which this Protestant group defined itself.[3] There was also a substantial Catholic minority within Northern Ireland, whose identity was linked to the emerging southern Irish state. This minority defined itself politically and culturally as Irish. Thus, the polarisation of the two communities was built from the inception of the state along religious and political lines. Religious affiliation came to define political identity. Ultimately, it was also the means by which the northern state characterised citizenship and loyalty.

The Government of Ireland Act 1920 sought to create two devolved Irish parliaments; one holding jurisdiction in the six counties of the north of Ireland, the other in the twenty-six counties of the south. The northern parliament envisaged under the 1920 Act quickly came into existence. The Act was the defining element of Northern Ireland's autonomy from British governmental interference, entrenched by a unionist major-ity in Northern Ireland's parliament.[4] In the south of Ireland the Act was the means to return a parliament of unopposed candidates, committed to intransigent republicanism who sought independence, not merely nominal legislative freedom from Westminster.[5] Elections in May 1921 were followed by a truce and a negotiated treaty which gave dominion status to the Irish Free State.[6] The limited autonomy granted by the Anglo-Irish Treaty was quickly outgrown by the fledgling Irish state. It forged its way to full independence by creating its own constitution in 1937; proclaiming a republic in 1948 and withdrawing from the British Commonwealth in 1949 and pursuing a strong foreign policy that actively dissociated Ireland from British policy priorities.[7]

Both parts of the island of Ireland are characterised by a history of political violence, historically derived from the coexistence of four conflicting cultures in Ireland – Gaelic, English, Anglo-Irish, and Ulster Protestant. This violence predates the revolutionary decade of 1912 to 1922, finding its roots in the native responses to the war of conquest waged in the sixteenth and seventeenth centuries.[8] The cultural antagonisms have a variety of components, including colonial conquest (English and Protestant), where elimination of the native (Catholic and Gaelic) culture was a political imperative; and more recently, as communal definitions of cultural identity have become rooted in the negation of other identities. One Irish taoiseach articulated the modern consequences of such negation as follows:

> In Northern Ireland, the conflict about national identity is increased because it coincides generally with a division in respect of religious belief, which in turn creates differences about philosophy and language. At times, the two communities in Northern Ireland, even when trying to reach out towards one another to find an accommodation, speak in such radically different language that they do not understand one another. What one side sees as a gesture of conciliation is seen by the other as an aggressive proposal simply because the modes of thinking are so different.[9]

The Northern Ireland substate came into existence by the threat of a violent reaction from the Protestant majority against its being subsumed into an all-Ireland entity. Its history from 1922 has been punctuated by brief bursts of civil disorder, compounded by underlying fear for the long-term security of the state.[10] Built on this foundation of insecurity, the state created structures to protect itself politically and militarily. The form of devolved government from the Westminster parliament which emerged in Northern Ireland had a direct bearing on the events which have unfolded in the jurisdiction between 1969 and 1994.

From the state's inception, the Protestant majority perceived its status to be threatened on two fronts: on the one hand, by the Catholic state on its doorstep, which had an explicit constitutional mandate to reunite the whole territory of the island;[11] on the other, by an internal Catholic minority which did not identify with the ideology of the majority and was viewed by the state as politically subversive. The practical difficulty for the Protestant majority controlling power was that the internal minority was not small enough to be eliminated completely as a direct threat to the legitimacy of the state. Conversely, the minority, while initially entirely reluctant to legitimise the state by participating in its creation, was thereafter politically and economically excluded from such partnership.[12]

The insecurity of the unionist community had a direct bearing on the nature of the state they created, which was ostensibly democratic in structure – elections and the one man, one vote principle were largely observed. However, behind the façade of democratic structures were practices of artificially manipulating electoral boundaries and the linkage of voting rights in local elections to a property ownership qualification. From its inception local government in Northern Ireland was designed to ensure that unionist representatives were in a majority, even in areas where nationalists dominated demographically. The *locus classicus* of this practice was in the city of Derry/Londonderry, where Catholic voting power was controlled by the manipulation of housing policy to prevent a demise of unionist supremacy on the local city council.

Political practices followed sectarian adherences. Both communities voted along religious and cultural lines. This ensured unionist domination of power, until Northern Ireland's devolved governmental powers were revoked by the British government in 1972. The constitutional nationalists who sat in the northern parliament were in the paradoxical position of being in parliament, but not of it. They recognised that they were fated to remain in permanent opposition and pursued a course of wavering participation,[13] occasionally withdrawing from parliament to signal their discontent.

Until 1972, the primary focus of unionist government was safeguarding the state. The agents of the state, primarily the Royal Ulster Constabulary (RUC) and such reserve forces as the B Specials, were overwhelmingly drawn from the unionist community, a fact which remains true today despite recent valiant attempts to change the demography of

the police force.[14] Both the creation and enforcement of law were historically associated with the politics of political domination. The neutrality
of the legal order was never ideologically defended, it was indisputably
linked to the political priorities of government. State security was primarily advanced through legislative mechanisms. Foremost of these was
the Civil Authorities (Special Powers) Act (Northern Ireland) 1922.[15]
This legislation drew heavily from the Defence of the Realm Act 1914
(DORA) and the Restoration of Order in Ireland Act 1920.

Under DORA, the British government was empowered 'during the
continuance of the present war [First World War] to issue regulations as
to the powers and duties of the Army Council, and of the members of
His Majesty's forces, and other persons acting on His behalf, for securing
the public safety and the defence of the realm'. The Restoration of Order
in Ireland Act became law on 9 August 1920. Under this legislation all the
DORA regulations which had been employed for counter-insurgency
purposes were readopted as Restoration of Order in Ireland regulations.
The main features of the Restoration of Order Act included the provision that court martials could virtually try all types of crime as well as
breach of the regulations, and special courts of summary jurisdiction
were created and powers were given to replace coroners' courts by military courts of inquiry.

With this impressive ancestry, the Special Powers Act came into existence, was renewed annually until 1928, made permanent in 1933 and
withdrawn in 1971. The Act allowed for internment without trial, retrospective criminal legislation, entry for search without warrant solely for
the purpose of interrogation, and a battery of other powers, and was consistently used against members of the nationalist community, rarely
against their unionist counterparts.[16] From the creation of the state, emergency legislation was entrenched and normalised as a daily part of state
procedure, becoming one of the primary focuses for discontent articulated by the civil rights movement of the 1960s. The centrality of emergency laws to the functioning of the unionist regime is an early indictor
of the abnormal political reality of the state. It teaches a wider lesson too,
that when the state is faced with crisis (whether actual or perceived) the
harnessing of law to manage the exigency is linked to and affirmative of
broader political goals.

Under international legal standards, 'emergency' is a concept that is
intended to invoke a finite and short-term crisis.[17] Simply said, the state

can only use emergency laws for limited periods of time. To facilitate this, international human rights law has created the mechanism of derogation, which refers to the legally mandated right of states to allow suspension of certain international obligations protecting individual rights in circumstances of emergency or war.[18] Derogations are not limitless nor are they open-ended. This means that the right of the state to regulate its internal affairs through the use of extraordinary law is restricted. Notwithstanding international and domestic legal constraints, the emergency in Northern Ireland became a synonym for normal state regulation. Any analysis of Northern Ireland's legal history informs us that this is a state which has never known anything but emergency rule. This remains the case regardless of the Good Friday Agreement, as the panoply of emergency powers remains fixed, despite repeated international and domestic calls for their repeal.[19]

The protracted use of emergency powers adds to the lack of clarity over the legal standards applicable to a jurisdiction experiencing prolonged internal crisis. In some states, including Northern Ireland, the emergency has become part of the problem not an inherent means for its resolution. Such a situation contravenes the basis for the resorting to extraordinary powers in the first place. The Questiaux Report argues that 'the [emergency] measure should – at the very least – apparently make it possible to abate or bring an end to the specific situation of danger'.[20] The use of short-term emergency powers can be a means to return to political and legal normality, but when the short-term becomes the long-term, any analysis of law needs to take into account the fact that the exercise of such powers creates social and institutional structures dependent on the continued existence of the abnormal. Unquestionably, Northern Ireland's emergency powers have had a profound psychological and political effect on the citizens of the state. These consequences also involve shaping the way in which the United Kingdom has managed the conflict.

A

CIVIL RIGHTS AND REFORM

By the 1960s the expression of discontent had changed in Northern Ireland. The minority community mobilised around a broadly based civil rights movement which sought inclusion in the legal and political

affairs of Northern Ireland. Equality of opportunity and an end to discriminatory practices were the key elements of reform sought. The response
of the unionist government was short-sighted and catastrophic: the civil
rights movement was characterised as a direct threat to the legitimacy of
the state itself. Due to the inability of the majority of unionists to
embrace reform, the seeds of violent civil disorder were sown. The pendulum swung from constitutional reform to violent backlash. State
responses to the civil rights marches varied from deeming them illegal,
breaking them up by force, or not preventing sectarian violence by militant loyalists being directed at peaceful protesters.[21] An escalation of violence seemed inevitable.

The RUC and the B Specials were linked inexorably with the perpetuation of abuse and discrimination.[22] They were the front-line response of
the state to the agitation of its minority on the streets. The unionist government was convinced that the civil rights movement was the Irish
Republican Army (IRA) in another guise. The unionist state sought to
protect itself by all means, and its agents were called upon to provide
the hard-line military response. For the minority community this
response could not be distinguished from the sectarian violence being
directed at it from entrenched loyalists. Continuous rioting and an explosion of sectarian violence throughout the summer of 1969 left the RUC
demoralised and unable to contain the spiralling sectarian strife and ultimately led to a decision by the British government to send in the British
army to restore calm.

B

CONTAINMENT – THE ROLE OF THE ARMY

The army's initial function was perceived to be a stopgap one, to provide
a mediating role to prevent further escalation of violence. Army intervention was initially regarded by sectors of the nationalist community
as their only protection from an impending pogrom. The immediate
consequence of the army's presence was that it abruptly embroiled the
British government in a situation which it little understood, but for
which it had effectively assumed responsibility. Military involvement
resulted in a short breathing space, as confrontations on the streets
subsided and a sense of potential political resolution was palpable.
But this relative calm in the winter of 1969–70 is more correctly

attributable to the nationalist and unionist communities assessing the promises of reform, than to better community relations fostered by army intervention.

The government misread the situation, regarding army intervention as capable of changing the internal political dynamics of the jurisdiction. There was an underlying supposition by the British government of the day that intervention and the subsequent potential for its withdrawal could effect the local political climate positively. This assumption has persisted throughout the course of the military deployment. More naive was the lack of foresight in the failure to predict that long-term military deployment might change the legal terms of reference for the conflict itself.

Allied with the introduction of the army, political pressure was placed on the Stormont government to introduce reform measures.[23] Changes did not materialise as quickly nor as profoundly as the reformist impulse within the nationalist community demanded. The result was that reformist leanings in some sections of the minority community were channelled in another direction. That direction was the protection of the community by means of political violence. This shift marked a sea change within certain segments of the nationalist community, which would subsequently remain on the fringes of democratic process, sustained by the belief that the Northern Ireland substate was incapable of reform. Hence, the momentum of the civil rights campaign became overshadowed by a splintering of the nationalist community into two distinct groups: those committed to constitutional politics and those seeking violent overthrow of the state.

Since 1969 the British army has remained in Northern Ireland. It was and remains ill-equipped for the communal policing functions it has carried out in the jurisdiction.[24] After 1969 the shift of political direction within the nationalist community resulted in increased political violence. That violence was fuelled by a deteriorating relationship between the army and the nationalist community. The military was now the front-line response to both public political confrontations and the violent showdowns of escalating paramilitary violence.

The governing unionist élite failed to recognise that constitutional repercussions would result from an extended stay in Northern Ireland by the army. They also overlooked the necessity of exercising parallel control over the extremist elements in their own camp to ensure a return to stability. In these failures was the genesis of the Provisional IRA (PIRA) and the death of the state in Northern Ireland. The imposition of direct rule from Westminster signalled the ending of the Stormont regime.

A twofold strategy has emerged from the United Kingdom government since 1969. First is a concentrated reliance on hard-line military tactics to 'solve' the conflict on the ground. Second, legal processes have been yoked to manage that conflict. The oscillation between the two has occasionally been interrupted by sporadic attempts to promote political initiatives. Almost three decades of sectarian, paramilitary and state violence followed.

A fundamental change in the cycle of internal strife came in August 1994, when PIRA declared a complete cessation of military operations, foreshadowing the hope that an end had come to the use of violence in Northern Ireland. Its ceasefire was quickly followed in October of the same year by a similar gesture on the part of the Combined Loyalist Military Command (CLMC). However, the fragile confidence of the emerging peace process was shattered in February 1996, when a PIRA bomb exploded in Canary Wharf in the docklands area of London. PIRA issued a statement declaring that a resumption of the 'armed struggle' was taking place, citing its frustration with the lack of movement on political talks as a motivating factor in that decision. Despite ample cynicism the republican ceasefire was resuscitated on 20 July 1997, and the peace process maintained its halting movements towards a comprehensive agreement. The slow pace of political transformation was predictably linked to the deep suspicions harboured by some parties in the *bona fides* of the republican movement, and their commitment to constitutional politics. Equally, nationalists, and to some degree the Irish government, were uncertain of unionist eagerness to embrace fundamental reform and to negotiate with all strands of Irish nationalism in concert. The election of a new Labour government, armed with a resounding majority in the House of Commons, facilitated a renewed interest in, and flexibility of, political movement which rejuvenated the three-stranded party and state discussions. The hothouse environment induced by an Easter deadline, assisted by the cajoling of the Irish, British and American governments, finally resulted in a historic moment of agreement for unionists and nationalists on 10 April 1998.

Notwithstanding the possibility of an end to the physical

manifestations of violence, Northern Ireland remains a society deeply scarred by its long history of conflict, and highly cynical of the possibility of breaking the cycle of sectarian strife. Continued violence and sectarianism following the signing of the Good Friday Agreement has served to emphasise how far Northern Ireland's peace process must still travel, and how far its enforcement remains locked in cyclical conversations about the righteousness of each side's broader conflict narrative. In the multi- and microscopic tasks that creating a new political edifice requires, provincial politics dominate. This politics of particularity seeks a definitive and legitimised version of mutually exclusive history, thereby giving impetus to one particular ideological reconstruction of past events over the other. There is a struggle to maintain competing versions of events by both sides of the political divide in Northern Ireland, which makes it difficult for each to accept complexities and nuances. This is not only true for participating political parties but also for the dominant state in the equation – the United Kingdom.

II
Phases in the use of force and the emergency cycle

The key to this analysis lies in the understanding that the use of force manifests clear patterns and phases of existence and transformation. Crucially these patterns are linked to the exercise of other mechanisms of control by the state, notably the exercise of emergency powers. This work identifies three key phases in the use of force since 1969. These phases are contemporaneously linked to the cycles of emergency powers exercised in the jurisdiction. Hence, I assert that the use of force, allied with exceptional legal regulation, serve mutually reinforcing purposes in a society experiencing extended internal strife. Also evident is that in these distinct phases the patterns of life-taking by the state illustrate a diminishing protection for the value of life when the state experiences crisis.

Before turning to the modern phase of the conflict, a reasonable question to ask is, what was the experience of the use of lethal force during the hiatus of unionist rule? Lethal force was not a flash point issue in this period and there are a number of reasons for this. Emergency legislation was firmly entrenched and lack of resistance to its imposition allowed threats to the state to be controlled within the confines of the Special

Powers Act. Furthermore, the resort to administrative detention, that being the internment of persons for extended periods without charge or criminal trial, was the means used by the state to respond to any flashes of subversion. In 1922 the Special Powers Act was used to intern 500 members of Sinn Féin and their sympathisers; in 1938, 827 men were interned on the basis of an alleged plot against the government; from 1945 to 1956 internment was used sporadically and it was resurrected widely to combat the threat of the 1956–62 IRA campaign.[25] Although the police functioned with a distinctly military character throughout the period of unionist rule, this did not result in their engagement in active counter-insurgency, hence this modern feature of lethal force deployment was markedly absent. Before the demise of the Stormont regime, organised resistance to state power either by committed, efficient and armed paramilitaries, or by peaceful nonviolent protesters, was not a feature of the Northern Ireland political landscape. Consequently, the police had not been challenged to meet these threats, which are typically confronted through the use or threat of force when public order is massively under siege. But Northern Ireland's political landscape was dramatically altered by the events following 24 August 1968 when the first civil rights march took place, protesting at the biased allocation of housing in the County Tyrone village of Caledon.

The first phase of the conflict in the jurisdiction, 1969–74, was a militarisation phase, characterised by the deployment of the army. According to the government's rhetoric, the military was fulfilling its role as an aid to the civilian power. This characterisation was strikingly inaccurate. In fact, this phase clearly manifested military primacy in Northern Ireland, with the police merely acting in tactical support on the ground. The militarisation phase corresponds most neatly to the traditional criteria for the use of emergency powers envisaged by international law. Like other western democracies, the United Kingdom functions as a willing participant to its international legal obligations. This means that it is obliged to fulfil certain legal requirements before it may resort to the use of exceptional powers in the domestic field. In order to invoke emergency laws, which *prima facie* violate the individual rights of citizens, there must be in place an exceptional situation which poses a discernible threat to the 'whole population and constitutes a threat to the organised life of the community of which the state is composed'.[26] The militarisation phase, dominated by images of a virtual civil war spiralling out of control, seems to contain all the necessary components required by domestic and international law to activate the extensive use of exceptional powers. That stated, any such powers remain subject to legal scrutiny.

The second phase, 1975–80, was the 'normalisation' phase, or in Northern Ireland terms, the 'Ulsterisation' phase, identified by the concept of police primacy, where power was ostensibly handed back to the police from the military. However, the police retained few civilian vestiges and were heavily militarised. Phase two, effectively, was militarised normality. In addition, the state harnessed the legal system as a means to combat internal insurgency through legal means. The normalisation phase was a recognition that internal crisis was not likely to be resolved expediently, and that the state faced a long haul in combating insurrection. However, the political calculation was made that extreme internal and external abnormality created a crisis of legitimacy for the state that must be addressed. This meant a rhetorical abandonment of the symbols of instability – the army, internment, special status for political prisoners – and their replacement with the ordinary tools of the state, the police and the courts. However, to facilitate this changeover, normal process was modified and reconfigured beyond all recognition. Thus, for example, the courts functioned, but jury trial was removed for a special class of offenders. In international legal terms the state continued to make use of the emergency doctrine to facilitate its reconfiguration of the domestic legal system and satisfied its external treaty obligations by using the derogation provisions of international human rights treaties. But, crucially, it operated internally as if the crisis was simply a criminal aberration, and remained in internal disavowal of a state of emergency.

The final phase, 1981–94, was the active counter-insurgency phase, marked in Northern Ireland by the ending of the republican hunger strikes.[27] This phase emerged from the failure of the ordinary criminal process, albeit severely modified, to yield the desired political results of neutralising the conflict, where legal and extra-legal models of response by the state to internal conflict were intertwined. In Northern Ireland the failure of the supergrass trials in the early 1980s, added to persistent levels of paramilitary violence, were strategic elements in the upsurge of counter-insurgency-type operations as a key component in the state's emergency arsenal. During this period modification of the legal regime continued, illustrated by the abrogation of the right to silence in Northern Ireland in 1987 and its subsequent removal in the United

Kingdom as a whole.[28]

Understanding the linkage between the use of force and these phases of conflict is of particular importance. First, strategy changes by the state designed to respond to internal threats inform us that the state is not a passive actor in situations of internal conflict. Specifically, it instructs us that the state has an array of legal and extra-legal measures open to it to confront exigency. Most significantly for this work, we should understand that the exercise of force is not a static phenomenon, it is tractable and responsive. It does not neatly fit within the paradigms of the normal use of force by states, because the situation in which force is exercised is not typical. The abnormality of context raises potent questions of accountability for the state. Moreover, it requires penetrating analysis of the appropriate legal definition for the experience of conflict itself.

III
Phase one, 1969–74
Militarisation: lethal force enters the political equation

The use of force to restore order has a long history in Ireland related to a long tradition of violence. Sending the army into Northern Ireland in 1969 was both a symbolic and a practical gesture. The symbolism was in the show of strength and the commitment signalled to militarism. The practical aspect of the deployment indicated that an exhausted and demoralised local police force could no longer cope with the civil disorder on the streets. The year 1969 saw an eruption of communal violence, precipitated by hostile and provocative acts, compounded by the misinterpretation of innocent and nonhostile acts by the nationalist community.[29]

The use of lethal force entered the political equation in Northern Ireland with the introduction of the army. Initially this was not the necessary outcome. The army was welcomed by many nationalists as a protector from hard-line loyalists and an untrustworthy police force. But the commitment of military forces did not stop the spiralling cycle of violence. As the empirical analysis of this study will demonstrate, the military commitment actually augmented state confrontation with its disaffected citizens. Arguably, this was because the commitment of troops was not accompanied by any fundamental constitutional change; direct rule was not canvassed at this point nor was change of the structures of devolved government. Troops were possibly intended as a minimum form of intervention, if the structures of the political and social order were not being reimagined. Ultimately, the military commitment represented a resort to crisis management without reflection on the underlying tensions which precipitated the civil disorder. The political calculation misunderstood how the very fact of a military presence, their unsuitable training for the task in hand combined with their lack of local knowledge would further inflame the volatile situation on the ground.

In theory the army was deployed in Northern Ireland in aid of the civilian power, which would suggest that it operated in hierarchical subservience to the police. However, over the past thirty years the lines of legal authority between police and army have been less than clear and the usual relationship between the two in a democratic society has been inverted. When the army was first deployed the General Officer Commanding (GOC) was entrusted by the British cabinet with securing overall responsibility for security operations. He was given full control of the deployment and tasks of the RUC when the police were used for security operations.[30] Thus, complete control of the military role of the police was assumed by the GOC on 19 August 1969, five days after their arrival.

Deciding what the military functions of the police were in 1969, as opposed to 'normal' policing functions, was no easy task. In effect, the army assumed responsibility for a multitude of duties to contain the civil unrest. The psychological and social impact of that assumption of control was the attachment of military characteristics to normal civic policing duties. There is little binding legal authority in English law concerning the rights and duties of individual soldiers when acting in aid of the civil power, and existing authority is largely related to the control of riot situations.[31] This confusion over the precise legal status of the army in Northern Ireland has remained almost wholly unclarified throughout their thirty-year deployment.[32] An early legal exception to this was the decision in *Hume v. Londonderry Justices*, whereby the courts found that the Stormont government was acting *ultra vires* the Government of Ireland Act by regulating the Special Powers Act for the use and deployment of the army in Northern Ireland.[33] The armed forces and regulation related to them were one of the reserve powers specifically denied to the devolved parliament in 1921.[34] The case was quickly followed by an

Act of Indemnity, legalising both the deployment of armed forces and all their acts from the moment of commitment.

Thereafter, the context in which the legal status of the military was most frequently raised related to their right to exercise force against citizens. The legal fiction of soldiers as ordinary citizens to explain their duties in preventing crime was the most persistent judicial rejoinder to the legal conundrum of extended military deployment. This had a definite effect on military parlance. As recently as 1996 Field Marshal Lord Carver was able to state that:

> A soldier differs from the ordinary citizen in being armed and subject to discipline; but his rights and duties in dealing with crime are precisely the same as those of the ordinary citizen.[35]

Some judicial pronouncements were far more circumspect. Lord Diplock sought to clarify the military position in a 1976 decision. He stated:

> There is little authority in English law concerning the rights and duties of the armed forces of the Crown when acting in aid of the civilian power; and what little authority there is relates almost entirely to the duties of soldiers when troops are called on to assist in controlling riotous assembly. When used for such temporary purposes it may not be inaccurate to describe the legal rights and duties of the soldier as being no more than those of an ordinary citizen in uniform . . . such a description is misleading in the circumstances in which the army is currently employed in Northern Ireland.[36]

Lord Diplock recognised the inaccuracy of characterising the soldier acting in aid of the civilian power as a mere 'civilian in uniform'. Nonetheless, there was evident political reluctance to facilitate the legal task of categorisation. Arguably, this is because legal ambiguity served to facilitate particular conflict management strategies that relied heavily on being able to exploit the legal lacuna over the official legal status of the internal strife.

The militarisation phase of the emergency is clearly indicated by the statistical evidence of responsibility for deaths in the 1969–74 period – the regular army are responsible for 90 per cent of all lethal force deaths in this phase of the conflict.

The army was demonstrably ill-equipped for the task in which they were engaged – in effect, a quasi-policing function in mainly urban areas, with poor training and a lack of local knowledge.[37] A particular

Figure 2 State agency responsible for lethal force deaths, 1969–74

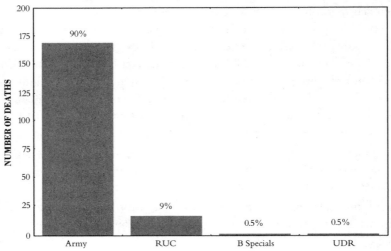

example of the problems of a lack of local knowledge derives from the
Bombay Street incident in Belfast on 15 August 1969. The incident
marked the army's first deployment in Belfast. Bombay Street was
razed by Protestant extremists as a response to the IRA gunmen taking
up position in Clonard monastery, allegedly to protect the small
Catholic enclave near the Catholic Lower Falls and the Protestant
Shankill. The army was under-manned and incapable of preventing the
burning of Catholic homes. They had relied principally on advice from
the RUC and during the burning were stationed in nearby Cupar Street to
protect Protestant homes from communal rioting. They were insufficiently aware of the geography of the area to discern how the religious
divide was practically manifested in housing arrangements. The result of
the Bombay Street arson was bitterness among Catholics about army
partisanship, reflected in the protection of Protestant homes at the
expense of Catholic homes.

There was a broad assumption in governmental circles that the army's
presence in Northern Ireland would be a short-term affair. The naive
conjecture that the Stormont government would put its house in order,
allied to an impending national election in the United Kingdom in June
1970, made long-term commitment inconceivable in the initial phase of
deployment. Drafting troops in at short notice meant that there was no
preparatory training for the particular conditions and tension that would

be experienced. In placing troops into Derry/Londonderry to contain communal strife on 14 August 1969 and subsequently into Belfast the following day to restrain potential catastrophe, there was no time to teach the legal niceties of arrest, due process procedures, or alternatives to the use of force.

A total of 188 persons were killed between 1969 and 1974. Of that total, 169 were caused by use of force being exercised by the regular military. Significantly, as figure 3 identifies, 65 per cent of those killed were indisputably unarmed at the time of death. Only 12 per cent of the deceased (23 persons in all) are confirmed to have been in possession of a weapon at the time of death. A further fifteen deaths are subject to dispute in this period, where state agent and eyewitness accounts are at variance. The empirical analysis places another fourteen deaths as being 'possibly armed', as the evidence available raises the possibility that the deceased might have been in possession of a weapon of some kind at the time of death but this cannot be established with absolute certainty. The figure of 188 represents 53 per cent of the total number of deaths resulting from the use of lethal force in Northern Ireland in 1969–94. Though there were a small number of criminal prosecutions arising in this first phase of the conflict, information relating to them is scant.[38] These cases

Figure 3 Armed status of deceased killed by lethal force between 1969 and 1974

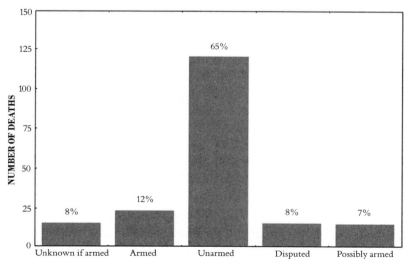

were not reported in the local law reports, hence primarily newspaper accounts survive of the proceedings, giving a limited insight into the application of the appropriate legal standards and judicial approaches to the facts and relevant law. The overall number of criminal prosecutions levied is small in proportion to the number of controversial deaths in this phase of the conflict.

This information raises highly problematic questions for the state in relation to the proportionality of the force exercised, and the lack of accountability for those deaths where there is no dispute that the deceased was unarmed. These matters will be addressed in chapter 2, which examines criminal accountability for the use of lethal force in the jurisdiction.

In the militarisation phase of the conflict reliance on the statutory-based emergency powers was limited. This tells us that the courts and attendant legal process were playing a minimalist role in the management of the conflict. The upsurge in violence emanating from the perceived failure of state metamorphosis was confronted by a military response, both symbolically and physically. In real terms the taking of life by the state was a front-line rejoinder to the political crisis it was experiencing. The terms of that retort are clearly delineated by a close look at the circumstances in which persons were being killed by agents of the state. These contexts are illustrated in figure 4.

Figure 4 Types of incident causing lethal force deaths, 1969–74[39]

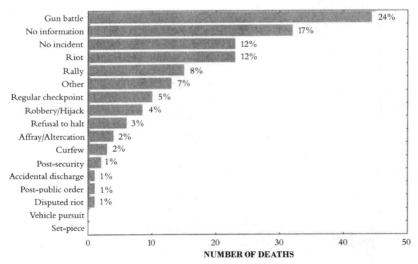

The evidence demonstrates that, contrary to general perceptions, a high number of deaths are recorded in the security context during the militarisation phase of the conflict – gun battles alone account for forty-five deaths in this period. This finding has potentially significant consequences for the categorisation of conflict in Northern Ireland during this period, as chapter 5 on the application of the laws of war will explore.

Many commentaries on the period 1969–74 assume that the majority of deaths were public-order related. This is in part a corollary of the high profile loss of life at the Bloody Sunday civil rights march in 1972 and the large number of injuries sustained by civilians in numerous situations of disturbed public order. However, at this historical moment, while insurgency against the state was ill-defined and sporadic, it was certainly present. Therefore many of the deaths which occur during the militarisation phase demonstrate that Northern Ireland was crossing a threshold which would make the legal standards of internal armed conflict relevant, though not acknowledged by the state.

During this phase large numbers of civilians were actively demonstrating against the state and sectarian acts were on the increase, and it is no surprise that many civilians were killed in this period, 121 in total (see figure 5 below). As individual cases demonstrate, many of the deaths

Figure 5 Status of deceased, 1969–74

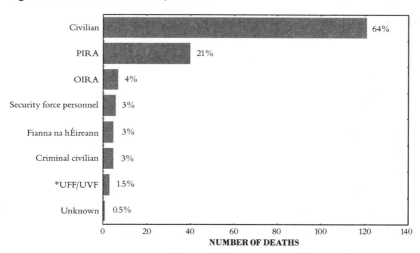

* It is acknowledged that the UFF and the UVF are entirely separate organisations; they are linked here to facilitate empirical presentation.

resulting from gun battles took place in crowd situations. The nexus of crowd gatherings and army responsibility is particularly in evidence in the first phase of the emergency. Crowd gatherings provided situations in which army units were more exposed, facilitating (perceived or actual) attacks upon them by subversives. Equally apparent was the army's lack of training for crowd control and using less harmful means of force to confront public disorder, so as to protect life meaningfully.

Employing the terminology of the European Court of Human Rights, it may be questioned whether the deployment of an ill-trained military force for quasi-civilian purposes was the most effective means to protect the right to life in this period. Clearly, this was not the language of the day, and governmental deployment of the military was not subject to any international judicial criticism at the time. What the evidence demonstrates is a quantifiable leap in the taking of life by the state at the point in which the state itself is in a moment of quantifiable crisis. What is also evident is that the majority of deaths are not of insurgents, members of paramilitary organisations or social outsiders, but rather ordinary civilians, many of whom were exercising their freedom to protest at the policies and structure of the state itself. As further empirical evidence in this work will demonstrate, the protection for life in situations of emergency is intimately tied to the status of the victim and his or her relationship with the state.

Figure 6 Geographical location of lethal force deaths, 1969–74

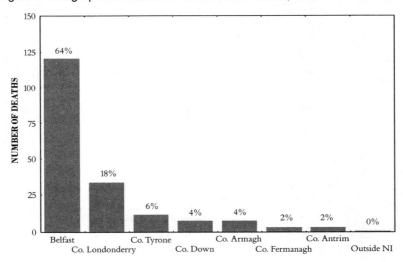

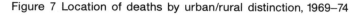

Figure 7 Location of deaths by urban/rural distinction, 1969–74

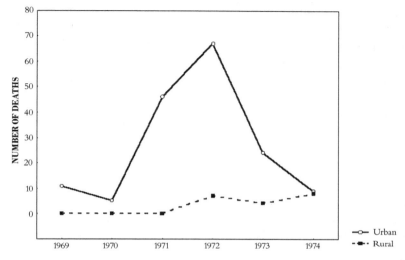

Figure 8 Status of deceased in Belfast, 1969–74

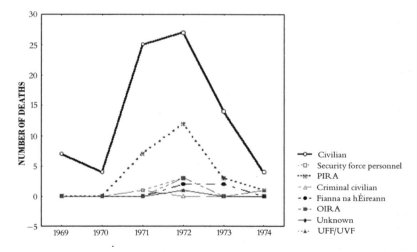

What is also patently evident is that the concentration of deaths in this phase took place in urban centres, notably Belfast, which was the focal point of confrontation between large crowds and the military. It was the place where civil rights marches, intercommunal rioting, forcible movement of persons from their homes and paramilitary responses to the military presence had their strongest expression. Thus, Belfast experienced loss of life caused by state agents on a scale far beyond any other part of the jurisdiction.

What is also cogently illustrated by the statistical evidence is that the majority of persons killed in Belfast were civilians. Out of the total 121 civilian deaths in the first phase of the conflict, 77 occurred in Belfast. In the same period fifty-five members of paramilitary organisations from both sides of the sectarian divide were also killed. Of these, three were members of the UFF/UVF, the remaining fifty-two belonged to various republican paramilitary groupings. Most of these deaths occurred in marginalised urban neighbourhoods within the city. It was these neighbourhoods which manifested the most serious problems of low socio-economic resources at the time and continue to do so thirty years on. The stratification of these communities was intensified not only by structural economic discrimination but by the politics of coercion which pointedly defined their relationship with the state.

A

THE EMERGENCY LAW FRAMEWORK IN THE MILITARISATION PHASE

Despite operational blunders when the army was first deployed, the numbers of persons killed remained relatively low during 1969–70. After 1970, with a motivated and restructured PIRA, the level of violent interaction between state and citizen rose sharply. In the same period the emergency regime was being reconfigured to counter new crises. In essence the state was seeking to use legal process to control the crisis. Draconian legislation to combat public disorder had been introduced in the form of the Criminal Justice (Temporary Provisions) Act 1970. This Act stipulated that persons caught rioting would be subject to a mandatory prison sentence of six months.[40] The army became the chief enforcer of this legislation.

Strictly there was no need for new legislation, as a wide variety of statutory and common law provisions creating powers of arrest for public order offences already existed. These ranged from breach of the peace at common law, grievous bodily harm and assault, to a plethora of charges for carrying weapons or the use of weapons. Such offences were created to be enforced by police officers, not by members of the armed forces, who lacked the skills and training to apply sophisticated discernment in arrest matters. The Criminal Justice Act was a means of making life easier for the army on the ground. It also represented a step away from a strict due process and proportionality model of criminal legal procedure. This move was later expanded by the state, notably by overhauling detention processes and reorganising the courts.

The use of the legislation further alienated the minority community, to whom it was incommensurably applied. The act also had the undesirable side effect of creating chaos in the magistrates' courts. It was repealed soon after its inception, following strong representations from the judiciary and the police.

At the beginning of the militarisation phase the most severe emergency measure used to restore order was curfew. The power to impose a curfew is found solely in the common law; it cannot be authorised by statute. On 3 July 1970 a curfew lasting thirty-four hours was imposed on the Catholic Lower Falls in Belfast. Sporadic gun battles took place during the curfew; five people were killed and sixty injured during the exercise. Tony Geraghty outlines the military expenditure during the curfew:

> In all, the soldiers had fired 1,454 rounds. This included seventeen rounds of .303 from sniper rifles, ten rounds of 9 mm from Sterling sub-machine-guns and 1,427 rounds from 7.62 mm high velocity ammunition, the NATO standard for battlefield use, from self-loading rifles. In addition, 1,600 cartridges and canisters of CS gas were poured into the narrow streets, penetrating every crevice.[41]

The curfew was intended as a means to exert direct control over the population, by allowing wide-scale searches of property to take place. It was, perhaps inevitably, a public relations disaster. Alienation of the minority Catholic community was one inevitable by-product of the imposition of curfews.

The precise legal basis of the July 1970 curfew has been argued by some scholars to rest in a novel extension of common law powers.[42] As proxy citizens army personnel may prevent violent crime and take all reasonable steps to prevent riot. This was the view endorsed by the courts in one of the few cases to arise from the imposition of curfew in Northern Ireland. In the words of the Crown solicitor, 'The soldiers in so doing [restoring the peace by occupying the area] are acting as citizens although they have greater resources.'[43] The courts at the time entirely ignored the link between the imposition of curfew and martial law rule. Martial law has been described as allowing the military 'in order to deal with an emergency amounting to a state of war [to impose] restrictions and regulations upon civilians in their own country'.[44]

Martial law has not been officially invoked in the United Kingdom since the seventeenth century. It is generally viewed as a Crown prerogative, though there is still some argument as to whether the prerogative has been superseded by statute. The imposition of martial law has clear consequences for the legitimacy and internal coherency of the state itself and is rightly perceived as an extreme measure. These stability factors and the proximate centrality of the constitutional relationship between Northern Ireland and the rest of the United Kingdom were cogent political reasons not to take the political step of officially proclaiming martial law in parts of Northern Ireland in the militarisation phase. However, given the escalation of violence in Northern Ireland in the summer of 1970, it is conceivable that martial law could have been declared in the jurisdiction. And given that martial law need not be publicly proclaimed to be in effect, nor that the ordinary courts have to be suspended,[45] there is strong evidence in Northern Ireland that in the early militarisation phase the army was operating on the ground as if, in fact, a state of martial law were in existence. The most cogent example of this is found in the imposition of the Falls Road curfew, which represented a dramatic shift of emphasis for the military. It was a move from peacekeeping to combat tactics, and the escalation had a profound effect on the community who experienced the change.

The question can be asked, however, if the legal status of the army's action makes any difference to an evaluation of the deaths which occurred during the curfew. If the curfew was a *de facto* imposition of martial law, the actions of the army remain theoretically subject to the sanction of the military courts. In reality, of course, that supervision is meaningless, given that the imposition of martial law is invariably accompanied by an Act of Indemnity to protect the military authorities from civil and criminal liability. As mentioned previously, the case of *Hume v. Londonderry Justices* underlines the precarious legal position under which the army operated until 1972.[46] After that date, while the army's actions and deployment were indemnified, the operational tactics of the military does not void the question of what the applicable legal regime was at the time. Nor should the Act of Indemnity detract our attention from the question of what the uncertain legal status of the army indicates about the status of the conflict itself. It should also leave

open the narrower question of the appropriate form of legal accountability for transgressions of domestic and international law committed by
soldiers on the ground during the period.

The most extensive emergency response by the state in the militarisation phase was the introduction of internment. Internment refers to prolonged administrative detention, during which persons taken into
custody are not charged with any offence, generally denied access to
legal counsel and other fundamental due process rights. After its introduction there was a dramatic leap in the number of lethal-force-related
deaths in Northern Ireland.

The introduction of internment was an operational and political
blunder and proved to be an unmitigated disaster. The Wilson Labour
government had been replaced by the Conservatives led by Edward
Heath. Internment had been an option on the 'respond' table for the
Labour government but was never activated; it was introduced by the
Heath cabinet for a variety of reasons. The unionist government had
grown disenchanted by the failure of the nationalist community to be
content with the small number of reforms which had been initiated;[47]
the creation of 'no-go' areas and the army's acquiescence to them
inflamed extremist positions within the Ulster Unionist Party; and
finally, there was a feeling that there needed to be a hard-line military
response to demonstrate the continuing strength of the state.

The army command opposed the introduction of internment from the
beginning.[48] Unlike the British government, they acknowledged the
partisanship of the RUC, the incomplete nature of the intelligence
information available and the alienating dangers of the measure.
Nevertheless, on 5 August 1971 the British cabinet agreed to allow
Northern Ireland Prime Minister Brian Faulkner to exercise the internment option. The detention procedure and its individual targeting of the
nationalist community provoked a surge of violence and an estrangement of moderate Catholic opinion from the governing authorities, surprising only to outside observers. The rise in violence is illustrated by a
sharp rise in lethal force incidents from 1971 onwards (see figure 1,
p. 17). That ordinary citizens were at the receiving end of the explosion
in the use of force is also demonstrated by the empirical evidence. Thus,
we note a nexus between the choice of emergency response and the
impact of that response on the protection of life by the state in an unstable
jurisdiction.

B

BLOODY SUNDAY AND COLLECTIVE CONSCIOUSNESS

The rising surge in lethal force deaths in the militarisation phase was compounded in January 1972 by the disastrous effect of the deaths of thirteen persons attending a peaceful civil rights protest in Derry/Londonderry. Multiple loss of life was caused when the Parachute Regiment opened fire on the march. Accounts of the incident vary, particularly in respect of the causal reason for military personnel opening fire on the protesters. The shooting began at the end of the rally. Some accounts link the shooting with the actions of the crowd in trying to climb over a street barrier. When they were forced back by the army deploying rubber bullets and spray from a water cannon, a stone-throwing battle commenced between the army and a group of youths. Dispute remains over which side fired the first shot; the sequence of events which led to the firing of military weapons is also disputed. Undisputed is the fact that all those killed were unarmed.

New evidence uncovered through the publication of statements taken from hundreds of civilians in the aftermath of the incident suggests that, in addition to firing live ammunition at the ground level, another regiment of the British army had fired on civilians from the heights of the city walls.[49] This evidence, combined with unrelenting public pressure, has led to the creation of a new Tribunal of Inquiry chaired by Lord Saville. Other members of the inquiry include Sir Edward Somers, formerly an Appeal Court judge in New Zealand, and Mr Justice William Hoyt, former Chief Justice of the province of New Brunswick, Canada. The inquiry held a preliminary hearing on 21 and 24 July 1998 and issued its rulings and observations on procedural matters. The tribunal stated that it had been convinced by the 'interests of justice' that families and the wounded were entitled to extended legal representation throughout the course of the proceedings.[50]

The official government inquiry into the incident in 1972 has been the subject of vociferous criticism – for the most part, the much discredited Widgery Report exonerated the Parachute Regiment, though some of its shooting was characterised as 'reckless'.[51] The repercussions of Bloody Sunday have become embedded in the cultural and political consciousness of Northern Ireland's nationalist community.[52] It represents a watershed in the relationship between minority community and state, cementing a history of coercion and disaffection, compounded by the state's willingness to exonerate the agents responsible for any acts which caused loss of life. The combination of this incident and the ongoing internment process indicated that due process had been entirely abandoned and that the military approach now dominated the political agenda.

Widespread communal violence followed the Bloody Sunday incident. The response of the Westminster government was to take the most expedient means of dealing with the crisis. Though the killings were carried out by the British army, the incident served as the death knell for the Stormont regime. Direct control of the internal affairs of Northern Ireland was taken away from the local regime and transferred to Westminster. The subtext of the British governmental response to Bloody Sunday was an unwillingness to leave internal security arrangements solely in the hands of the local unionist politicians. The Northern Ireland parliament was prorogued and direct rule was imposed in March 1972.

Militarisation was evident in the number of troops on the streets in Northern Ireland in 1972. That year saw the highest levels of military commitment to Northern Ireland, a total of 22,000 troops on the ground.[53] It was also the most violent year of the conflict. There were 10,628 shootings, 1,853 bombs planted, 470 deaths, 27.4 tons of explosives found, and 531 persons were charged with terrorist offences.[54] It was also the year that the highest number of deaths were recorded from the use of lethal force by the security forces.

The escalation of violence was a clear indication that militarisation had not solved the Northern Ireland problem. The British government quickly realised that the strategy of militarisation alone succeeded only in raising the levels of conflict – the state found itself in a catch-22 situation. To abandon the military approach would be to open up the sectarian divide and unleash the potential anarchy of all-out intercommunal violence. To rely on the military solution alone alienated the nationalist community and fuelled the extremist violence of PIRA, Once there was a high military presence in the jurisdiction, withdrawal or deployment was no longer a purely military decision. It played into the emerging political dynamics of both nationalist and unionist communities. A high level of military commitment spelt reassurance to one community and increasing alienation to the other. The greater the military's visibility, the harder politically any discussion about its removal became.

Militarisation was no longer a short-term solution, it had become a part of the long-term problem. Not only had the military deployment lasted longer than expected, but the emergency itself was entrenching and becoming part of the long-term calculation. The management of both was the key issue for the British government to address in 1972. What emerged was a realignment of the militarisation policy and a promotion of a legalised emergency regime. The first small steps to this end came with the recalibration of the internment process in 1972. The process was formalised by the introduction of judicial hearings, which were not trials in any meaningful sense, but served to legitimise the detention of suspects by providing an aura of legality.[55] From 1973 onwards the British government engaged in the process of finding alternatives to internment and confrontational approaches to the management of crisis. Their Trojan Horse was the commission under Lord Diplock, set up to examine the criminal justice system and the manner in which it could be modified to more effectively facilitate prosecution of terrorists.[56] Its recommendations were to provide the means to change the response of the state to the internal crisis facing it. It became a catalyst for the cosmetic changes to the shell of internal strife, enabling its normalisation and entrenchment.

IV
Phase two, 1975–80
Normalisation: the politics of Ulsterising the conflict

The policy of normalising the conflict was born out of the failure of interment, the limits of overt militarisation within democratic structures, and a recognition by the British government that the crisis in Northern Ireland was not a short-term affair. The Diplock Report in 1972 was the stepping stone to facilitating the transition from militarisation to normalisation.[57] The report laid the foundation for a governmental strategy which was to deal with the conflict by changing its external terms of reference. The dominant political objective of the mid to late 1970s was to eliminate the political context of the violence, effectively neutralising political legitimacy for the opponents of the state, and re-establishing the legitimacy of the statist order. This was undertaken by invoking and entrenching a criminalisation doctrine, to defuse the political roots of the conflict. Fundamentally, defusing the political context of the violence meant criminalising the actions of those engaged in violence or subversiveness against the state. In this way any legitimisation for violence was removed.

This change was initiated on two levels. First, a fresh approach was directed at the status of prisoners founded on the recommendations of the Gardiner Report.[58] This concentrated on the removal of special category status for those convicted of politically motivated offences after 1976. Special category prisoners had been allowed a status similar to that afforded prisoners of war under the Geneva Conventions.[59] They were allowed to wear their own clothes and were not required to undertake prison work. Giving political status to those persons violently opposing the state was the legal acknowledgement of a loss of political legitimacy and the creation of opposing centres of power within the state. As will be discussed later, it was also strong evidence to indicate that at this point the conflict in Northern Ireland had moved firmly out of the human rights framework and was viewed by the state as a low-intensity armed conflict. The United Kingdom government might have sustained such a political position had the conflict, as first envisioned, been quickly resolved. Once a more long-term prognosis was revealed, the political response was more circumspect. According political status to republican and loyalist prisoners was politically uncomfortable for a state wishing to avoid the external conclusion that another post-colonial débâcle existed in Northern Ireland. Equally unpalatable was any overt validation of the applicability of the laws of war to an internal crisis, thereby admitting of a crisis of constitutional legitimacy for the United Kingdom within its own internationally confirmed borders. Instead, the legal system became the primary means to combat the increasing political violence.

The normalisation strategy was rooted in recommendations of the Diplock Report itself. This response by the British government is important in telling us that once a crisis prolongs, the stamp of legality is a key aspect of governmental control within the emergency law model. Achieving political normalisation was the rationale for using the court system but modifying it to combat terrorist violence. The crime-control model swung the pendulum firmly towards a legality model for dealing with subversive activity.[60] The criminalisation model was a critical feature in the attempt to defuse the political stalemate which was emerging in Northern Ireland in the early 1970s. The use of ordinary

courts to process terrorist violence had the effect of normalising and chan-
nelling state responses in a specific and externally validated way. As long
as the courts functioned, and due process was not completely abrogated,
the moderate majority and international perception was that the conflict
was being managed in the appropriate manner. It also gave backing to
the position that the crisis was an internal criminal problem rather than a
low-intensity conflict activating the applicability of the laws of war.
However, in order to 'manage' the scale and nature of the paramilitary
threat, quite severe modifications to the traditional criminal process were
required. These modifications were to have severe implications for confidence in the impartiality and neutrality of legal process.

The transformation of the criminal justice process was achieved by
generating two pieces of legislation, the Emergency Provisions Act and
the Prevention of Terrorism Act. Though the products of differing gesta-
tions, they retain the central similarity of extraordinary legal powers
created to function within the confines of the ordinary. They are currently in force as the Northern Ireland (Emergency Provisions) Act
1996 (EPA) and its counterpart the Prevention of Terrorism (Temporary
Provisions) Act 1989 (PTA). The current EPA is an evolved version of a
piece of legislation first passed in 1973.[61] Its forerunner repealed the
Special Powers Act,[62] which symbolically represented to the minority
community the dominance and undemocratic nature of the state.
However, the 1973 legislation paradoxically re-enacted many of the
same provisions.

Both the PTA and EPA 'are designed to obtain convictions in cases
involving those suspected of paramilitary activity, based on confessions
obtained through prolonged detention and intense interrogation'.[63] The
centrepiece of the EPA is the removal of jury trial for defined scheduled
offences. At the core of the Diplock system is the concept of 'scheduling'.
Scheduled offences are those offences specifically listed and contained in
Schedule 1 of the EPA, If charged with such an offence, the panoply of
emergency arrest, detention and trial processes accrue to the citizen
charged. Research has indicated that up to 40 per cent of those charged
and processed under the Diplock system were involved in the commission of offences with no political motivation, but which could not be
descheduled by definition.[64] Powers in the legislation include road blocking powers, proscription and related powers, offences of collecting information and training, possession for terrorist purposes, directing the

activities of a terrorist organisation; formerly racketeering provisions were included (these have now been transferred to the ordinary law).

The PTA was enacted in 1974 following the killing of twenty-one people in bombings in Birmingham pubs in November 1974.[65] It was derived from the 1973 EPA legislation,[66] and the Prevention of Violence (Temporary Provisions) Act 1939,[67] which had been enacted for use against an earlier IRA campaign. Although the PTA was originally intended to expire after only six months, it has endured to the present. It is a grim reminder of the tendency of the transient to become permanent. Initially, the PTA was subject to renewal by parliament every six months, but in 1976 it was re-enacted subject to yearly renewal.[68] The statute was updated and overhauled in 1984[69] and 1989.[70] As with the EPA, there have been a number of major reviews and yearly assessments of the PTA,[71] These reviews have been proclaimed widely as independent of the state and vaunted at international forums as neutral and protective processes that have the potential to rein in the state in its use of crisis powers.[72]

A

DUE PROCESS RIGHTS UNDER THE EMERGENCY REGIME

In the normalisation phase due process rights were the focal point of legal modification for the state. Due process protections are the most frequently and extensively limited rights for the individual under emergency regimes. This is particularly true of Northern Ireland. These rights are the most vulnerable to governmental intrusion and limitation, and are one of the most effective vehicles for streamlining the response of the state to crisis. Thus arrest, detention and trial are pivotal points of institutional response for the state. In Northern Ireland, from its creation, the criminal justice structure was key to harnessing the response of the state to internal exigency. The use of the criminal justice structure has a number of distinct advantages for the state in responding to crisis. First, it has a useful symbolic effect, in allowing the state to claim that crisis is under control because ordinary process is apparently utilised, notwithstanding the fact that the ordinary criminal justice system may be severely modified in order to contain crisis. Nonetheless, the appearance of normality is maintained. Second, legitimacy is maintained by the use of legal sanction as opposed to extra-legal measures. However, the experience in many jurisdictions (including the United Kingdom) is that extra-legal measures are part and parcel of state response but are partly concealed by the overt response of the criminal justice system.[73] In Northern Ireland these concerns have centred primarily on allegations of a shoot-to-kill policy by law-enforcers and allegations of collusion between members of the security forces and loyalist paramilitary organisations.[74]

Arrest and detention was a critical feature of the normalisation regime. In particular, section 14 of the PTA was the primary legal means created to facilitate extended detention in Northern Ireland. Section 14 (4) and (5) allow an initial arrest period of forty-eight hours, which can be extended for up to five days on the order of the Secretary of State for Northern Ireland. These arrests, while taking place within the PTA legal framework, have a significant relationship with the EPA powers. This is because persons arrested under 'terrorism provisions' become subject to special provisions governing access to solicitors and notification of arrest. The substantive limitations on basic due process rights under section 14 cannot be underestimated. While the law-enforcer is required to have a reasonable suspicion that the arrestee has been involved in the 'commission, preparation or instigation of acts of terrorism', the majority of those detained have been released without charge.[75] In fact, the vast majority of those arrested have been released without charge within two days.[76]

Section 14 was the means of gathering information, seeking informers and collating information on discrete communities and individuals, with the cost of limiting the rights protection of arrested citizens. It facilitated classic counter-insurgency techniques within a sanctified legal model. It was the outward face of normalisation, as arrest statistics were vaunted as proof that the battle against terrorism was being won. But the water was muddied by the fact that arrest alone was not sufficient to halt paramilitary violence and what occurred within the arrest framework did not always sit comfortably with a legality model and Western democratic practices.

From its 1974 inception, section 14 has been interlinked with sustained concerns about the conditions of detention in holding centres in Northern Ireland and ill-treatment of persons detained. The adverse conditions in Castlereagh, Belfast, the primary detention centre for emergency arrests, have been widely publicised.[77] They include lack of natural daylight, failure to keep cells clean, no resources for exercise, lack of access to reading material, and physically small holding spaces. The United Nations Human Rights Committee recommended in July 1995 that Castlereagh detention centre be closed as a 'matter of urgency'.[78] Furthermore, there is no statutory basis for the existence of the interrogation centres in contravention of international legal requirements. Paragraph 40 of the Body of Principles on the Right to a Fair Trial, drawn up and presented to the UN Sub-Commission on Prevention of Discrimination and Protection of Minorities in June 1994, states: 'Detainees shall be housed in places *established by law* for that purpose and duly identified [emphasis added].'[79]

The use of seven-day arrest powers in Northern Ireland has been the basis for the United Kingdom's derogation from its legally mandated international obligations. The seven-day detention power has been found by the European Court of Human Rights to contravene the principles of protection set out under Article 5 (3) of the treaty, requiring that those arrested and charged with any offence be brought 'promptly' before a court. In the *Brogan* case, detention under the PTA, which amounted to four days and six hours, was deemed to fall below the European Convention standard.[80] Rather than repealing the legislation and bringing the detention period into line with international standards, or alternatively creating some form of judicial oversight of the process, the government opted to derogate from its international obligations, under Article 15 of the European Convention and Article 4 of the International Covenant on Civil and Political Rights. The government's choice to initiate the derogation is itself controversial. There is clear evidence that the derogation in 1988 was entered as a response to an adverse court decision, rather than reacting to the strict necessity for its use as required by international law.[81]

B

THE CORNERSTONE IS MODIFIED – COURTS AND TRIAL

The abrogation of trial by jury in Northern Ireland in 1973 was one of the most fundamental inroads on the protection of due process rights in the jurisdiction. It was also the central plank of the normalisation policy. The Diplock Courts have been plagued by controversy since their inception.[82] Tied to the coercive arrest and detention process, concerns about judicial case-hardening, the high level of confessional-based convictions and the manipulation of the rules of evidence to ensure convictions, the courts have been severely discredited domestically and internationally.[83]

Diplock trials are characterised by a number of problematic procedural aspects whose overall effect is to limit protection for the rights of accused persons. The laws of evidence have been significantly changed in order to accommodate a modified legal system whose primary focus was (and remains) conviction of offenders associated with political disorder.[84] Furthermore, the abandonment of the common law Judge's Rules and their replacement by a statutory standard has resulted in lower standards for determining the admissibility of evidence in these courts.

C

THE EARLY TRIUMPH OF NORMALITY

The alliance of the legal system with the political priorities of the state was no new phenomenon in Northern Ireland.[85] The Northern Ireland legal system was allied with the central forces of the substate from its inception – the unionist government had the power to appoint magistrates. These lower courts were particularly significant as they tried the bulk of 'political' crimes prior to the creation of the Diplock Courts. The Senior Bar and the judicial branch was dominated by Protestant legal actors. It was not until the passing of the Butler Education Act in 1947 that large numbers of Catholics attained legal education and entrance to the legal profession.[86] Of the seven judges on the High Court in Northern Ireland in 1970, three had been Ulster Unionist Party MPs at Stormont, a fourth was the son of an Ulster Unionist government minister. There was a widespread perception that the legal profession was neither representative of nor responsive to the diverse ethnic make-up of the jurisdiction.

The imposition of new emergency laws met with no legal challenge or resistance from the domestic guardians of due process and constitutionality. Any such commentary was reserved for concerned outsiders.[87] This is not an experience unique to Northern Ireland. The judicial branches in numerous countries facing states of exception have proved consistently faint-hearted in addressing misuse of emergency powers or inappropriate extension of executive powers.[88] Harnessing the courts to process the political crisis facing the state was simply a continuation of previous practice for the institutional structures of the substate in the 1970s. This was precisely what had taken place between 1922 and 1969. The courts had routinely dealt with and legitimised the use of the Special Powers Act. Northern Ireland had been under a permanent state of emergency since 1922, facilitated by the use of special powers and advanced by an acquiescent and willing legal establishment. Those external factors had not changed by the time of the EPA's introduction. What was different in 1973 was the extent to which that legal structure was relied upon to define political policy. Once the legal strategy was in operation, it confirmed the political dynamic. The Diplock Report was an *ad hoc* response to the crisis emanating from the failure of internment. The structure created was the means to facilitate the normalisation of a state of emergency. Ultimately, its normalisation ensured that the legal system redefined itself by reference to abnormality, leaving behind the need to examine the irregularity which accounted for its modified structure.

D

LETHAL FORCE IN THE NORMALISATION PHASE

In understanding the evolution of increased protection for the right to life in the normalisation phase, an analysis of the changing relationship of control on the ground between the police and army is critical. In the

Figure 9 Fatalities caused by state agents, 1975–80

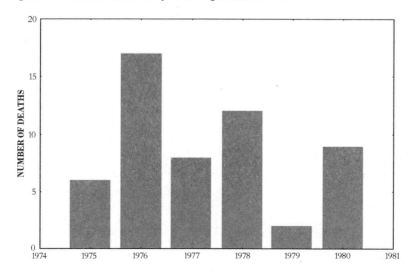

militarisation phase of the conflict the RUC had been required by sweeping political circumstances and their own mismanagement to abdicate responsibility for policy and security matters to the army. The abdication of police responsibility created an upsurge in deaths resulting from the use of lethal force by the military. This fact demonstrates the negative correlation between extreme exigency, the agents' responsibility for controlling it, and the protection of citizens' lives. By 1973 the perception that short-term solutions were unlikely to resolve the conflict meant that the British government wanted responsibility for law enforcement to shift back to local law-enforcers. The reasons for this were entirely politically motivated. The policy of normalisation, or Ulsterisation, sought to place management of the conflict in local hands. The symbolic re-establishment of the RUC as the primary and visible law-enforcers had an immeasurable public relations value. It was a means to once again change the terms of external and internal reference on the conflict. It signalled in a visual and tangible way a return to normality and played down the strife as a mere criminal problem that was under legal (not military) control.[89]

The use of force by agents of the state drops dramatically in the normalisation phase. This is not to suggest that force is exercised in a comparable manner with an ordinary democratic state which is not facing internal insurgency. The comparison here is strictly with the earlier phase, the militarisation phase. There are three reasons for the decrease in fatalities. First, the changeover in agency responsibility, where the army plays second fiddle in large crowd situations to the police. Second, the army itself is adjusting to its role in a civilian situation, adapting to the local environment, learning to read the ground rules more cogently. Finally, the emphasis on legal structure to control the conflict essentially moves the crisis off the streets, which had been the dominant site of confrontation during the militarisation phase.

The distribution of fatalities caused by agents of the state between 1975 and 1980 is distinctly lower than in the 1969–74 period. A total of fifty-four persons were killed in this phase of the conflict by members of the security forces. The lower number of fatalities is also correlated with a lowering tempo of violence in this period. The high point of communal street demonstrations against the Stormont regime had passed, in effect taking away the focal point of large scale confrontation between state and citizen. These had also been the focal point of state life-taking as a

Figure 10 Types of incident causing lethal force deaths, 1975–80

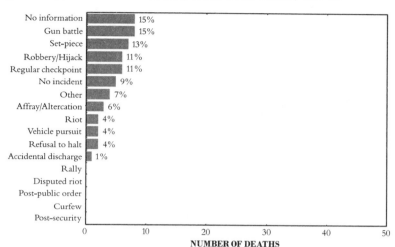

means to combat internal dissent. Thus, citizens' lives were better protected simply because there were fewer public opportunities where citizen and state came into open conflict. This did not mean, of course, that the state had placed a higher objective value on the lives of dissenting citizens. This fact is cogently proven in the active counter-insurgency period which was to follow in the 1980s.

Between 1975 and 1980 the taking of life occurs in changing circumstances. These circumstances parallel the political dynamics of the period. The number of persons killed in gun battles dropped from 24 per cent in the first phase of the conflict to 15 per cent in the second phase. Curfews, rallies and riots have become less significant as a causal basis for lethal force deaths. As we will notice in the analysis pertaining to the final phase of the conflict, public order deaths reassert themselves on public consciousness in communal responses to the republican hunger strikes. Thus, seven deaths in 1981 result from the use of plastic bullets in situations of disturbed public order. However, this particular context of death is not a feature of deaths occurring in the normalisation phase.

An examination of deaths in the normalisation phase illustrates the inauguration of a small but discernible shift in agency responsibility. This shift throws light on how conflict management changes over time with the entrenchment of an emergency. Although the regular army is still primarily responsible for loss of life (thirty-six deaths in total), overall

Figure 11 State agency responsible for lethal force deaths, 1975–80

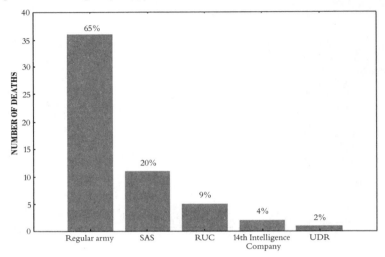

numbers of fatalities (fifty-four) are much lower. What occurs in this period is the initial activation of specialist military units, assertively engaging in counter-insurgency. Empirical information indicates that specialist units were responsible for thirteen deaths in the normalisation phase of the conflict.

The year 1978 is particularly revealing, as specialist military forces are dramatically utilised with botched effect. The Special Air Service (SAS) was officially committed to Northern Ireland in 1976 – the official announcement of its deployment on 7 January followed a number of incidents in south Armagh earlier in the year. Directly preceding the announcement was an incident in which ten Protestant workmen, travelling on a bus, were murdered in a unambiguous sectarian act in Kingsmills. The presence of the SAS in Northern Ireland was not new. From the start of the conflict individual members of the squadron had been seconded to the regular army. The official announcement was a calculated political act, with propaganda value. It was designed to comfort those who sought a tough military approach to paramilitary violence. It signalled a change of tactics by the state to the republican paramilitaries and in particular to the geographical location of south Armagh.

The 1978 specialist military operations were entirely unsuccessful for a number of reasons. Primarily, the public relations value of killing dangerous terrorists was lessened because not all those killed were terrorists, but indisputedly civilians. Furthermore, a number of terrorists were unarmed when fatally shot. This aspect of their deaths gave rise to the allegation that the state was engaging in a shoot-to-kill policy, alienating moderate nationalist opinion and creating political embarrassment for government ministers. However, 1978 is an anomaly in the normalisation phase, as the overt use of specialist units was abandoned until the resumption of active counter-insurgency in the 1980s.[90] There was also a realisation that the killing of paramilitaries on 'active service' or otherwise gave a propaganda coup to the republican movement.

The deployment of undercover units in situations likely to cause loss of life requires an exercise in political balancing by the security forces. Will the potential loss of life and resulting community alienation be outweighed by the security advantages of successful confrontation? For a considerable time after the 1978 débâcle the answer was no; the SAS remained in Northern Ireland but its expertise was concentrated on intelligence and surveillance. However, the question of active engagement against those violently opposing the state was not far away from the political agenda. The response to the balancing question was to have a very different answer in the 1980s.

E

NORMALISATION UNDER STRESS

The optimism which breezed in with the normalisation policy soon experienced its first seedlings of disillusionment. In 1975 allegations of ill-treatment of detainees in detention centres surfaced in the jurisdiction. The allegations gained credence as they were confirmed in 1978 by international observers from Amnesty International and could not be easily dismissed as republican propaganda. The allegations related initially to the ill-treatment of detainees during internment in the militarisation phase of the conflict. A series of high profile cases to the European Court of Human Rights was the first indicator that Northern Ireland's detention procedures were about to receive unwelcome external scrutiny.[91] The RUC became the focus of attention as the cases highlighted how reliance on confessions, facilitated by relaxed rules of evidence, could lead to systematic abuses of individual rights in violation of international law. While the cases under consideration related to the earlier phase of the conflict, the heart of the observers' examination related directly to the methods still being utilised in the normalisation phase to control the civil strife. It was only a matter of time before the linkage between the interrogation methods being used in both phases would be made. The peephole on the militarisation phase opened up a Pandora's box on the normalisation phase.

International pressure mounted as Amnesty International's report sustaining allegations of ill-treatment was followed by a European Commission decision on the Irish government's case alleging violations of the European Convention on Human Rights by the United Kingdom government.[92] The commission report was soon followed by a decision of the European Court, which found that the five techniques of interrogation specifically addressed in the Irish complaint constituted inhuman treatment under the convention. The consequence of the decision was to focus attention not only on what happened during the internment period, but upon concurrent practices in detention centres in Northern Ireland. They struck at the core of the governmental response in the normalisation phase. Both the report and the European Court decision highlighted the shift from confrontation in the streets to reliance on the courts and their attendant processes to control conflict. In the normalisation phase the primary security strategy was prosecution through the modified court system. Eight out of every ten prosecutions relied on confessional evidence alone to secure conviction.[93]

The European judgment had a deterrent effect on the use of these interrogation techniques, which were the main prop of the machinery to ensure conviction for terrorist offences. This marginal shift was forced by the recommendations of the Bennett Report in 1979. The Bennett Committee had been activated by the government as a means of limiting the loss of confidence in the administration of justice caused by the confirmation that ill-treatment of detainees had taken place. The committee recommended access to solicitors for detainees after forty-eight hours in custody, the monitoring of cells by close-circuit television, and proper training for interrogators.[94] Unwanted external scrutiny and additional constraints on the interrogation process cemented the conclusion that legal process alone was not 'winning the war'. This led to another shift in emphasis in the early 1980s and a change in governmental strategy to achieve a containment of violence.

V
Phase three, 1981–94
The alliance of active counter-insurgency and extraordinary law

On 27 October 1980 seven republican prisoners in the Maze prison began a hunger strike in protest at the removal of political status. This hunger strike was the culmination of earlier protests, which first began in 1976: from the point at which special category status was denied to republican and loyalist prisoners, the former refused en masse to comply with prison rules. The most compelling example of this was the 'dirty protest', so named from the refusal of prisoners to wear prison uniforms, resulting in their confinement to cells and the practical consequences of refusing to avail of the inadequate toilet facilities within those cells.[95] It has also generally been overlooked that a minority of loyalist prisoners participated in the so-called 'blanket protest'. This minority was largely unsupported, morally or practically, by other loyalist prisoners and external organisations.[96] The hunger strike was abandoned on 18 December 1980, after it appeared that the government was committed to concessions and dialogue with the prisoners. Intentional food deprivation recommenced in March 1981 following the failure of that dialogue. The response of the nationalist community to the perceived inflexibility of the United Kingdom government during the seven-month protest, in which 10 hunger-strikers (7 PIRA, 3 INLA) died, created a political watershed in Northern Ireland. This political metamorphosis goes some way to explaining the change in direction for conflict management in the jurisdiction in the 1980s. The hunger strikes produced grassroots support for republicanism which was both unexpected and threatening for the state. The election of Bobby Sands, the first hunger-striker to die, to the Westminster parliament was followed by considerable electoral success for Sinn Féin in successive local government and general elections. By June 1983 Sinn Féin had obtained 13.4 per cent of the electoral vote in Northern Ireland.[97]

Quantifying the effect of the hunger strikes on security policy is not straightforward. The subsequent high electoral support for Sinn Féin compounded the view in certain governmental quarters that there was a hard-line element in the nationalist community, actively supportive of the politics of violence. The tactics of negotiation would not reposition this hard-line constituency in relation to their views on the internal political structures of the United Kingdom. Sinn Féin support was read as a failure of the policy of normalisation, because it illustrated that the policy had floundered among a considerable segment of the nationalist population. In military terms, a simplistic read would see votes for Sinn Féin as a network of support for an ongoing campaign of violence. Practically translated, that meant safe houses, a flow of information about the state and its agents, and an unwillingness to lend support to the forces of law and order.

With this analysis in hand, a more systematic return to active counter-insurgency was predictable. What the dissection failed to recognise was that the high point of support following the hunger strikes was intimately linked to what one commentator describes as 'a tribal voice of martyrdom, deeply embedded in Gaelic, Catholic, Nationalist tradition'.[98] The point being, that initial electoral success by republicans can be linked to emotive responses evoked by the historical analogies of martyrdom, as opposed to direct and unequivocal support for political violence.

A

SETTING THE STAGE FOR ACTIVE COUNTER-INSURGENCY

While the hunger strikes laid bare a grim moment of political consciousness misunderstood by the state, the stage for what followed had, in fact, been set much earlier. By the late 1970s the state had come to realise that the policy of normalisation was not producing the intended long-term results for conflict containment. The hunger strikes merely confirmed this political fact. When police primacy became a pivotal political reality, the seeds were sown for active engagement against those violently opposing the state.

By the end of the 1970s the RUC was emerging as a self-confident, modern police force. When Kenneth Newman was Chief Constable, strong emphasis was placed on modernising the force and integrating the RUC into mainland police structures and practices, while maintaining a parallel militaristic and civilian role. The militaristic function was evidenced by its sophisticated weaponry, the centralisation of intelligence and its role in processing detainees under the emergency legislation. Its rising political importance, allied with internal beliefs about its military capacity, created the assumption that the police were capable of taking on active counter-insurgency within the jurisdiction. Thus, the evolution of the RUC is crucial to conceptualising the re-emergence of a policy of active counter-insurgency, and its reformulation when police control proved to be an utter failure.

The police gateway to active counter-insurgency found its inception in the centralisation of intelligence in the RUC Special Branch from 1977 onwards. Traditional hostility between the police and army over intelligence sources was temporarily abandoned, with the creation of integrated intelligence centres called Tasking and Co-ordination groups. The first was created in 1978 and was based at Castlereagh in Belfast. Increased RUC control over intelligence sources led to the development of further specialised units within the police apparatus. The year 1980 saw the conception of Divisional Mobile Support Units (DMSUs), specialised units trained in militaristic responses to riot and crowd-control situations. These were intended to provide flash-point support when the 'ordinary' police were unable to cope. Incrementally the policy of specialisation was pursued within the RUC, This involved creating Headquarters Mobile Support Units (HMSUs), specialist units to support ordinary police in rural areas. Finally, spearheading the developing hierarchy were the Special Support Units (SSUs).

All these units were sustained by informer information, which was, in turn, facilitated by extended detention powers, and remained the mainstay of the police response to terrorism. The SSUs were to become especially important. They were SAS-trained, with an emphasis on firearms training and reactive responses to situations of threat. The next logical step, from a police point of view, was to activate the use of these units to specifically combat the paramilitary activity ever present in Northern Ireland. This view was given political credibility by the unfolding events in Northern Ireland in the early 1980s.

B

THE ANATOMY OF POLICE FAILURE:
THE POLICE AND COUNTER-INSURGENCY

In 1982 the police dabbled directly and ineptly in overt counter-insurgency. Between 11 November and 12 December six individuals were fatally injured by RUC MSUs in County Armagh. Five of the dead were members of republican paramilitary organisations, the sixth was a civilian. All six deaths occurred in controversial circumstances.

Two weeks prior to the first deaths, those of PIRA members Gervaise McKerr, Sean Burns and Eugene Toman, three police officers were killed when a large bomb blew apart the car in which they were travelling in Kinnego, County Armagh. Linking these two incidents is problematic. Nonetheless, commentators have suggested that the three deceased PIRA men were linked to a PIRA active service unit that had set up the Kinnego incident.[99] The fatal confrontation was preplanned on the basis of informer information, the three men having been under constant surveillance for a considerable time before their deaths.[100] They were unarmed when killed and an approximate total of 109 bullets were discharged into their vehicle. In 1984 three policemen were subsequently charged with and acquitted of the murder of Eugene Toman.[101]

Two other incidents were also characterised by excessive use of force. On 24 November seventeen-year-old Michael Tighe was shot as he entered a hayshed which was under surveillance by an MSU, On 12 December Seamus Grew and Roddy Carroll, both members of the INLA, were shot in a confrontation with undercover police shortly after crossing the border from the Irish Republic. Both were unarmed at the time of the incident. Constable John Robinson was charged with and acquitted of the murder of Seamus Grew.[102]

These incidents provoked local and international condemnation. A series of inquiries into the deaths failed to dampen nationalist fears that a shoot-to-kill policy was being operated against republican paramilitaries. The most notable was the Stalker inquiry, started by Deputy Chief Constable John Stalker of the Greater Manchester police on 24 May 1984. The police foray into military confrontation had backfired, confirming the army's evaluation that they were inherently unsuitable to the task of counter-insurgency. The political calculation was quickly made. In short, active counter-insurgency by a theoretically civilian police force would always be subject to greater public scrutiny than any similar action on the part of the army and should be avoided.

Compounding the failure of the RUC to successfully assume a counter-insurgency role was the collapse of the 'supergrass' system to obtain convictions for terrorist offences. The dubious practice of supergrass trials came into use after the ending of the hunger strikes.[103] The process was heavily backed by the police, who provided the raw material to make it work. The trials resulted from informers turning Queen's evidence against former alleged accomplices. Their willingness to give such evidence occurred within the confines of protective police custody, and was additionally safeguarded by a system of plea bargaining to protect themselves from punitive criminal sanction. The trials were discredited by the fact that in numerous cases accomplice evidence was uncorroborated, the element of inducement undermined the voluntary nature of the evidence, and the reliability of the witnesses was open to serious doubt.

Supergrass operations amounted to a more sophisticated form of internment, as those charged with offences on the strength of supergrass evidence were held on remand for up to two years before trial. The conviction rate was initially high – by the autumn of 1983 three major supergrass trials had resulted in the conviction of 56 of the 64 defendants (88 per cent), with 31 of these convictions (55 per cent) resting solely on the supergrasses' uncorroborated testimony.[104] On appeal, however, the bulk of the convictions were overturned. The Court of Appeal has nonetheless repeatedly denied that 'the procedures and rules of evidence applied in the "supergrass" trials failed to guarantee the basic right to a fair trial'.[105] In the final analysis it seems that the judiciary were unwilling to sustain convictions based on flawed and largely uncorroborated sources. Their willingness to be independent of political pressures was

Figure 12 Types of incident causing lethal force deaths, 1981–94

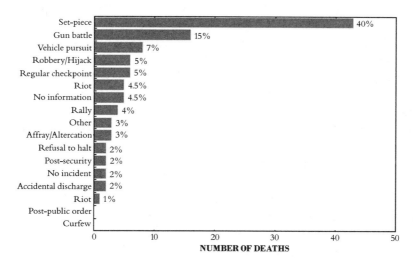

the most significant factor in the collapse of the supergrass system.[106]

The abandonment of the supergrass trials, combined with the removal of the military option for the RUC, shifted the counter-insurgency balance back in favour of the army. From 1983 onwards the politics of confrontation were largely in the domain of the specialist army units, primarily the SAS,[107] The RUC was relegated to the function of providing backup to such operations and providing the informer information that allowed preplanning for military 'set-piece' operations. The resounding political message was that police primacy did not extend to mounting counter-insurgency operations against PIRA,

I use the term 'set-piece' to describe the particular kind of specialist operations leading to the use of deadly force which emerged in the third phase of the conflict. The features of these set-piece operations give a grim indication of a discernible shift in state policy as regards the use of force in the 1980s. First, the deployment of specialist units meant that when force was exercised, the soldiers shot to kill. In many preplanned military confrontations the evidence suggests that arrest in the context of these operations did not constitute taking the suspect into custody; it meant eliminating a threat, even if that meant killing the suspect. The decision not to seek custody seems invariably linked with the status of the deceased. Between 1981 and 1994, 40 per cent of all incidents involving the use of lethal force occurred in the set-piece context. The dominant affiliation of those killed in this period in the set-piece context was to paramilitary organisations. Notably, as figure 13 illustrates, the majority of those killed during 1969–94 belonged to PIRA,

It is a harsh political reality that it is easier for the state to 'sell' the necessity for taking the lives of members of paramilitary organisations than to manage the fall-out when uninvolved civilians are killed by agents of the state. Ensuring that the taking of life occurs within a legally permissible framework is not without importance in the planning and execution of these operations. The external perception that legality is the normative context for death has both a public relations and a legal value. The planners of these operations in this third phase realised the potential political embarrassment and alienation (usually of moderate nationalist opinion) which could result from an operation where it appeared that the rules of due process had been entirely abandoned. When life-taking seemed to operate outside the legal framework there was the unwanted possibility of criminal prosecutions against the security forces, which were

Figure 13 Paramilitary affiliation of deceased, 1969–94

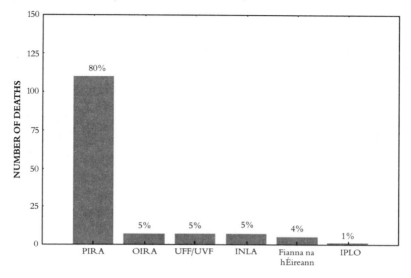

undesirable for two reasons. First, the careers of individual soldiers who were simply following orders were placed at risk. Second, sources of military intelligence might be compromised.

The fact that the suspected paramilitaries were armed and were, allegedly or actually, engaged in unlawful activity gives both a legal justification under domestic criminal law to use force and provides sufficient rationale within the army's own internal guidelines.[108] Arguably, domestic legal standards leave a gaping hole in accountability by excluding from the legal evaluation of life-taking in these particular incidents the maximal use of force, the deployment of specialist units and the persistent resort to informer information.

It is important to qualify my analysis at this point. I do not suggest that there is a political text which explicitly gives a green light to active counter-insurgency under new rules of engagement – it is unlikely that any such document exists. But what this work does illustrate is the fact that there was a discernible shift in the empirical patterns of state confrontation with paramilitary actors in the 1980s in Northern Ireland. These involve real and meaningful changes in the scale of a particular type of confrontation with anti-state actors and they invariably involve the use of lethal force, resulting in the deaths of paramilitary members, or civilians mistakenly identified as paramilitaries. Without fail, they involve specialist units of the military, trained to shoot to kill, not to wound or incapacitate.

These facts can lead to various political conclusions which are not the function of this analysis. Rather, in legal terms they illustrate a shifting approach to a permanent emergency situation, which displays unacknowledged low-intensity armed conflict characteristics. They also point us to a diminishing value for the protection of life in a prolonged conflict. In particular, it seems that suspicion or actual membership of a proscribed organisation in Northern Ireland substantially weakens the right to life of those thus suspected.

C

PARALLEL EMERGENCY MODIFICATIONS
DURING THE COUNTER-INSURGENCY PERIOD

The Northern Ireland emergency itself was also modifying during this third stage of conflict management. The most cogent feature of this period was the trend to completely normalise the emergency by transferring emergency powers into the ordinary law in order to cope with civil strife.[109] Thus, the invisible barrier between the ordinary and the extraordinary was in a process of being entirely swept away by the state. The prime example of this is the abrogation of the right to silence, first enacted in Northern Ireland in November 1988, now extended to the rest of the United Kingdom. While not a part of the emergency regime *per se*, its introduction was premised on the perceived difficulty in processing paramilitary defendants in the criminal justice system and allied to expansive predetention powers.

The removal of the right to silence was a clear extension of the emergency regime into the ordinary criminal law. Following the 1994 ceasefires in Northern Ireland, Secretary of State Sir Patrick Mayhew announced a 'powerful, authoritative and independent' review of anti-terrorism laws.[110] This most recent review of emergency legislation, submitted by Lord Lloyd and Mr Justice Kerr, recommends the imposition of permanent counter-terrorist (emergency) legislation upon the normal legal framework as part of the ordinary law.[111]

The outcome of the review process illustrates the extent to which the normalisation process has advanced. The basis for their conclusion rests largely on two propositions. First, that terrorism presents an exceptionally serious threat to society. Second, that terrorists have proven particularly difficult to apprehend without recourse to special offence schedules and additional police powers.[112] The report sets out five distinguishing features of terrorism, and concludes that their particular characteristics justify the creation of special legislation.[113] There is no broad engagement in this review with the historical, social and political context in which the use of emergency laws was developed and refined in Northern Ireland. Parallel to this is a myopic assessment of the threat facing the United Kingdom from terrorism and an unwillingness to intellectually engage with the potential of the ordinary legal system to cope with changed circumstances.

The Lloyd review indicates how the use of emergency powers for extensive periods has a distinctive effect on the establishment, which comes to rely upon it legally and politically. The normalisation of emergencies not only creates profound legal trenches but has a discernible effect on the mindset of those who operate within them, and who come to view legal structures through the prism of the abnormal. A practical illustration of this phenomenon in Northern Ireland was the complete retention of the emergency framework throughout the entire period of the ceasefires and beyond. This is generally indicative of how difficult it becomes to dislodge crisis powers once they have become institutionalised within the state.

No emergency review has been couched in terms of a commitment to dismantling thirty years of permanent emergency. This is illustrative of the complete ease with which the exception has become the norm in Northern Ireland, and the danger that the exception will become the norm in the United Kingdom as a whole. The long-term use of emergency powers becomes a convenient basis upon which to usurp the protections that all citizens are entitled to under the treaty protections of the European Convention on Human Rights and the International Covenant on Civil and Political Rights. When a state creates a permanent piece of anti-terrorist legislation, drawn and modelled on pre-existing emergency structures, what we are witnessing is a slippage of emergency laws into ordinary law. This legal act is no less the creation of a permanent emergency than doing so by passing an act of parliament which has the word 'emergency' in its official title. It is also indicative of how the emergency phenomenon evolved once again during 1981–94, where the exception has, in fact, become entirely normalised.

The first step towards internalisation of the legally exceptional is the willingness to intellectually rationalise the process of normalising the abnormal. In relation to the right to silence, the localisation of the initial legal changes to Northern Ireland, couched in the language of the exception, lulled many observers in the United Kingdom into assuming that its effects would always remain local to an aberrant situation. In this context, the Lloyd recommendations are not as surprising as one might think. They fit a neat paradigm that localisation is not a feature of governmental practice in relation to the use of crisis powers. Complete normalisation of emergency powers ultimately requires that those facets of emergency authority which identifiably demonstrate difference be made ordinary. This has the effect of limiting the heightened scrutiny of law. Its most worrying aspect is that it actually changes the terms of the discussion itself. That is to say, the process of normalisation changes the debate about the emergency by seeking to redefine the emergency as a normal facet of everyday life. The Lloyd Report is key to this evolving approach in the United Kingdom, as 'emergency' is redefined as an inevitable, if not banal, feature of modern social existence.

D

COUNTER-INSURGENCY RE-ESTABLISHED

The preplanned confrontations in the counter-insurgency phase are more sophisticated than their 1978 forerunners. An example is the Loughgall incident in which eight members of a PIRA active service unit and an innocent civilian were killed by an SAS unit while attacking a small police station in County Armagh in 1987. The PIRA unit was heavily armed and information is limited about the precise details of the incident.

On 8 May 1987 a PIRA active service unit attacked the village RUC station with a large construction site digger loaded with 200 lbs of explosives. However, the unit had been under heavy surveillance by the security forces and it is likely that the military had informer information giving advance notice of PIRA's intentions and its specific target.[114] Though never officially confirmed, commentators agree that members of the SAS were involved in the specialist unit monitoring and actively participating in the Loughgall operation.

With meticulous planning, the SAS went into position within and around the police barracks many hours before the attack took place. Mark Urban has argued that the positioning of the troops inside the barracks was crucial for legal purposes – the military was thus provided with a clear self-defence justification by virtue of the explicit threat posed by the PIRA unit.[115] This remains the case notwithstanding the fact that the military were aware of the precise nature of the threat before it was deployed to respond to it. Troops were also placed at key locations within and around the village to prevent the escape of any PIRA members.

Figure 14 Set-piece incidents, 1977–92

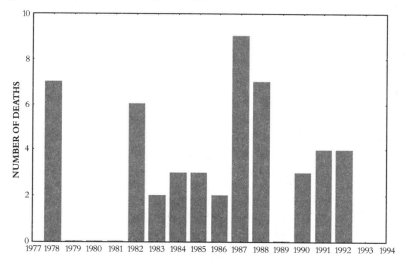

The exact sequence of events precipitated by the arrival of the PIRA unit in the digger and a blue Toyota van is unclear. When they got to the station gunfire commenced almost immediately and the bulk of the shooting seems to have come from the SAS.[116] The bomb detonated, blowing up the digger and flattening a major portion of the station and nearby buildings. The expenditure of firepower was massive, killing eight PIRA men as well as fatally injuring Anthony Hughes, an uninvolved civilian.

The death of this civilian raises serious questions about the manner in which the military operation was conducted. Hughes and his brother Oliver were driving through Loughgall, and upon hearing the massive explosion, they sought to reverse their vehicle and move away as quickly as possible. Soldiers in the vicinity opened fire on the car; Anthony was killed, but Oliver survived, despite being hit at least four times. There is no doubt that the SAS opened fire without warning and without seeking to ascertain who was in the vehicle; and there was no attempt to disable the vehicle or to use minimum, rather than maximum, use of force. The SAS also fired on another car driven by a woman, with her young daughter in the passenger seat. Both escaped serious injury. Immediately after the shootings the area was totally sealed off by armed police – a clear indication that the police operated in a 'mop-up' function to the military power. No press or public access was permitted to the police station and its environs.

This incident raises many sensitive issues. First, was the use of such massive and deadly firepower inevitable or justifiable, given the advance information available to the security forces? Second, could the PIRA unit (or individual members of the unit) have been arrested at the scene of the incident? Finally, given the circumstances of Anthony Hughes's death, what were the operational orders governing the actions of the soldiers at the scene? This case has been deemed admissible by the European Commission on Human Rights.[117] The controversial circumstances, the lack of meaningful domestic inquiry, and the relationship between counter-insurgency and protection for the right to life will make for

Figure 15 Location of set-piece incidents, 1969–94

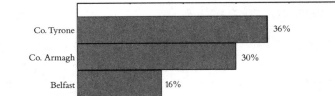

interesting review by the European Court and Commission.

Of the 40 paramilitaries killed in set-piece incidents, 29 were armed at the time of death. The large percentage of those armed (and the military's official position that those who were unarmed were subjectively believed by individual soldiers to be armed) gives rise to a clear legal implication – that relevant self-defence provisions of domestic law would automatically apply to military use of force.

Whether intended or not, the manner in which the use of lethal force developed served specific military and political functions at crucial junctures. From a military point of view the selective elimination of dangerous terrorists, whom the courts were failing to process, served a useful purpose in defeating a particular threat to law and order at a particular time. This value was always balanced against the danger of creating martyrs or killing innocent bystanders and further alienating the nationalist community. The political benefit was weighed by an evaluation of that alienation and how it would affect mainstream political processes. If one were to take the extreme view that the hunger strikes had revealed a nonparticipatory and disaffected nationalist community who were not worth wooing politically, then the benefits outweighed costs.

It is interesting to note that these deaths are predominantly confined to specific geographical areas. On one reading, we can surmise that these areas are so 'republican' that the effect of lethal force killing does little more than confirm local opinion on the partisan nature of the security forces. The dangers for the body politic in Northern Ireland only came when such incidents affected moderate opinion about the security forces and the control exercised over them by the state.

It is also interesting to note that the use of force has been significantly used less frequently against loyalist paramilitaries in comparison with their republican counterparts (see figure 16, p. 70). This can be explained on a number of levels. First, if one accepts the thesis that lethal force performs a political function for the state in controlling insurgency, it is obvious for historical reasons that a loyal Protestant community would not be considered a threat to the secure status quo. Thus, there exists no political rationale to use force as a mechanism of control against that community. Second, in the class of lethal force deaths caused by the police or local part-time military forces, such as the B Specials or UDR, there is some validity to the assumption that the overwhelmingly Protestant make-up of these bodies would make it less likely, for psychological and social

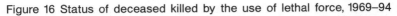

Figure 16 Status of deceased killed by the use of lethal force, 1969–94

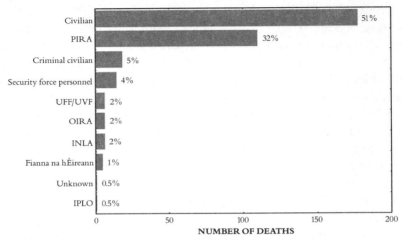

reasons, for their arms to be exercised against their own communities.

In the early part of the conflict the security forces were not made the object of attack by the majority community. There has been a minor shift in this pattern following the signing of the Anglo-Irish Agreement in 1985, with the emerging loyalist view that the security forces were the cutting-edge of its enforcement.[118] In a divided society where conflict becomes normalised, an army working in aid of the civilian power finds itself communally and individually required to identify hostile elements. Thus, the pitting of identified segments of the nationalist community against the state (real or imagined) also becomes a road map for the military in its relationship with that community. That road map becomes part of the unstated background in which lethal force is exercised.

VI
Conclusion

The use of lethal force represents an exercise in control and legitimacy. In the normal course of events in a healthy and functioning civil society lethal force is an aberration for the state. Against such a background, the protection of citizens' right to life lives up to its cherished rhetorical position – the taking of life is sanctioned only by justificatory or excuse rationale established by constitutional or criminal law.[119] In the entrenched emergency context of Northern Ireland, the taking of life became a systematic response exercised with political flexibility, and constituted an alternative mechanism to control aspects of the internal crisis facing the state. Modifications to the criminal justice system and attendant procedures, restrictions on freedom of expression for the press, draconian powers of stop and search, militarisation of certain communities on a par with martial law, all failed to stem the continuing violence. The essentially political nature of that violence was virtually unaddressed by a lack of political dialogue and agreement. As a result, the state operated on a variety of levels to control civil disorder – the strategic exercise of force by its agents was merely one choice on that continuum of control.

2

Patterns in the use of force and the response of the criminal justice system

The exercise of lethal force by agents of the state in Northern Ireland has manifested distinct patterns, which points to conspicuous and diverse phases in the use of force in the jurisdiction. In maintaining that between 1969 and 1994 there were three distinct phases to the Northern Ireland conflict, this work intertwines the exercise of force with a profusion of other contemporary political/legal elements. At this point, however, the analysis takes a concrete look at the particularities of lethal force in that period, seeking to flesh out the variety of forms in which lethal force was exercised. Distinguishing the legally significant characteristics of these incidents leads to penetrating conclusions about the ability of the criminal justice system to facilitate transparent legal accountability in a situation of low-intensity conflict. Most importantly it charts the extent to which the Northern Ireland legal system was capable of and willing to respond to the changing patterns in the use of lethal force experienced on the ground.

Mapping the response of the legal system requires a close look at the application of criminal sanction to the use of lethal force. The criminal justice system in Northern Ireland has been under close scrutiny for a number of years, notably in its dealing with lethal force deaths. The paucity of criminal sanction resulting from these incidents has created the perception within segments of the community and its citizenry that state agents operate with virtual impunity. Information concerning the application of criminal sanction to state agents who exercised force causing death during the first phase of the conflict is limited and generally overlooked. A recently published compendium which chronicles all deaths resulting from the Northern Ireland conflict between 1966 and 1999 illustrates *inter alia* that a small number of prosecutions concerning the exercise of force took place in this phase.[1] However, as there are no published legal reports of these cases, there are still many outstanding and unresolved issues which confirm the lacuna of state accountability generally identified in this chapter. First, what standard of legal proof was used and applied in the cases concerned? Second, where convictions were sustained, information is still missing concerning the outcome of appeals (if any). Finally, it is not known whether soldiers were subject to internal military sanction (for example, suspension, dismissal) following these criminal proceedings. Between 1974 and 1994, this study has identified that 24 prosecutions involving 34 persons have been taken in relation to lethal force incidents, and only eight law-enforcers have been convicted of criminal offences arising from the use of force exercised while on duty.[2] The matrix of controversial and persistent loss of life caused by agents of the state, together with subsequent lack of legal sanction, has created sharp divisions between the two communities in Northern Ireland about the impartiality of the rule of law.

I
Establishing context

In order to assess the adequacy of the law controlling the use of force, it is necessary to take a close look at the context in which death occurs. By 'context', I mean the broad factual circumstances leading up to and inclusive of the moment of death itself. The comprehensive contexts of lethal force deaths, added to the personal assessment of the law-enforcement officer at the moment force is exercised, has had a direct bearing on the evaluation of criminal responsibility for deaths. It is not only the moment of death but the extended context in which it has occurred that has had a profound effect on shaping public perceptions, legal categories and the legal status of the conflict.

The statistical evidence reveals that there are discernible patterns exposed by the contexts of lethal force deaths. These patterns have two distinct elements. First, patterns of state action related to the precise moment of individual deaths. Second, patterns related to what was happening around the deceased and the state agent when force was exercised. Both these elements show that state responses have altered significantly during different phases of the conflict. This tells us that there is a direct and immediate relationship between state strategies to exercise control over conflict and the ensuing experiences when lethal force is exercised. The most striking intersection relates to the shifting affiliation of state agents responsible for deaths and the type of individual being killed between 1969 and 1994. This leads to the preliminary conclusion that modifications to the practices of the security forces in relation to the use of force have a direct relationship with political strategies being pursued by government at different points of the conflict.

The distinctive strategic and military component of these modifications has evolved with the endurance of the conflict. In acknowledging this fact, patently revealed by the statistical evidence, it is nonetheless important to reaffirm that there has been no abdication of the democratic framework in Northern Ireland. That is to say, that while military imperatives have grown and modified with the prolonging of the conflict, the actions of state agents remain technically within the framework of a rule of law state, and the taking of life must consistently be framed in that context.

Figure 17 Types of incident causing lethal force deaths, 1969–94*

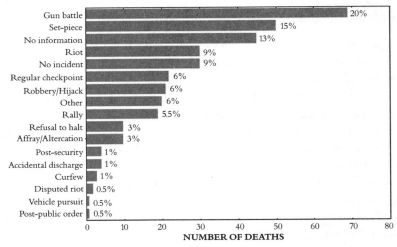

* For graphs giving separate analyses of the three phases of the conflict see figure 4 (1969–74), p. 34, figure 10 (1975–80), p. 53, and figure 12 (1981–94), p. 61.

Figure 17 establishes the variety of situations in which individuals have been killed by the use of lethal force in Northern Ireland between 1969 and 1994.[3] There are seventeen distinct categories defined by this statistical analysis.[4] For the purposes of clarity, I will reduce these classifications to three broad areas of concern. First, those fatalities which occurred in 'security' situations. The circumstances of these deaths relate directly to the conditions of conflict, and the actions of the security forces are generally contextualised by reference to a perceived terrorist threat. This category includes set-piece incidents, gun battles, checkpoint deaths, vehicle pursuits, refusal to halt when called upon by the security forces, and post-security incidents (alleged or *de facto*), which refers to deaths which occurred after a security-type incident has taken place.

Second, those fatalities which resulted from weapons being employed in public order situations. The majority of deaths here resulted from the use of force exercised in response to the existence of a threat or a perceived threat from public demonstrations. Many of these deaths are indisputably linked to the political nature of the conflict. Nonetheless, they are differentiated from the security category of deaths because they do not have the overriding rationale, from the security forces' viewpoint, of preventing paramilitary activity. This broad category includes riots, disputed riots, rally, curfew, affray or altercation, and post-public-order incidents.

The third category encompasses disparate elements, many of which have resulted in as much public controversy as those deaths in the security or public order classifications. They include deaths resulting from accidental discharge of a weapon, robbery and hijack, deaths where there is no obvious external context within which to place the fatal discharge of a weapon ('no incident' category), and deaths where there is insufficient information available to classify appropriately within other frameworks ('other' category).

In identifying these categories and outlining the legal consequences which attach to each, it is possible to distinguish which specific contexts notably eschew legal accountability. The category where this has been most controversially absent is where deaths have resulted from planned confrontations. In the final phase of the conflict, 1981–94, this research has identified that over 40 per cent of all lethal force deaths were the product of set-piece, or preplanned, confrontations. Not surprisingly, such encounters and their lethal outcomes received saturation publicity. In common with other security category deaths, these incidents had the common feature of the application of maximal force and the apparent failure to prioritise due process mechanisms as the most appropriate means to manage suspected transgressors of the law. This subcategory of cases is particularly problematic from the point of view of normal legal accountability.

A

PREPLANNING – RECONSTRUCTING THE INCIDENTS

Security-linked deaths account for 45.5 per cent of all deaths included on the data base underpinning this study. Of all the subclassifications which fall into this category the most contentious have been the set-piece deaths. These operations are characterised by the exclusive use of specialist military or police units, responsibility lying principally with three agents: the SAS, the 14th Intelligence Company[5] and the SSUs of the RUC, This study has established that forty of the fifty persons killed in set-piece operations were members of paramilitary organisations, their deaths occurring particularly in the third phase of the conflict. A number of such operations have resulted in the deaths of innocent bystanders mistakenly identified by the specialist military units as members of paramilitary organisations. In these cases an outstanding concern is that no attempt was made to distinguish between the uninvolved civilian and members of paramilitary units. This failure adds fuel to the speculation that these operations have the singular aim of eliminating paramilitary threats at all costs and that no accommodation is made for any other unforeseen eventuality.

Set-piece operations typically involve the security forces acting or being aware of the actions of others on the basis of informer information. In short, the agents responsible for death may be aware of the movements and planned activities of the deceased prior to death. For example, some set-piece operations have involved arms caches being staked out, with the security forces waiting for members of paramilitary organisations to arrive and collect the deposited weapons. The criminal proceedings taken against two SAS soldiers arising from the shooting of sixteen-year-old John Boyle is instructive here.[6] Having discovered weapons in a local graveyard, the youth informed his father, who immediately passed the information to the local police. The information was forwarded to the SAS, who subsequently staked out the scene with the view to waiting for the persons who had deposited the weapons to arrive. What resulted is a matter of unresolved controversy. It is certain that the youth returned to the scene, perhaps out of curiosity, and was killed by the soldiers dug into their surveillance position. The soldiers claimed that he had picked up one of the weapons and pointed it at them in a threatening manner. They were acquitted of all charges.

Other situations in this category have included the deceased being followed by the military or the police for extended periods during the time immediately preceding their deaths. Finally, it has been claimed that some set-piece incidents result from the attempt to apprehend the deceased because he was allegedly engaging in (or about to engage in) illegal activity. In these cases it seems that the law-enforcers were aware that such activity was taking place before they confronted the deceased.

Since 1981 lethal force deaths have occurred in markedly different circumstances than in the two preceding phases of the conflict. The choice to use specialist units has coincided with the emergence of the set-piece as the primary context in which individuals were killed by the use of lethal force. The deployment of such units was not mere chance. In particular, the use of the SAS had a definite political and military value. Its political value lay in demonstrating a hard-line approach to the regulation of the conflict on the ground. This is borne out by the unit's long history of involvement in situations of counter-insurgency in post-colonial situations.[7] Its military value lies in applying the uniquely structured training given to members of the SAS, The squadron is composed of cellular units, consisting of highly skilled soldiers particularly selected out of regular army units.[8] The regiment usually takes officers for three-year tours of duty, and they return to their parent regiment when their attachment is complete. Training for the regiment is specialised and intensive, concentrating particularly on physical endurance and expert weapons-training. A fundamental and obvious question arises as to whether the training of these units is compatible with the policing function that they are intended to undertake in a jurisdiction such as Northern Ireland, where they technically operate in aid of the civilian power.

Members of the 14th Intelligence Company have been responsible for a number of deaths since 1969. This study has attributed four deaths to the undisputed responsibility of this unit.[9] However, Mark Urban has ascribed responsibility for a number of other deaths to this unit.[10] The inability to verify these assertions independently means that these deaths will be categorised as falling under general army responsibility. Overall, however, the role of the 14th Intelligence Company is principally defined in terms of intelligence gathering. This has usually involved the setting up of observation posts or other forms of surveillance, facilitating the more direct role of other units such as the SAS,

The MSUs of the RUC were the product of its internal restructuring following the advent of police primacy as a political priority in the 1970s. These units were trained along SAS lines in 'speed, firepower and aggression'.[11] The counter-insurgency units were viewed internally as a necessary accessory to the development of specialised surveillance units within the RUC,[12] The militarisation of the police was not a new event for Northern Ireland. The Hunt Report of 1969 acknowledged firmly that the most striking difference between the RUC and other police forces in the United Kingdom was that it fulfilled a military as well as a civilian role.[13] The new departure for the RUC in 1982 was the willingness to confront PIRA within the terms of reference normally reserved for the specialist army units.

One prevalent criticism of the security operations involving these agents is that the intelligence information available to them was not utilised to prevent the necessity of using force. Such preventative measures would include making safe weapon sites, thus eliminating the possibility that the weapons could be used against members of the security forces, or indeed, against members of the public. Technological advances mean that equipment is available to the security forces that would have allowed them to neutralise the danger to themselves of weapons found in arms caches; for example, weapons could be fitted with electronic devices, allowing their location to be tracked.[14]

Most importantly, these operations were criticised for failing to arrest suspected members of paramilitary organisations when it was clear that they were unarmed and not posing a direct threat to the security forces. The lack of such pre-emptive measures, prioritising arrest rather than exercising force, has led to some speculation that arrest may not have been the prime consideration for such operations. Prior information gives the security forces substantial, though certainly not guaranteed, opportunity to ensure that suspected paramilitaries are arrested and processed through the courts. While the extent of such information is not known to the general public, and the use of Public Interest Immunity Certificates (PIICs) has excluded its consideration in legal proceedings arising from lethal force deaths, the perception abounds that such information was used as a means of providing a lawful excuse to use force rather than as a means of avoiding it. This leads to the inference that in such operations a legality model of procedure is suspended in favour of a counter-insurgency model.

Judicial dicta has excluded the possibility of taking the planning and any prior knowledge available to the security forces into account when legally assessing these deaths. Instead only the immediate circumstances of the decision to use force can be evaluated.[15] Arguably the planners of such operations would have been aware that judicial dicta had excluded the examination of informer information and the setting up of these confrontations at criminal trials. Wider evidence, which might go to prove that arrest was a viable alternative to the use of lethal force, can generally be relied upon to be excluded in the court's evaluation of the individual soldier's or police officer's response to the alleged threat posed by the person who is subsequently fatally injured. Although it cannot be proven, it seems virtually unavoidable that such knowledge of judicial practice has had a direct effect on security policy.

The propensity of these operations to lean towards a counter-insurgency model of state behaviour is further illustrated by looking at whether those killed in such operations were armed at the time of their death. A feature of these preplanned confrontations is that despite the fact the suspected paramilitary members were frequently armed, eye witnesses and forensic evidence attest that their weapons were not fired. It is not always clear on the available empirical evidence that the deceased were given the opportunity to surrender themselves to the state. The Gibraltar inquest inquiring into the deaths of Mairead Farrell, Sean Savage and Daniel McCann is instructive on this point:

A: [Soldier E] As I have said, it was a start of a yell and then almost instantaneous firing.

Q: [Mr McGrory, counsel to the families] You mean with almost a split second between?

A: [Soldier E] I said before, yes, almost a split second and it was go.

[later]

Q: [Mr McGrory] ... but in terms of a warning to McCann it was pretty useless?

A: [Soldier E] Yes, I would say it was. They obviously could not understand it, I suppose.[16]

Arguably, some might declare that a law-enforcer is not compelled to place himself in physical danger in order to facilitate the possible surrender of an armed and dangerous offender. The criminal law recognises this by allowing the use of force for the lawful protection of self and others when facing an immediate and pressing danger. But this lawful right to exercise force is also informed by the principles that underpin a rule of law state, those being that the law-enforcer is under an obligation to use force only as a last resort and to seek to have those who are suspected of transgressing the law processed by the courts. Preplanned operations raise serious concerns because there has been a consistent resort to maximal force without obvious attempt to pursue less deadly means to apprehend offenders.

To understand why these set-piece deaths follow a particular pattern in terms of a lack of warnings, a glimpse at the training of SAS soldiers is instructive. In military terms this type of incident is usually regarded and referred to as an 'ambush'. That phrase has a specific meaning. A leading military text refers to it as follows: 'An ambush is a surprise attack by a force lying in wait upon a moving or temporarily halted enemy.'[17] After many of these set-piece incidents it was stated that the encounter with the paramilitary members was accidental, that the security forces 'happened to come upon' suspects unwittingly. This was rarely the case. A consistent feature of these operations was that specialist units were aware of the impending arrival or actions of the alleged paramilitaries. This information was generally facilitated by the use of local informers. It is important to state that the use of such information is not *per se* in contravention of domestic criminal law. Nonetheless, there are ethical dilemmas inherent in reliance upon such information. The dilemmas are compounded in the context of the additional complex features associated with lethal force incidents in Northern Ireland.

The available empirical information reveals that the action of the specialist units in these incidents was typically to concentrate heavy fire on the threat as soon as it revealed itself. When the suspected paramilitaries were carrying weapons, opening fire immediately could be justified in the aftermath of the incident in terms of the threat perceived by the soldiers. The legal dilemma is that if no attempt is made to arrest by calling for the surrender or by limiting the use of reactive firepower, the action may amount to extra-judicial execution. The problem invariably lies in the proof of this allegation. There have rarely been any eyewitnesses or survivors, and the only authoritative version of events to emerge is a military one.

B

PREPLANNING – LEGAL AND POLITICAL IMPLICATIONS

The legal basis of the use of force is discussed in detail later in this chapter. Suffice it to say at this point that the exercise of force is not derived from a carte blanche authority to use weapons *per se*, Rather, the right to use a weapon is derived from statutory provisions and common law rules which couch the right in justificatory or excusable terms.[18] The guiding principle is that arrest of a suspected offender is always the preferred goal of the law-enforcer. As already discussed, features of set-piece operations give grim indications of a discernible shift in state policy as regards the use of force in the 1980s, and the deployment of specialist units meant that when force was exercised, the soldiers shot to kill. This occurred in part because the nature of a soldier's training in such units means that the decision to open fire on a target was a decision that would signify that the soldier would continue to fire until the 'threat' was eliminated – in other words, that the targeted individual would usually not survive the encounter.

Set-piece incidents have rarely come before the courts.[19] Three criminal proceedings which are classified by this study as preplanned encounters leading to fatalities all resulted in the acquittal of the accused law-enforcers. The paucity of criminal sanction has created ongoing public discussion, particularly where the available information concerning certain incidents suggests that there was no attempt to arrest suspects. This is not to say that legality or, more correctly, the appearance of legality, is unimportant to the planning and execution of such operations. On the contrary, it is of paramount importance. What I suggest is that legal accountability was frustrated by increasing sophistication in the organisation of these operations. In short, the basis upon which these counter-insurgency operations were carried out ensured that they 'fitted' neatly within the prevailing legal framework. To ensure that the normative legal framework was applicable, informer information was critical. It was this information which provided the opportunity to confront members of paramilitary organisations when they were identifiably posing a threat to the state. The threat they posed, both subjectively and objectively, was the basis for using force within the law.

Thus, the consistent theme of deaths in the preplanned category is the assumption on the part of the security forces that the individual killed was a member of a paramilitary organisation and was believed to be engaged in illegal activity at the moment of death. From a military standpoint such confrontations fall into a 'clean kill' category of death.[20] The arms carried or believed to be carried by the suspected paramilitaries, or the belief that they were engaging in unlawful activity gave a *bono fide* legal justification under domestic criminal law to use force. It also provided sufficient rationale for using force as defined by the military's own internal guidelines.[21] Self-defence could be argued because the deceased was carrying weapons or posing a threat to the soldiers at the time of encounter.

Section 3 of the Criminal Law (Northern Ireland) Act 1967 could also be invoked on the basis that the action of the law-enforcers was taken to prevent crime or in the attempt to effect a lawful arrest. This raises some very difficult questions. Where law-enforcers seem to be operating within the technicalities of the law, bringing a criminal prosecution is difficult. It requires sophistication to recognise that the spirit of the law itself may be subject to manipulation by the actions of those required to uphold it. The apparent applicability of specific provisions of domestic criminal law in the United Kingdom to these preplanned confrontations does not necessarily imply that the taking of life was legally justifiable. The appearance of legality can be deceptive and requires resourceful deconstruction.

Preplanned incidents are clearly differentiated from other incident types. From 1981 onwards they became the primary context in which individuals were killed by the use of lethal force in Northern Ireland. This is amply illustrated by figure 14, p. 67. Legal responsibility and criminal culpability for such deaths is the same as for deaths in any other context – the applicable law is not different in formal definition. In the few cases that have come before the courts regarding the actions of state agents during such incidents, the courts have not distinguished the set-piece as a distinct form of planned encounter with members of paramilitary organisations by the state. Judicial interpretation has failed to acknowledge that these incidents are different from other lethal force incidents. Thus, a uniform standard of interpretation is applied throughout. This has entirely excluded consideration of preplanning, maximal use of force, and the choice of specialist units as an abstract matter for such operations. The failure of the courts to address these matters has created a huge problem for accountability in the use of force in Northern Ireland. It has provided the means for the use of force to function as a mechanism of conflict control for the state itself.

II
Other elements of the security classification

Preplanned incidents are not the only incident types which fall into the broad security category outlined on pp. 73–6. The remaining context classifications are linked in two significant ways, particularly the gun battle, vehicle pursuit and checkpoint classifications. First is the assumption made about the status of the victim. The state has consistently offered as a political defence to its action in taking life the belief of law-enforcers that the deceased was engaged (or believed to be engaged) in paramilitary activity at the time of death. This means that the state maintains that its own security was threatened (or believed to be threatened) by the actions of the person who was subsequently killed. Life-taking by the state has a quantifiably different accounting process in such circumstances. The rhetoric of threat and counter-threat is part of a much larger political equation, in which actual use of lethal force plays only a minor role. The assertion of political context further places the taking of life away from the ordinary due process model which applies in jurisdictions not facing internal crisis and instability. This is because states experiencing protracted internal conflict not only face questions about the lawfulness of force in a particular context but the legitimacy of the state itself. This background has obvious effects on the efficacy of domestic criminal accountability.

The second link between gun battles, vehicle pursuit and checkpoint classifications is that the use of force is maintained to be reactive. Lethal force is exercised as a response to a direct threat to persons or property, forcing immediate action. Gun battles have provided a significant context of death in Northern Ireland since 1969. On the available information for this study it was ascertained that sixty-nine persons were killed in gun battles since that date. Of those killed, thirty-eight were members of paramilitary organisations at the time of the incident. Evidently, such deaths fall securely into the variety of situations envisaged by law in which force can be used by the law-enforcers of the state. However, the statistics further reveal that twenty-nine uninvolved civilians were also killed in gun-battle situations, a high number which begs the question as to the efficacy of training methods, the accuracy of fire in gun-battle situations (predominantly occurring in urban areas) and a failure to discriminate between civilian and lawbreaker. Where low-intensity conflict is being subsumed within the ordinary criminal justice system it is imperative that highly evolved training be given to law-enforcers to ensure that clear distinctions are made in practice between serious transgression of the law endangering persons, and transgression which does not reach this standard. It is the activation and implementa-tion of these important distinctions that are the ultimate protection for the right to life in any jurisdiction. This is particularly true in a situation of low-intensity conflict, where the applicable legal norms have a ten-dency to blur.

A

CHECKPOINT FATALITIES – EXCESS IN DUBIOUS CIRCUMSTANCES

One particular context in the security classification deserves close atten-tion – those deaths which have occurred at checkpoint situations. This study ascertains that 22 persons have been killed at such locations, 10 of whom have been civilians and 6 criminal joyriders (see figure 18, p. 85). The checkpoint locale is entirely controlled by the security forces. As such, it is their responsibility to ensure that the planning and administra-tion of checkpoint functions is undertaken in a manner which prevents confusion on the part of the intersecting public.

The army's own guidelines in the 1972 version of the Yellow Card, which outlines the occasions upon which a soldier may open fire, con-tained a provision which allowed that a vehicle which failed to stop at a checkpoint could be fired upon.[22] This provision is not included in the 1980 revised version of the Yellow Card. Evidently there was a discern-ible policy shift between 1972 and 1980. This can be attributed to the fact that a significant number of civilians had been killed in controversial cir-cumstances at checkpoints. Moreover a soldier had been charged with manslaughter following such use of force at a checkpoint situation.[23] Despite the exclusion of the specific provision which facilitated opening fire simply on the basis of a failure to halt a vehicle at a checkpoint, the use of force in such contexts continues to be controversial. The Yellow Card has been subject to recent judicial commentary in the March 1994 appeal by Private Lee Clegg on his conviction for the murder of teenager Karen Reilly. Here there was overt judicial disapproval of the amended portion of the Yellow Card pertaining to firing upon vehicles:

> Whilst we recognise that it is desirable that soldiers should have guidance as to the circumstances in which they should open fire and that the Yellow Card was drafted to give short and simple instructions which could be easily understood by soldiers in respect of firing at a car which has injured another person. The literal meaning of para 5. b. read with para 5. a. (3) is that a soldier may open fire to arrest any person who has deliberately driven a car at a person and has injured him, irrespective of the injury ... Therefore we consider that it would be desirable for the army authorities to redraft the Yellow Card to make it clear that the mere fact that an actual injury has been caused by a car does not justify a soldier in opening fire.[24]

The use of lethal force against joyriders has been a notable problem. In the cases resulting in fatalities law-enforcers have consistently claimed that they believed the stolen car to contain determined terrorists resisting arrest. In effect, by raising the stakes of suspicion, the legality of using force is measured against a different scale dependent entirely on the perceived status of the victim. More problematic, as this chapter will reveal,

Figure 18 Victim status at vehicle checkpoints, 1969–94

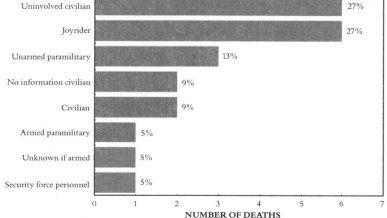

has been the widening of legal justification for opening fire on fleeing suspects by the United Kingdom's courts. This widened basis for using force leaves the minor offender in a very precarious position if he seeks to flee from state agents when he is incorrectly assumed to belong to a paramilitary organisation.

The prevalence of joyriders was and remains a persistent problem in urban areas, and is a symptom of economically and socially marginalised city communities. There can be no doubt that a car being driven at high speed by a minor, unable to fully control the vehicle, presents a potential threat to both the public and the security forces. However, there exists a number of methods to stop such vehicles without causing death or serious injury to their occupants. These include the use of caltraps and road spikes, which cause damage to the vehicle but not to those within it. It would seem preferable that military training should focus on debilitating the vehicle and that these methods be consistently employed in areas where joyriding has proved to be a persistent problem, to avoid the use of lethal force against young car thieves. In short, law-enforcers should be taught the use of minimal rather than maximal force. The particular problems with vehicle deaths demonstrate the practical enforcement dilemmas of deploying the military to undertake large-scale law enforcement. These issues become acute when the military undertakes quasi-policing tasks in a situation of extended exigency.

III
Fatality in the context of public order

Fatalities resulting from the use of force in public order situations have a number of common distinctive features. The most salient feature is that the majority of persons killed in these circumstances were civilians with no connection to or affiliation with paramilitary organisations. These deaths do not typically involve preplanning in the sense that the preparation for the law-enforcement operation creates a certain inevitability to the use of force. Rather, the systemic problem which arises from an examination of these deaths is the mundane and habitual recourse to the exercise of potentially lethal force as a means to control crowd situations, to the exclusion of other, less severe, responses.[25]

Such patterns of state response require explanation. The development of a policing and military culture which sustains and reinforces the regular resort to excessive force is one rationalisation. This means that, over time, exceptional practices of response have been entrenched in the conceptual and practical mindset of state agents, making it difficult for them to envisage alternative solutions to recurring problems. Equally, there has been a persistent trend towards the militarisation of crowd/ state encounters in the United Kingdom as a whole since the 1980s. One example of this was the use of militarised constabulary during the miners' strike in the early 1980s. In this respect Northern Ireland is not entirely unique in its public order experiences.

However, what distinguishes the jurisdiction is a police force which has consistently exercised militaristic functions within the state, operating in its embryonic stage as a stalwart of a politically polarised discriminatory regime. Furthermore, since 1969 the distinctive policing culture of Northern Ireland has been inexorably linked to the deployment of the British army to undertake regular policing duties. Notably, the regular army holds a disproportionately high responsibility for deaths by the use of lethal force since 1969 in public order situations. Of the 350 deaths by the use of lethal force under review here, the regular army holds causal responsibility for 240.

The application of force in numerous situations where the state fears that disorder may result from a convergence of assembled crowds has been contentious since the start of the conflict in 1969. First, the abstract issue of the use of lethal force in crowd control situations *per se* has been subject to political wrangling, given its inevitable arbitrariness in such contexts. Moreover, this leads to the specific contention that whilst the total amount of force employed by the security forces may be proportionate to the scale of the disorder experienced, the potential injury suffered by the arbitrarily selected citizen is likely to be disproportionate to the offence (if any) committed by him or her.[26]

Second, public demonstrations in Northern Ireland have an expansive political context. Invariably they are the expression of political inclusion, exclusion or protest. Often the rationale underpinning the appropriation of public space is a psychological confrontation with the symbols and ordering of the state, and not merely a casual intersection between the governed and the government. Thus, the use of lethal force in such context sends far deeper signals to the protesting community than might be imagined to arise from a particular exercise of control over some gathering or demonstration. The controversial role of the state's response to public demonstrations in the militarisation phase of the conflict is emblematic of a more profound struggle over identity and control in Northern Ireland.

Most deaths in the militarisation phase took place in a context of disturbed public order, or the stated perception of disorder by law-enforcers. The highest number of deaths by the use of lethal force were experienced in this phase of the conflict also. Doubtless, many fatalities resulted from indiscriminate force being exercised at assembled crowds as entities, instead of being directed at particular subgroups within the crowd, whose actions the security forces may have sought to curtail. The general aiming and execution of force at crowds, rather than at clearly identified individuals within it, may contravene principles of proportionality and immediacy which are implied in the applicable criminal law standards. Section 3 of the Criminal Law Act 1967 (see pp. 97–9), the salient domestic legal standard in this context, seems to envisage force being used only when it is required to overcome individual resistance or to contain a direct threat posed by one individual to another. However, there is a genuine concern as to whether section 3 covers the issuing and carrying out of blanket instructions to use force against a group or crowd.

Arguably, many deaths which have occurred in the context of public demonstrations have resulted from a lack of planning on the part of the state, whose agents have not considered other means which would avoid the necessity of using force. For example, the deployment of the army on the streets of Belfast in 1969 was characterised by planning ineptitude. The catalogue of failure includes the oversight of not acquainting soldiers with the most basic geographical knowledge of the city to ensure that they could distinguish one side of the sectarian divide from the other. Furthermore, a conspicuous lack of numerical strength left them easily overwhelmed by events on the streets at the time. These facts raise broader issues about the suitability of marshalling the military in legal situations which are in the twilight zone between an emergency confinable within the normal law of the land and a low-intensity conflict which is not. The problems are most evident when the military stretches the boundaries of legal permissibility in the ostensibly normal legal structure, but accountability is lacking because of the ill-defined nature of the legal situation as a whole.

A

THE NON-LETHAL LETHAL WEAPONS

The review of public order fatalities would not be complete without some reflection on the use of plastic and rubber bullets. This study has identified that seventeen persons were killed between 1969 and 1994 by the use of these weapons. The rubber bullet was first introduced to Northern Ireland in 1970, and its plastic counterpart made its appearance in 1973. Plastic bullets have been regularly used in crowd situations, despite internal and external criticism of the practice.[27] For example, during the republican hunger strikes in 1980 and 1981, seven persons were killed by these weapons. Only one criminal conviction was sought in relation to state use of plastic bullets; it concluded in an acquittal.[28]

The weapon has always been described as 'non-lethal' by official sources, a portrayal not sustained by the high number of persons fatally injured by its use, which has proved to be indiscriminate in crowd situations,[29] both by design and deployment. By its nature the weapon is arbitrary, exposing as it does the persons nearest the user to the greatest risk, though they may not actually be engaged in such illegal behaviour as would sanction the use of regular weapons which have the same lethal effect.

Reliance on weapons such as plastic bullets to control riot situations represents a commitment to maximal force policies by the state. There are safer means available to disperse crowds and contain demonstrations. These include water cannon, ultrasonic sound devices and flashing lights, added to the plethora of electronic and laser devices designed to impede anti-social behaviour in crowd situations without causing loss of life or serious injury.

The ideal situation would be to ensure adequate training of law-enforcers in crowd situations to pre-empt the need to use force against the public. Though the scale of plastic bullet use has fluctuated, with a recent upsurge in response to the perceived threat of loyalist gatherings during the marching season, its continued existence as a resource to the security forces undermines the state's commitment to protect life.[30] This was confirmed by the November 1998 report by the United Nations Committee Against Torture (CAT), which expressed its concern about the continued use of plastic bullets as a means of riot control in Northern Ireland, and expressly called for an abolition of their use.[31]

The current policy indicates that containment of public disorder is sought at any cost. The consequence of this extreme form of intervention is hostile community/state relations, particularly where the state is perceived to respond aggressively to mass political demonstrations. It adds to the perception that force is the sole means of arbitration conceived of by the state as a means to contain community discontent, however that political expression is manifested. Additionally, the failure to apply sanctions (internal or criminal) to excessive use and abuse of plastic bullets sends a strong signal to law-enforcers that a high threshold for acceptable force in crowd control situations is maintained in the jurisdiction. Law-enforcers on the ground will continue to operate within an upwardly defined threshold where policy dictates allow such interpretation.

IV
Typology of victim

Aside from the above identified commonalities of context, the empirical data also reveals a number of personal and group characteristics common to the subjects of the use of force. The personal histories of lethal force victims present a variety of social backgrounds, age, gender and religious affiliations. Despite this distinct and real diversity, there are a number of common characteristics that emerge when one examines the victim group as a whole. Charting these commonalities is of enormous significance, both legally and politically. If all lethal force deaths are merely the product of their own unique set of circumstances, then scrutiny of state action is limited to each individual case on its own merits and solely within its own terms of reference. Alternatively, when one charts a group commonality between victims and circumstances in the use of force, a different standard of scrutiny may apply to state action. In short, this may illustrate the need for a heightened standard of review, especially in the legal realm. If, as this study demonstrates, there are notable patterns of state behaviour to be traced in the exercise of force, the necessity for accountability is elevated considerably. Moreover, and most significantly, the existence of patterns may also reveal something about the nature of the conflict itself – providing a mechanism to shed light upon the appropriate definition of conflict under domestic and international law.

A

RELIGION

The fact that the overwhelming number of victims were drawn from the minority community in Northern Ireland has significant social and political consequences.

Figure 19 Religious affiliation of the deceased, 1969–94

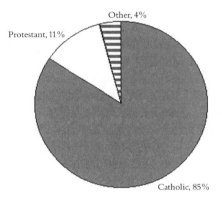

Other, 4%

Protestant, 11%

Catholic, 85%

These statistics demonstrate the extent to which one community has disproportionately carried the burden of fatalities resulting from the exercise of force by the state. While there has invariably been a social consciousness in the minority community of that burden, highlighted at particular times by high profile loss of life, there has been an absence of indisputable factual evidence to demonstrate that truth independently. If we acknowledge that lethal force has, in fact, been a prevalent and widespread component of the minority community's experience within the state, then this acknowledgement, in turn, must validate and reinforce the minority's perception of the state and its agents.

This is particularly true at a juncture where Northern Ireland is seeking to reinvent itself as a place where both communities can live together and transcend their communal differences. In a sense both communities are required to enter into a new contract with one another and with the state they inhabit. Genuine revitalisation of civil society as a means to support that transcendence means that the experiences of discrete communities must be confronted. The marked encounter of one community with the exercise of lethal force over the other is a part of this equation.

On a more practical level, it has had enormous consequences for the perceived neutrality and independence of law and legal process in the jurisdiction. In short, there can be no avoidance of revisiting the effects of lethal force, if the state and its communities are seeking the reassertion of a neutral and legitimate legal order.

B
PARAMILITARY STATUS

The empirical evidence presented by figure 13, p. 63, relates solely to those individuals whose status has been defined as belonging to a paramilitary organisation at the time of death. It demonstrates clearly that the overwhelming majority of those killed were members of one paramilitary organisation, PIRA, This is not unexpected – since 1969 PIRA has been at the forefront of paramilitary violence directed at the state and its agents. It was the paramilitary organisation with the largest active membership, the greatest access to military hardware, and the highest level of both real and tacit community support which facilitated its ongoing conflict with the state for twenty-five years.

C
GEOGRAPHICAL LOCATION OF LETHAL FORCE DEATHS

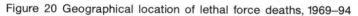

Figure 20 Geographical location of lethal force deaths, 1969–94

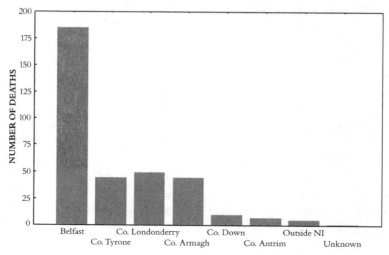

As figure 20 illustrates there are striking concentrations in the locations where lethal force incidents took place. Belfast, the largest urban centre in Northern Ireland, is the site of 53 per cent (185 deaths) of all lethal force incidents.

Belfast has been a city characterised by all facets of the conflict – intensive sectarian divides, the ghettoisation of communities, extensive destruction of property, daily disputes between the security forces and the nationalist community and heavy militarisation. For over two decades, the city was at the heart of the conflict in Northern Ireland. Thus, the scale of fatalities resulting from the use of lethal force is unremarkably found here. Nonetheless, this also informs us that the use of lethal force has been disproportionately absorbed by one city. Estrangement from the state has a high concentration in certain and particular communities, with a resulting burden upon the state to rebuild its relationships with geographical particularity.

The city of Derry/Londonderry and counties Tyrone and Armagh fall in behind Belfast as the secondary sites of lethal confrontation by the state. Derry/Londonderry's fatalities were extensively experienced in the first phase of the conflict in Northern Ireland. The city sustained heavy loss of life on Bloody Sunday. Since that time the psychological burden of that loss has remained with the families of those killed and the community as a whole.

The concentration of loss in Tyrone and Armagh has some interesting aspects. Lethal force in these areas is associated with the later phase of the conflict, notably in the state's counter-insurgency actions against paramilitary organisations. Loss of life in Tyrone and Armagh has largely taken place in rural communities and engendered far-reaching sentiments of alienation from the state. The tactical use of counter-insurgency measures in particular geographical locations is intimately linked to state perceptions of the political 'costs' of operation in these districts. Arguably, those areas perceived of as 'hard-line' have experienced a particular brand of lethal force use which is not consistent throughout Northern Ireland. Tyrone in particular has a high concentration of incidents involving specialist military units, frequently assisted by informer information, and a targeting of suspects with paramilitary affiliations. Therefore, responding to the effects of the use of force in these communities is markedly different than the more diffuse experience of force in other locales in Northern Ireland.

D

GENDER AND AGE OF THE VICTIMS

Analysis of the age and gender of lethal force victims reveals distinct patterns. The vast majority of victims (95 per cent) were male; women (5 per cent) were statistically less likely to be subject to the use of force throughout all three phases of the conflict.[32]

Figure 21 Distribution of deaths by gender, 1969–94

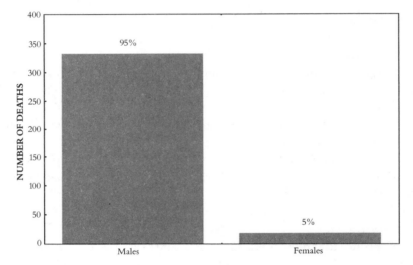

Of those victims killed by the use of force whose age is known, 17 were under 15 years; 4 were female. A further 46 victims were aged between 15 and 17 years, 3 of which were females. The largest concentration of deaths lies in the 18–25 age group: here, 151 young male adults died. These statistics are particularly striking in identifying the overall youthfulness of those killed by lethal force in Northern Ireland in this time frame. In the 26–35 age band there were 77 victims, of whom 3 were female. And in the 36 plus age band there were 49 deaths, 6 of which were female.

It bears reflection that the numerous deaths within the age band 18–25 may have profound social and psychological consequences which are not immediately apparent. In social and familial terms, the loss of young men means the creation of single parent families and dependants. In psychological terms, their youth carves them out a generation lost to their

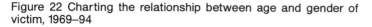

Figure 22 Charting the relationship between age and gender of victim, 1969–94

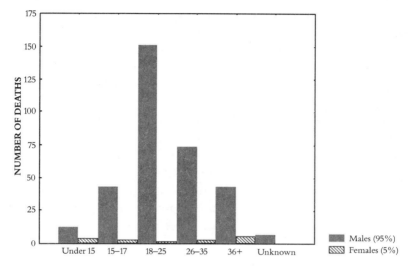

communities, many becoming martyrs and personifying the tarnished relationship between their communities and law-enforcers. In this light, the significance of accountability becomes pronounced as the potential to rebuild those relationships is kept to the fore.

E

CONCLUSIONS

A distinct 'average type' emerges from the statistical information: that victim is male, Catholic, and aged between 18 and 25 years. This stereotypical picture can serve to re-emphasise the sense of historical victimisation that has been articulated by the nationalist community.

The identification of a victim prototype leads to a serious assault on the position that the use of lethal force is a random, unpredictable act, dependent on circumstantial factors alone. It also indicates the limits of the individualistic model of criminal legal accountability for the use of force in a society experiencing internal conflict. Individually oriented process is not mandated to examine these broader social and political concerns. Rather, its function is to determine the guilt or innocence of a particular person charged with a particular offence. The criminal law is not marked by a preoccupation with the experience of group in a society, whereby individual acts exercised on a systematic scale have exclusionary and possibly discriminatory effect on one community. In most ways the ordinary law may be structurally incapable of responding to these kinds of systemic violations. Furthermore, it does not have the definitional capacity to accommodate such experiences of group loss. Thus, the identification of a group or community experience of negative state action requires imagination in order to address exclusion and anomie sympathetically and openly.

Stereotypes do not always fully explain social perspectives but they are important indicators of why a group or community may feel a particular way about the state they live in. If, as these statistics demonstrate, there is an empirical basis for the sense of historical victimhood, acknowledging that is a first step towards rehabilitating relationships between state and community. The next step is to think of imaginative ways to confront that experience within the confines of the state itself.

V
Criminal legal regulation of the use of force

The lack of criminal sanction to the use of lethal force in Northern Ireland has been the subject of vociferous criticism.[33] The perception abounds that deadly force is exercised with virtual impunity by the security forces. Furthermore, the lack of sanction is believed by many to have had a structural effect on the planning and execution of security operations where the use of force is envisaged by state agents as a likely possibility. Statistical evidence confirms the lack of accountability – criminal sanction is rare. As previously outlined, between 1974 and 1994 this study has identified that only 24 prosecutions involving 34 people have been taken against members of the security forces.[34] Of this number, only eight state agents have been successfully prosecuted. As with the pursuit of any criminal process, the Director of Public Prosecutions (DPP) will only seek trial where he feels that there exists a reasonable probability for a criminal conviction for the state. The high level of acquittals in relation to the number of cases pursued indicates that the issues of accountability go far beyond the mechanics of a decision to prosecute in these cases. Rather, they attest to immense problems with the existing statutory and judicial framework.

Such difficulties are not a new phenomenon to Northern Ireland. In its own time, the Special Powers Act gave rise to similar problems of accountability in relation to the exercise of lethal force. Section 7 of that Act allowed that force could be used by any officer when effecting arrest related to any crime or offence against the regulations contained in the legislation. Given the laxity in definition associated with many of the offences defined under the Act, the power to use force was extraordinarily wide and subject to few meaningful controls.

There are two statutory provisions in place governing the exercise of force in the jurisdiction. The first is Article 88 of the Police and Criminal Evidence (Northern Ireland) Order 1989 (PACE). This provision has never been litigated and its scope of application is generally not relevant to the majority of cases under review in this study. The second and most pertinent to this work is section 3 of the Criminal Law (Northern Ireland) Act 1967. Many legal commentators view section 3 as lamentably lax in definition. While the European Court of Human Rights has not directly addressed the legal standard itself as an abstract matter, there is a distinct possibility that section 3 stands in contravention of international standards which protect the right to life. Equally subject to controversy has been domestic judicial interpretation of this legal standard. Judicial dicta in this arena has lacked precision, consistency and intellectual honesty. Clearly, judges who operate in a state experiencing internal conflict face daily challenges unknown to their brethren in other jurisdictions. Yet, as Article 1 of the United Nations Basic Principles on the Independence of the Judiciary stresses, judicial independence is the core value of a state seeking to function in compliance with the rule of law. Nowhere is this responsibility of impartiality more severely tested than in cases where agents of the state appear before the courts charged with serious offences. As the Lawyers Committee for Human Rights points out:

> Unfortunately, ongoing concern has been expressed by human rights organizations and others in Northern Ireland in relation to the judicial treatment of cases involving the exercise of lethal force by members of the security forces subsequently charged with serious offences, including murder, manslaughter and grievous bodily harm. Judicial activism in these cases raises a number of issues. These include fair trial concerns, overtly political commentary by certain judges and the application of legal standards that do not conform to international norms of due process.[35]

Post facto legal regulation of the use of force is critical for three reasons. First, because high profile acquittals direct attention to the inadequacies of the legal use of force domestically and internationally. Second, unequivocal international legal standards on the protection due to the right to life give a solid basis for evaluating domestic law. These assessments throw the inadequacies of domestic regulation into sharp relief. Finally, legal regulation is open to the possibility of legislative change, thereby creating the possibility for genuine accountability. Thus, the goal of critique is to encourage changes to the normative legal structure, whose effect will be to ensure behavioural adjustments by those persons who have the legal right to exercise force in the jurisdiction.

A

A CLOSE EXAMINATION OF THE STATUTORY STANDARDS

Section 3 of the 1967 Criminal Law (Northern Ireland) Act provides:

(1) A person may use such force as is reasonable in the circumstances in the prevention of crime or in effecting or assisting in the lawful arrest of offenders or suspected offenders or of persons unlawfully at large.

(2) Subsection (1) shall replace the rules of the common law as to the matters dealt with by that subsection.

This legislative provision came into existence following the recommendations of the Seventh Report of the Criminal Law Revision Committee.[36] Neither preparatory committee nor parliamentarians could have envisaged that the section would become the guiding legal framework for the use of force in a situation of prolonged internal conflict within the United Kingdom. Above all else, it must be understood that this legislation was originally intended for normal policing situations, where a police officer might occasionally be called upon to discharge his weapon in the course of his law enforcement duties.

In the context of its application in Northern Ireland, section 3 is entirely limited by its gestation process. It was not designed with an armed police force in mind, much less a situation in which, for thirty years, the military worked both in aid of the civilian power and in a position of authority to it. It was certainly not designed to cope with a jurisdiction in which the legitimacy of law-enforcers is questioned by a sizeable segment of the population. Judicial interpretation of section 3 has avoided overt acknowledgement that the police and army are not working within the constraints of 'normal' community law enforcement in Northern Ireland. In short, a provision which was created with the unarmed police forces of England and Wales in mind was transplanted to Northern Ireland, taking no account of the distinctions between the practice and politics of the two jurisdictions.

In Northern Ireland prevention of crime has had a historically different internal coherency for law-enforcers and policy-makers. The primary operational criteria for the police and army during the last three decades has been active counter-insurgency – combating terrorism has been the policing priority in a situation of prolonged civil unrest. This means that the tactics and methods of policing and law enforcement differ from the norm of other jurisdictions which do not face similar problems. Prevention of crime has a different spin in Northern Ireland, where security force personnel have been acutely aware of paramilitary violence and the significant personal danger they face in the completion of their ordinary duties.

Yet in numerous court cases state policy has sought to ignore this anomaly and to insist that counter-insurgency operations are within the normal scope of policing duties. Clearly, this position results from the political imperative of 'normalising' the conflict, as set out in chapter 1. The effects of such a policy plainly undermine the integrity of the ordinary system of legality. Setting up ambushes and using informer information to intercept members of paramilitary organisations are situations for which section 3 of the Criminal Law Act was never designed to cope; however, the state has vigorously asserted that such actions are not abnormal. Instead, the attempt is made to harmonise them within the ordinary criminal justice model – in short, to make them fit within the legal framework of section 3. To do otherwise would be to admit openly that different rules are in operation, to acknowledge that military solutions are being sought, rather than due process through the criminal justice system. What results is a normalisation of abnormal responses by the courts.

A symbiotic relationship has been developed between the ordinary criminal law and the emergency situation within which the law operates. In some circumstances aspects of the emergency are used to bolster and justify magnified responses of the normal criminal law. In other circumstances the ordinary criminal law is the mechanism used to structure adaptation to the emergency, therein normalising the emergency response. Thus, the advantages of using the ordinary criminal process works both ways for the state. The emergency is used to justify applying criminal norms to selected or newly created prohibited acts; alternatively, the fact of emergency is rhetorically used to justify departures from the protections of the normal criminal process for suspected offenders. The identification of seventeen different contexts in which lethal force incidents in Northern Ireland have taken place demonstrates the difficulty in applying one standardised legal norm to rationalise the use of force in all contexts. It points to the difficulties which courts face in confronting a variety of lethal force experiences, which must be subsumed and considered under a fixed legal standard.

Legal review is most problematic in those contexts which fall into the security classification. Security-related deaths are unique to a situation of disturbed civil order. The exigencies of an emergency situation were certainly not factored into the thinking behind the adoption of section 3 – resultantly applying a uniform and inflexible standard creates dilemmas. For example, there is a mammoth difference between exercising force in a preplanned security operation and its occurrence by way of accidental discharge of a weapon. These differences relate not only to the intention of the person discharging the weapon but also to the operational context in which the weapon is fired. Section 3 works on the premise that a generalised standard which holds the law-enforcer accountable in one of these contexts in a court of law works in all the contexts. This is not the case. However, the courts continue to apply a 'one size fits all' standard that fails to fully accommodate the situations requiring accountability that arise on the ground.

Both the positive legal standard and its subsequent judicial interpretation fail to identify that the use of force is exercised in hugely varying circumstances. As a result, when prosecutions for lethal force fatalities come before the courts in Northern Ireland, an attempt is made to ensure that a standardised version of events is presented. Even a brief overview of the case law reveals that law-enforcers, giving evidence about the circumstances of various deaths, disclose striking similarities in the nature and the content of their evidence across widely differing circumstances. It usually works along the following lines. The defendant states that he either felt that his life was in danger or that if the deceased had escaped, he would engage in unknown unlawful activity. Furthermore, there is a conspicuous similarity in the descriptions by law-enforcers of suspected paramilitaries 'reaching', 'pivoting', 'pointing' and 'swinging' towards them with real or imagined weapons.[37] In Northern Ireland this explanation has become the defence of sudden movement — the alleged movement of the deceased being responsible for the subsequent actions of the policeman or soldier.

It is critical to understand that with frequency this isolated moment in the sequence of events which led to a fatality is detached as the determinative aspect of negating criminal liability. This is facilitated by a judicial unwillingness to sceptically confront assertions about the truthfulness of perceived threat and the exclusion of operational preplanning from judicial scrutiny. The end result is few prosecutions and fewer still successful convictions.

A brief look at Article 88 of the PACE(NI) Order 1989 is merited at this point. The article states that 'Where any provision of this Order ... confers a power on a constable ... the constable may use reasonable force, if necessary, in the exercise of the power.' This statutory provision has never been subject to review by the courts, so it remains to be seen how the test shall be interpreted. However, a few cursory observations may be made. The inclusion of the 'necessity' criteria in tandem with the 'reasonableness' requirement suggests that this is a stricter standard of review than that under section 3 of the 1967 Act. What one cannot predict is, even if the wording of the legal standard were reformulated to the seemingly higher standard of necessity, whether stricter judicial control would follow. Rather, it is possible that even with such a statutory reform, judges would continue to rely on the jurisprudence related to the reasonableness standard of section 3, with all of the problems that that has entailed in the past.

It seems evident that the power under Article 88 extends only to police officers who are exercising an arrest power which is conferred by PACE, This would leave the 1967 test applying to crime prevention or arrests sought under non-PACE laws, such as the PTA and the EPA, It seems at preliminary view that the inclusion of the right to use reasonable force for PACE-related law enforcement may in fact be a widening of the factual circumstances which give rise to the use of force. If this is the case, the development is an unwelcome one, as it does little to tighten controls on the use of force, extending rather than limiting the possibilities for its use.

B

COMMON LAW JUSTIFICATIONS:
THE INSIDIOUS ASSAULT OF REASONABLENESS

At common law an individual is entitled to use force in defence of others or in self-defence.[38] The degree of force used must be reasonable in the circumstances. There has been an ongoing academic debate as to the relationship between section 3 of the 1967 Act and the common law provisions. Some writers have argued that the common law defence was subsumed by the statutory enactment.[39] Others maintain that the common law defences survive statutory enactments, and should remain a distinct defence.[40] The argument seems resolved by judicial dicta which has maintained the defence in the English courts.[41] Northern Ireland's judges have adopted a similar approach.[42]

Both the common law defence and the statutory provision share the guiding principle of reasonableness. The term has become crucial in evaluating the actions of the security forces when deadly force is exercised by them. Before 1967 the law required 'apparent necessity' before an officer of justice might use deadly force.[43] The reasonableness concept was imported into the statutory structure by the Seventh Report of the Criminal Law Revision Committee.[44] Sean Doran points out that the move to the reasonableness criteria represented 'a departure from the more traditional "rule-based" model of criminal law'.[45] The move to this broader definition was intended to allow a greater inclusion of circumstances when evaluating the situations in which force was used. At the time it was felt that 'reasonableness' was a concept that juries could easily understand. In practice the concept has been interpreted overinclusively, threatening to shift emphasis from the immediacy of the law-enforcer's reactions to a selective myriad of surrounding circumstances.

Interestingly, the Diplock Report, which prompted the enactment of the EPA in Northern Ireland, did not suggest changes to the reasonable force criteria of either the statutory or the common law and no such change was incorporated into the PTA or the EPA, On this basis, the reasonableness concept in purely formalistic understanding ought to have remained objectively unchanged by the exigencies of the situation in Northern Ireland. But 'reasonableness' is a broad and malleable concept and its fluidity has facilitated its broad interpretation in the light of the emergency situation. This further reflects the extent to which a relationship has been cultivated between the emergency and the normative structure, with the capacity for the distortion of both systems.

When analysing the reasonableness concept, academic writers have partitioned it into two primary subcomponents:[46] first, a proportionality requirement, and second, a necessity element. Proportionality implies an equality of response to the threat posed between individuals. On a crude analysis this means an equality of arms. The reaction to a threat should not be excessive, but measured to respond to the danger posed. Applying the proportionality principle requires measuring competing harms.[47] The question to be asked is whether, on an objective assessment, the harm that might result from the use of lethal force (death or serious injury) is less than the harm that might follow from allowing an individual to escape arrest or continue to carry out an unlawful act.

Historically, applying the proportionality test was facilitated by the distinction between felonies and misdemeanours. The law-enforcer, before deciding whether to use force, could ascertain the gravity of the illegal act by applying the distinction. The distinctions no longer exist in the criminal law, but they have some continued use in providing an indication of how the proportionality principle might appropriately be applied in particular circumstances.

Seventeen contexts in which law-enforcers are required to make judgements which weigh proportionality into the scheme of their responses have been identified in this work. The exercise of this judgement by soldiers and policemen in Northern Ireland has repeatedly created controversy and concern. The high number of civilian deaths in the jurisdiction resulting from the use of lethal force illustrates the deficiencies of judgement, as figure 16, p. 70, demonstrates authoritatively.

Other indicators attesting to the lack of rigorous application for the proportionality principle are the statistics on the numbers of minors killed by the use of force. A total of 17 children under the age of 15 have been killed by lethal force, and a further 46 victims have been aged between 15 and 17 years of age. The regular army bears a high responsibility for deaths in both age bands. All children killed by the use of force were fatally injured by soldiers, as were thirty-four teenage deaths.

As a subsequent examination of the case law will illustrate, the principle of proportionate force has been developed to enhance deterrence, by allowing the security forces to use lethal force not only for grave crimes but also where there is only a suspicion that a crime has been committed.

The fact that the killing of a fleeing offender who offers no resistance and is not suspected of any specific offence can be justified demonstrates how far away from the proportionality principle the Northern Ireland courts have moved. This legal principle was established following the case in which Lance Corporal Jones was acquitted for the murder in 1974 of Patrick McElhone, a Tyrone farmer, who had sought to flee from a group of soldiers undertaking a search operation while they were questioning him.[48] The deceased was clearly unarmed at the time of the shooting, and the soldier discharged his weapon solely on the belief (mistaken) that McElhone was a member of PIRA attempting to run away.

C

THE NECESSITY COMPONENT OF REASONABLENESS

'Necessity' can be read in a number of competing ways. It can be interpreted as meaning that the least violent measures must be used to avert the threat encountered. This interpretation could activate the resort to lethal force. Glanville Williams argues that the averting theory has two sub-components: the immediacy principle and the nonexcessive force principle.[49] The immediacy principle requires that the threat faced must be actual and at hand. Thus, a latent or potential threat is an insufficient basis upon which to exercise force. Nonexcessive force implies that minimal, not maximal, force should always be exercised. In essence this is a proportionality test, couched in the language of minimalism rather than one of balancing. One practical interpretation of this principle is that a law-enforcer should always be shooting to wound, rather than to kill.

If the necessity principle were actually applied in practice by judges, such a strict interpretation would distinctly limit the circumstances and the manner in which lethal force could be exercised. Unfortunately, the reformulation of the fleeing felon rule in the Northern Ireland Attorney-General's Reference case in 1976 has moved the courts in the jurisdiction far away from enforcing the necessity component of the reasonableness rule.[50] This case followed Jones's acquittal for the murder of Patrick McElhone. The Attorney-General sought a clarification of the law after the decision, which was provided by the House of Lords. The Lords essentially validated the use of lethal force against a fleeing suspect who is solely suspected of belonging to an illegal organisation.[51] Allowing the legal standard to legalise the shooting of an unarmed individual who is not suspected of any particular offence but merely of membership in a proscribed organisation has considerably weakened the protection for the right to life in Northern Ireland. In this case it was also accepted that Patrick McElhone was 'an entirely innocent person who was no way involved in terrorist activity'. The Lords affirmed the claim of Jones that he genuinely believed McElhone to be a PIRA suspect as he fled away from him. They also accepted that the soldier 'had no belief that the deceased would immediately engage in terrorist activity'.[52] The abandonment of the necessity principle could not be clearer.

In a more general vein the nonexcessive force principle has been abandoned by training procedures which teach the application of force as a total elimination of threat by shooting at the torso of the suspected lawbreaker, rather than shooting to wound. Evidence of this practice is illustrated by the data in figure 23. The information is based on an evaluation of the medical determinations of deaths at coroner's inquests into lethal force deaths in Northern Ireland. Notably, gunshot wounds to the torso are the primary cause of death for most victims. It is abundantly clear that shooting to kill is the direct objective of the decision to open fire, given that the physical target is that part of the body which is the most vulnerable to fatal injury.

Figure 23 Medical determination by juries in inquests concerning lethal force deaths, 1969–94*

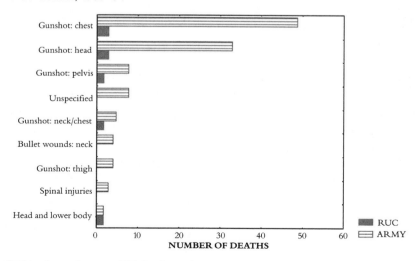

* This data relates to 137 deaths only.

The use of the necessity paradigm is not entirely failsafe. While it is possible that a stricter adherence to the necessity principle would strengthen the legal standard of reasonableness, weaknesses are also present in the conceptualisation of this canon. Dicey argued that strict necessity encompassed the notion that any steps may be necessary, and thus legally justifiable, in an immediately threatening situation. This wider view of necessity might even include the validation of anticipatory self-defence as part of the necessity test. It indicates that it is potentially capable of as loose an application as a broad reading of reasonableness has had in the recent past. In short, glowing academic endorsement for the concept of necessity gives it a more positive shine than the results of practical application may actually demonstrate. Ultimately, much depends on the interpretation undertaken by judges in individual cases, rather than on the semantics of language that guides them.

D

PARTICULARISING REASONABLENESS IN NORTHERN IRELAND

The two academic subdivisions of necessity and proportionality seem to neatly explain the application of the reasonableness concept. In practice, however, they have not been widely or rigorously used as objective conceptualisations to guide judges in particular cases concerning the use of lethal force. In Northern Ireland the twin concepts of proportionality and necessity do not create the framework within which the reasonableness criteria is determined. Instead, the courts have ducked espousing generic criteria, preferring to take a case-by-case approach. Each case is evaluated on the specific facts pertaining to a particular incident. For example, in the 1987 *Heggarty* case, Lord Chief Justice Hutton stated:

> Rather the tribunal has to put itself in the position of the accused and to decide whether or not the force used was unreasonable taking account of the pressures and dangers to which the accused was then exposed (or the dangers to which others were exposed) and the time (which may be only a second or two) in which the accused had to come to a decision.[53]

The concentration, then, lies on the events and actions immediately prior to the discharge of a weapon by the law-enforcer. The emphasis is on the 'facts', which are collected from witnesses and forensic evidence but primarily from the law-enforcer's own recollection of events and apprehensions. The approach entirely individualises each lethal force incident, thus precluding judicial admission that there are patterns evident across lethal force fatalities coming before the courts.

For example, in the context of the limited judicial evaluation of pre-planned operations, each set-piece incident is viewed in isolation as a 'chance encounter' with members of paramilitary organisations thought to be acting illegally or posing a threat to others. At the trial of Constable John Robinson for the murders of Seamus Grew and Roddy Carroll, the RUC version of events was that the car carrying the three deceased drove through a police roadblock, thereby activating the police response. Substantive examination was not given by the court to the fact that the two men had been under constant surveillance that same day, and that a plethora of information was available to the officers about their movements immediately prior to their deaths.

Reasonableness has become the evaluation of individual responses rather than an objective legal norm by which the individual's actions are compared to an objective standard composed of specific components such as proportionality and necessity. The courts have refined a subjective test, where the belief of the law-enforcer is the primary focus of inquiry. Moreover, the courts have placed a strong emphasis on the anxiety and apprehension felt by the law-enforcer in such a situation. In the Attorney-General for Northern Ireland's Reference case, Lord Diplock stated:

> The jury would also have to consider how the circumstances in which the accused had to make his decision whether or not to use force and the shortness of the time available to him for reflection might affect the judgment of a reasonable man.
>
> ... the jury in approaching the final part of the question should remind themselves that the postulated balancing of risk against risk, harm against harm, by the reasonable man is not undertaken in the calm analytical atmosphere of the courtroom after counsel, with the benefit of hindsight, have expounded at length the reasons for and against the kind and degree of force that was used by the accused; but in the brief second or two which the accused had to decide whether to shoot or not and under all the stresses to which he was exposed.[54]

In this approach much emphasis is placed on the anguish of the officer's decision. This methodology builds a bond of sympathy with the accused, facilitated by the use of legal categories which stress subjective belief over objective assessment:

> The jury would have also to consider how the circumstances in which
> the accused had to make his decision whether or not to use force and the
> shortness of time available to him for reflection, might affect the judg-
> ment of a reasonable man.[55]

That is not to say that the use of the subjective legal category itself is
misplaced. But rather that its method of construction creates a momentum to empathy with the action of the state agent facing criminal review.
The courts have also confirmed that the accused is to be given the benefit
of mistaken apprehension; that is, if he fired a weapon on the basis of a
factual assessment which was mistaken, he must be 'judged against the
mistaken facts as he believes them to be'.[56] The courts have gone further
in holding that the accused is to be judged on the mistaken beliefs
'regardless of whether, viewed objectively, his mistake was reasonable'.[57]
Consequently the sole means to dispute the honesty of the defendant's
subjective belief is to demonstrate that it was so entirely unreasonable
that it could not have been honestly held. But this has proven a
Herculean task in the Northern Ireland courts.

All of the criminal cases heard in Northern Ireland have articulated a
subjective component in testing the veracity of the law-enforcer's belief
in exercising deadly force. In short, judges have endorsed the application
of the legal formulae that would facilitate testing the reasonableness of
subjective belief:

> If, however, the defendant's alleged belief was mistaken and the
> mistake was an unreasonable one, that may be a powerful reason for
> coming to the conclusion that the belief was not honestly held and
> should be rejected.[58]

The court is required to examine whether the belief which prompted the
resort to lethal force was genuinely held. If not, the *mens rea* (the requisite
intention to undertake a criminal act) for a culpable criminal offence is
proven. Reaching this threshold of unreasonableness has proven consistently elusive in Northern Ireland. The reason is simple. In examining the
context within which individual soldiers and policemen have exercised
the use of force, the courts have given unyielding standing to the legal
category of 'circumstance'. Reasonable beliefs have skated into the
appropriation of personal appraisals of proximate and imagined threats
in the territory of Northern Ireland. This signifies that in practice the
objective test is almost meaningless.

E

REASONABLE BELIEFS?

At what point does subjective belief become unreasonable in these cases? Justice MacDermott, acquitting Constable John Robinson for the murder of Seamus Grew in 1984 stated: 'policemen . . . are not required to be "supermen" and one does not use a jeweller's scale to measure what is reasonable in the circumstances'.[59] In acknowledging that law-enforcers face overwhelmingly difficult choices, a rule of law state still demands their accountability for the exercise of deadly force. Policemen or soldiers may not be supermen but we should not presume that they are omnipotent either. This leads to a more practical question. When do the courts choose not to believe a version of events presented by the security forces when persons are killed by the use of lethal force? During litigation in all lethal force cases it has proven difficult for the prosecution to demonstrate that law-enforcers have reached the objective standards of unreasonableness, primarily because of the contextualisation that accompanies the soldier or police officer's stated belief. When it is accepted as a direct contextualisation for each individual death that the law-enforcer is threatened with 'armed insurrection', undermining the stated subjective beliefs of the accused is virtually impossible for the prosecution. Lethal force prosecutions are haunted by this background contextualisation, because it favours the accused's position that he honestly (though mistakenly) believed himself or others to be under threat.

Equally significant to the creation of an honest belief in the minds of the law-enforcers is the information given to them prior to or during the planning stages of a security operation. The Gibraltar case is a prime example of how imparting particular information to the soldiers on the ground greatly contributed to their perception of the threat posed by McCann, Farrell and Savage.[60] In the operational briefing given to the British surveillance team and the military personnel (including all the SAS soldiers) the following assessments were included:[61] that a PIRA unit intended to attack the changing of the guard ceremony in Gibraltar on the morning of 8 March 1988; [62] specific information was given as to the past criminal records of the three suspects, categorising them as 'dangerous terrorists';[63] the belief that a blocking car would be used in the operation;[64] and the likelihood of various kinds of bomb detonation.[65] No doubt, the cumulative effect of this information was to heighten the perception of the soldiers as to the threat posed by the three deceased.

Two practical points arise at this juncture. Are the subjective beliefs of law-enforcers bolstered by the empirical evidence adduced by this study? Two particular areas of assessment demonstrate the extent to which subjective beliefs are not reinforced by the factual evidence. The first pertains to the issue of whether those killed were armed at the time of their death and therefore posing an immediate and practical threat to the law-enforcer.

Figure 24 Armed status of victims in lethal force incidents, 1969–94

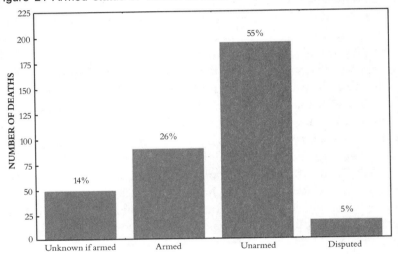

Figure 24 illustrates the available information on the armed status of victims at the time of death. It shows us that 55 per cent of the victims (194) were unarmed at the time of their death; 5 per cent (18) are disputed (that is to say that the security forces allege the deceased was armed and this assertion is contested by eyewitnesses and/or forensic evidence); and in 14 per cent of the cases it is not known if the deceased were armed. The 'unknown if armed' category refers to those incidents where there are no eyewitness versions of events, but the evidence available suggests that the deceased may have been armed. Twenty-six per cent (90 persons) were armed at the time of their death on the available evidence. It should be noted that within this armed category fall persons killed who were technically armed and posing a threat to the law-enforcer but whose weapons were infinitely less sophisticated than those carried by members of the security forces. This would include persons throwing stones and petrol bombs. In a number of these cases the exercise of force by the state seems to have taken place with a considerable lack of proportionality to the nature of the threat faced.

A further important subcategory to examine is the corpus of civilian deaths. As figure 16, p. 70, reveals, the majority of persons killed by the use of force in Northern Ireland were civilians. This fact alone creates a genuine concern that state agents have frequently erred in the exercise of judgement when determining which persons constitute a threat to them and which do not. This determination is further supported by a close examination of the contexts in which civilians have lost their lives.

Figure 25 Types of incident in which civilians were killed by lethal force, 1969–94

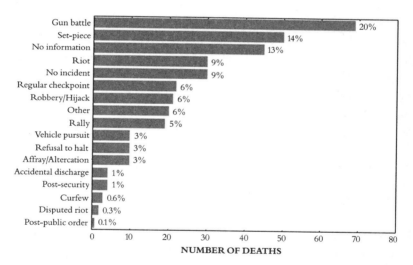

Figure 25 reveals that leaving aside the category of gun battles and riot in which collateral damage to bystanders may be difficult to avoid, the largest number of civilians were killed when there was no incident whatsoever occurring to shape the law-enforcer's belief that he was under threat. This evidence creates very serious doubts about the desirability of elevating subjective beliefs to unassailable heights in the domestic criminal courts.

F

EXTENDING THE CIRCUMSTANCES

Judicial elevation of subjective reasonableness has been balanced by solid expansion of the legal category of the 'circumstances' in which lethal force incidents occur. In short, the circumstances have become the defining rationale for reasonable action. Traditionally, the use of lethal force was judicially evaluated in terms of response to an immediate situation. Criminal responsibility was determined on the justification of that response to a direct and immediate threat. The Northern Ireland courts have incrementally transformed that approach. The 'circumstances' of life-taking now include a variety of proximate and abstracted particulars. They include hostile territory, undefined future threats to persons and property, bad neighbourhoods and potential ambushes. As a result, the duty to minimise confrontation (the minimum force principle) has been undermined, if not abandoned. The approach is illustrated by Lord Chief Justice Hutton's acquittal of two soldiers for the murder of Fergal Caraher. Following a declaration of the charges pending against the soldiers, the opening page of his decision immediately proceeds with the following contextualisation:

> On 30 December 1990 about 10.00 am a patrol of Royal Marines left their base at Newtownhamilton to carry out a number of tasks in and around the small village of Cullyhanna in Co. Armagh. *The village of Cullyhanna, and the countryside around it, is in an area where PIRA terrorists are very active, and carry out frequent attacks on the security forces* [emphasis added].[66]

From the outset, the judicial stage constructs a rationalisation for the subjective fear which is invariably raised by the accused. One of the most controversial aspects of expanding the context doctrine relates to the appropriate course of action to follow when faced with a fleeing suspect. This has resulted in approving the use of deadly force against an escaping suspect who may be suspected of no more then membership of an illegal organisation. It seems excessive that such membership, no matter how undesirable the affiliation, should be the basis for taking the life of a citizen.

In all the cases mentioned here the defence raised by the accused was section 3 of the Criminal Law (Northern Ireland) Act 1967. Force was exercised to prevent a suspected lawbreaker fleeing custody. Section 3 permits the use of force in two distinct circumstances: effecting an arrest and preventing crime. When the suspect is evading arrest the application of force is at its most exposed juncture and shooting a fleeing suspect has always been a matter of controversy.[67] Historically the rule operated with limitations derived from the distinction created between felonies and misdemeanours in the criminal law. However, these limitations are markedly absent in both the statutory provisions and judicial interpretation of the positive law. This is starkly evidenced by the fact that courts have maintained the right of law-enforcers to shoot at an individual who is solely suspected of membership in an illegal organisation. This laxity is compounded by judicial approval of the exercise of force well in advance of the actual criminal offence being carried out. The leading case on the matter, the Attorney-General's Reference, is highly instructive here. Lord Diplock states:

> the accused had reasonable grounds for apprehension of imminent danger to himself and other members of the patrol if the deceased were allowed to get away and join armed fellow-members of the Provisional IRA who might be lurking in the neighbourhood . . .

He continues:

> In the other scale of the balance it would be open to the jury to take the view that it would not be unreasonable to assess the kind of harm to be averted by preventing the [deceased's] escape as even graver – the killing or wounding of members of the patrol by terrorists in an ambush, and the effect of this success by members of the Provisional IRA in encouraging the continuance of the armed insurrection and all the misery and destruction of life and property that terrorist activity in Northern Ireland has entailed.[68]

Other courts have gone even further than judicially approving the use of force against a fleeing suspect who might at some future time commit an unspecified offence. In 1976 the Court of Appeal characterised the use of deadly force as a means of maintaining army authority in a particular area. Justice Jones found that

> if the deceased . . . had been permitted to run away when legally called upon to halt . . . there might . . . have been a resultant discomfiture of the forces of the law, and encouragement of the Provisional IRA to further resistance to the Army, and it could be seen by those in the area hitherto uncommitted to the IRA as a demonstration that the army was ineffective to enforce its authority.[69]

The use of deadly force in this case is viewed as a mechanism to command the loyalty of the local community. What the judge in question fails to recognise is that the consequence of deaths caused by the use of lethal force may only serve to alienate the community from state agents. The act of the law-enforcer may in fact bring about the end which the courts state they seek to avoid.

It is also clear that the geographical location of the death has become an objective context in itself, and a factor justifying the resort to lethal force by police officers and soldiers. In the first instance trial arising from the death of Patrick McElhone, Justice MacDermott spoke very specifically about the site of the incident. In his elucidation of the reasonableness concept he concentrated particularly on the geographical location, stating that the incident occurred in 'a "bad" area – which in the present context means an area in which IRA men operate or come from'.[70] (See figure 20, p. 92, which outlines the geographical distribution of fatalities in Northern Ireland. This reminds us that the concentration of lethal force deaths in distinct geographical locations has resulted in the notion of 'bad areas' filtering into practice, with a high correlation between perceived problem areas for the state and lethal force use.)

The concept of reasonableness, then, is not directly tied to the action taken by the law-enforcer but to the wider context in which that action occurred. Arguably, that context has been artificially constructed by the courts. It is not that the evaluation of context can be removed from assessment by judges or that excluding examination of wider issues is a better approach. What is missing is a lack of balance in the courts' methodology. First, there is a distinct overemphasis on the circumstantial context to the exclusion of its relevant and objective link with subjective belief. Second, disproportionate judicial emphasis on the 'circumstances' in lethal force cases has been given at the expense of undertaking objective assessment and using the proportionality test. It is worth noting that judicial embrace of relevant circumstantial context has been abjectly missing in a number of controversial non-lethal-force cases. In particular, the Casement Park trials of Patrick Kane, Michael Timmons and Sean Kelly illustrate the exclusion of charged atmosphere, crowd fear and the events of previous days in the same geographical location from consideration, when the three accused were convicted of the horrific murders of two off-duty British soldiers using an extension of the law of common purpose.[71] On 19 March 1988 the two soldiers, David Howes and

Derek Wood (accidentally) drove into the funeral cortège of Kevin Brady. Brady had been killed in a loyalist attack on 16 March upon the funeral of the three PIRA members killed in Gibraltar. Surrounded by mourners, one of the plain-clothed soldiers produced a gun. The angry and frightened crowd, convinced that another attack was under way, proceeded to drag the soldiers from their car, and disarmed them. They were dragged to Casement Park, beaten and searched, finally being thrown over the low wall of the park, where they were driven away and shot repeatedly by two armed men. Scores of men were arrested for their involvement in the incident. Over twenty were convicted of offences ranging from murder to perverting the course of justice, though the problematic decision is that handed down by Justice Carswell in the cases of Kane, Timmons and Kelly. Most important in contextualising these convictions is the fact that neither of the men who actually killed the two corporals was apprehended. The conclusion may be drawn that the benefit of context is only given to state agents accused of serious offences and not to their civilian counterparts.

It bears reminding that the wide definition of circumstances has a one-sided aspect. Circumstances such as informer information, intelligence surveillance and stakeouts of suspicious sites are precluded from evaluation. The use of Public Interest Immunity Certificates in cases where these issues are raised prevents the courts from a full examination of the entire and relevant context preceding the exercise of deadly force. The intellectual approach is undeniably flawed. There is an articulated focus on the precise moment of weapon discharge. However, this is amplified by selective reference to broad security concerns that go to support the subjective beliefs of the law-enforcer in his decision to open fire. The inconsistency of this practice is revealed by looking closely at the *Farrell* case, which exposes the limited choices available to the courts in defining the circumstances.[72] The case arose from the deaths of three unarmed men by four soldiers during an attempted robbery outside a bank in Newry, County Down. The House of Lords when evaluating the circumstances appropriate for review rejected the wide test of 'the circumstances in which the operation is conceived and planned and in which the preparatory steps are taken as well as those in which the final decisive act is performed'.[73] They opted instead for the narrow test of 'the circumstances in which they [the soldiers] were placed'. Clearly, there would seem to be two sets of judicial rules in operation. First, in incidents which are not preplanned, everything is relevant to assess reasonableness. This invariably leads to acquittals for criminal offences when the law-enforcer's subjective perceptions are added to the 'hostile territory' argument. Second, in preplanned incidents, everything is excluded except the subjective threat felt by the law-enforcer. Predictably, this also leads to acquittals for criminal conduct where honest subjective belief is taken to trump objective factual circumstances, which would tend to impute criminal responsibility.

VI
Assessing the arbitrators – judges in Northern Ireland

Any judge who is assigned the responsibility of assessing the criminal culpability of a state agent for the exercise of deadly force has a difficult task. The duties of such judges are doubly difficult in a state that suffers violent and ongoing civil strife. This is in part because the courts themselves, despite consistent self-depiction as neutral, impartial and nonpolitical entities, are an institutional site for the wider struggles that define a divided society. Thus, the judiciary itself plays a part in the wider social events that shape the state's existence.

Judicial oversight of lethal force fatalities has been ceaselessly controversial. Lethal force deaths are tried in Diplock Courts in Northern Ireland and constitute a unique subclass of cases which are manifestly different from other cases tried in these courts. The trials differ markedly in substance, tone and outcome, by comparison with the trials of defendants who are not members of the security forces. These trials are also marked by a distinct form of judicial activism and the persistent recourse to political commentary by individual judges on the appropriateness of bringing criminal proceedings against law-enforcers acting in the course of their duties. Judicial interventions in these cases are complex and contradictory, and judges struggle to balance the apparatus of fixed legal categories with their own ideological inclinations.[74] It is also apparent that judicial interventions in these cases have modified over time. These modifications result from changes in the judicial relationship to other state institutions and changes in judicial personnel.

Why is judicial pronouncement so important in these cases? Clearly, judicial intervention is less direct than the political action of many other state institutions. It is episodic and on a case-by-case basis, making only brief forays into the regulation or validation of the use of lethal force by the state. Yet it is critical for a number of reasons. The way in which courts deal with particular issues of law have profound implications for wider social constructions within the state. The validation of the state through the legal system sends an enormously powerful message to communities, both loyal and disaffected, within that state. In lethal force cases it is abundantly clear that the construction of legal categories by the courts had had a precise and identifiable impact on the practices of law-enforcers on the ground, or at least in how they articulate those practices. Furthermore, action by the judiciary frequently tells us how they see the relationship between the particular issue before them and the wider narrative of societal strife. And, in so far as the judiciary has greater prestige than other state apparatus, judicial interpretations may have relatively greater persuasive value, or legitimating power, than the actions of the state itself.

A

THE RELATIONSHIP BETWEEN INVESTIGATION AND TRIAL

Criminal trials related to the exercise of deadly force have a markedly different tone and outlook than others where similar offences are charged. The disparity first arises in relation to distinctions in pretrial procedures in Northern Ireland, when members of the security forces are charged with serious offences. From the outset, there is the presumption that no crime has been committed by the state agent when a person is killed by the use of force. As numerous interviews with legal counsel for this work have confirmed, it is assumed by the investigating authorities that the state has the right and the authority to exercise force against citizens in defined circumstances.[75]

No soldier or police officer has ever been detained for seven days in a holding centre in connection with serious incidents which occurred while on duty that may have breached domestic criminal law. In many cases the law-enforcer is not suspended or relieved from duty pending internal and external inquiry into his action, but rather continues to carry out normal duties as if nothing had occurred. Access to counsel of choice is never denied to agents of the state under investigation for scheduled offences. Security force witnesses speak freely to their lawyers prior to police interviews or give their statements in the presence of their lawyers. In contrast, citizens detained and questioned under the emergency laws are routinely denied access to counsel,[76] and when access is granted to lawyers after the first forty-eight-hour detention period, typically it amounts to no more than a half-hour conference between solicitor and detainee.[77] In a sworn affidavit to the High Court solicitor Barra McGrory stated:

> It has been my experience that the police have deferred legal access in practically all arrests under section 14 of the Prevention of Terrorism Act 1989 either for 24 hours or 48 hour periods and that immediate access to a solicitor by a detainee in Castlereagh is now the exception rather than the rule.[78]

By comparison, no police officer or soldier charged with such serious offences as murder and manslaughter has ever been denied access to counsel at any point, and their right to have legal counsel present during questioning by investigators has never been limited.

Such disparate practices mark the vast difference between the investigation of lethal force deaths and all other offences in Northern Ireland arising under the rubric of the emergency situation. More often than not it seems that law-enforcers who were causally responsible for a deadly assault are treated as witnesses to an incident rather than potentially culpable suspects.[79]

This fact is cogently illustrated by the prevalent practice whereby members of the security forces simply hand over their statements to the police during lethal force investigations. This means that their statements are prepared elsewhere and are not subject to the controls of the investigation procedure. In lethal force cases involving soldiers, the investigation practices are even more problematic. Soldiers' statements have frequently been prepared in tandem with an army lawyer. In some cases there has simply been no access to the soldiers by police until a military debriefing has taken place. Moreover, in numerous cases soldiers do not entertain (and are not required to answer) further questions on the particulars of their statements or the details of the incident itself.[80]

These matters are never highlighted in the trial process, and when they do arise they are not taken to indicate evidence of the problematic nature of these cases as a distinct class. If it were acknowledged that investigative process in lethal force cases manifests peculiar characteristics which may go to the heart of the security forces' claims about a particular death, judicial process might contemplate the claims made by state agents a little more sceptically. Arguably, investigative process is a fundamental component in understanding the overall context of a lethal force fatality, and may shed some light on the precise circumstances in which an individual was killed.

It is interesting here to compare the assessment made by Northern Ireland judges of situations in which civilian witnesses have not given their statements directly to the police. The perilous consequences for such civilians is disclosed by the *Caraher* case. While acquitting two soldiers for the murder of Fergal Caraher and the attempted murder of his brother, Lord Chief Justice Hutton drew sharp and negative inferences from the decisions taken by civilian witnesses to give their evidence to a solicitor rather than directly to the police.[81] He stated:

> It is clear that before going to the police station each civilian witness saw the same solicitor, Mr Tiernan, and prepared a written statement which he gave to Mr Tiernan ... I am satisfied ... that the civilian witnesses gave untruthful answers on oath in the witness box when they said that there was not a pre-arranged plan to give written statements to Mr Tiernan, and that some of them gave untruthful answers when they said they did not refuse to answer questions to the police. It is quite contrary to commonsense to accept that civilian witnesses all went and gave statements to Mr Tiernan, and that he accompanied them to the police station and told the police that they would answer no questions, without some sort of plan or arrangement between them and, possibly, some other third party or parties.[82]

The civilian witnesses had stated that they were fearful of the consequences that might befall them as spectators to a serious incident in which two unarmed young men were seriously wounded by the military, one of whom had died. Their failure to trust the police in a community where police public relations were virtually nonexistent was impugned by the judge, and stood instead as persuasive evidence of the civilians' lack of reliability.

The double standard is conspicuous. Prepared statements by members of the security forces charged with serious offences have never been maligned judicially. The latitude given to the security forces is apparent in the murder trial arising out of the death of sixteen-year-old John Boyle, shot by two SAS soldiers staking out an arms cache. Both handed in prepared statements to the police following the incident. Lord Lowry found that:

> In reality these considerations do not increase the likelihood of guilt
> because, at worst, they could do no more than support the inference of
> a desire on the part of a superior authority to protect men who might or
> might not be guilty.[83]

Such procedure is never viewed as indicating pre-arranged planning or
ulterior motive but excused as, at worst, simple maladministration.
Similar persuasive arguments have never been applied to civilian evidence. Clearly, there exists an acceptance for irregular procedure in relation to lethal force deaths. It adds to the presumption in these trials that
the security forces are not guilty of a criminal offence when lethal force is
exercised.

B

THE CONDUCT OF TRIALS

By the conduct of proceedings, any court seeks to reconstruct a particular
event or series of events. By and large, as the earlier portion of this chapter
has pointed out, such occurrences are abstracted from much of their
history and context, though not all. Clearly, certain 'relevant' defences
and arguments shape the manner in which the narrative of a particular
death and the response of the law-enforcer will be reconstructed. What
this invariably achieves is that the actuality of death is denuded of much
of its actual and most significant social and practical consequences.

At this point it is useful to reflect on the conduct of the lethal force
trials themselves, because they tell us much about the functionality of
judges in the wider social strife from which many of these cases arise.
Observers have noted that sympathy for members of the security forces
charged with serious criminal offences is a persistent theme in judgments.[84] For example, while acquitting three policemen on 5 June 1984,
in connection with the deaths of McKerr, Toman and Burns, which
would give rise to the Stalker inquiry, Lord Justice Gibson stated:

> Doubtless when deciding whether to bring this prosecution on such
> tenuous evidence, the grave consequences likely to result from it,
> regardless of the outcome of the charge, were carefully weighed. I
> speak not of the inevitable suspense and worry to the accused or the
> additional danger which they are now likely to face because their iden-
> tities and appearances have been publicly exposed by this trial. I am

thinking of the more widespread effects among other members of the police and indeed the armed forces generally. When a policeman or soldier is ordered to arrest a dangerous criminal, and in substance, as in this case, to bring him back dead or alive, how is he to consider his conduct?[85]

On one level this sympathy towards members of the security forces is understandable. Judges in Northern Ireland, and particularly those sitting in the Diplock Courts, are reminded daily of the misery and violence visited upon the community by the action of paramilitary organisations. The judiciary itself has been under considerable threat from the same organisations. Judges and their families have been guarded around the clock by members of the security forces, upon whom their personal protection has depended. There is a natural affinity with the enforcers of law and order who belong to an establishment (in the broadest sense) to which the judiciary is also bound. However, this should not result in police officers and soldiers being placed above the law.

The rule of law requires that judicial hearings conform to a uniform standard of evenhandedness. If standards vary according to the status of the defendant, then the essence of fair trial is impugned. The trials of law-enforcers have seen the development of judicial doctrine which is unduly favourable to the accused. This has been accompanied by a loss of confidence in legal processes as a means of restoring accountability for the use of force. The *Bohan and Temperley* case is instructive.[86] The evidence presented by the soldiers was that the sixteen-year-old youth, with no involvement in paramilitary activity (and whose father had reported an arms cache to the police), had picked up a rifle and pointed it at them in a menacing fashion. Lord Lowry argued that 'the strength of this defence is its simplicity'. The simplicity position ignores how such a defence could be manipulated – there were no witnesses to the incident other than the two soldiers. The absolute reliance of their version of events to the exclusion of other possibilities is problematic. This is highlighted by the characterisation of one of the soldiers by the same judge as 'an untrustworthy witness, eager to make unmeritorious points'.[87] Yet both soldiers were acquitted of all charges.

The tendency to give the benefit of the doubt to the law-enforcer, particularly where the circumstances point to the need for a rigorous review of the security forces' actions, is also evident in the case arising out of the death of teenage joyriders Karen Reilly and Martin Peake. This case has been the subject of extensive litigation and public scrutiny. Private Lee Clegg was initially convicted of murdering Karen Reilly by opening fire on the back of the car in which she was travelling after it had passed through an army checkpoint (and when there was no longer an imminent threat of danger to the soldiers from the vehicle).[88] On retrial he was exonerated by Mr Justice Kerr on the charge of murder, based on fresh forensic evidence to the court. This new evidence demonstrated that it could not be proven that Clegg had opened fire after the joyriders' car had passed his position. He was nonetheless convicted of the lesser offence of attempting to wound with intent the car's driver, Martin Peake. This judgment was given despite the judicial characterisation of Clegg's evidence at retrial as a 'farrago of deceit and untruth'.[89] Clegg was released on bail pending an appeal on his conviction for attempted grievous bodily harm. Clegg was acquitted of all charges on appeal.

Both trials give a tremendous insight into the judicial reasoning methods employed when dealing with lethal force cases. The sympathies of Justice Campbell are evident in the first trial when he said that he regretted he had no choice but to sentence Clegg to life imprisonment (the applicable law meant that the lesser charge of manslaughter was unavailable). When the case first went to appeal Sir Brian Hutton stated:

> There is one obvious and striking difference between Private Clegg and the other persons found guilty of murder. The great majority of persons found guilty of murder, whether they are terrorists or domestic murders, kill from an evil and wicked motive ... [We] have no doubt that as he commenced the patrol he had no intention of unlawfully killing or wounding anyone.[90]

Unusually in this case, Constable Gibson, the policeman accompanying the army patrol, gave evidence to the first trial court that after the shooting took place he saw the soldiers inflict an injury on a member of their patrol, Private Aindow. The injury, it seems, was intended to support the soldiers' assertion that the car had injured one of their party, thereby activating the legitimate defence of self-defence in opening fire on the vehicle.[91]

Justice Campbell's appraisal of this evidence bears some close inspection. In examining Constable Gibson's oral evidence, he made significant play of the fact that the constable had given two accounts of the incident. The first, written the morning following the fatalities, made no mention of a deliberate injury inflicted on one soldier by the others. The policeman's stated reasons for the differences in his statements were explained by a growing realisation that he had a moral and legal duty to tell the whole truth.[92] The judge's construction of the first statement as 'lies' shows little understanding of the institutional context in which the constable's dilemma was located, and his own admission that there were powerful forces at play, resulting in his wish not to 'get the soldiers into trouble'.[93] The methodology employed by the judge in examining the evening's events lack rigour and imagination. It is particularly troublesome because it fails to scrutinise the soldiers' actions after the lethal shooting had taken place, and it lacks an overview of the collusive nature of their conduct, breaking down each soldier's version of events as complete in its own right and ignoring the necessary links to the group response.

It is this group response to the events which has a direct bearing on the establishment of criminal liability. Most ineptly, by posing one of the central questions of the case obliquely, its significance to overall events is entirely lost: rather than asking whether the injury on Private Aindow was delivered by other soldiers, the judicial focus shifts (contrary to the weight of evidence) to whether the Astra car carrying the teenagers struck him.[94] Subtly, the burden of proof is shifted from the soldiers themselves, and the self-defence provisions, activated by the potential threat of the oncoming car, become the focal point. Posing the question in this manner facilitates a convenient avoidance of a central issue, entirely undermining the evidence given by Constable Gibson and other civilian observers that the injuries received by the soldier were wholly unrelated to the actions of the vehicle. While the judge finds that Private Aindow was not struck by the Astra vehicle driven by the teenagers,[95] the overall presumption that it did so pervades the decision:

> Having considered the evidence, I find it impossible to understand how this car could have struck Private Aindow, where he is said to have been struck, without hitting or mounting the kerb.

The subsequent paragraph continues inconsistently:

> Private Aindow said that after the car struck him his left leg was very sore and when the car had passed out of sight he made his way down to below the gypsy encampment where Lance Corporal Boustead was setting up a cordon and he made him sit down.[96]

The implication of Justice Campbell's reasoning is that the soldiers are consistently being given the benefit of the doubt disproportionate to the presentation of actual physical and witness evidence.

While the judge ultimately and conclusively holds that the soldiers did in fact deliberately inflict an injury on Private Aindow, the significance of this fact is underplayed in this judgment.[97] The relationship between the fabrication of a story *post-facto* to justify the use of force and the lack of legal justification for exercising force in the first place is never examined. The soldiers are given the benefit of the applicable common law and statutory provisions, despite the evidence that the group decision to inflict an injury on a member of the patrol subverts the rationale upon which they used their weapons in the first place.

When handing down the decision of acquittal in lethal force cases, judges have frequently commented that the cases should not have come before them, and members of the security forces have been praised for the actions they have taken. Even though it was pronounced almost twenty years ago, the most infamous judicial dictum remains Justice Gibson's 'posse' direction. Directing a jury in a civil trial for compensation taken against the Ministry of Defence by the widow of an unarmed man shot during a bank robbery in Newry the judge stated:

> If you watch wild west films, the posse go ready to shoot their man if need be, if they don't bring them back peaceably they shoot them. And in the ultimate result if there isn't any other way to open up to a man [*sic*] it's reasonable to do it in the circumstances.[98]

The comparison of the forces of law and order with an unruly posse is unfortunate. In so far as lethal force cases are concerned, it shows judicial thinking in a harsh and unattractive light.

Judgments in such cases create a political dynamic. This was evidenced by the criminal trial of three RUC officers for the murder of Eugene Toman in November 1982.[99] Justice Gibson gave rise to a political storm by announcing to the prosecution that they never had 'the slightest chance of sustaining a conviction'. Following in the footsteps of his posse direction, he commended the RUC officers for their 'courage and determination in bringing the three deceased men to justice; in this case, the final court of justice'. The comments provoked outrage. They were viewed by many as judicial endorsement of a shoot-to-kill policy in Northern Ireland. Politicians from both the north and south of Ireland stated publicly that the judge had overstepped his judicial remit. Amid calls for his resignation, the judge took the unprecedented step of calling a press conference to clarify his comments. At that conference he denied acquiescing in a shoot-to-kill policy. He stated, 'nothing was further from my mind, nor would I contemplate that for a second, that such a view was tenable'.[100]

C

THE JUDICIAL LANGUAGE OF ARMED CONFLICT

One final disturbing aspect of many judgments arising from lethal force prosecutions in Northern Ireland is the misapplication of international legal standards and terminology. One manifestation of this is the use of phrases in judicial decisions such as 'quasi-war situation', 'armed insurrection' and 'hostile territory'. These militaristic phrases are used as a means to contextualise the use of lethal force in numerous circumstances. However, they are not without implication and have, in fact, precise legal definition under international law. Their misappropriation blurs and confuses the application of domestic legal standards. It is important to stress that no state of war or armed conflict officially exists in Northern Ireland. This has been expressly confirmed by the House of Lords in a decision concerning the use of lethal force. In 1977 in legal argument before the House of Lords it was clearly stated that:

> In spite of the fact that in Northern Ireland the security forces are working in active service conditions and often in conditions with which the ordinary law was not designed to cope and in regard to which there are few legal precedents, the security forces are not entitled to any special privileges, nor are they operating under the laws of war.[101]

If the laws of war were applicable, the relevant legal standard of review in some of the lethal force incidents would be the Geneva Conventions and the 1977 Protocols I and II Additional to the Geneva Conventions. Judges should be aware that the use of humanitarian law terminology may have legal and political implications, which are profoundly uncomfortable both for them and the state itself.

Following the Diplock Report of 1972, the United Kingdom engaged in a process of criminalising the Northern Ireland conflict. The rules of law which apply to the use of force are not emergency rules or military rules. Neither can the ordinary law in respect of the use of force be modified by military considerations. The persistent resort to humanitarian law terminology signals an acceptance by the judiciary (albeit unconscious or unofficial) that a state of armed conflict exists which, in turn, modifies the obligations and duties of members of the security forces. Such an approach is contrary to the international legal obligations of the United Kingdom government, which has signed treaty agreements protecting the right to life. That right is nonderogable under international law, even in an emergency situation. Judicial dicta on this matter in Northern Ireland suggest that there is either a lack of knowledge of the relevance of international law or a deliberate intention to ignore it. This issue is explored in depth in chapter 5.

VII
The appropriate charges?

Criminal proceedings are generally sought by the DPP only where it believes there is a reasonable chance of a successful outcome. The high number of acquittals in relation to the total number of prosecutions sought in relation to the exercise of deadly force is an anomaly related uniquely to this class of case in Northern Ireland. One reason repeatedly cited for the lack of will on the part of the prosecuting authorities to bring criminal proceedings in these cases is the 'all or nothing' choice as regards charging a member of the security forces with a criminal offence after an individual has been killed by the use of lethal force. This situation has in part been brought about by judicial dicta which has limited the circumstances in which a charge of manslaughter can be preferred against a member of the security forces who fatally discharges a weapon during the course of his duties. The technical rules pertaining to the preferment of charges are critical to understanding the obstacles here. Tom Hadden has characterised the problem as follows:

> [the problem] arises from four interrelated legal rules: first the rule that an intent to inflict serious bodily injury is sufficient to sustain a charge of murder; secondly the rule that a conviction for the lesser charge of manslaughter is not permissible where lethal force is deliberately used; thirdly the rule that in assessing the legitimacy of the force used only the circumstances immediately facing the soldier or policeman can be taken into account; and finally the rule that a conviction for murder can only be sustained if it is proved beyond reasonable doubt that

the defendant did not honestly believe that the use of lethal force was justified.[102]

The most basic quandary regarding preferment of charges lies with the legal construction of criminal intent. The rule that an intention to cause serious bodily injury is treated as an equivalent to an intention to kill is a disincentive to charging members of the security forces involved in lethal force incidents. In most situations when a law-enforcer discharges a weapon they do so deliberately. There is an intention to prevent an act, to protect oneself or another person. The weapons training that a law-enforcer receives ensures that he realises what the consequences of discharging a weapon will be, usually death or serious injury. The law assumes that law-enforcers intend the probable outcome of their actions. Consequently, the charge deemed appropriate when a law-enforcer deliberately discharges his weapon is murder. The obstacles to obtaining successful convictions for murder in relation to actions by members of the security forces has already been outlined.

Proving the *mens rea* of murder creates particular problems in lethal force cases. The required proof is that the accused had the necessary intention to kill or to cause serious injury to another person. This is the crux of criminal intention. Proving this deliberate intention on the part of a law enforcer operating in difficult political circumstances is a serious bar to obtaining criminal convictions. The standard defences previously outlined give a justifiable reason to use a weapon. The issue then returns to the reasonableness of the beliefs held by the law-enforcer which resulted in their resort to the use of a weapon. Where a court accepts that the soldier or police officer genuinely believed the version of events presented, it is bound to acquit the accused of the charge of murder.

A

AN ALTERNATIVE – THE DOCTRINE OF EXCESSIVE DEFENCE

Courts in the United Kingdom have expressly rejected the doctrine of excessive defence.[103] The principle was adopted in both the Irish Republic and in Australia, deriving its validity from the common law.[104] However, it has recently been abandoned in Australia, on the basis that its formulation was too difficult for juries to understand,[105] though it continues to operate effectively in the Irish jurisdiction. Arguably, the adoption of this doctrine might be a useful means to address some of the persistent problems that have plagued lethal force prosecutions in Northern Ireland. Judges in the jurisdiction have also acknowledged the limitations of the current regime and called for statutory change in this direction. In upholding the first conviction of Private Lee Clegg, Northern Ireland's Lord Chief Justice stated:

> But this court considers, and we believe that many other fair-minded citizens would share this view, that the law would be much fairer if it had been open to the trial judge to have convicted Private Clegg on the lesser crime of manslaughter on the grounds that he did not kill Karen Reilly from evil motive but because, his duties as a soldier having placed him on the Glen Road armed with a high velocity rifle, he reacted wrongly to a situation which suddenly confronted him in the course of his duties.[106]

The adoption of the doctrine of excessive defence recognises that in certain situations individuals have the right to use force, whether that be in self-defence, to effect arrest or to prevent a crime. However, it acknowledges that this right can be exercised excessively, upon objective evaluation by the courts. This means that a person with the legal right to use force can overreact and use more force than was necessary in a particular situation. Such a reality is borne out by the situations which have given rise to numerous lethal force fatalities, whereby members of the security forces argued that they felt threatened, but their belief to that effect was entirely mistaken, and the force used was completely out of proportion to the reality of the situation encountered.

Many commentators have called for a change to the legal standard relating to the use of force in Northern Ireland.[107] The excessive defence doctrine would remove the 'all or nothing' difficulty; it would allow that a charge of murder could be reduced to manslaughter, recognising both the culpability of and mitigating circumstances facing the accused in the exercise of deadly force. Tom Hadden has argued persuasively that its adoption would deal with the problems posed by the current construction of criminal intent in these cases.[108] A statutory change on this highly sensitive matter would give greater flexibility to the prosecuting authorities and the courts, facilitating the potential for meaningful accountability in the arena of lethal force in the jurisdiction.

VIII
Non-binding rules on the use of force

Both police and army have in place internal guidelines which more precisely define the circumstances in which force can be exercised in the
jurisdiction than does the criminal law. However, these guidelines have
no binding legal force and failure to adhere to the internal rules has no
criminal or civil legal consequences for a law-enforcer. Nonetheless they
are important to examine, because well-formulated internal policy
guidelines can provide an informal mechanism by which sanctions are
enforced for breach of accepted norms.[109]

The rules governing the use of firearms by soldiers are set out in a
document entitled 'Instructions for Opening Fire in Northern
Ireland'.[110] More commonly known as the Yellow Card, the document
is officially classified, but its contents have become widely known
through its presentation into evidence at various legal processes following the use of lethal force by soldiers. It is issued to all soldiers serving in
the jurisdiction, who are expected to be familiar with its contents. The
reasons for the issuance of such guidelines are self-evident: soldiers who
are generally trained in the mechanics of battle engagement are suddenly
thrust into an unknown role, requiring them to act as an aid to the civilian power. They are expected to carry out many of the duties that would
normally be exclusively reserved to the domain of police forces. In other
words, it is a task for which they may be untrained and unsuitable. The
Yellow Card is a means of giving soldiers basic information in an acces-
sible form, which allows them some knowledge of the legal parameters
within which they must now operate.

The Yellow Card has been considerably modified since it was first
introduced. Initially it contained over twenty separate rules, while the
current version now runs at six. The original version was problematical
as it contained too much information for the average soldier to readily
absorb. As a result, there was a danger that the fundamental principles
were being lost or ignored. Simplification sought to concentrate on
basic principles that were easily understood by all army personnel.

The constraints imposed by the Yellow Card are, in theory, quite considerable. The rules emphasise the use of minimum force, the theory of
last resort and the issuing of clear warnings before resorting to the use of
firearms. The problem lies in the implementation of these rules – they are

generally ignored or abused in practice. Of equal concern is the fact that the difference between the internal military standard and the standard of criminal legal culpability is vast. It is quite conceivable that both ordinary soldiers and those with command responsibility engaged in operational planning are aware of the difference. That may mean that they are also aware that a failure to adhere to the internal standard will not have any serious consequences for them.

The Yellow Card imposes a higher standard than current legal regulation in relation to the decision to use force in particular circumstances. The document concentrates on the validity of using force only when there is an immediate threat to life of self or others. The area of greatest difference is in respect to the fleeing offender. The Yellow Card does not seem to allow for the use of force simply to prevent someone from escaping. This rule would seem to apply even if the offender is a member of a paramilitary organisation. In short, the Yellow Card maintains the validity of the immediacy and proportionality tests in the exercise of force by a soldier.

However, judicial dicta on the Yellow Card has been dismissive, persistently stressing that breach of this document has no value in helping to ascertain the guilt of an offender charged with either murder or manslaughter. In 1975, at the murder trial following the death of Patrick McElhone, Justice MacDermott stated:

> For my part, I consider this card to be something which exists for some reason of policy and is intended to lay down guidelines to the forces, but in my view it does not define the legal rights of members of the security forces. No doubt it contains much sound advice, but I can readily understand that to many soldiers, and perhaps to others too, it is to say the least of it a difficult document.[111]

Justice MacDermott confirmed that a failure to follow the instructions contained in the document would not imply that the soldier's conduct had been unlawful. The views are echoed by Lord Chief Justice Lowry in the *McNaughton* case in the same year.[112] The soldier concerned was charged with attempted murder. The shooting had taken place after a bomb explosion in the vicinity of the soldier's patrol unit, which encountered John Walsh coming from the direction of the blast. Walsh alleged that he had been ordered to climb over a nearby fence by the accused and was subsequently shot on the basis that he was attempting to escape. In the course of his judgment, the judge reiterated that the Yellow Card was only a policy document, remarking:

> There was, of course, at the same time in existence what is called the yellow card, something the contents of which, it seems, are largely dictated by policy and are intended to lay down guidelines for the security forces but which do not define the legal rights and obligations of the forces under statute or common law.[113]

In both cases the judges identify that there are reasons of policy dictating the creation and use of the Yellow Card. Those reasons are not difficult to ascertain. They include clarification of broad legal guidelines, control over the actions of soldiers performing policing duties, and emphasis on the principles of proportionality and minimum force. Northern Ireland judges have always linked the existence of the Yellow Card with policy, but have never articulated what those policy considerations might be. Moreover, they have never sought to catalogue the extent to which the Yellow Card enforces the policies underlying the enforcement of the criminal law itself. Instead of recognising the value of an interplay between operational rules and legal standards, and acknowledging that one can complement the other, the courts insist that the two are completely divorced.

The RUC also maintain operational guidelines on the use of force. These guidelines have never been officially published, and the absence of public knowledge on their contents is regrettable. However, they have been alluded to in the criminal trials of police officers charged with serious offences arising from the use of lethal force. At the trial of Timothy Hanley, following the death of Kevin McGovern, a young agricultural student shot by him in 1991, Detective Chief Inspector McFarland gave evidence to the court on the content of the police regulations. Justice Nicholson paraphrased his evidence as follows:

> He agreed in cross-examination that it was a detailed document, that the police had no equivalent of the Yellow Card issued to the soldiers which, he agreed, was more direct, could be read more quickly and memorised. He agreed that as to paragraph 3 which dealt with circumstances for the use of firearms, an attack or suspected attack with the use of a coffee jar bomb would justify the use of firearms. He said that a police officer was entitled to use his firearm in appropriate circumstances, was trained to think independently and act independently; aimed shots were preferred to warnings, that there was no justification on firing aimed shots at a suspect except in self-defence; there was a

serious threat to that patrol by an IRA unit; firing into the air was the safest form of warning shot; if he himself thought that he was to be fired on he would fire for effect.[114]

It would be both expedient and desirable that the differences between the legal standards and the operational standard be clarified. While doing so, it may be possible to maintain a higher operational standard for the army in particular. As Tom Hadden points out:

> it is thought desirable to set a stricter standard in the operational Army rules and in so doing to provide a margin of safety for individual soldiers against any possible civil or criminal proceedings.[115]

What must be remedied is the current situation in which the operational standard is undercut by persistent judicial devaluing. Judges must not forget that internal rules of conduct can act as a powerful control tool within institutional settings. The operational guidelines, if enforced by internal disciplinary procedures that aim to control the exercise of force by law-enforcers, can facilitate the protection of the right to life within the state. But for this to occur, the state and courts must be seen to value the internal controls themselves. If this does not happen, a strong signal is sent to the law-enforcer that the internal rules are meaningless and that no adverse consequence follows from ignoring them entirely.

IX
Reforming the law

Calls for reform of the law regulating the use of lethal force in Northern Ireland have been persistent and vociferous.[116] The lack of accountability for deaths resulting from the use of deadly force has had a quantifiably negative effect on the relationship between communities and the state. Rethinking the law in this arena is a crucial element of rebuilding fractured relationships with all of Northern Ireland's diverse communities, and it is all the more crucial now, as Northern Ireland enters another phase, the post-conflict endeavour of peace-building. Law conveys and transmits a complex set of attitudes, values and theories about the way in which a society functions. When its structures and values represent, reinforce and legitimise a social order which is exclusionary, privileged and unaccountable, the pervasive effects on the health of a society cannot be underestimated.

Lethal force deaths have created presumptions that the rule of law operates dysfunctionally in the jurisdiction. In some communities extensively affected by the use of force the perception pervades that the state has acted with legal impunity in taking life. In the creation of a bipartisan pluralistic society, it must be persuasively confirmed that soldiers and police officers, like all other citizens, are subject to the law and must act within the law. Failure to hold the agents of the state accountable when they act outside the boundaries of the law impacts profoundly on the legitimacy and impartiality of the legal system and of the state itself.

The practical legal quandaries are as follows. First, the standard allowing the use of force is exceptionally broad and seems ripe for statutory redrafting in a form which is more responsive to the reality of practical situations in which the need to use force arises. It is interesting to note that the British Labour Party proposed such statutory modification in recent years.[117] More particularly, the reasonableness standard is in dire need of statutory reformulation to ensure that it conforms with the European Convention on Human Rights standard of necessity. This may be achieved *de facto* with the incorporation of the European Convention into domestic law which will require domestic judges to interpret the reasonableness standard in a more stringent manner.

Second, the unavailability of the lesser charge of manslaughter creates a legal straitjacket, the result of which has been a clear unwillingness by the DPP to proceed with cases against members of the security forces. There is a demonstrated need for a greater range of charges to be available to the prosecuting authorities. Such a move has already been welcomed by the courts, which are unhappy with the limitation imposed upon them as a result of the 'all or nothing' options presently in place.

The adoption of the excessive defence doctrine would be a marked improvement on the present situation. It would help to restore credibility and accountability, allowing the prosecuting authorities to pursue sanctions in cases which currently would simply not come before the courts. A number of other options to tighten the legal standard exists. One is the adoption of a new statutory offence which might include the new offence of 'reckless discharge of a weapon'. Such an offence would have a number of advantages: it offers a broader spectrum in the choice of charges; it may be easier to sustain convictions for this offence than for the offence of manslaughter; and it facilitates further controls on the use of lethal force.

The Standing Advisory Commission on Human Rights also

suggested the introduction of a further offence of breaching a statutory code, directly regulating the loose operational rules which apply to the discharge of weapons within law enforcement agencies themselves.[118]

What all this tells us is that there is no shortage of proposals for reform of the present regulatory system with its acknowledged weaknesses. What is ultimately required is political will to initiate and administer such changes. Northern Ireland is in the embryonic stages of reconfiguring its internal social relations. This is not an easy task. In transcending conflict, it is important that the state remains mindful of the structures and policies which have been at the heart of the conflict itself. Restoring meaningful accountability and disavowing impunity is a fundamental aspect of transformation. The use of force in Northern Ireland has created long-standing alienation and hurt for individuals and communities. In reshaping society it is important that the legal structures which have proven inadequate to respond to that fact be re-imagined, so that the future will be faced on a different premise. That is, the premise that the lives of all citizens are equal and equally valued by their state.

3

Other mechanisms of accountability – the inquest procedure

Inquests in Northern Ireland are inexorably linked to the controversy surrounding many disputed deaths.[1] The reason for this is a simple one – most disputed killings have not been subject to criminal prosecution, and there have rarely been any public inquiries into these deaths. Civil compensation has been limited, has lacked publicity, or has simply been denied.[2] As a result, the inquest absorbs the expectations of the public and the next of kin for legal remedy following a disputed death. Correspondingly, this creates many unrealistic expectations about the inquest and its ability to deliver meaningful accountability when death is caused by an agent of the state.

In many jurisdictions inquests have come under considerable pressure from disparate sources. Their role has been limited by improved scientific methods for determining the causes of death by specialists including pathologists, toxicologists and medical experts. Further, the inquest's independent functions have been diminished by heightened co-operation between coroners and law-enforcement officers. These general limitations are true for Northern Ireland. However, some additional caveats apply to the inquest process in the jurisdiction.

The legal regulation of inquests in Northern Ireland has been subject to penetrating changes. These alterations are related to the functioning of inquests in a protracted conflict, and raise serious concerns about the adequacy of the amended model in the jurisdiction. Analysis of these changes demonstrates the diffusion of crisis responses by the state into the ordinary legal system, particularly at the points where the ordinary law must confront the emergency.[3] It is well documented that emergency laws confer extraordinary powers on the state, giving it the capacity to respond speedily and unencumbered by the restraints and the protection of individual rights. Less comprehensively analysed is the extent to which the pattern of utilising extraordinary law affects the way in which the state manages pre-existing institutions that play a role in conflict management. In Northern Ireland the widespread and long-term use of emergency legislation has created the psychological conditions under which ordinary law and legal structure have also been incrementally modified. Legal changes to the structure of the inquest process reveal some of this 'normal/abnormal' interaction. What must also be clear is that this diffusion occurs despite a political rhetoric of normality, which insists that changes to legal structures are simply routine or the product of other policy imperatives.

In Northern Ireland the point that starkly highlights the modification to the inquest process is a comparative one. In short, there are significant differences between the law regulating inquests in England and Wales and in Northern Ireland. The differences between the Northern Ireland inquest and its English counterpart do not lie merely in their varying legal powers but also in distinct practices, peculiar to inquests in Northern Ireland, which reflect an abnormality of process, refined partly in response to the nature of the conflict itself. While the vast majority of the day-to-day work carried out by inquests has little to do with the emergency in the jurisdiction, the points at which the institution and conflict intersect have proven critical for the legal standing of the inquest itself.

This chapter shall address both the practice and law of inquests in Northern Ireland. As the inquest remains the primary mechanism for accountability when life is taken by the state, it is crucial to outline whether that function is performed adequately and fairly. Equally, the viability of domestic forms of legal accountability is a measure of whether the state is in conformity with its international obligations to protect life. The analysis also gives an extraordinary insight into the 'cross-over' phenomenon – this term describes the way in which ordinary law and legal process is substantially altered when it plays a role in managing a prolonged low-intensity conflict.

I
History of the inquest

In order to understand the current limitations placed upon the inquest, it is necessary to trace its historical development. The office of coroner dates back to medieval times.[4] Historically, the primary role of the office was to safeguard the fiscal interests of the Crown.[5] The coroner's function was to secure custody of the king's revenue, principally the revenue accruing from fines and forfeiture.[6] In addition, the coroner occasionally exercised the sheriff's jurisdiction, inquiring into such matters as unexplained deaths, treasure troves and deodands.[7] The creation of the coroner's office is believed to be a direct result of the attempts of Henry II to curb the powers of the sheriffs.[8] The office was linked from its inception to the administrative rather than the judicial side of government.

The role of the coroner expanded in the Middle Ages. Throughout the thirteenth and fourteenth centuries there were usually four coroners assigned to each English county, and by the nineteenth century, the coroner's role in cases of sudden or unnatural death was well established. However, despite the widening of his role, by this time the status of the coroner's office was in decline. This was due to the increased participation of the medical profession at the coroner's inquest, which downgraded the political status of the coroner's role, as the inquest came to have both medical and legal functions. In the twentieth century the coroner's inquest has been legally subordinated to the investigative function of the police and the DPP, This was confirmed by the Coroner's (Amendment) Act 1926, which acknowledged that the primary duty of investigation and prosecution for unlawful death rested with the police.

Thus, over time the role of the coroner's inquest has been incrementally limited. Prior to the passing of the Criminal Law Act 1977, the inquest jury had the power to return a verdict indicting a person of murder, manslaughter or infanticide; the coroner then had the power to commit the person identified for criminal trial. In such cases the inquest took the place of a preliminary investigation by a magistrate and the inquisition took the place of the indictment. This procedure was abolished by the 1977 legislation.[9] A coroner's inquest can no longer charge a person with any offence.

The subordination of the inquest is also evident in the new provisions which facilitate the adjournment of proceedings. In England and Wales, when criminal proceedings commence in respect of a death which is concurrently under review by an inquest, the inquest can now be adjourned pending resolution of those proceedings.[10] In Northern Ireland a similar provision applies.[11] Further, the police may ask the coroner to adjourn the inquest for twenty-eight days or longer if there are grounds to believe that a person will be charged with murder.[12] It is now established practice that if an inquest takes place after relevant criminal proceedings have concluded, the cause of death must not be inconsistent with the criminal determination.

Abolishing the indictment function of the coroner's inquest reflected concern for the protection of those individuals whose rights might be prejudiced during criminal prosecution by the outcome of a prior inquest proceeding.[13] The changes also indicate a transformation in outlook on the purpose of the inquest, which is now viewed as a purely inquisitorial process. Reflecting this, the inquest has been restructured as a neutral fact-finding entity and, consequently, any involvement in the allocation of legal fault for a death would undermine this capacity.[14] Such a division of labour makes complete sense in a situation where the ordinary criminal process has the primary function of investigating a death and bringing criminal charges if necessary. In such a situation the inquest can take a back seat. However, this historical transformation of the inquest only makes sense when the criminal justice system is able and willing to carry out its prosecutorial function. The problems arise with such changes when there are serious weaknesses evident in the ordinary or modified criminal process, and the inquest may take on a significance for accountability that is unmatched by its legal capacity. In situations where the state is experiencing prolonged crisis, and where public confidence in legal process has diminished, certain legal mechanisms may take on a symbolic significance that is not concomitant with their actual powers.

II
Regulation of inquests in England and Wales

Inquests in England and Wales have a straightforward mandate. A coroner must hold an inquest in cases of violent or unnatural death;[15] and is obliged to sit with a jury if a death occurred in police custody or as a result of police action.[16] English and Welsh inquest juries still retain the power to bring in verdicts. The Brodrick Report,[17] initiated by government as a review of the operation of the coroner's office, recommended strongly that verdicts be replaced by findings of fact. This recommendation has thus far not been accepted in England and Wales. Currently, juries choose from an array of verdicts including, 'natural causes', 'addiction to drugs', 'unlawful killing', 'accident', and 'misadventure', which are not mandatory choices but 'suggestions' made by the Lord Chancellor.[18] Until 1980 juries could add a rider to their verdicts, but the Brodrick Committee recommended that this power be removed. The change was facilitated in the revised Coroner's Rules 1984.[19] In England and Wales the coroner retains the power to make a report where he believes action needs to be taken to prevent a fatality recurring in a similar situation.[20]

In England and Wales, unless a suspect has actually been charged with murder, an inquest will proceed into a suspicious death. If an individual has been charged with a lesser offence than murder, there is no requirement that the inquest be suspended pending the outcome of criminal proceedings. This can only occur if the DPP requests an adjournment. However, coroners do not have the power to simply adjourn an inquest indefinitely.

III
The politics of regulating inquests in Northern Ireland

The coroner's inquest in Northern Ireland has a very different history from its English/Welsh counterpart. Tom Hadden characterises it in this way:

> There have long been substantial differences from the prevailing British model in the law and practice of inquests in Northern Ireland. The Lord Chancellor and ministers of the Northern Ireland Office have repeatedly portrayed these differences as of minor significance. But this position is hard to sustain. The more important issue is how far the differences may be attributed to official fears that inquests into disputed killings by the security forces may cause problems for the authorities and how far to the more systematic adoption of the recommendations of the Wright and Brodrick Reports both by the Unionist government and under Direct Rule.[21]

The duties of coroner in Northern Ireland are set out in the Coroner's Act and the Coroner's Rules.[22] Prior to the legal reform in 1959, which produced the Coroner's Act, there were pre-existing differences between the English law regulating inquests and Northern Ireland law regulating inquests. This was strikingly true in respect of deaths caused by agents of the state. It is evident that from an early point such deaths were viewed as being a potential source of political embarrassment and friction. Thus, the legal regulation of such deaths was customised.

The Special Powers Act, which remained an effective statutory provision until 1973, created the competence to prohibit holding an inquest in a designated case or class of cases.[23] Section 10 of the legislation, which prohibited inquests, further allowed the Minister of Home Affairs to conduct an inquiry in lieu of an inquest if the minister alone considered the circumstances appropriate. It was also open to the minister to apply for a military court of inquiry rather than an inquest if the military authorities so requested.[24] A situation in which a soldier killed a civilian was specifically enumerated as a circumstance in which a military court would appear desirable.[25] However, the legal position on inquests set out in the Special Powers Act was not a novelty – earlier draconian legislation embodied in the Restoration of Order in Ireland Act 1920 gave wide and exceptional powers to military commanders. These also

Figure 26 Inquest status by victim status, 1969–94

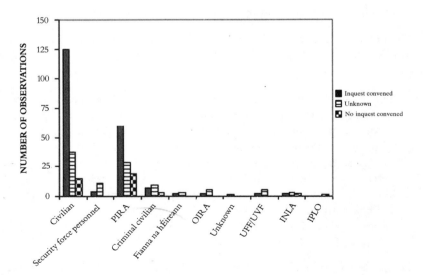

included instituting military inquiries into violent deaths caused by army personnel, rather than allowing for the initiation of coroner's proceedings.

Thus, historical legal prohibitions on holding inquests in Ireland illustrate the political recognition that these proceedings were a potential source of embarrassment for the state, which was heightened when state agents caused deaths. The potential for the inquest to once again become a lightning rod for discontent was self-evident after 1969. The source was the large numbers of deaths caused by the military and the police in the context of renewed sectarian violence and the response of the state to the civil rights movement.

A distinct pattern of legal regulation for inquests has emerged in Northern Ireland and legal rules governing inquests have changed significantly in the jurisdiction in the past thirty years. Many of these changes simply parallel recommended modifications in the reports produced by the Wright and Brodrick Committees.[26] Some might argue that the changes merely reflect local efficiency in streamlining a particular legal process. An alternative and provocative interpretation would suggest that reconstruction of the inquest procedure was responsive to political events in Northern Ireland, and the interaction of legal process with these events. This view concurs with the overall thrust of this book: that law is not a neutral bystander in situations of prolonged emergency.

A

VERDICTS V. FINDINGS

In some notable contexts the modifications to the inquest structure have gone further than the changes proposed by the official governmental committees, which, in itself, indicates the presence of the political backdrop. This is significantly illustrated by the legal changes relating to the issuing of verdicts in Northern Ireland. Currently, Northern Ireland inquest juries must issue verdicts that are confined to a statement of who the deceased was, and how and when he or she died.[27] In short, not only has the power to issue verdicts been removed but also the manner in which the fact-finding is undertaken has been severely circumscribed.

Circumscribing the inquest's declarative power has an interesting chronology in the jurisdiction. The restrictions commenced with the practice of confining the jury to a fixed range of verdicts available from a rigid list.[28] This followed logically from the recommendation of the Wright Report, which advocated that questions of civil and criminal liability should not be considered by juries and that the power to commit persons to trial from the inquest should be abolished.[29] In England the Coroner's Rules of 1953 implemented these proposals, and the Coroner's Act (Northern Ireland) 1959 had the same effect. The Brodrick Committee had also strongly recommended that the determination of legal culpability should be removed from the inquest's fact-finding function. In England and Wales this was achieved by abolishing the verdicts of murder and manslaughter in 1977.[30]

In Northern Ireland these changes were put in place at a much earlier stage. After 1969 a disturbingly large number of open verdicts were recorded at inquests when death had been caused by an agent of the state. The paucity of criminal prosecutions subsequent to such verdicts became the focus of public attention. Thus, when the recommendations of the Brodrick Committee were being implemented these political

Figure 27 Inquest jury results in lethal force cases, 1969–94*

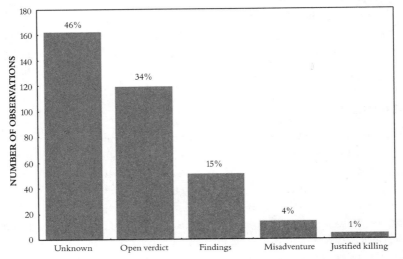

* This representation collapses two varying sets of data: information pertaining to the issuing of findings, and information related to the period when juries were legally permitted to issue verdicts. However, the information demonstrates cogently the high number of open verdicts issued (119 in all). Note that information is not available as to the outcome of inquest proceedings related to 162 deaths.

anxieties were to the fore of political thinking. Hence, the abolition of verdicts was taken a step further in the jurisdiction. The move to substitute findings for verdicts in every case would appear to have been precipitated by the overwhelming number of 'open verdicts' returned on deaths caused by members of the security forces.

The requirement that the jury issues only findings poses very practical problems. Some inherent contradictions arise in the task that they are given. On the one hand, they are told that they are not concerned with issues of criminal liability; on the other, they are left to reach a conclusion as to how the deceased came to die. In many situations it is difficult to separate out one question from the other. In certain cases the jury has taken an entirely minimalist position, going no further than the most cursory description of how a death came about. This approach is illustrated by the death of Charles Breslin. The jury's findings stated:

> We the jury unanimously agree that Mr Charles Breslin met his death on the 23rd of February 1985, in a field at the rear of 36 Fountain Street, as a result of gunshot wounds to the head and trunk. The incident took place at approximately 4.55 a.m.[31]

In this case the inquest findings gave no more information to the public than did newspaper reports the day following the incident.

Despite substantial impairment of the jury's function as findings replaced verdicts, some juries have performed extremely well. Certain juries under the coroner's direction have used the requirement to give findings as a means to give a detailed and comprehensive overview of the context of death. Such detailed findings have occasionally pointed to lapses on the part of state agents, which indicate some criminal sanction to be appropriate. For example, in the inquest concerning the death of Brian Robinson (an active member of the Ulster Volunteer Force) struck by gunfire in 1989 while fleeing a murder scene, the jury decided that Robinson had been shot while unarmed and lying on the ground. The DPP subsequently reopened its file on the case. The jury investigating the death of Seamus McElwaine in 1986 decided that two rounds of ammunition, with an interval between each round, had been fired at the Maze prison escapee. Inevitably, the jury's findings led to the conclusion that a *coup de grâce* had been administered to the deceased. In many cases juries have also altered the draft findings placed before them by the coroner. This indicates the capacity of juries to be independent-minded and to exercise rational and autonomous judgement on the facts that are presented to them. Equally, it is this tendency to be independent-spirited which causes such concern to the authorities, and which has been shackled by the removal of the verdict power.

The public response to these changes has been muted. Few citizens come into routine contact with inquest proceedings, and, therefore, knowledge of these changes is not widespread nor widely felt. On the other hand, for those individuals who come to an inquest with the perception that it will provide an accountability forum for the death of a family member, the changes have created significant resentment. For this group the alterations are not seen as the neutral implementation of governmental policy on inquests generally, but as a means of minimising official discomfort where deaths have been caused by agents of the state, where the inquest finding has merely become declaratory. The change from verdicts to findings has limited the power of the inquest to act as a check against either the discretion of the police not to fully investigate and the discretion of the prosecutor not to criminally prosecute.

Removing the capacity of Northern Ireland's inquest juries to issue verdicts has another important dimension – the loss of validation given by lay participation in a judicial system sorely lacking undisputed legitimacy to both communities in the jurisdiction. Restrictions on the involvement of the jury can have significant consequences for perceptions about the legal system as a whole. This is particularly true in Northern Ireland, given the wider lack of civilian participation in the trial of scheduled offences in the non-jury Diplock Courts. In a situation where public confidence in the legal system is at low ebb, effective lay participation plays an important part in regulating public perceptions and instilling confidence in the legal system. It is for this reason that the limitation of the role of the jury, in the removal of the verdict power, has had wider consequences in Northern Ireland than it might have had in another jurisdiction.

B

COMPELLING WITNESSES

Another notable feature of the Northern Ireland inquest process relates to the rules which pertain to compelling witnesses. In 1963 a specific rule was introduced in the jurisdiction which decreed that the person suspected of causing a death was a noncompellable witness.[32] This rule expressly prohibits a coroner from compelling any person 'who is suspected of causing the death or has been charged or is likely to be charged with an offence related to the death' from giving evidence at the inquest. There is no comparable legislation in England and Wales. One reason for the change may have been the concern that forcing such a witness to give evidence might only result in a refusal to answer questions during the proceedings on the grounds of self-incrimination. This view is misleading. There was no evidence of a consistent refusal of such witnesses to answer questions during inquest proceedings. Furthermore, the rules on self-incrimination continue to function adequately in England and Wales and there is little evidence to suggest that they are insufficient to protect potential witness-suspects in Northern Ireland. What seems clear is that there was a particular concern in Northern Ireland about witnesses with causal responsibility for the death of a person giving evidence to inquests. Probing this further, it is not likely that the average citizen's self-incrimination was of such enormous concern to the state. Rather, there was a particular class of compellable witnesses who were judged to be in need of evidential protection. This class of witnesses were agents of the state who might be compelled to appear before an inquest, having been causally responsible for the death of a citizen.

This provides another insight into the normal/abnormal discourse in the jurisdiction. If agents of the state were operating within the 'normal' rule of law framework, there should be no reason why they would not give evidence at inquests when they exercised force against citizens. However, when agents of the state function in a legally ambiguous situation, and their actions may be specifically directed at containing counterinsurgency, there may be every reason for the state to avoid minute legal scrutiny of their actions. Such examination might require a formal acknowledgement that the ordinary rules do not apply. This has serious consequences for the narrative which the state has sought so hard to impose on the conflict over the years.

In practice this noncompellability rule means that members of the security forces directly responsible for causing a death never attend inquests to give evidence. Consequently, these central witnesses cannot be cross-examined nor are they required to swear their testimony under oath. It is very doubtful that this interpretation of their recommendations was envisioned by the Wright and Brodrick Committees – notably and by contrast, law-enforcers who have caused a death by the use of force in England and Wales remain compellable witnesses.

The noncompellability rule has been the subject of protracted litigation in Northern Ireland, its most direct challenge coming in the *McKerr* case.[33] The inquest arose from the deaths of Gervaise McKerr, Eugene Toman and Sean Burns, three unarmed members of PIRA, by an RUC undercover unit in November 1982. At an early point in the inquest proceedings, a direct challenge was made to rule 9 which facilitated the non-appearance of the police officers causally responsible for death. Counsel for the next of kin argued to the Northern Ireland Court of Appeal that the rule modified the substantive law relating to the compellability of witnesses and was beyond the 'practice and procedure' allowed by section 36 of the Coroner's Act 1959, making it *ultra vires* the Act. The Court of Appeal agreed, maintaining that witnesses whose answers might self-incriminate nonetheless remained compellable witnesses.[34] The court further found that rule 9 was inconsistent with section 17 of the Coroner's Act 1959, which empowered the coroner to issue a witness summons for any witness whose attendance he thought necessary to the inquest. The Attorney-General appealed the decision to the House of Lords, which unanimously overruled the Northern Ireland Court of Appeal. The Lords held that rule 9 was a valid rule regulating practice and procedure at inquests. Stressing the inquisitorial function of the inquest, they felt that it was 'misleading in the context of the Coroner's inquest, to describe the compellability of a witness as an "important" common law right'.[35]

The judgment strongly advocated against the imposition of standards from other courts and tribunals to inquests. The court strongly defended its view that the coroner's inquest is not an adversarial process, and resisted any perceived attempt to transform it into such. The point missed by the court is that for the inquest to carry out that inquisitorial function adequately, it is important that those individuals responsible for causing a death be present to give their version of the facts. To have such witnesses present need not automatically turn the coroner's court into an adversarial proceeding.

In England and Wales the coroner's court functions adequately without the equivalent of rule 9. Persons cannot refuse to be a witness simply because they might subsequently be charged with an offence connected with the death.[36] As Tom Hadden has noted:

> In the McKerr case the fact that the decision has resulted in a signifi-
> cantly different rule of procedure operating in Northern Ireland from
> that in Britain, on the basis of some passing reference in a nineteenth-
> century Irish case, was scarcely mentioned.[37]

The weakest aspect of the House of Lords' decision in *McKerr* was the
conclusion that rule 9 did nothing more than extend protection to citizens falling within specified categories. The Law Lords concluded that
compelling these citizens to give evidence might expose them to the
embarrassment of having to invoke the privilege against self-incrimination. To build the case for noncompellability of witnesses in Northern
Ireland on the foundations of their potential embarrassment is to expose
the weakness of the judicial approach to the matter. The case has created
the perception that a malleable set of legal criteria has been constructed to
respond to the problems which arise when members of the security forces
give evidence at inquests. Such perceptions do little to endear the inquest
process to the public at large and compound wider ripples of discontent
with the rule of law in Northern Ireland. It has profound long-term consequences for the rule of law itself, particularly now that the Good Friday
Agreement seeks to normalise both societal structures and the law that
regulates them.

C

THE ADMISSIBILITY OF STATEMENTS
MADE BY NONCOMPELLABLE WITNESSES

Given that the individual who may have caused a death is not a compellable witness, another acute issue rests in the status of any statements made
by that person which are admitted during the inquest process. By and
large, coroners in Northern Ireland have admitted the statements of
noncompellable witnesses and the practice has produced some notable
litigation.

The objections to admitting such statements are self-evident: their
authors cannot be cross-examined by legal counsel, leaving no means to
challenge a witness about the veracity of the statement made and to point
out inconsistencies. Deciding how much weight to accord to such statements is also problematic. In numerous cases where a disputed death is
under scrutiny the only eyewitnesses may be the members of the security

forces who were involved in the incident. Weighing evidence in such circumstances is a difficult task for the jury, the absence of security force witnesses making it impossible to clarify disputed evidence. In recent years the Belfast Coroner John Leckey has stated that juries must be wary of such statements, as their authors cannot be cross-examined on the facts disclosed.[38] Finally as the contents of these statements are not attested to under oath, their authors cannot be subject to any subsequent prosecutions for perjury.

Legal challenge to the practice of admitting statements came during the *Breslin and Devine* inquest in 1987. By way of judicial review, counsel for the next of kin contested rule 17 of the Coroner's Rules, the legal basis for admitting these statements into evidence.[39] Rule 17 allows that the coroner may admit a document into evidence, if he considers that the attendance of its author is unnecessary and the document is produced from a source deemed reliable by the coroner.[40] Prior to the 1980 rules, which came into effect the following year, any written evidence, with the exception of the postmortem report, would not have been admissible in evidence unless the coroner was satisfied that there was good reason why its author should not attend the inquest in person. The changes heralded by these rules have resulted in manifest erosion of the obligations of a witness. This has resulted in a radical realignment of the inquest procedure.

Both the first instance court in the *Breslin and Devine* case and the Court of Appeal found for the applicants on the grounds that the admission of unsworn statements was outside the ambit of rule 17. Both courts were of the view that rule 17 was confined to statements which were formal or uncontroversial. However, the victory was a pyrrhic one, as the Court of Appeal confirmed that the statements were nonetheless admissible on the basis of the coroner's common law power to receive hearsay evidence.[41] On appeal to the House of Lords the decision on the common law power was upheld, and in addition the Law Lords found that the coroner was acting within his power to admit the statements under rule 17.[42] Counsel for the next of kin also submitted this issue for review to the European Commission of Human Rights. They contended that the lack of access to the statements of those who gave evidence constituted a violation of Article 6 of the European Convention.[43] The commission declared the application inadmissible on the grounds that the inquest proceedings did not involve the determination of a civil right or a criminal charge within the meaning of the convention. In order that the commission be able to apply the due process provisions of Article 6, it must first be satisfied that such potential negation of civil rights or criminal consequences would follow the disputed state act. The commission was not satisfied in this instance that that was the case.

The domestic legal decision on rule 17 is markedly out of step with the intention which seemed to underpin its legislative creation. The parallel English provision, rule 37 of the 1984 Coroner's Rules, makes clear that where written evidence is admitted without subsequent oral testimony, the coroner has a number of obligations to fulfil. Before admitting written statements, he must make a public announcement of his intention to do so and in that process he must describe the maker of the statement and identify him by name. Any person with legal standing may see a copy of the statement and can object to the admission of the document into evidence.[44] The reasons for accepting that evidence cannot be given in person seem to be strictly construed, envisaging illness or a physical inability to attend the inquest.[45]

Without exaggeration, it seems that the English provisions have as their primary objective the desire that the authors of relevant statements should be called as witnesses at inquests. Any exceptions to this general rule are to be strictly defined. The House of Lords seems to have overlooked this long-established interpretation of the rules in their examination of the matter in the Northern Ireland context. This again reveals the subtle effect of the particular circumstances of the Northern Ireland conflict on the interpretation of ordinary law. There is no overt mention of the unique context in which force is exercised in the jurisdiction, though this was the evident background of the case before the House of Lords. Rather, there is a subtle spill-over between the particularity of the decision before the court and the wider background to the case, coming from a jurisdiction in which distinct formula has emerged when the state exercises lethal force.

The practical effects of admitting unsworn statements are profoundly negative. The next of kin feel aggrieved that the persons causally responsible for a death are not being called to give account of their actions in the legal forum which seeks to establish the manner in which the death came about. For this reason, at the inquest into the death of Tony Harker his family refused to participate as a form of protest at what they viewed as a fundamental inequality of process, resulting from the admission of such unsworn statements.[46]

IV
Distinct problems associated with the Northern Ireland inquest

Northern Ireland inquests have been subject to protracted domestic and international criticism. Invariably, the disquiet chiefly revolves around those inquest proceedings which investigate deaths resulting from the use of lethal force by an agent of the state. The outstanding procedural problem is a simple one. Such inquests are subject to interminable delays, a large number being outstanding for up to ten years;[47] some have notched up sixteen-year delays in opening proceedings.[48] Yet by law the coroner is required to hold an inquest 'without delay'.[49] The legal standard is far removed from practice in a significant number of cases, controversial deaths being the most problematic in terms of delay.

Figure 28 contains an analysis of delays based on 184 cases involving lethal force deaths. Of these cases, only 4 deaths were subject to inquest within 28 days. In the 1–6 month category there were 48 cases; in the 7–12 month category, 51 cases; the 13–24 month category, 51 cases; and finally there were 30 cases with an excess of two years' delay. These frustrating delays have a distressing effect on the next of kin. Equally, the state's ability to move on is held in abeyance in that there remains an ongoing expectation that the legal process must kick in at some point.

Figure 28 Delays in Northern Ireland inquests concerning 184 disputed deaths, 1969–94

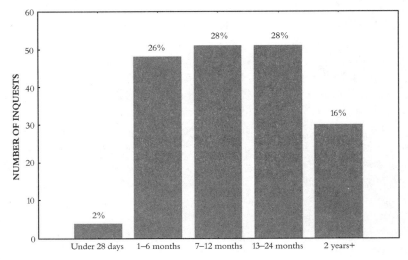

There are also wider effects on the perception of justice within the legal system. The delays heighten the sense of abnormality with the inquest system in respect of a particular class of cases. It accentuates the difference between ordinary and extraordinary functions of law within Northern Ireland.

Why are such extensive delays a characteristic of Northern Ireland's inquests during 1969–94? One of the primary reasons for the delays is the link between inquests and police investigation in the jurisdiction. In practice, inquests in Northern Ireland do not commence until the coroner is informed by the police or the DPP that proceedings may be opened.[50] In other words the coroner does not control the timing of the inquest. Lethal force deaths complicate this practice further: in these cases the decision to prosecute a police officer or soldier invariably involves consultation with the Attorney-General. Appreciating that an additional administrative layer of consultation may add to the delay in these cases should not mean a failure to acknowledge the ability of the Attorney-General to proceed quickly if a case is elevated to an internal status of importance. It serves to stress the lack of urgency that the state is perceived to attach to these particular deaths by the use of lethal force. More problematic is the possibility that the internal decision-making layers are used as a means to slow down legal process in this class of cases generally.

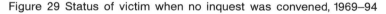

Figure 29 Status of victim when no inquest was convened, 1969–94

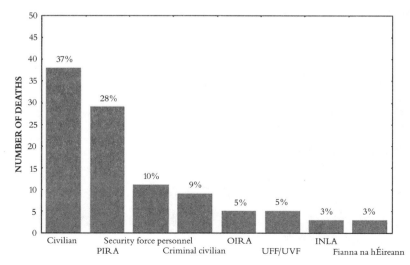

The investigation by the police into a lethal force death can place the coroner in an impossible position. If the coroner is not satisfied that police investigations are efficient or fair, he has few options available to him, especially where these investigative issues hamstring his ability to proceed with the inquest. This concern is amply illustrated by the inquests into the deaths of Seamus Grew and Roddy Carroll in 1982. Here, the coroner, Gerry Curran, simply resigned, citing 'irregularities in the police file'.[51] His resignation came in 1985, three years after the deaths had occurred during which time his attempts to resuscitate the inquest proved fruitless. This case exemplifies the fact that notwithstanding the willingness of individual coroners to undertake an open and thorough investigation into a controversial death, their ability to do so can be seriously undermined by other state actors.

Figure 26 (p. 140) gives an overall view of the status of inquest proceedings between 1969 and 1994. The data is based on 350 cases. Of this total, inquests are known to have taken place in 59 per cent of the cases. The smaller number of cases where it is known that inquest proceedings did not occur constitute 11 per cent of the total. As figure 29 illustrates, the majority of these cases relate to deaths which involved a member of a republican paramilitary organisation. However, a significant number of civilian deaths also have not been subject to inquest scrutiny. Notably,

Figure 30 Inquest status

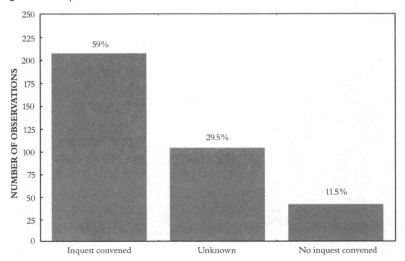

there is a high proportion of cases (103) where it is not known if an inquest took place at all. This large number is explained by a loss of records registering deaths in the early phase of the conflict. Furthermore, as many deaths in the militarisation phase were unreported in the media and received little internal or external attention, it has been difficult to ascertain what legal processes followed.

A

ADJOURNING INQUESTS

Inquest delays are further compounded by the practice of adjournment. Northern Ireland coroners share a common power of adjournment with their English and Welsh counterparts. The differences between the jurisdictions lie in the manner in which the power is exercised. The Coroner's Rules in both jurisdictions provide that the police can require a twenty-eight-day adjournment, during which they consider whether to charge any person in connection with a fatality.[52] As Tom Hadden has noted:

> British practice reflects the underlying purpose of the rule by making it clear that it is the Coroner who is in control and by enabling the police or the prosecuting authorities to be summoned to give an account of themselves if there is an apparently unreasonable delay.[53]

In England and Wales the provisions to adjourn only apply where the charge being considered by the police or the DPP is a serious one, usually murder. By contrast, adjournments in Northern Ireland can follow on all charges, even minor ones. Furthermore, a practice has developed in Northern Ireland whereby the police are granted indefinite adjournments. (By contrast, coroners in England and Wales have no power to adjourn an inquest indefinitely.) This is an inversion of the usual practice and reflects the extent to which the police play a dominant role in the legal proceedings concerning lethal force deaths. Adjourning inquests without setting a date for their resumption has compounded the systemic delays in the inquest process. By illustration, the inquest which convened to investigate the deaths of nine persons in Loughgall in 1987 opened and adjourned in September 1990 and did not reopen for a further eight years.

The relationship between the police and the coroner on the matter of adjournments leads to the very strong impression that it is the prosecuting authorities who control the timing of the inquest. This creates serious issues for the inquest process, in terms of its externally perceived neutrality and independence. When the death being investigated by the police was caused by the police themselves, the matter is even more delicate.

In the early 1990s a number of these controversial inquests were also being litigated in other forums. Judicial review proceedings sought to clarify a number of issues which went to the heart of whether inquests in these cases could act as meaningful fact-finders. They concerned such issues as the compelling of witnesses, the physical screening off of witnesses and access to internal investigative reports into lethal force deaths.[54] This crucial litigation also meant that many legal practitioners handling controversial deaths were reluctant to force coroners to commence proceedings while litigation, with potentially significant practical effect on their own cases, was being decided. Undoubtedly this also had a compounding effect on the issue of delays.

All of the practical and legal problems outlined here clearly have a serious effect on the speedy commencement and conclusion of inquests. It can be argued, however, that they are not the fundamental reason for delays. Procrastination is also a product of a lack of political will. Decisions not to convene inquests or to adjourn them indefinitely point to a pattern of procedural manipulation with serious implications for the state. Delaying inquests is a telling sign of a lack of commitment to open and accountable investigation in conformity with international standards. The Brodrick Committee recommended that inquests should commence soon after a death and be completed within seven days.[55] International legal standards such as the Principles on the Effective Prevention and Investigation of Extra-Legal, Arbitrary and Summary Executions require that investigation into deaths caused by the state be prompt and impartial.[56] Self-evidently, current practices in Northern Ireland fail the efficiency test and raise severe doubts about the fairness component.

It is worth pausing to reflect on the practical problems that dawdling in the inquest process incurs. Any time-lag in fact-finding poses many practical difficulties. Not least of these is that the memories of witnesses become dim or unavailable, which undermines the factual enterprise itself. The February 1993 inquest into the death of Aidan McAnespie is sharp proof of this. The incident causing death occurred in February 1988; the inquest was delayed for five years. In the intervening period, one of the key witnesses, an elderly man, had died.

For the next of kin delays thoroughly provoke a sense of frustration.

Generally speaking, families are only notified of the opening date for the inquest. They are usually not informed of the reasons for the delays by the coroner and depend entirely on their own legal representatives to keep them up to date on the progress of the state's investigation. Moreover, their legal representatives may be no better informed by the state than they are. The evidence suggests that the state takes little interest in ensuring that the next of kin and their legal counsel are fully aware of all that takes place within the state's remit related to the death.[57] Legal counsel representing the interests of the deceased do not gain access to evidential or forensic material any earlier if delays occur. Families hang in a limbo of irresolution and hesitation, unable to move on with their lives while the legal proceedings remain dormant. This leads to a strong suspicion on their part that public investigation into lethal force deaths caused by state agents are curtailed by official policy. Manoeuvring the legal process may indeed have wider causes, related to the manner in which the state seeks to control the narrative of the conflict that it validated by law. All of which has serious consequences for the integrity of law in situations of entrenched conflict, where there will always be a tension between the state's desire for a wide margin of discretion in its internal actions, and its need to be seen to be living up to its rhetoric of democracy and accountability.

V
The problems of evidence

Control of and access to evidence during inquest proceedings remain a highly contentious domain. There are two facets to this issue: first, that legal regulation of access to documentary evidence has been inconsistent and ill-defined for the next of kin; second, that the practice of coroners regarding access to evidence has been inconsistent. An unwavering consistency in relation to evidence at inquests has been that the police always have access to postmortem reports and other reports before family legal counsel. Recommendations made in a recent Home Office circular concerning deaths in police custody,[58] now adopted in Northern Ireland, have the capacity to affect the regulation of pre-inquest disclosure substantially in this jurisdiction. However, it remains open to question whether in controversial cases involving the use of force the police will maintain transparency in their investigative methods, given the extent to which wider issues of state conflict management are implicated in lethal force deaths. However, until now during formal proceedings the next of kin's legal representatives feel unfairly disadvantaged in comparison to the institutional representation.

The most frequent complaint by nonstate lawyers before and during inquest proceedings into lethal force deaths is the lack of access to forensic and postmortem reports in sufficient time to allow for adequate preparation. Practices in relation to the postmortem report vary most noticeably, as it lies within each coroner's discretion to release copies of the report to what are termed 'properly interested persons'.[59] In recent years, for example, the Belfast coroner has consistently released copies of postmortem reports. However, other coroners do not have the same policy. The inquest proceedings concerning the death of Fergal Caraher illustrate the point – the coroner refused to grant the family access to the postmortem report.[60] These inconsistencies highlight the need for a coherent policy on family access to the postmortem report. Equally, the creation of a uniform policy should place an emphasis on facilitating open and transparent investigation. This means that unless there are compelling legal reasons to refuse access to such documentation, the starting point should favour availability.

Other forms of evidential material have raised grave concerns about the fairness of the inquest procedure. The *Breslin and Devine* inquest raised the issue of access to photographic evidence.[61] When the inquest began family legal representatives had not seen any of the photographic evidence, which formed a significant part of the state's justification for its use of force.[62] All the institutional legal representatives had been given ample time to review these exhibits. During the proceedings the legal representatives of the next of kin sought a declaration by way of judicial review that they were entitled to receive a copy of all the photographs put into evidence.[63] The coroner ruled that legal counsel for the next of kin were only entitled to examine the material within the physical confines of the courthouse. They were not permitted to take the materials away overnight for detailed scrutiny. Each day duplicate copies of photographic materials were made available to them, but were collected by the RUC when the courthouse closed. The distinctions being made between state and nonstate legal representation could not have been more conspicuous.

The judicial review proceedings required the court to examine rule 38 of the Coroner's Rules, which allows coroners a discretion to decide which 'properly interested persons' should view either the postmortem reports or other reports. The reviewing court denied the application for access on two primary grounds. First, the court maintained that the procedure for supplying documents at inquests was a matter for the Lord Chancellor alone and they could not find that there had been improper or unlawful exercise of that discretion in this case. Second, that in order to facilitate access to documentary evidence, the Lord Chancellor was required to seek the concurrence of the coroner. There was no indication that the coroner was prepared to change his position and he could not be legally mandated to do so. The court argued semantically that the discretion given to the Lord Chancellor under rule 38 (2) contemplated the exercise of his discretion after the inquest was completed. This could not be activated during the course of an inquest, as was sought in the application before them. This clearly implied that even if they had not found otherwise, the case before them was perceived of as entirely moot.

While the court acknowledged that a right to inspect materials existed for nonstate legal representation at inquests, it was not prepared to imbue that finding with any practical meaning. Meaningful inspection requires that legal counsel have the time to discharge their professional skills adequately and competently. This is difficult to achieve while simultaneously appearing before the coroner in a fraught and controversial inquest. Inspection has to allow adequate time to gather information and detail from the documents under view. Without this, the right to inspect has no substance.[64]

The decision in this case principally revealed an unwillingness to make the inquest process an inclusive one. It demonstrated a formalistic and doctrinaire approach to the governing legal rules and evinced little sympathy for the difficulties facing the legal representatives charged with representing the interests of the next of kin. A profusion of similar decisions followed on matters related to the transparency of the inquest process.

The new rules regarding pre-inquest disclosure are specifically aimed at regulating access to information at inquests which result from death in police custody but also include deaths which result from the action of a police officer in the purported execution of his duty.[65] The enumerated categories seem clearly to bring these rules into play where death has been caused by the use of lethal force. The circular characterises the interests which emerge at inquests following controversial deaths as follows:

> In such circumstances [controversial death], disclosure of information held by the authorities in advance of a hearing will help to provide reassurance to the family of the deceased and other interested persons that a full and open police investigation has been conducted. It will also ensure that the families and their legal representatives will not be disadvantaged at inquests.[66]

The circular outlines that the existing law determines documentary evidence produced by the police during an investigation to be the property of the force commissioning the investigation. It clearly outlines that the coroner has no power to order the pre-inquest disclosure of this documentation. Thus disclosure of evidence is on a voluntary basis and dependent on the good offices of the facilitating police force.

The circular, and the recent acceptance of its applicability to Northern Ireland, is a positive step forward in acknowledging the frustration and limitations which result from the current situation of non–disclosure to the next of kin and their legal representatives.[67] However, it is not clear how the new guidelines will work in practice, particularly in respect of outstanding lethal force inquests in the jurisdiction. Given that the discretion to disclose lies with the police, and following the concerns that have been raised by this study about the adequacy of the police investigation itself, there is no firm confirmation that disclosure will be the norm for all future inquests. Moreover, as the use of Public Interest Immunity Certificates in recent years has demonstrated, state institutions have generally sought to limit the disclosure of information during the inquest process. While the new guidelines provide much needed clarification of the legal rights of the next of kin, whether they will transform into genuinely transparent process in the practice of lethal force inquests remains an open question.

There can be little doubt that the overwhelming effect of these pronouncements was to convince the average observer that legal élites in Northern Ireland have had little interest in making the inquest an evenhanded occasion. More than that, it indicates how high the stakes ride for the state in such proceedings. A tremendous amount of legal energy is spent protecting the state and its agents at lethal force inquests. This is not because inquests themselves are such momentous legal occasions, but in the context of lethal force deaths, they are usually the only form of legal review that takes place. When these deaths are indicative of broader policies facilitating conflict containment which the state is anxious to avoid scrutiny of, it is the legal inquiry that must be contained. In a nutshell, this has been the recent history of legal developments concerning the inquest in Northern Ireland.

A

PARITY OF ACCESS TO WITNESSES

Any witness to a death caused by state use of force is critical to the inquest process. Witness ability to recall and describe in detail the sequence of events which led to the death are the foundations upon which effective fact-finding is based. Following most deaths, witnesses give evidence to the investigating police as a matter of course. The status of and access to their statements has evolved into a matter of considerable controversy.

Witness statements are always seen by the police, the coroner, counsel to the coroner and legal representatives of the police and army before the inquest begins. Until now no such privilege has been uniformly extended to the legal representatives of the next of kin. Once the inquest begins, practice governing access to these documents has varied between coroners. In some cases counsel may be given access to some statements before the inquest starts, but rarely has all documentation been available for examination. For example, when the inquest into the deaths of Gervaise McKerr, Sean Burns and Eugene Toman reopened in 1992, the family lawyers were given four witness statements, although there were thirty-nine persons named on the official witness list for the inquest.

Legal challenges to the practice of excluding full access as a general principle was first raised in 1980. In the case of *Re Mailey*, the court held that witness statements were only proofs of evidence,[68] merely indicating what a person might disclose in oral evidence and, therefore, not conclusive. Hence, they were not covered by the rules of disclosure. Since 1980, when this case was decided, the issue of access to witness statements has been rekindled by developments in relation to the appearance of witnesses at inquest hearings.

Prior to 1981, written evidence, with the exception of the postmortem report, was not admissible in evidence unless the coroner was satisfied that there was good reason why its author would not attend the hearing in person. This meant that all admissible evidence was generally dependent on its oral validation. However, changes in the Coroner's

Rules meant that the coroner was given the discretion to dispense with the attendance of any witness at an inquest.[69] What the changes to the rules meant was a move from the arena of legally enforceable and reviewable obligations to wholly loose and discretionary control by individual coroners. In practice this meant that at inquests concerned with lethal force deaths security force witnesses who were directly responsible for the deaths did not appear to give evidence. Their written statements then came to have a greater significance for the inquest process.

The *Breslin and Devine* inquest brought the legal question to the fore. During the inquest, as well as requesting sight of photographic evidence, legal representatives for the next of kin also sought, by way of judicial review, to require the coroner to make the written statements available to them. The request was rejected at first instance.[70] On appeal the reviewing court followed the precedent of the Blair Peach case.[71] In this decision the court placed its emphasis on the inquisitorial nature of the Coroner's Court and the limited objectives of the process. Acquiescing in the request to allow access was characterised as a means of transforming the Coroner's Court into an adversarial process and the Appeal Court entirely rejected such a move. There is a self-evident paradox in this decision. While it is clear that the inquest has a legally limited mandate, in relation to the particular class of lethal force cases it functions as the sole legal inquiry. This means that such a decision in relation to documentary access fails to acknowledge the larger political context of inquests in a society where legal process has been fundamentally altered to accommodate perpetual crisis. The Appeal Court may not desire that the inquest takes on any vestige of adversarial process, but, despite what the legal rules may say, the decision fails to recognise that this function has occurred by virtue of societal expectation.

Until this point legal regulation of access to evidence highlights the manner in which the courts view the legal representatives of the next of kin. Evidently, the legal status of 'properly interested persons' fails to give them the same standing accorded to the institutional legal representation. It remains to be seen whether the changes in the practices related to pre-inquest disclosure affect the relative positions of state and family counsel. Given, however, that the disclosure of documents is intimately linked to the question of witness compellability in Northern Ireland, the sceptics might foresee limited changes to documentary access in the disputed lethal force category of cases. There can be no change to the existing patent inequality until family·legal counsel is granted a higher status. A recognition of higher standing does not imply that the Coroner's Court will become adversarial in nature – it simply means that the inquest will become a fairer and more equal process for all its participants.

Equal status for the legal representatives of the next of kin at inquests has been affirmed in the Canadian and American jurisdictions, based on a reliance upon common law principles,[72] and early English cases confirm the right of counsel to question and cross-examine witnesses.[73] There exists a definitive legal pedigree confirming rights of participation for nonstate counsel. What has been lacking is a modern jurisprudence of equality to make that participation meaningful. Equal access to documents is a fundamental component of that parity.

There can be little doubt that effective participation by family counsel would greatly enhance public confidence in the inquest procedure. Exclusion of counsel by limiting legal participation tends to confirm public perceptions that the inquest is merely a state 'whitewash' or at best an inadequate inquiry.[74] Ultimately, both private and public interests are served by full and meaningful participation.

B

THE INADEQUACIES OF INVESTIGATION

It is important to reflect upon the relationship between the inquest and the state investigation which usually precedes it. The inquest does not take place in isolation. In order to review the events leading up to and causing a death, the coroner must have access to evidence, information and witnesses. He does not have an independent investigation team at his disposal. Rather, he must rely on the police to undertake the collection of evidence for him. Moreover, which witnesses to call to give an account of a controversial death at inquest is a delicate matter, and the coroner is essentially dependent on the police investigation to provide relevant witnesses. The ability of the coroner to call such witnesses depends on the thoroughness of that process. Rather than gathering information independently, the inquest serves as a stage from which the coroner presents information collected by the police. If the investigation is inadequate, the picture of events presented at the inquest may be inaccurate.

Case-by-case analysis for this research has demonstrated serious flaws in the questioning of witnesses after lethal force incidents. For example, following the death of Kevin McGovern in September 1991, the police failed to question many of the key eyewitnesses after the incident. An independent human rights organisation, the Committee on the Administration of Justice, carried out a door-to-door investigation in the days following the death and discovered that preliminary interviews had not been carried out with a number of persons who had relevant information to the police inquiry.

Numerous interviews with legal representatives of the next of kin has revealed the lack of consistent guidelines in the choice and questioning of witnesses at the site of a lethal force death or in the aftermath of the incident.[75] An additional problem arises when many witnesses who have not been contacted by the police are unwilling to come forward and offer what information they may have. Typically, they fear bringing undue attention to themselves and their families. In a number of cases witnesses to these incidents have been subjected to arrest and detention by the police.[76] Kevin McGovern's death is also instructive here. Following the student's death, his two companions (also students) were arrested and held overnight by police in Gough barracks. Both young men were severely traumatised by the police shooting of their friend on a narrow country road near a small Cookstown housing estate. They were released with neither apology nor acknowledgement that the arrest was a compounding ordeal following a very difficult experience.

It is not surprising that such occurrences have perpetuated an unwillingness on the part of many witnesses to volunteer information. As this study has revealed, the majority of lethal force victims have been Catholic and the bulk of the fatalities have occurred in urban areas. In the urban ghettos of Northern Ireland, many of these deaths have occurred in Catholic neighbourhoods. All this serves to limit the extent to which persons who may have information to offer about a death caused by an agent of the state would choose to do so – a reality that has had a profound impact on the inquest process.

A coroner cannot be judicially reviewed for failing to call witnesses who have not been interviewed by the police. Legal representatives for the next of kin complain frequently that their lack of input into selection of witnesses and the exclusion of others in the investigative process has a direct bearing on the coroner's selection. Judicial review offers no meaningful remedy in practice for any inadequacies in the investigative process. This is because the legal emphasis on the discretionary nature of police investigations creates judicial unwillingness to open up this arena to constant public second-guessing through the mechanism of judicial review.

VI
National security and the inquest process

In recent years inquests in Northern Ireland have become further embroiled in controversy as the assertion of state national security interests has dominated inquest proceedings. National security claims have invariably been heralded at inquests by the use of Public Interest Immunity Certificates by the state. This has led to strident claims that it has become impossible for inquests to function properly because national security constraints limit their most basic capacities. A number of issues converge here. First, the state has increasingly resorted to national security claims where it seems that the inquest may stray into examination of areas pertaining to operational and security practices in Northern Ireland. Second, legal representatives of the next of kin have consistently sought to test the state's limitations on the information to come before the court. These challenges have the common thread that inquests cannot perform their task without such information, and that a fundamental inequality of process is imposed as a result of acquiescence in state-centred claims.

For certain information to be classified as 'privileged' in a legal proceeding, a claim must be made by the government minister whose department is concerned that such information should not be publicly released through court hearings,[77] and PIICs are usually issued by the Secretary of State for Northern Ireland or the Secretary of State for Defence. They have customarily sought to prevent the presentation of particular types or areas of evidence at inquests. The claim to public interest is usually made on either a 'contents basis' or a 'class basis', which means that the objection may relate to specific facts contained in specific documents or to a class of documents because of their collective character.[78] Public interest immunity is an exclusionary rule that in theory applies equally to all parties.[79] Thus, in the public interest certain information is excluded from the public domain on the grounds that to release it would be harmful to the state's interest, and ultimately, to the public's interest.

Usage of PIICs has increased in Northern Ireland in recent years, their frequent appearance has been akin to a scattering of confetti in the jurisdiction. They have been particularly associated with high profile inquests investigating the deaths of members of paramilitary organisations by specialist military units. Such inquests include the Gibraltar, *McKerr* and *McElwaine* proceedings.[80] The issuing of such certificates goes to the heart of the matter under examination in this book. That is, the extent to which the state deploys legal process as a means to avoid scrutiny of its conflict management strategies. The PIIC is a legal device. Clear legal rules apply to its invocation and its review by the courts. But the essence of what a PIIC seeks to do is to exclude review. Thus, one uses the law to avoid the law. Observers ought to be very wary when a state consistently seeks to avoid substantive oversight, when that avoidance is linked to the management of conflict and the actions of state actors within it.

What concerns many observers is that there exists no independent mechanism to review the issuing of PIICs. When the certificate is presented to the court it falls to the coroner or judge to weigh the value of nondisclosure against the interests of justice and the public's more abstract right to know. This test is the sole means under the present method of legal regulation to ensure that nondisclosure of information cannot simply be imposed on the whim of a government minister. In practice, the test is weak. There is strong judicial dicta to suggest that where a PIIC contains statements of fact expressing the minister's opinion, these expressions are taken as authoritative.[81] Lord Reid makes that case persuasively:

> Full weight must be given to it [the minister's view] in every case, and if the Minister's reasons are of a character which judicial experience is not competent to weigh, then the Minister's views must prevail.[82]

In most cases where the PIIC is issued on the grounds of national security, the courts are reluctant to override the decision of the minister in question. This is grounded in the natural reluctance of courts to interfere with the domain of the executive. The working assumption for most judges is that the minister is acting on substantive grounds, which apprehend danger to the state. In such cases the courts disinclined to intervene; nonetheless, they continue to insist on their legal right of oversight.

Generally speaking, judicial assumptions are made about the good will and *bona fides* of government ministers who invoke national security concerns. However, the controversial Matrix Churchill case has severely undermined belief in this innate good will.[83] The three defendants in these criminal proceedings were accused of being parties to the export of machinery to Iraq at a time when such export was unlawful. When they sought to have additional governmental documentation pertaining to their applications for export licences made available to the court, a PIIC was issued to prevent disclosure. The presiding judge decided that to deny access to some of the documents might result in a miscarriage of justice. Subsequent access to the relevant documents resulted in an acquittal of all three. Clearly, the government ministers who issued the PIIC had ascertainable political motives to avoid public disclosure of the documents. The certificate was used as a means to bypass public accountability for government policy at the expense of the defendants' case.

Matrix Churchill was a unique case. However, it does not stretch the imagination too much to see that the possibilities for similar manipulation are present in Northern Ireland, where the state is anxious to preserve a particular narrative on its actions and wants to ensure that the definition of the conflict as provided by the legal system does not differ from its own political rhetoric. Thus, screening information from the public and the courts during the investigation into lethal force incidents should continue to raise concern.

A

PUBLIC INTEREST IMMUNITY IN NORTHERN IRELAND

The use of PIICs in Northern Ireland's inquests has been a feature of the overt counter-insurgency phase of the conflict. Invariably, these certificates are issued when specialist military or police units have been involved in a fatal shooting. In almost all these inquests the certificate pertains to operational matters prior to the shooting incident. Usually this means that information as to whether the deceased had been under police or army surveillance prior to their death is not disclosed to the jury. Without fail, the effect of the certificate is to decontextualise the resort to lethal force; the death is therefore examined in isolation from the events which led up to it. As a result, the picture of the incident which emerges from the inquest may be distorted or inaccurate.

The *McKerr* inquest directly raised some of these concerns. The inquest opened for the third time in May 1992 and a number of issues arose in relation to public interest immunity. When the inquest convened, a PIIC was submitted to the coroner, covering significant portions of the evidence to be addressed during the proceedings. Under cross-examination, the official submitting the PIIC revealed that the Secretary of State had not read all the relevant documentation prior to signing the certificate. In short, the certificate was issued *pro forma*, in the assumption that the state would not be questioned too closely about the manner in which the decision to exclude information was made. Public interest seems ill-served by officials signing exclusionary documents whose contents they are not familiar with. Contrary to the all-embracing justification that they are serving the public, the operating principle seems to be, the less the public know the better.

Substantively, several other issues were addressed in relation to the PIIC in this case. The inquest had been preceded by unprecedented publicity. There was extensive public and media commentary on the facts and details of the three deaths under legal examination.[84] Thus, counsel for the next of kin argued that much of the information which the state sought to protect was already in the public domain. Despite the veracity of counsel's point, the coroner rejected this attempt to limit the perimeters of the PIIC,

Furthermore, government information, gathered by way of internal official inquiry into the deaths of McKerr, Toman and Burns, was to engender even more controversy at the inquest. During the proceedings the coroner ordered the Chief Constable by writ of *subpoena* to submit the Stalker and Sampson Reports to the inquest. (These were the reports which were requisitioned by the government following the shoot-to-kill débâcle of police involvement in active counter-insurgency in the winter of 1982.) The Chief Constable sought to have the writs set aside,[85] and during the judicial review proceedings the Secretary of State issued a PIIC, It certified that the information contained in the Stalker Report should not be revealed because its publication would be likely to cause serious harm to the fight against terrorism and prejudice the interests of national security. Brice Dickson summarises the state position as follows:

> The PIIC identified two grave concerns in relation to national security. One was the integrity and efficacy of the relevant security forces in their efforts to counter the terrorist threat and the other was the protection of the lives and safety of those involved, of their families and of persons

who have provided or may provide information and intelligence to the security forces.[86]

Justice Nicholson weighed public interest in the integrity of the criminal investigation process against the public interest in disclosure of information. The process was found to favour the integrity of criminal process and the Stalker and Sampson Reports were deemed not relevant to the coroner's inquest. He then went on to set aside the writs of *subpoena* on the grounds that national security would be threatened by the production of the two reports.

PIICs have also been to the fore of the litigation emerging from the *McNeill* inquest. The case concerned the deaths of Eddie Hale, John McNeill and Peter Thompson who, while robbing a bookmaker's premises in west Belfast, were shot by British undercover soldiers in January 1990.[87] McNeill, the driver of the getaway car, was unarmed when shot sitting at the driver's wheel of the vehicle. Replica weapons were found connected to Hale and Thompson at the scene of the incident. They were shot as they ran from the betting shop. Eyewitnesses reported that no warnings were issued before the soldiers opened fire. The PIIC was signed by the Secretary of State for Defence and attested that the terrorist campaigns of violence in Northern Ireland threatened national security in a direct and immediate way. The litigation concerning the PIIC in this case should be explained by reference to established practice in relation to these certificates. The doctrine of public interest immunity has legally developed in relation to the production of documents. Practically speaking, this means that upon issuing the certificate the Minister of State attaches a list of documents to which the public interest attaches. The list serves an important function for the recipient of the certificate. The coroner can have access to the listed documents, allowing him to decide whether the minister's concerns are justified. However, when the state seeks to expand the boundaries of public interest immunity to nondocumentary sources, this process of assessment becomes much more difficult.

In the *McNeill* case four soldiers had been directed to give evidence at the inquest and the PIIC issued sought to limit the manner in which the soldiers would give their evidence. The certificate pertained to three of them and outlined that they should only give evidence from behind a screen, hidden from view of the general public and visible only to the coroner, the jury and the legal representatives of the state and the next of kin.[88] The coroner refused to accept the certificate, ruling that the PIIC was essentially a tool for dealing with documents and not appropriate in situations where there were no documents and only oral evidence was being given.[89]

The decision of the coroner was appealed by way of judicial review by the Minister of Defence. Justice McCollum found that the doctrine of public interest immunity was never intended to restrict PIICs solely to limitations on disclosure of information contained in written documents. The Court of Appeal affirmed that the PIIC can be an appropriate vehicle for limitations on oral as well as written evidence.[90] The decision was then remitted to the coroner for a fresh determination, with a healthy impetus for him to reconsider the Secretary of State's view on the national security dimensions of the issue. Nonetheless, on appeal Sir Brian Hutton succinctly confirmed the court's right of review:

> The question whether a witness should be screened is a matter relating primarily to the administration of justice which has to be determined by the court, and . . . the court is not precluded from determining that issue because of a certificate of the Secretary of State in relation to matters of national security.[91]

Confirming the right to review in matters which touch on national security is not inconsequential. However, the right to review is meaningless unless courts are prepared to do more than rubber-stamp an executive resort to national security. Review may be a chimera unless it is supported by judicial willingness to find that the state may have overstepped the bounds of its claim to national security.

While some commentators have argued that it is difficult to quarrel with the technical finding that PIICs can be an appropriate vehicle for limitations on nondocumentary evidence,[92] others caution on the general principle advanced here. The practice of screening witnesses has important consequences for transparent legal process. Screening has become a feature of most inquests involving specialist military and police units. In these cases the witnesses most centrally concerned with the death exercise their privilege under rule 9 not to attend the inquest to give evidence. The military personnel who are called to give evidence are usually peripheral to the events which relate to the death under examination. This means that from the outset the inquest proceedings lack the appearance (and substance) of a complete and open process. When witnesses are shielded, only the coroner, jury, and the legal representatives have the opportunity to assess their demeanour. The relatives of the deceased have no such opportunity, thus becoming even more marginalised and excluded from the process.

The extent to which this exclusion can be further compounded is illustrated by the PIIC issued in the *McNeill* case. The certificate originally given to the coroner on the opening day of the inquest was later modified. The amendment sought to exclude properly interested persons who were not legally represented from viewing the screened witnesses. However, as many families do not qualify for legal aid, it is conceivable that they could choose to represent themselves.[93] Legally speaking, a 'properly interested person' is entitled to ask questions of witnesses and to conduct himself or herself as would a legal representative.[94] The manifest implication of this amendment was that the Ministry of Defence did not trust the next of kin to view the military witnesses. Such a position shatters any illusions of the equality of all before the law. The result is that a properly interested person without legal representation would be treated less favourably than a properly interested person with legal counsel. In the *McNeill* case the coroner expressed his concern over the provision, but as all the families involved were legally represented, neither he nor the reviewing courts were required to issue a legal opinion on the matter.

In this case, when the coroner refused to accept the PIIC, his decision underscored an important point, virtually ignored by the appeal courts. When the application was made to permit screening, the Ministry of Defence stated that its policy position was to uniformly seek anonymity for undercover soldiers giving evidence. In his initial decision, the coroner stressed that this stance could lead to a situation where the Crown could apply for a soldier to be screened if he had killed a person during the course of his duties and subsequently stood trial. If, however, the charge related to a minor motoring offence, unconnected to the same soldier's official duties, no such privilege would be sought. The net effect is that for minor offences undercover soldiers could give evidence in open court, but where serious offences were alleged, soldiers would be given the benefit of screening.

Most inquests into non–lethal–force deaths in Northern Ireland occur at least a year after the death in question. In the *McNeill* case three years ensued before the inquest was convened. As with other army units in

Northern Ireland, members of undercover units perform tours of duty in the jurisdiction and frequently, by the time the inquest opens, the individuals called to give evidence have usually completed their tour. Therefore screening in such circumstances may be completely unnecessary. The position taken by the Ministry of Defence and supported by the courts, however, is not to examine whether screening is warranted in each individual case, but to attempt to affirm a blanket ban on all undercover soldiers giving evidence in open court.

It is undesirable that a prohibition on open evidence should be accepted as a norm for giving evidence and such a policy has a number of serious consequences. It differentiates unfairly between undercover soldiers and members of ordinary army units in their treatment before the courts. The practice also fails to acknowledge that on a daily basis local police officers give evidence in trials related to scheduled offences and none have sought to be screened from the public. In security terms, a greater threat is posed to the lives of these individuals who live and work in Northern Ireland than to undercover soldiers living in army barracks on short terms of duty. The difficulties posed for the judicial process by screening were forcefully acknowledged by the coroner presiding over the Gibraltar inquest:

> The reality seems to be that unless the witnesses are screened I may not be able to have a meaningful inquest and of course if they are screened it would be a flawed inquest in any case.[95]

When the state is seen to be complicit in the death of a citizen, open proceedings would demonstrate its willingness to have its actions examined. Yet, PIICs, whether pertaining to screening or to documentary evidence, give the strong impression that the state has something to hide. They serve to heighten the impression that the security forces will not be subject to rigorous review. Justice is ill-served by a lack of transparency. As Lord Diplock has noted:

> As a general rule the English system of administering justice does require that it be done in public ... If the way that courts behave cannot be hidden from public ear and eye, this provides a safeguard against judicial arbitrariness, or idiosyncrasy and maintains the public confidence in the administration of justice.[96]

VII
Public participation in the inquest

Section III of this chapter outlined the manner in which the shift from the use of verdicts by inquest juries to the issuance of findings has negatively affected public participation in the inquest process. Additionally, public participation at inquests has been substantially affected by a variety of practices which have subtly sought to exclude and undermine the collective nature of the inquiry.

One of the inquest's historical and contemporary functions is to alleviate public concern over sudden, unexplained or suspicious deaths. It is intended to be a forum in which concern about loss of life is examined and some measure of satisfaction is felt by the public and next of kin. The cornerstone of this functionality lies in the openness and accessibility of inquest. Two facets of Northern Ireland's inquest rules and procedure undermine this basic function. The first is the legal power of the coroner to exclude the public from the hearing 'in the interests of national security'.[97] Unless the coroner can be shown to have acted unreasonably there is no other means to test the validity of his judgment. The provision makes nonsense of the stated rationale for the inquest itself with its potential to exclude the members of the community, whom the inquest procedure is intended to reassure. A basic practical problem encountered by families and members of the public attending inquests has been the limitation on physical access to the courtroom. This is usually accomplished by the practice of limiting public seating. For example, at the *Breslin and Devine* inquest, counsel for the next of kin argued that rule 5 of the Coroner's Rules had been breached by the practice of limiting access to public seating in the courtroom.[98]

At this inquest the police had block-reserved seating for potential witnesses in the courtroom, many of whom did not attend to hear other evidence. Most of these potential witnesses were members of the security forces, unlikely to sit through the long weeks it would take to conclude the inquest. As a result, there were vacant seats inside the courtroom each day, while, outside, family members and others who wished to hear the proceedings were not admitted. The decision concluded that there had been no breach of rule 5, because the public had been admitted to the extent that the capacity of the courthouse (excluding reserved seating) allowed.

What the practice revealed, however, was the unwillingness of the coroner and the police to be flexible when presented with a practical problem which revolved around a matter of concern to the relatives of the deceased. In such situations the relatives feel that they are being deliberately excluded from the proceedings. It heightens their sensitivities and adds to their doubts about the meaningfulness of the process. Such exclusionary practices also have perceptible effects on public opinion about inquests. They serve to augment concerns about the deaths under examination rather than to assuage them. They create the sense, justifiable or not, that the state has ulterior motives in minimising public access to the process of review. They also serve to highlight the differences between inquests into controversial security force deaths and all other inquests to which such practices are never applied. What emerges with these disparate practices is two-tier legal process. On the one hand is the 'ordinary' system, and on the other, the 'extraordinary'. Nevertheless, the state persists in advocating the view that all is ordinary. There is no overt acceptance that the legal system is modified to facilitate the state's own response to an internal crisis.

Lastly, a compounding exclusion is the unavailability of legal aid for inquests. The failure of the government to implement relevant statutory provisions has created conspicuous monetary hardship for those caught up unwittingly in the inquest system.[99] In order to be legally represented at an inquest most families have to pay for legal services privately. For many this has led to additional financial burdens following the death of a family member. Because the majority of lethal force victims are male, aged between eighteen and twenty-five and often the primary breadwinners for a family, the fiscal consequences of paying for legal representation in long-running and legally complex inquests should not be underestimated. The RUC and the army are invariably represented at inquest proceedings: their legal representation is paid for out of public funds. This disparity is a bar to the principle of equality which ought to underpin such proceedings.

VIII
Conclusions

Having outlined the numerous difficulties which confront the inquest process in relation to lethal force deaths, some contextualisation is necessary. Notably, inquests into disputed deaths are but a small fraction of the total number of inquests which take place each year in Northern Ireland – most are uncontentious affairs. Generally, an inquest is only required when the deceased has not been seen by a doctor either after death or fourteen days before death.[100] In such situations there is rarely a dispute over the cause of death or any issue of potential civil or criminal proceedings. Medical cause of death is usually the sole issue before the coroner and jury. Obviously, questions of national security never arise in such cases. In Northern Ireland, concerns about the efficacy and fairness of inquests have concentrated on proceedings related to disputed state killings.[101] (This is not the case in England and Wales, where there is an ongoing campaign to improve the status and standing of inquests.[102]) Nonetheless, there is a broad range of issues which merit attention in a substantive review of the functions and practices of the coroner's inquest. This is made all the more urgent by the extension of modifications to the structure of the inquest in the jurisdiction, intended to strengthen the procedure when it confronts aspects of the emergency, to the ordinary cases that compose most of the inquest's daily work.

One solution advocated to deal with the problems encountered with inquests in Northern Ireland is simply to impose a parity of law and practice based on the current English and Welsh model. Parity would have the advantages of restoring verdicts and making all witnesses compellable. But this solution is limited in a number of respects. It fails to recognise the shortcomings of the coroner's inquest in England and Wales,[103] which include the lack of advance disclosure of witness statements, the lack of status for legal representatives of the next of kin, and the inability of juries to make recommendations to any responsible party to prevent future deaths. Furthermore, this solution would not address the problems imposed by the use of PIICs, the uniform practice of screening certain witnesses, and the more delicate issue of deficiencies in police investigation and its impact on the thoroughness of inquests.

Bringing into line inquest processes in these jurisdictions would certainly solve some of the most blatant disparities between them, perhaps thereby restoring some confidence in the Northern Ireland inquest, but would fundamentally fail to confront the issues that arise in respect of controversial deaths. In short, this is a good formal means by which to proceed but fails to account for the particularity of the Northern Ireland situation which has given rise to the local modifications in the first place.

Lethal force deaths may only be one class of case that come before the inquest but they have a profound and complicated nexus with the reality and the management of the conflict itself.

As far as the inquest process is concerned, the central question that must be faced is that of its proper role in such an ambiguous legal situation. Again and again, judicial dicta has stressed that the inquest is not an adversarial process. Reviewing the *McKerr* application for judicial review, Justice Nicholson has put it as follows:

> It is unfortunate that, despite the clear statements of judges in the past, the public are still unaware of the limited scope of the coroner's inquest to which Carswell J, numerous divisional courts, the Court of Appeal and the House of Lords have drawn attention. But it is also unrealistic to fail to recognise that in an inquiry of the present kind the coroner has almost an impossible task in preventing the inquest from developing into an adversarial contest and that it is difficult for the lawyers to refrain from taking up adversarial positions when their clients expect them to do so.[104]

In recent years English and Welsh courts have also repeatedly stressed the limited nature of the coroner's inquest.[105] In short, they have confirmed that the purpose of the inquest is extremely limited and is not to be used as a means to facilitate a general inquiry into extraneous matters. In describing the how, when and why of inquests Sir Thomas Bingham MR has said:

> 'How' is to be understood as meaning 'by what means'. It is noteworthy that the task is not to ascertain how the deceased died, which might raise general and far-reaching issues, but 'how ... the deceased came by his death', a more limited question directed to the means by which the deceased came to his death ... There can be no objection to a verdict which incorporates a brief, neutral, factual statement ... but such a verdict must be factual, expressing no judgment or opinion.[106]

Generally, the need for thorough investigation of most ordinary deaths is mostly satisfied by the limited nature of the coroner's inquest. In such cases, the wider context, or 'why' of a death, may be entirely ascertainable without the need to probe the events or actions leading up to the moment of fatality. However, this is certainly not true of controversial deaths, especially when the state bears causal responsibility for loss of life. The greater expectations placed on the investigation into such deaths is compounded in Northern Ireland by the fact that inquests have been the sole forum of accountability for deaths by use of lethal force. Thus, unrealistic expectations are raised for a legal structure that within its current boundaries is incapable of providing the reassurance and accountability sought by the next of kin and the watching public. Inquests are also fundamentally incapable of resolving the competing social and political narratives that are raised when the state uses force in a situation of protracted internal crisis. The question arises, in which forum, if any, can such issues be addressed and resolved?

A

PUBLIC INQUIRIES

This leads to the question of whether or not other forms of state investigation are more appropriately suited to the task of investigating lethal force deaths. There is a public precedent for such inquiries in the Widgery, Scarman and recently convened Saville tribunals.[107] In addition, many unofficial public inquiries have been initiated in Northern Ireland, the most comprehensive being the public inquiry into the death of Fergal Caraher.[108] In England and Wales inquiries have been held into controversial deaths resulting from the Clapham, Zeebrugger and King's Cross disasters. In total twenty-two tribunals have been set up under the Tribunals of Inquiry (Evidence) Act 1921. Evidently, such tribunals are rare occurrences, convened when it is necessary to preserve the integrity of public life which has been threatened by a crisis of public confidence.[109] As Dermot Walsh notes:

> The purpose of such a Tribunal of Inquiry is not to establish the guilt or innocence of the parties allegedly involved, but to establish the truth, if any, behind the allegations which have led to the crisis. Where the report exposes wrongdoing, the task of taking the necessary corrective action falls elsewhere. The Tribunal's value lies in its capacity to persuade the public that the full facts have been established, and generally to assist in restoring public confidence in the integrity of government.[110]

Tribunals convened under the 1921 Act are endowed with comprehensive legal powers. They are vested with all the powers, rights and privileges of the High Court in respect of compelling witnesses to attend and to submit to examination, and they can compel the production of evidence. Witnesses before such a tribunal are entitled to the same immunities and privileges as they would be entitled to if they were witnesses to civil proceedings in the High Court. Such a tribunal must also sit in public and be open to the public, though powers of exclusion do exist in defined circumstances. The tribunal has a clear mandate of being an inquisitorial proceeding, designed to elicit the truth.

Both official and unofficial inquiries have resulted from the public's desire to know more and be firmly reassured about the circumstances of a particular loss of life. This is attested to by the long-standing public campaign in Derry/Londonderry to reconvene a public inquiry which would fully and independently investigate the events which led to thirteen deaths in the city in 1972. The impetus to create a tribunal usually comes from the affected communities in which the deaths occur, with the express desire of preventing other deaths from occurring in similar circumstances. Such inquiries underscore the importance of accountability and openness and the value placed on these principles by the ordinary citizen.

An obvious question is whether such inquiries are more satisfactory than inquests in fulfilling the expectations placed upon them. The answer here is variable. Much depends on the nature and scope of the inquiry. A public inquiry with wide-ranging powers to call witnesses and evidence is a genuine step forward on the constraints presently limiting inquests. However, the method of establishing a tribunal is critical to its subsequent abilities. For example, the Widgery Tribunal was instituted by parliamentary resolution. This mechanism has the benefit of democratic participation and a broad political validation of the need for an inquiry. Thus, the broadest powers of inquiry are to be found in the initiation of a resolution by both Houses of Parliament under the 1921 act. There are, nonetheless, some notable drawbacks to the parliamentary procedure. Primarily, parliament can circumscribe the ability of any tribunal by giving limited terms of reference, or by appointing powerless overseers. The mechanism is also hostage to the political will of government and the ability to mobilise members of parliament with a variety of interests across party lines. This means that it is only for exceptional cases that such a tribunal will be initiated.

Local political circumstances in Northern Ireland following the Good Friday Agreement make it unlikely that the local multi-party Assembly would convene the necessary political will to reopen inquiries into past lethal force controversies. The Westminster parliament is equally unlikely to be convinced of the desirability of such an enterprise in the present political circumstances.

Of course, to require a public inquiry in the case of every disputed death would involve a significant change in legislative patterns and state responses to lethal force deaths. The fiscal costs of creating such inquiries is also a negative consideration, likely to impede substantial reliance on the procedure. It is also worth pausing again to reflect on the mandate of the inquiry mechanism. It shares some similar characteristics with the inquest, in that its function is neither adversarial nor combative. According to Dermot Walsh:

> The Tribunal of Inquiry by contrast [to the High Court] is set up speci-
> fically to find the truth. It is expected to take a positive and primary role
> in searching out the truth as best it can . . . Ultimately, the task facing
> the Tribunal is to establish the truth, not to make a determination in
> favour of one party engaged in an adversarial contest with another.[111]

Those who expect a tribunal to supplant the criminal courts will be disappointed. Nonetheless, tribunals have the symbolic potential to assuage many of the concerns that have arisen in respect of the use of force by the state in Northern Ireland over almost three decades.

The Saville Tribunal reinvestigating the events of Bloody Sunday will be closely watched to ascertain whether there is a genuine willingness on the part of the state to acknowledge its responsibility for civilian loss of life and the inadequacy of its previous attempts at accountability. In a ruling on the matter of anonymity for soldiers, Lord Saville outlined the role he saw for the tribunal:

> The Tribunal has as its fundamental objective the finding of the truth
> about Bloody Sunday. It regards itself as under a duty to carry out its
> public investigative function in a way that demonstrates to all con-
> cerned that it is engaged in a thorough, open and complete search for
> the truth about Bloody Sunday.[112]

However, the attempts by the tribunal to engage in such an open and transparent process are being hotly contested by the agents of the state. Rulings by the tribunal in December 1998 on the issue of anonymity for soldiers giving evidence were litigated throughout the spring of 1999. The Divisional Court concluded that the tribunal had made a number of errors on the matter of anonymity and quashed the ruling of the tribunal insofar as it related to the seventeen soldiers who had applied for judicial review. Its reasons included:

> (1) We are satisfied that the present Inquiry did misunderstand the
> nature and extent of the anonymity granted to the applicants
> [the soldiers] by Lord Widgery, and that this misunderstanding
> played a significant part in the Inquiry's reasoning process when
> arriving at the decision under challenge . . .
> (3) We are satisfied that the Inquiry did misinterpret the Security
> Service Threat Assessment . . .[113]

The tribunal was given leave to appeal the Divisional Court's decision. The Court of Appeal upheld the Divisional Court's judgment.[114] In May 1999 the tribunal rejected automatic anonymity for all soldiers giving evidence to the tribunal, but explicitly provided for individual soldiers to apply for anonymity on the grounds that it was justified in their own particular circumstances. Lord Saville couched his decision in the following manner:

> After the most anxious consideration we have concluded that on the
> basis of the material presently available before us our duty to carry out
> a public investigation overrides the concerns of the soldiers and does so
> even if the Widgery assurance continues to apply.[115]

The soldiers have again sought judicial review of that decision. The litigation on the matter continues in the domestic courts.

Should the Bloody Sunday inquiry prove fair and transparent there may be expectations that a similar legal process would satisfactorily examine other legally unresolved lethal force deaths in Northern Ireland. However, no matter how positive the Saville Inquiry, it seems unlikely that it will prove to be the start of a series of similar investigations.

The Bloody Sunday inquiry is the culmination of years of intensive lobbying and consensus-building across political and social constituencies to convince a wide public of the need to reopen the investigation on these thirteen deaths. No other deaths caused by the state in Northern Ireland have the same wide emotional force, creating an unstoppable momentum to investigation.

B

ALTERNATIVE MECHANISMS

There have been calls for the complete abandonment of the inquest process in the United Kingdom.[116] These calls suggest that the chief role of the coroner has become associated with and limited to the verification of the medical autopsy. Thus, the historical functions of the office are now discharged by other institutions and nothing is added to the autopsy by the findings of the jury. The legal framework ought to be abandoned for a medical process of determination, which would involve less state expense and limit cumbersome procedures following unexpected deaths.

These views entirely ignore the potential of the inquest to work as an effective democratic check, by informing the public through its public proceedings and record. They disregard the community's need to verify the context and causation of death and facilitate the prevention of deaths in similar circumstances. Process has an independent value of its own that serves as a legitimising rule in community perceptions of governance. The inquest, as a process, fulfils needs that cannot be accomplished by merely ascertaining the cold medical facts of a death as a medical matter.

But, as this analysis points out, there are lacunae to be filled. This is particularly evident in cases concerning controversial deaths in which state agents bear causal responsibility. Therefore some rethinking of the inquest is necessary for these kinds of cases. One option is to split the functions of the inquest in two. Noncontentious deaths could be examined under a reformed version of the current model, the overarching function of this inquiry would remain the medical determination of death. While the medical inquiry predominates in this model, the legal implications of medical findings should not be ignored. The medical determination requires the benefit of a structured legal framework with evidential rules, defined rights of participation for the next of kin, and a meaningful result which satisfies the need for genuine accountability. However, controversial deaths, such as those caused by the use of lethal force, require a different legal format.

Clearly, controversial deaths are ill-served in the current model. Effective investigation into these deaths requires a move away from the inquest into a formalised legal inquiry with wider terms of reference and stronger legal protections for the next of kin and the public interest. An interesting comparative model to examine in this context is the Scottish method for investigating controversial deaths. Rather than using the coroner's office, the duties of the coroner in these cases are subsumed into the legal office of the procurator fiscal. In cases of sudden or suspicious death, the procurator issues a warrant to the sheriff, who holds an inquiry sitting with a jury of seven.[117] The evidence for the inquiry is collected by the procurator fiscal and not by the police.

As pointed out previously, one of the outstanding criticisms of the coroner's inquest in Northern Ireland is that the office merely serves as a stage from which the coroner presents information collected by the police. The advantage of the Scottish approach is twofold. First, the status of the sheriff adds to the weight of the proceedings. The sheriff is not only a judge of the Scottish local civil court but also a judge of the criminal court of summary jurisdiction when he sits with a jury. The sheriff is a legal officer and his court has been described as 'by far the most important of the inferior criminal courts'.[118] Although the verdict of the sheriff's inquiries may not be used to determine any question of civil or criminal liability, the status of the office and the wider scope of the inquiry lends a greater credence to the exercise of factual determination following a controversial death. It should also be noted that interested parties, usually the next of kin, have the right to appear personally and address the inquiry. The Scottish model bears the strong influence of the civil law systems of inquiry, in which the investigating magistrate assumes overall responsibility for the police investigation.

Drawing on the Scottish model, one can envisage an investigative inquest that would have the necessary remit and powers to fully examine lethal force incidents. A revised structure should have wide terms of reference in its examination of investigative, evidential and legal issues. Its legal powers should mirror the rights and privileges of the High Court in relation to witnesses and evidence. Both the legal representatives of the state and those of the next of kin should have the right to provision of services from public funds to facilitate full and equal representation of all interests. The investigative inquiry should not supersede the function of the criminal courts. Its aim should remain a commitment to fulfil a fact-finding function competently, and to alleviate public concern when death is caused by an agent of the state.

Tinkering with the inquest process seems insufficient to alleviate the major concerns that have emerged in recent years. Any viable reform requires that the inquest will revitalise the meaning of fact-finding and ensure confidence in the rule of law. Northern Ireland faces many new challenges in the process of peace-building. Not least of these is a revamping of those legal processes which have been identified as partisan and incapable of fulfilling the needs of accountability and transparency in a divided society. The inquest is one such structure in need of urgent overhaul.

4

International law and the use of lethal force

I
When all else fails

While this work has thus far primarily concentrated upon the functioning and capacity of law in a domestic context, such analysis is
only a narrow part of a wider frame. Sovereign states such as the United
Kingdom no longer operate in legal isolation. Rather, supra-national law
has a distinct and sophisticated interplay with the domestic arena. This
has not always been the case. Historically, situations of internal conflict
were an unregulated area for international law. The state was presumed
to have an absolute right to regulate its internal affairs as it saw fit, and
nowhere was this more true than in times of exigency. However, the
Second World War irrevocably transformed the idea of state sovereignty. The post-war system of multilateral human rights treaties
created both internal and external obligations for states. These obligations
were created by the states themselves, as were their concurrent mechanisms of enforcement.

The international human rights system had the effect of internationalising the manner in which states behaved in the domestic realm.
No longer could states that had entered into human rights treaty obligations assume that the manner in which they treated their citizens was
solely a matter for their own discretion. They were now to be held
accountable to consentually agreed standards that would hold up a
mirror to their internal practices, even when they were experiencing
internal crisis.

Despite this contextualisation, the recourse to international law is generally thought of as an option of last resort when human rights violations take place. In the ideal world national courts are in the best position to process human rights violations: they are located in the territory where violations occur, they apply laws that perpetrators cannot claim to be ignorant of, and they have immediate and practical access to the factual evidence. Equally, there are important psychological consequences in ensuring that national courts carry out this task: local courts demonstrate a willingness to be active rather than passive in the face of human rights violations; fair domestic process allows for confidence-building in the idea of law itself; and this form of accountability can assist meaningful institutional-building in a divided society. It is only when the domestic system has failed to remedy human rights violations in any meaningful way that the international legal order steps in.

In Northern Ireland loss of life resulting from the use of lethal force is evaluated through the prism of the protection accorded to the right to life in international law. The local legal order has proven patently unable to respond adequately to violations of the right to life. Thus, lack of domestic accountability has led to redress being sought outside the jurisdiction.

II
Evaluating international standards on the right to life

The right to life has mighty rhetorical force. Contained in all international human rights treaties[1] it is a nonderogable right, meaning that the state cannot in any circumstances deviate from its protection. The inclusion of the right in the international law of human rights reflects the acceptance of a number of self-evident principles. First, that its protection ascribes a value to human life itself. Second, that there is an intrinsic value to each life, reflected in the assumed egalitarianism of the right. At least in principle, each human being has the same right to life without distinction, which derives from a validation of each person's unique humanity. Thus, all human lives must be regarded as having an equal claim to preservation simply because life itself has an irreducible value.[2] Finally, the right has pre-eminence, in that its presence is a logical prerequisite to the existence of other rights. Thus, other rights exist in a relationship of dependency derived from the validation of this right.

The right to life is protected by a number of positive, post-war, international legal standards, committed to the centrality of rights discourse in the new world order. The right to life has a longer pedigree under international humanitarian law, where certain prohibitions on the methods and means of warfare are rooted in a tradition that elevates the right of individual survival and limits the methods for terminating human existence, even in war. Whether the right to life has attained the status of *jus cogens* remains a subject of considerable debate. *Jus cogens* is understood to mean that a particular state practice has reached the status of being a pre-emptory norm of international law. Thus, such a norm cannot be limited or derogated from by agreement between states in their relationships with one another.[3] Some argue vociferously that the right to life and its subjects has attained this lofty status; others are more circumspect, noting that even if a portion of the right can be placed in this category, intense dispute still rages over the definition of that morsel.

Discussions on the right to life are significantly different in tone than similar conversations about other rights. Life and its protection are concepts that raise strong and varied emotions, no less even where the polemic is directed at limiting protection for particular reasons. The right is often described as both inalienable and indefeasible. An indefeasible right is one that is incapable of being annulled or made void without consent. An inalienable right is one that is incapable of being alienated, surrendered or transferred, even if one wishes to do so. In ascribing such strong metaphysical stipulations to individual ownership of life, we gain an inkling of how difficult interpretation of the orbit of this right may be. Kevin Boyle reiterates the point that there is something profoundly different about this right that places it in a different evaluative category:

> [It] is essential, to give full weight to the nature of the right to life as the *foremost* right, that it be treated as conceptually different to all others despite sharing characteristics with other rights of being subject to exceptions.[4]

The consequences of affirming the foremost ranking of this right not only affects our perceptions of the right itself but also the manner in which exceptions are made or limitations placed upon it. There is a relationship between the core status of a right and the manner in which exceptions to its realisation will be interpreted. Therefore, while it is accepted that the right to life is subject to exemptions, either by positive law or judicial interpretation, which is an aspect of its commonality with other rights, the status of the core is not unrelated to how limitations may be construed.[5]

A

EUROPEAN PROTECTIONS

When domestic legal remedies for loss of life prove insufficient in Northern Ireland the most readily available supra-national remedy comes under the European Convention on Human Rights. However, despite the deaths of 350 persons in the jurisdiction under review in this study by the use of lethal force since 1969, only 10 individual cases have been lodged with the European Commission.[6] However, increasing use is being made of the convention structure. This is explained by greater familiarity on the part of local legal practitioners with international remedies and the notable success of the high profile Gibraltar case in substantiating a violation of the right to life by the United Kingdom. This chapter examines how the European Convention on Human Rights articulates its protection for the right to life, how the jurisprudence of the supra-national system defines deficiencies of domestic law, and whether international review has clarified the legal status of the Northern Ireland conflict in any way.

The European Convention was conceived and drafted in the decade following the Second World War. The experience of that war had a profound effect on the European states, which came together to draft a regional charter with the aim of protecting individual rights and freedoms.[7] The convention followed from the establishment of the United Nations Charter, inaugurating multilateral protection for human rights as a matter of international concern. The charter's preamble states that the 'Peoples of the United Nations' are determined to 'reaffirm faith in fundamental human rights, in the dignity and worth of the human person, in the equal protection of men and women and of nations small and large'. Article 55 of the charter mandates respect for 'human rights ... without discrimination'. A Universal Declaration quickly followed the charter, giving greater specificity to the latter's human rights dimension. Article 3 of the Universal Declaration holds that 'everyone has the right to life, liberty and the security of the person'.[8]

The European states were quick to follow with accelerated agreement on a regional human rights convention and attendant implementation institutions and the European Convention was signed in Rome on 4 November 1950 and came into force in September 1953. The defining feature of the convention was the provision made for the effective enforcement of rights. Its radical departure was the means made available between state and individual citizens to access a supra-national legal structure, which had the standing to hold domestic states accountable for the manner in which they treated their own citizens.

The right to life is protected by Article 2 of the convention and is framed as follows:

1 Everyone's right to life shall be protected by law. No one shall be deprived of his right to life intentionally save in the execution of a sentence of a court following his conviction of a crime for which this penalty is provided by law.
2 Deprivation of life shall not be regarded as inflicted in contravention of this Article when it results from the use of force that is no more than absolutely necessary:
      (a) in defence of any person from unlawful violence
      (b) in order to effect a lawful arrest or to prevent the escape of a person not lawfully detained
      (c) in action lawfully taken for the purpose of quelling a riot or insurrection.

Hence, the protection for the right to life is framed in an unusual way. Article 2 opens with a broad and generic statement, which sets out the framework to protect the right to life. The article then proceeds to establish limits on the right, prescribing the circumstances in which the right to life can be limited or taken way.

The nexus of a broadly enumerated right, followed by a series of limitations, is clearly paradoxical. It is a clear manifestation of the tension between rhetorical absolutes and the practical necessities of regulating individual behaviour in society. Not only does Article 2 set out an individual right to life, it also defines a state right to take life in particular circumstances. However, the state right to take life, or at least to balance one set of individual rights to life against others, can be seen as a necessary corollary to the dictates of community, an aspect of the choice to live in society. It is equally arguable that the permitted justifications for taking life undermine the substantive content of the right to life itself. As Kevin Boyle points out, it is noteworthy that one of the objections to the United Kingdom's enumerative approach in the drafting of the International Covenant on Civil and Political Rights, specifically the right to life provision of that treaty (Article 6), was the concern that to specify the occasions when it would be legitimate to kill might appear to endorse killing in such circumstances.[9] This tension is inherent under Article 2 because states choose to spell out the circumstances under which life's protection can be limited. Other international treaties have avoided this conundrum by resisting explicit text as far as limitations are concerned, being satisfied to remain focused on the articulation of a generic rule protecting life.

The requirements of Article 2 place explicit duties on the state. J.E.C. Fawcett argues that 'it is not life, but the right to life, which is protected by law'.[10] This forces us to reflect on whether the article in fact sets out an unequivocal right to life. Though it is generically described as a 'right to life' article, on closer examination we see that this is an article imposing certain legal obligations on the state in relation to the protection of human life. It is not exclusive protection for life *per se*, If the obligation on the state is to protect life, how far does that extend? It would seem that the practical effect of that obligation is not to deprive an individual of his/her life capriciously. The outright limiting factor on intentional deprivation of life is due process – any intentional taking of life must be authorised by a legally sanctioned process in adherence to legitimate norms subject to the due process protections contained in Article 6 of the convention.[11]

How wide is the scope of governmental obligation to be interpreted? It would seem to extend to a duty to abstain from acts that would needlessly endanger life.[12] But how far does the state have to go to protect life? Convention jurisprudence states definitely that the state is not required to take extraordinary measures to protect the individual. In the case of *X v. Ireland* the applicant complained of the failure of the state to continue to provide him with a personal bodyguard following threats from an assassin.[13] In this case, the European Commission of Human Rights located the assessment of the right to life between two strategically defined positions. First, the general protection given by state laws designed to protect life; second, the particular and unique needs of the individual applicant in relation to protecting his defined right to life. The state was found to have satisfied its first obligation of providing general protection for the right to life. What the applicant had sought came under the second heading – unique and personalised protection by the state. The commission was clear that states could not be required to give such protection. It stated: 'Article 2 cannot be interpreted as imposing a duty on the State to give protection of this nature, at least not for an indefinite period of time, which is what in effect the applicant requests.'[14] In short, the commission was of the view that Article 2 did not impose a positive obligation on states to give the kind of personal protection sought by the applicant.[15] Nonetheless, the commission has on several occasions voiced the opinion that a state's obligation under Article 2 should not be viewed as wholly negative, but that it also includes positive aspects.[16]

The European Court of Human Rights' 1998 decision in the case of *Osman and Osman v. United Kingdom* underscores the articulation of this positive obligation.[17] The applicants submitted that under Article 2 of the convention the United Kingdom had been under a positive obligation to protect the life of the deceased Ali Osman. He was killed by his young son's former teacher, who had developed an obsessive attachment to the boy and had threatened the entire family on a number of occasions, and had allegedly subjected them to ongoing harassment. The applicants submitted that the convention was breached by the failure of the police to take adequate steps to protect the family.

Following the commission's report, the court asserted that the positive burden of Article 2 upon a contracting state could include an explicit obligation to safeguard life. The court stated that this implied, in well-defined circumstances, 'a positive obligation on the authorities to take preventative operational measures to protect an individual whose life is at risk from the criminal acts of another individual'.[18] The commission had similarly argued that it could go as far as requiring the state to take preventative steps to protect life from known and avoidable dangers.[19] However, mindful of the excessive burdens that a broad reading of this principle might place on the police, the court balanced its position with the view that 'such an obligation must be interpreted in a way which does not impose an impossible or disproportionate burden on the authorities'.[20]

Thus, in order for the protection obligation to be activated, the authorities must be proven to have known that there was a 'real and immediate' risk to identified persons from third parties. Furthermore, it must be verified that the authorities failed to take measures available to them, which would have avoided the known risk.[21] The court was not satisfied that in the particular circumstances of the *Osman* case the police knew or could have known of the explicit and immediate danger posed to family members from the actions of their son's former teacher. However, while concluding that there had been no infraction of the right to life protection under the convention, the court determined that Article 6 (1) had been transgressed by the exclusion of adjudication on the merits of the applicants' civil case as a result of an exclusionary rule applied by the United Kingdom courts .[22]

A number of brief conclusions can be drawn from these decisions. First, that the state's primary obligation to protect life is a generic and generalised one. The European Commission is unwilling to articulate a *lex specialis* which would demand tailored and individualised life protection for citizens. Second, that the general obligation rests significantly on the existence and enforcement of positive law and the completion of general and ordinary enforcement duties by agents of the state. This is the case even where the state (and its citizenry) is facing unusual threat. Third, that the European human rights system is loath to place undue burdens on the state, whether these be financial or administrative in nature. There is unstated judicial balancing being undertaken here, acknowledging that the 'nightwatchman' state may be the model of modern government and that undue burdens of law enforcement may be viewed as unwarranted domestic interference. Fourth, that while the court may be reluctant to declare violation in this kind of case in terms of Article 2, its emphasis on right of access to a domestic remedy with substantive due process protections may be a positive new direction. Finally, these decisions demonstrate the articulation of the general duty to protect life but not special duty, the latter being more onerously constructed, making the threshold of its applicability far beyond the reach of the average citizen.

The extent of positive state responsibility goes to the heart of any discussion on extra-legal killings, where state agents may not be directly responsible for deaths, but have colluded with those orchestrating such killings.[23] Self-evidently, the state is not held to account for the failure to protect life in all possible situations of danger. Such an interpretation would be both impractical and unreasonable. However, the convention was drafted with the actions of state agents in mind. It is their actions, not the potential actions by other nonstate actors, which may affect the right that the article protects. On a side note, it seems evident, despite the lack of judicial qualification on the matter, that if the state fails to create a system of legal accountability, which holds those who deliberately take the lives of others criminally responsible, that failure may breach the principles contained in Article 2.

The litmus test for state protection is firmly rooted in the enforcement of ordinary legal steps designed to safeguard life. The positive measures of protection revolve around the effective functioning of the criminal justice and judicial systems, and the mechanisms of investigation within the state that support them. Torkel Opsahl describes it as follows:

> The protection required must operate on several levels, having preventative as well as repressive functions: through prohibition of acts causing loss of life and through regulation and limitation of certain risks, as well as through provision for enforcement procedures and sanctions, in particular through criminal or civil responsibility.[24]

These are the key elements of protecting life 'by law'; in effect, ensuring that legal process works where life is taken and that its effective administration acts as a bar to both citizens and state agents in their actions. Violation of the right to life under the European Convention seems now to rest on the principle that where governments fail to observe these positive principles, they will be found liable of violation. The Gibraltar decision, in particular, has crystallised this approach by the European Court.

B

ALLOWABLE FORCE UNDER THE CONVENTION

The basic protection given by Article 2 is the prohibition on the deliberate taking of life by the state, with certain defined exceptions.[25] These enumerated situations create a legal legitimisation for taking life. They include life taken in defence of others,[26] effecting lawful arrest,[27] and in quelling riot or insurrection.[28] At minimum, there is an allowance for 'life endangering force' in pursuance of certain specified aims. This is the paradox of Article 2, that in protecting life, provision is made for lawfully depriving it. The specified limitations envisage situations where the actions of individuals may mean that they pose a direct risk to other members of society. In such circumstances, their personal rights are trumped by the rights of others to protection. Taking life is not a one-dimensional choice made in a vacuum bereft of balancing considerations, it is intimately coupled with the realisation of others' rights.

The taking of life by the state in these defined circumstances does not mean that such action cannot be held up to scrutiny when life-taking force is exercised. Article 2 is clearly composed of a number of under-lying principles in the articulation of a state's priorities. The first is the principle of necessity and Article 2 (2) acknowledges this by the incorporation of the phrase 'absolutely necessary'. This means that life cannot be taken on a whim nor as a pre-emptive measure. When life is taken by an agent of the state, it must be a choice of last resort.

One basic problem is setting criteria by which to judge, in any particular set of circumstances, whether the use of force was no more than 'absolutely necessary'. In the Gibraltar case the European Court specifically addressed the definition of 'absolute necessity', stating that it was a 'stricter and more compelling test' than that which is normally applicable in determining whether state action is necessary in a democratic society.[29] The second issue, arising in extreme cases, is whether absolute necessity can include deliberate killing. This is a problematic question, given that deliberate killing seems to be excluded *per se* under the general protection of Article 2 (1). Practical realities indicate that member states allow for premeditated killing in such circumstances as self-defence and defence of others. Nonetheless, it is possible that Article 2 (2) can still be interpreted restrictively. The permissibility of deliberate killings under Article 2 (2) is always limited to the specific legitimate aims outlined in the article and no further. One possible corollary to the 'absolute necessity' principle is the requirement of minimum force. This mandates that when force is exercised, the least destructive means possible must be used to achieve the ends sought.

The second principle underpinning Article 2 is that of proportionality. In essence, this means that the use of force to take life must correspond to a threat of similar magnitude facing the user of force. On a crude reading, this could mean parity of weaponry. It inherently implies that the response in using force must correlate to the seriousness of the specific offence suspected. Thus a minor misdemeanour can never be a reason to exercise lethal force. Proportionality is always dependent on the specific factual circumstances of each case and the subjective assessments of those analysing the controlling factors around them. The principle of proportionality has been repeatedly invoked explicitly and implicitly by the European Court and Commission. The discussion of individual cases will elucidate this theme further. At this point suffice it to say that force which is not proportionate to the aim pursued could never be 'absolutely necessary' under the convention.

C

CASE LAW OF THE CONVENTION

The European Convention provides two formal mechanisms to enforce protection of the rights it contains: the interstate procedure, and the individual complaint process. States initially articulated the view that the interstate machinery was the best means to most effectively hold states accountable for violations of human rights.[30] However, this has not been the case. This mechanism envisaged one state taking formal legal procedures against another, based on a failure by the latter state to ensure the protection of its own citizens within national boundaries. The mechanism is rarely used and subject to the overriding constraint of *realpolitik*, States tend to view it as a purely political mechanism, which is used to exert political leverage selectively against one another. The nexus of intertwined relationships in an integrated European Union means that fiscal and social implications follow from interstate cases, not immediately apparent from the nature of the alleged violation. State sovereignty also remains an entrenched bulwark. Many states are reluctant to interfere in the domestic affairs of other states, even where violation of fundamental rights guaranteed by all states is involved. An unwritten supposition is that such action by a state could lead to the complainant state's own policies towards its own citizens being examined, and no state seeks to have its own backyard under international review.

Only a small number of interstate cases have been brought concerning Article 2 violations. In *Ireland v. United Kingdom* the Irish government alleged *inter alia* that a number of persons had been killed by members of the British security forces in Northern Ireland in circumstances not justified by the invocation of the second paragraph of Article 2.[31] Disappointingly, this part of the complaint was declared inadmissible because of the failure to furnish evidence of administrative practice, requiring the local remedies rule to be complied with. Elsewhere, in a series of applications involving Cyprus and Turkey, Cyprus accused Turkey of having murdered citizens.[32] The cases were declared admissible and the Council of Ministers found a violation of Article 2 by Turkey.[33] As the scarcity of these cases indicate, there has been an abject lack of interstate cases generally and a notable lack of cases invoking Article 2 in particular. This in part explains the absence of a comprehensive jurisprudence on the protection due to the right to life in the

European human rights regime.

The individual complaint mechanism has been the primary vehicle for pursuing alleged right to life violations under the convention, though the paucity of case law is also noteworthy here. The majority of these cases have come from Northern Ireland, alleging violation of the right to life by the United Kingdom government. The European Commission has examined five cases in total on the specific issue of the use of lethal force in Northern Ireland. The right to life has been examined in other contexts, including the rights of the unborn child,[34] and the right of a father to prevent termination of a pregnancy.[35] More recently, in a number of cases the commission and court have encountered applications concerned with the relationship between extradition and a violation of right to life. For example, in *D v. United Kingdom* the applicant was an alien drug courier whose country of origin was St Kitts.[36] Having entered the United Kingdom in January 1993, he was apprehended carrying illegal drugs and sentenced to six years' imprisonment. While incarcerated, he was discovered to be suffering from AIDS, His application resulted from the United Kingdom's intention to return him to St Kitts, where he had no accommodation, family, moral or financial support and no adequate medical treatment. Following the *Soering* decision,[37] the court found a violation of Article 3, but did not feel it necessary to examine the complaint under Article 2.[38]

The *Farrell* case was the first before the commission on the matter of state use of lethal force. The case involved the killing of James McLaughlin, Sean Ruddy and Robert Anderson, suspected terrorists who in fact turned out not to be terrorists at all but felons engaged in a robbery. The commission set out the facts as follows in its decision on admissibility:

> On the night of 23 October 1971, in Newry in Northern Ireland, the applicant's husband and two other men were shot dead by a patrol of four British soldiers. The applicant's husband and the two other men were together attempting to rob two other men who were leaving money in the night safe of the Provincial Bank in Hill Street. The four soldiers were stationed on the roof of a two-story building overlooking Hill Street, and they had an uninterrupted view of the bank and the street. They were in command of one of their number, Soldier A. The Officer in charge of the patrol, described as Officer X, had information that on the night of 23 October 1971 a terrorist attack would most

probably be made on the bank. He had directed the patrol to take up fixed positions on the roof of the building. He did not have men in fixed positions at the ground level.

From their position on the roof, the patrol could not be seen from the street below. Having been called to the front of the roof by Soldier B, Soldier A saw three men cross the road to the bank and there was a scuffle with the two men already there. After about 10 to 15 seconds, Soldier A called 'Halt'. The three men stopped what they were doing and looked up and down the street. One of them shouted 'Run' and the three men took to their heels. Soldier A cocked his rifle and shouted 'Halt! I am ready to fire.' The men did not stop. He fired and the three soldiers with him also fired. It is not disputed that the soldiers fired to kill.[39]

In *Farrell* the central issue to be resolved was whether the degree of force permissible in effecting arrest could ever include deliberately lethal force.[40] The question was never publicly addressed as the case was settled following the commission decision on the matter. The United Kingdom government paid a substantial amount of compensation to the applicant, and the grounds for the settlement between the parties were not made public. The applicant had also claimed that there was negligence on the part of those who planned the military operation that led to her husband's death.

Though this part of the complaint was found inadmissible by the commission for failure to exhaust domestic remedies, the commission implicitly confirmed that such claims could give rise to a violation of Article 2. This issue was left dormant for many years but was to prove critical to the outcome of the Gibraltar case in September 1995. Much of the governmental submission in *Farrell* concerned whether the 'reasonableness' standards of domestic self-defence provisions was one and the same as the 'necessity' standard contained in Article 2.[41] This issue has been addressed in chapter 2, detailing the applicable criminal standards relevant to the exercise of lethal force in the domestic context.

The next case to examine the use of lethal force by the state concerned the death of a thirteen-year-old boy from Belfast, Brian Stewart.[42] The boy was killed in October 1976 following the deliberate discharge of a plastic bullet. In its factual appraisal the commission confirmed that the deceased had been part of a riotous crowd of approximately 150 persons, engaged in throwing various impeding objects at an 8-man military patrol. Even though the factual assessment was and remains highly disputed, the commission agreed that the discharge of the soldier's weapon was lawfully taken for the purpose of quelling a riot under Article 2 (2) (c) of the convention. The commission stated that paragraph 2 of Article 2 does not primarily define situations where it is permitted to kill an individual, but it does define situations in which force is allowed, which may, as an unintentional consequence, result in the deprivation of life. The commission stated:

> The Commission . . . considers that Article 2 paragraph 2 permits the use of force for the purposes enumerated in sub-paragraphs (a), (b) and (c) subject to the requirements that the force used is strictly proportionate to the achievement of the permitted purpose. In assessing whether the use of force is strictly proportionate, regard must be taken to the nature of the aim to be pursued, the dangers of life and limb inherent in the situation and the degree of risk that the force employed might result in loss of life. The Commission's examination must have due regard to all the relevant circumstances surrounding the deprivation of life.[43]

The commission also examined the concept of 'necessity' in relation to the enumerated exception of Article 2. Drawing heavily from *The Sunday Times v. United Kingdom* decision, it outlined that in that case 'necessity' was determined as meaning (1) a pressing social need; (2) the 'necessity' test included an assessment of whether the interference with the convention was proportionate to the legitimate aim pursued; and (3) the qualification of the word 'necessary' with the adverb 'absolutely' indicated that a stricter and more compelling test of necessity had to be applied by the court.[44] The case arose when the *Sunday Times* challenged an injunction which prevented the publication of an article concerning the cases of children born disabled as a result of their mothers taking a drug Thalidomide during pregnancy. The injunction had been imposed on the grounds that publication would be a contempt of court. The European Court found that there was an interference with the right to freedom of expression under Article 10 of the convention.

In the *Stewart* case the use of lethal force was found to be necessary in a situation of public unrest, where the factual context was expressly linked to attack upon soldiers by a hostile crowd. The commission also noted that riots involving loss of life were common in Northern Ireland; such riots often provided cover for sniper attacks on soldiers; the evidence (according to the commission) demonstrated that plastic bullets were less dangerous than alleged; the soldier who fired was trained and experienced in using plastic bullets; and the soldier's aim had been disturbed and deflected at the moment of discharge.[45] The commission found that there was no implied duty of retreat for the soldiers in the face of mounting violence.[46] Whether this is still in fact good law following the Gibraltar decision will be teased out later.

The *Stewart* case reveals a tangible obstacle for complainants, singularly unresolved across a spectrum of cases – that is, the complete absence of critical evaluation by the European Court of the domestic finding of fact. When a case comes before the commission, domestic legal remedies have been exhausted and the version of fact presented (and usually accepted) as authoritative is that decided upon by these procedures. This unequivocal approval by the European Court and the European Commission fails to take account of the limitations of domestic legal process. In a situation of entrenched emergency, such as that in Northern Ireland, it ignores the perceived lack of impartiality by the legal apparatus to a significant portion of the community. The commission and court have been undifferentiating of factual and legal judgments from Northern Ireland despite the imposition of extraordinary legal norms, the manipulation of legal process in the Diplock Courts, and an inadequate and hamstrung inquest procedure. Despite the capacity to engage in independent fact-finding, the commission has only done so in the early intergovernmental cases and intermittently in recent cases coming from the Turkish state.[47] This issue will become more relevant as Protocol II has come into force for the convention system. Protocol II removes the two-tier commission/court structure created when the European Convention first came into operation, replacing it with a permanent and expanded court, functioning in grand chambers and mini-chambers.[48] Unless the reformulated court is prepared to be activist or critical in their fact-finding assessments, the prognosis for right to life protection may be limited in the long term.

This point is particularly relevant in light of the commission decision in the *Kelly* case.[49] The incident occurred in January 1985. Paul Kelly, with four other youths, was driving a stolen car in west Belfast. While failing to stop at a military checkpoint when directed, the car was fired upon. Kelly was fatally injured when the soldiers fired twenty rounds of ammunition into the vehicle.[50] The deceased's father brought an action for negligence against the Ministry of Defence in local courts. The application was unsuccessful. The European decision on admissibility was cursory and limited. The commission accepted, without reservation, the finding of fact by the High Court in Northern Ireland. This finding had accepted that the soldiers believed the occupants of the car to be desperate terrorists intent on making an escape from an army roadblock. It ignored evidence of a practice of teenage joyriding in the city of Belfast, and did not consider the possibility that the soldiers ought reasonably to have considered whether the car contained teenagers who had stolen the vehicle. The commission stated:

> The shooting . . . was for the purpose of apprehending the occupants of the stolen car . . . in order to prevent them carrying out terrorist activities. Accordingly, the action of the soldiers . . . was taken for the purpose of effecting a lawful arrest within [Article 2 (2) (b)].[51]

Accepting the domestic finding of fact meant that, within its definition, the use of force could neatly fall under the Article 2 (2) exceptions. The judgment was contextualised in terms of the background of terrorist killings in Northern Ireland, opening the door on the judicial use of a plethora of context justifications as a means to circumvent the strict applicability of state responsibility for the enforcement of the right to life.

Article 2 has no 'clawback' clauses and is not subject to the privilege of derogation. The *Kelly* judgment was a blunt attempt to institute such limitations through the judicial side door. The commission was also guilty of a fundamental misunderstanding of applicable domestic law. It is evident that they believed the soldiers involved had the right to arrest Kelly and his companions, which was not the case. Soldiers in Northern Ireland have no power to arrest on the grounds of prevention of crime; they may only arrest in connection with specific crimes already committed.[52] The inherent paradox of the domestic court's decision is also apparent – the soldiers had the right to fire to prevent flight, but no corresponding power to arrest.[53] As Sarah Joseph points out:

> One reading of the Commission decision in *Kelly* is that the Commission endorsed the use of potentially lethal force to stop the escape of persons suspected of no specific crime, but who were reasonably assumed by law enforcers to be likely to commit unspecified future crimes. Here, the Commission mistakenly considered this point in relation to Article 2 (2) (b). However, the use of force in such

circumstances could nevertheless be justified under Article 2 (2) (a) i.e. in order to defend others from violence.[54]

The *Kelly* decision would seem to suggest that the right to life of suspected terrorists diminishes drastically if they attempt to escape from law-enforcers. The problems of the reformulated fleeing felon rule, as applied in the domestic law-enforcement context, have already been outlined. The cameo appearance of this approach in international human rights jurisprudence is very problematic. The premise of the decision is all the more problematic when there is no direct apprehension of what kind of offence such a fleeing person is likely to undertake, and when exactly they are likely (if ever) to engage in such activity.

The most controversial decision emanating from the European Convention system on the right to life was the first case in which the court itself directly examined the deliberate taking of life by law-enforcement officials. The Gibraltar case also represents a bright-line being drawn, which moves the jurisprudence of the convention away from the direction being taken by the commission in the right to life arena. The case[55] concerned the killing of Mairead Farrell, Daniel McCann and Sean Savage by SAS soldiers in March 1988. All three were members of a PIRA active service unit, in Gibraltar to carry out a bombing mission. They had been subject to intense surveillance prior to their deaths, and were the object of a massive counter-insurgency operation, comprised of both local and specialist forces. The backgrounds of the three deceased were well known to the authorities. Farrell and McCann had been previously imprisoned for bombing and related activities.

The commission decided that the suspects were effectively allowed to enter Gibraltar with the intent that they be picked up by the surveillance operation at a later strategic moment and place.[56] Security forces gave evidence at the inquest, accepted by both the commission and court, that they believed the attack would be carried out by way of a car bomb. Varying evidence was given about the mode of detonation of this potential device. The inquest evidence, persuasive to the court, was that some form of remote control device would be used to detonate the bomb. It was also conceded by soldiers giving evidence to the inquest that once it became necessary to open fire on a suspect, they would continue shooting until that person was no longer a threat. The Gibraltar jury returned lawful killing verdicts by a majority of nine to two.

The court first confirmed that the exceptions in Article 2 indicate that its provisions extend, but are not limited to, intentional killing. Article 2 was accepted to apply not only to situations where it is permitted intentionally to kill an individual, 'but describes the situations where it is permitted to "use force" which may result, as an unintended outcome, in the deprivation of life'.[57] The stricter protectionist tone of the court is set in paragraph 149:

> In this respect the use of the term 'absolutely necessary' in Article 2.2 indicates that a stricter and more compelling test of necessity must be employed from that normally applicable when determining whether state action is necessary in a democratic society, under paragraph 2 of Articles 8 to 11 of the Convention. In particular, the force used must be strictly proportionate to the achievement of the aims set out in sub-paragraphs 2 (a), (b) and (c) of Article 2.[58]

The court confirmed from the outset that any exception to the right to life will be narrowly and strictly construed. Thus, by extension, the value of human life is emphasised over other rights, an unstated creation of a hierarchy of norms within the convention order.[59] The elevation of life's protection is an obligation, which, by reason of the importance of its subject matter, gives it an uncommon status, generating a corresponding legal interest in enforcement. The significance of the right to life in a democratic society is also underscored:

> In keeping with the importance of this provision in a democratic society, the Court must, in making its assessment, subject deprivations of life to the most careful scrutiny, particularly where deliberately lethal force is used, taking into consideration not only the actions of the agents of the state who actually administer the force but also all the surrounding circumstances including such matters as the planning and control of the actions under examination.[60]

The emphasis on the role of this right in the democratic order also signals an equality approach, whereby the status of the victims, in this case as terrorists, is not a means to lessen the value of the right to them *per se*, Equally, the decision to widen the responsibility of the state for its actions and decisions leading up to the moment of life-taking is an important step in expanding the concept of what protecting life actually means.

The applicants had placed great emphasis on the disjunction between the domestic legal standard (Article 2 of the Constitution of Gibraltar)

and the European Convention Article 2 criterion.[61] The court held that
its mandate did not extend to examining *in abstracto* the compatibility of
national provisions with the requirements of the convention.[62] It noted
that, on the face of it, the convention standard appeared to be stricter.
This discrepancy was smoothed over by the government's contention
that their domestic standard was interpreted and applied in such a
manner as to negate any differences of protection.[63] The court failed to
engage in a substantive examination of the government claims, being
content that the cursory affirmation of similar application resolved the
positivist differences. Such curt dismissal is regrettable, given that the
only manner in which the claims of discrepancy can be addressed is by
thorough examination of domestic practice. Arguably, given the complexity of the case, it was outside the court's ability to examine what
would in fact prove to be a Pandora's box. It is to be hoped that in
other cases government affirmation will not create a presumption in
the state's favour that practice is in conformity with the convention's
standard.

On the accepted facts, the court held that the actions of the four soldiers who carried out the shooting did not breach Article 2. The soldiers
had stated that they continued to fire at the suspects until they were physically incapable of any further movement. This was to prevent any one
of them detonating the remote device that the soldiers believed they were
carrying. As a result, Mairead Farrell was hit by 8 bullets, Daniel McCann
by 5 and Sean Savage by 16. The soldiers claimed they had honestly
believed the three deceased to be capable of detonating a device from a
distance, and had been briefed in such a manner as to discount other possibilities.[64] Having accepted the commission's factual assessment that the
deceased were all shot while standing, or in the momentum of fall, there
was no assessment as to whether any one of the three were incapacitated
at a point where their lives might have been saved, notwithstanding the
use of force.

Had the court stopped here, as in earlier commission decisions, the
state would have been entirely absolved of any responsibility for the
deaths. The mistaken beliefs of personnel would perform an absolving
function, as the act of killing would be entirely justified on the grounds
of these beliefs. But, the court went further, and, in doing so, widened
the mantle of state protection, preventing the moment of death alone
from becoming defining of liability. Instead, the moment of death

became merely a culmination of a series of events that led to its certainty. The court found that the instructions and information relayed to soldiers A–D 'rendered inevitable the use of lethal force'.[65] It seems that it was this inevitability, the closing off of other options from an early point in the operation, which profoundly impressed the court and opened up the examination of the control and organisation of the operation.

On the facts accepted by the court, the principals in Operation Flavius did not observe the three suspects cross the border. However, the court accepted that had a more rigorous border surveillance operation been mounted, the suspects might have been arrested at an early point. The court seemed struck by the fact that if the intention of the operation was to prevent injury and destruction in Gibraltar, the suspects' paradoxically easy access to the jurisdiction rendered that objective almost meaningless.[66] The failure to arrest the three suspects, objectively speaking, put their lives at greater risk. It is this postulation, this framing of the right to life, as a right which belongs to those transgressing the law as much as to those who observe it, which is at the heart of the court's judgment. More correctly, it lends weight to the hypothesis that it is the *right* to life that is equally protected by the article, not life itself. The *McCann* case accepted that the action of killing did not render those who carried out the killing open to liability, but the right to life of the three acknowledged terrorists was still given value and required guardianship. This portion of the judgment takes us in an entirely different direction from the *Kelly* decision. As Sarah Joseph states:

> It is arguable that their [the court's] inclusion of the border entry as a 'relevant factor' indicates that the refusal by the authorities to risk the 'escape' of dangerous persons, thereby risking the reasonably foreseeable death of those persons, is not justified. To put it another way, the subsequent killing by the authorities of those persons should not be deemed 'absolutely necessary' within Article 2 (2). This implication indicates that the *Kelly* case was wrongly decided; killing in order to prevent future violence is not 'absolutely necessary'.[67]

The court accepted that the intelligence support units had made a number of incorrect assessments which were conveyed as factually precise to the soldiers on the ground.[68] In short, these assumptions did not make sufficient allowances for any other contingencies.[69] The close examination of the state's operational planning reveals the scrutiny which the court was prepared to undertake. The right to life has emerged from the *McCann* decision as a strict scrutiny right, subject to enhanced review.[70] This embryonic formalisation of a special review formula for the right to life is all the more interesting in that it stands in marked contrast to the rational basis review that seems to be the predominant theme of other rights reviewed under the convention. It is too early to tell, and the jurisprudence is too limited to predict, where the European Court will take the doctrine and whether, as in the United States, heightened scrutiny (in the latter case, constitutional) will be limited to 'discrete and insular minorities'.[71] The heightened scrutiny is not only focused on the outcome of the state's action but more significantly on the means by which the state came to act in a particular way, which results in an extraordinarily high level of inspection overall. The decision evidences an unwillingness to base the protection of life on the 'worst-case-scenario' approach argued strenuously for by the state. To concede this argument would be to facilitate any suspect or fleeing felon being predetermined as inculpated of the worst and most socially dangerous behaviour.

In this line of analysis the court also turned to the decision to deploy specialist forces in this type of operation. Given that these soldiers were trained to shoot to kill at situations where they had to engage their weapons, their deployment made it highly unlikely that such 'dangerous' suspects, who were expected to resist arrest, could ever be brought to trial. One reading of this approach seems inconsistent with the early determination that there was no premeditated shoot-to-kill policy in respect of the three deceased. The inconsistency here may be explained by the court's declaration that a high burden of proof and evidence was needed to find the state liable for a systematic and approved policy of extra-judicial acts.

The reflex action of the soldiers was to kill, and thus the court was propelled to find that their training was incompatible with the degree of caution expected by law-enforcement officials in a democratic society, even when dealing with dangerous terrorists. Their deployment stood in marked contrast to the standard of care expected of ordinary police forces, which emphasises the legal responsibilities of officers at the moment of engagement with offenders.[72] This approach further accentuates that an equal standard of care is due to all transgressors, no matter the heinousness of their alleged activities. Suspecting an individual of terrorist activities does not absolve a state from guaranteeing that individual the same due process rights as any other citizen or offender. On the sum of the inadequate operational planning, the state was found to have failed in its obligations under Article 2 (2) of the convention.

Despite the advancement made on a rigorous right to life defence, the judgment contains one significant area of weakness, which concerns the court's assessment of the adequacy of the domestic investigations (the inquest proceeding).[73] Counsel for the applicants and various *amicus briefs* stressed the necessity of ensuring legal protection for the right to life with forceful accountability mechanisms. In other regional human rights systems effective accountability has become the motif for governmental guardianship of the right to life. The weaknesses of the Gibraltar inquest included, *inter alia*, lack of independent police investigation; the failure of forensic experts and others to follow standard scene of crime procedures; the failure to contact all independent eyewitnesses; and the exclusion of certain crucial evidence by the use of Public Interest Immunity Certificates.[74]

The court outlined that the right to life, read in tandem with Article 1's requirement that states 'secure to everyone within their jurisdiction the rights and freedoms defined in [the] Convention', mandated 'some form of effective official investigation when individuals have been killed'.[75] However, the court refused to prescribe in any fashion what the standards of effectiveness ought to amount to and entirely glossed over the incompatibility of the inquest's shortcomings with the United Nations Principles on the Effective Prevention and Investigation of Extra-Legal, Arbitrary and Summary Executions, forsaking the opportunity to link together the specialist UN 'soft' law standards with the 'hard' treaty law of the convention. It was content to view the fact of official inquiry, the presence of witnesses and a voluminous transcript as illustrative of a fair and open process, when it might be claimed that, like the Emperor, the inquest was exposed.

Nevertheless, the approach of the majority, overall, evinced a much stricter scrutiny of the state party's assertions than is normally manifested in relation to other convention violations.[76] It is noticeable that express mention of the margin of appreciation doctrine is absent, marking the right to life arenas as one of the few bastions that the doctrine has left untouched in the European system. The margin of appreciation has been defined by the commission as allowing a state, when it acts in certain areas of domestic law, 'a certain measure of discretion in assessing the extent strictly required by the exigencies of the situation'.[77] Given the sensitive subject matter of the application, and the national security tone of the respondent government's defence, other courts might well have given greater leeway to the state. The European Court was effectively saying to the state that in the calculation of acts which are likely to cause loss of life, the state faces strict scrutiny of its actions and justification no matter whom the victim.

The endnote on the matter was the procedural decision not to award damages to the applicants (though their legal costs were paid by the United Kingdom). Given that liability was established, and damages are frequently equated with the value of the life lost, the message from the refusal to award compensation could imply a lack of worth accredited to the lives of the deceased. Equally, the court may have felt that the sensitivity of the decision itself was a burden to the respondent state, which would be exacerbated by pecuniary award. No substantial reasoning was offered by the court to elucidate its thinking on this matter.

The Gibraltar case also allows us to reflect on some wider issues related to state protection for rights in situations of conflict. It is clear from the foregoing discussion that the reality of an ongoing internal conflict in Northern Ireland was not considered persuasive to the court as a basis for weakening the obligations of the state in respect of the right to life. This was true both in the court's unwillingness to formally define conflict as a compelling contextualisation for state action, and in its reluctance to allow the existence of internal conflict to operate as a *de facto* reason to give greater permissibility to state use of force. This is extremely significant. The reasons underpinning that significance require looking at the Gibraltar incident through another legal prism, that of the international law of armed conflict.

It is possible that in practice (as opposed to the formal legal standards applicable to such a surveillance and interception operation) the SAS soldiers tasked with apprehending the three suspects were actually operating as if an entirely different legal standard applied to their actions. It could be argued that they were operating on the ground as if a situation of armed conflict with all its own specialised legal norms were the rules of the game. Thus, both by deploying a particular kind of military force, and by the manner in which the operation was planned, it could be suggested that the state was tacitly behaving as if the combatancy rules of international humanitarian law applied in their engagement with the three paramilitary actors. But the state was concerned that the 'normal' rules of law were seen to apply to their actions. This tells us an enormous amount about the way in which a state, experiencing internal conflict, wants to have it both ways. It sees a pressing security need to respond to paramilitary violence. Equally, it does not want to acknowledge politically that the laws of war apply to the conflict situation. It would prefer to have the capacity to respond using active counter-insurgency measures, drawn from the methods and means of armed combat, while maintaining the shell of ordinary law and applying the theory of political normality.

In the Gibraltar case the European Court recognised the need for states to respond to paramilitary activity, but stated that this did not lessen the strict requirements of protection due to all citizens, including those transgressing the law. The court avoided making any legal assessment about the status of conflict in Northern Ireland, despite the glaring messages inherent on this matter in the incident being examined. Finally, however, the court ruled, in effect, that the state cannot have it both ways. If the state contracts into an international human rights structure on the basis of its democracy and accountability, it will be held to those standards.

D

RECENT DEVELOPMENTS IN THE
EUROPEAN COURT'S RIGHT TO LIFE JURISPRUDENCE

A series of recent cases sheds further light on where the European Court of Human Rights has taken its jurisprudence on the right to life since the Gibraltar case. The signs are that judicial protection for the right to life continues to augment. This remains true even in those situations where the state is experiencing internal crisis. In 1997 the court once again examined Article 2 of the convention in the *Andronicou and Constantinou* case.[78] These two deaths resulted from police intervention in a violent domestic dispute. A young Cypriot man, Lefteris Andronicou, was heard beating his fiancée, Elsie Constantinou, in their apartment in late December 1993. Local police established that Andronicou was armed and refusing to allow the young woman to leave the building.[79] After a day-long standoff special police forces (MADD) decided upon armed intervention. As they entered the apartment and following continuous and unsuccessful negotiations, a mêlée ensued and tear gas bullets were fired into the residence. However, one officer, instead of firing tear gas bullets, inadvertently fired two live rounds. The first officer to seek entry into the apartment claimed that he saw Andronicou pointing his weapon directly at him. Andronicou fired his weapon and shooting continued on both sides. One officer was injured and both Andronicou and Constantinou were killed.

By a narrow margin of five votes to four, the court decided that there had been no violation of Article 2. The majority took the view that it was not sufficiently proven that the operation had not been organised and planned in such a way as to minimise the potential loss of life. This emphasis on planning underscores the new review standard developed in the *McCann* decision. Thus, once again it is not solely the moment when the lethal discharge of a weapon takes place which is under scrutiny but the broader context in which a fatality occurs. (This may have major implications for any further cases which involve preplanning in the use of lethal force emerging from Northern Ireland.) The majority held that, given the circumstances, despite the unfortunate loss of life, the use of force did not exceed the test of 'absolutely necessary'. They felt that the police officers had sought to protect the life of Elsie Constantinou as well as their own lives, and were within the perimeters of Article 2 (2) (a) in using force.

In the *Kaya v. Turkey* decision the European Court once again took an in-depth look at the exercise of force in an intense emergency situation, where the state claimed the deceased was an active and dangerous terrorist, and family and witnesses claimed otherwise.[80] This is an extraordinary decision, notably in its emphasis on the state's investigative duties following the exercise of lethal force. The facts of the incident were highly disputed and there were significant gaps of information consequent on the lack of witness availability and the paucity of official investigation after death. What is known is that the deceased, Abdulmenaf Kaya, was killed by Turkish security forces in the village of Dolunay in the province of Diyarbakir, south-eastern Turkey. The state alleged that a gun battle had taken place between up to sixty members of the security forces and a group of terrorists on 25 March 1993. They claimed that Kaya was among the group of terrorist assailants. After the shooting ended, the security forces undertook an extensive search of the area and discovered Kaya's body alongside an automatic assault gun. Later that day a government doctor and public prosecutor were flown to the scene. The body was found to have suffered a large number of entry and exit bullet holes. Further, Kaya's legs were both broken as a result of blows he had received. It was not disputed that he was wearing farming and not paramilitary clothing. Kaya's brother (the applicant) claimed that a number of local villagers were witnesses to the events that day. He also alleged that the deceased had been deliberately killed by the security forces in circumstances where there were no threats to their lives. He further contended that the state failed to carry out an independent and effective investigation, in breach of Article 6 of the convention.

Given the scarcity of information available, the commission undertook its own independent fact-finding process. However, this was hampered considerably by the failure of Kaya's brother and other local witnesses to appear before them. Nonetheless, the commission stated its grave doubts about segments of the Turkish government's version of events. The lack of evidence would not allow the court to conclude beyond a reasonable doubt that the deceased had been killed in the circumstances alleged by the applicant. This meant that there was no breach of Article 2 in this context.

This portion of the decision is interesting, as it reveals the court's manifest discomfort with the state's version of the incident. However, even though clear probative standard was applied, it was not in a position to counter the version of events presented by the Turkish government. The problem that emerges is complex. In situations of high intensity emergency, where the state is engaged in active counter-insurgency against paramilitaries, hit-and-run skirmishes between state and nonstate forces are not extraordinary.[81] International courts are in an odd position here. If we assume the government's version of events to be truthful, the human rights body is examining deaths which take place in an emergency context, but arguably also in a low-intensity conflict situation where the rules of humanitarian law may be dually applicable to the situation under review. Formally, international human rights courts are not empowered to apply a standard of review which is based on humanitarian law – a complementary but different realm of international legal obligation on states. This formal exclusion might suggest that international human rights courts should not be in the business of reviewing such situations at all. But this is not the case. The European Court of Human Rights has not indicated that it views such situations as inherently nonjusticiable. On the contrary, it continues to hold states accountable to the standards that they have contracted to, understanding that the prism of review may be somewhat false, given the contradictions of the conflict situation on the ground.

Assuming that the state version of events is not entirely frank, other issues arise. As recurrently transpires in such active counter-insurgency situations, the state does not always behave honourably in its use of force.[82] Thus, civilians become the casualties of undeclared low-intensity warfare. The greatest practical difficulty for a human rights court in this situation, whether the victim is a civilian or combatant, is access to evidence and facts. In many emergency situations, such as that which currently prevails in south-east Turkey, access to nonstate sources of information is arduous. Consequently, there may be few, if any, witnesses to such events, or they may be unwilling to come forward, fearful of the repercussions for themselves and their families if they do.

However, the court demonstrated its willingness to be both farsighted and innovative in its examination of this case. Unwilling to simply abandon the allegations with a curt dismissal of Article 2 on the grounds of a lack of empirical evidence, it examined the issue of investigation. Following the impressive lead of the Inter-American Court of Human Rights in the *Velasquez Rodriguez* case,[83] and moving further than it was prepared to do in the *McCann* decision, the European Court directly linked a lack of effective investigation with a violation of Article 2.

The court commenced by recalling that the legal prohibition on arbitrary killing would be meaningless if there existed no procedure for reviewing the lawfulness of the use of force by states. Thus, the obligations of Article 2 of the convention, allied with the state's general duty under Article 1, mandate that a state *must* carry out an effective official investigation when one of its agents is involved in the exercise of lethal force. Most importantly, the court emphasised time and again that the right to life was only meaningful where procedural protections were in place to ensure that the exercise of force was subject to independent and public scrutiny. Linking meaningful investigation to the core undertaking of what a state is required to do to protect life creates a deeper protection for the right to life by law. It also means that the court further augments its heightened scrutiny standard for Article 2, first developed in the *McCann* decision. Notably, the European Court of Human Rights is now increasingly in line with United Nations soft law standards for the protection of life. In particular, the decision complements the standards of review developed in the UN Principles on the Effective Prevention and Investigation of Extra-Legal, Arbitrary and Summary Executions.[84]

Particularly interesting in light of a number of similar cases like *Kaya* in Northern Ireland is the firm declaration by the state that because this was a 'clear-cut' case of lawful killing by the security forces, the state was dispensed from having to comply with anything other than the minimal legal formalities. The Turkish position on this matter was entirely rejected. The court also noted its disapproval of the public prosecutor's unquestioned assumption that the deceased was a terrorist who had died in a physical confrontation with the security forces. It was critical of the lack of thorough scene-of-crime analysis: the failure to take statements from the soldiers at the scene of the incident, and the absence of collaboration from villagers who might have heard or seen the incident. Clearly, the court is asking for state authorities who confront such cases to be far more circumspect and inquisitive of their agents' *bona fides*, The European judges assumed that an independent prosecutor could have looked into the case, one who would be open to the possibility that the soldiers might have been criminally culpable during his investigative process.

Finally, the court held that the prevalence of armed clashes and the high incidence of fatalities in Turkey did not absolve the state from their absolute responsibilities under Article 2 of the convention. This is a confirmation of the nonderogability of the right to life, no matter what form of crisis the state is facing. In conclusion, a violation of Article 2 was sustained on the basis that the state had failed to maintain an independent prosecution system for investigating allegations of unlawful killings of the security forces.

The case highlights the court's recent willingness to stretch the boundaries of protection on the right to life. It should be evident that this has not been an easy course for the European Court to chart. In both the *McCann* and *Kaya* cases, the state has made impassioned claims that those killed were terrorists posing an immediate threat to the state and its agents. The clear background to both cases are situations of entrenched emergency and low-intensity conflict. Nonetheless, the court appears to be safeguarding its stance that, whether the deceased is an ordinary citizen or a member of a paramilitary organisation, a substantive measure of life protection is due to them. That protection is not solely limited to the moment of fatality, but extends before the death to the planning of an operation which may apprehend a suspect, and after the death when the state must thoroughly and independently investigate if their own agents acted with due consideration to the right to life of the deceased. This is a sea change in European jurisprudence with significant implications for the examination of lethal force cases in Northern Ireland and elsewhere.

E

ADMINISTRATIVE PRACTICE AND THE RIGHT TO LIFE

One issue which arises tangentially from the Gibraltar case, which the court did not address (and the applicants did not argue), is the matter of administrative practice in the context of systematic life-taking by agents of the state. Administrative practice means that the human rights violations under review are not simply a one-off aberration, but rather reflect a coherent policy by the state, sanctioned at some level of government or by the institutions of government. In jurisdictions such as Northern Ireland lethal force is neither an isolated nor a random happening. Furthermore, a series of Turkish cases, pending before the European Commission, highlight many of the problems associated with the protection of life in a situation of emergency, but further demonstrate the capacity of a permanent emergency to function as concealment on the existence of a low-intensity conflict within the state. There are very real obstacles to ensuring that systematic violations of human rights are adequately confronted by the procedural constraints of the European convention. Two problems are evident. First, the convention was conceived of as an individual complaint apparatus – group rights are conceptually underdeveloped in the convention jurisprudence.[85] Therefore, widespread practices of human rights violation are difficult to confront procedurally. Second, the convention contains no *locus standi* for class action *per se*, Where states are carrying out gross and systematic violations of rights, there are limited tools within the convention machinery itself to confront such practices.[86]

To raise the issue of administrative practice is to undermine a central feature of the European human rights identity. That is to say, European states do not conceive of themselves as having problems related to systematic human rights violations. This is largely, though not universally, true. Any such admission is potentially destabilising of the political support enjoyed by the supra-national court and commission. States are loath to admit human rights violations, but are more graceful where the state violation can be explained away as an individual aberration. In other words, the consequences for a state of being deemed a gross violator of human rights may be quite extensive in political terms, when participation in international human rights structures is a defining feature (externally and internally) of its constitutionalism and democratic standing. Furthermore, as membership of human rights regimes is increasingly deemed to be a precursor to the membership of the élite international economic communities, the significance of being found to breach the human rights rules may be augmented.[87]

We should also note that for states who are found to be in violation of human rights norms the political presentation of that fact is not without significance. This has two aspects: first, the servicing of a domestic political audience, which may punish a democratic government electorally for its policy failures, or which may lose the confidence of significant internal communities; second, alliances with the external political community of nations upon which both democratic and nondemocratic states depend. These complex relationships underpin state unwillingness to be categorised as a persistent violator of human rights. It is always easier for states to present a human rights violation as an aberration from the normal practices of good governance, than to admit that violations are widespread and defining of the experience of government for citizens. To some extent the *Ireland v. United Kingdom* case demonstrates the point.[88] Here the United Kingdom government accepted that ill-treatment of internees occurred and issued the public undertaking that the five interrogation techniques used would be suspended and never employed again. There was a clear political benefit to that acknowledgement, which went hand in hand with the position that what had occurred was a unique situation which would not happen again.

Arguably, the European human rights system has been complicit in hiding the extent of violations by certain states. The court has colluded with these 'problem' states, treating each violation as if it were the sole violation ever to appear before it, even if the same state repeatedly appears before it in respect of the same types of transgression. The recent onslaught of cases from Turkey to the court proves the point succinctly. As Reidy, Hampson and Boyle have concluded:

> [In] over 60 cases from South East Turkey declared admissible, the
> Commission has found in each case that the applicants did not have an
> adequate remedy at their disposal to address their particular complaints
> . . . the question of how many cases are necessary in which applications,
> raising essentially similar complaints, are admitted by reason of a lack of
> effective remedies, before the conclusion is reached that there is a prac-
> tice of violation of the right to an effective domestic remedy?[89]

The perpetuation of similar kinds of violations is indicative of more rudi-
mentary problems with the contracting state, which the court and commission have been reluctant to respond to. A toleration of administrative
practice violations could be read as a green light to states which entertain,
and fail to stop, on-going lethal force practices by their agents. This
tolerance not only creates individual human rights violations but also
causes a discrete and insular class of group right violation.

Some precedents exist in the European system to acknowledge that
widespread practices of human rights violations occur. Its first mention
came in the *Greek* case.[90] Here, the commission observed that:

> where there is a practice of non-observance of certain Convention pro-
> visions, the remedies prescribed will of necessity be side-stepped or ren-
> dered inadequate. Thus, if there were an administrative practice of
> torture or ill-treatment, judicial remedies prescribed would tend to be
> rendered ineffective by the difficulty of securing probative evidence,
> and administrative inquiries would either not be instituted, or if they
> were, would be likely to be half-hearted and incomplete.[91]

Explicit recognition of administrative practice in an individual petition
came in the *Donnelly* case.[92] The case arose following allegations of brutality and ill-treatment after the introduction of internment without trial
in Northern Ireland in 1971. The commission considered the application
in light of the rule contained in Article 26 of the convention which
required the exhaustion of domestic legal remedies before supra-national
legal consideration. The specific issue addressed was whether the exhaustion requirement should be eased in the context of alleged administrative
practice. Initially, the commission found that there was nothing in the
European Convention which prevented an individual from raising a
complaint of administrative practice, in so far as *prima-facie* evidence was
offered to substantiate the allegation. It further found, assuming *prima-
facie* evidence, that the requirement to exhaust domestic remedies under
Article 26 was inapplicable.[93] In its final decision on the matter the

commission took the opportunity to refine the concept of administrative practice.[94]

It appears that *prima-facie* proof of an administrative practice produced by an applicant at the admissibility stage raises a rebuttable presumption only that the domestic remedies are inadequate.[95] This means that the commission will now examine the effectiveness of the domestic remedies before waiving the requirement to bypass them. The pitfall of this approach is that it places the applicant in a catch-22 situation. If the applicant fails to undertake any domestic legal procedures, and if a waiver is not given when administrative practice is alleged, then the case may be declared inadmissible for failure to exhaust local remedies. It limits the possibility of using the administrative practice claim as a means to circumvent the procedural hurdles of the convention. Nonetheless, administrative practice can remain a fundamental part of any application alleging violation of the convention.

In examining the right to life, administrative practice may be a crucial issue. This is especially true for the case study underpinning this book. The number of deaths, and the failure to prosecute those responsible, points to a tolerance for the use of lethal force in Northern Ireland. Chapter 1 notes historical patterns in the use of force in the jurisdiction and varying strategies adopted by the state from 1969 to 1994 in respect of life-taking. The patterns identified are consistent with policy decisions having tremendous influence on the deliberate choice to exercise force by agents of the state.

The *Donnelly* decision on administrative practice raises one other issue of significance both generally and in particular to Northern Ireland. The commission, in its final decision, leaned to the view that administrative practice was defined only by tolerance at the highest levels of government.[96] It seems that tolerance at the lower and middle levels of government does not suffice to constitute administrative practice (even if that tolerance is frequently demonstrated), when the state takes reasonable steps to prevent recurrence. The reasonableness of such steps is not defined. In Northern Ireland, investigations such as the Stalker and Sampson Inquiries would likely be read by this standard as 'reasonable' responses by the state, despite their paltry outcome.[97] These inquiries indicated low-level tolerance for the excessive use of force.

The prevailing European standard proves problematic to the demonstration of administrative practice as it has been experienced in Northern

Ireland. Proving that there was high level authorisation, or, at least, tolerance, for a policy allowing excessive use of lethal force, faces evidentiary obstacles which are insurmountable for the average applicant. There has been no concrete evidence of tolerance at the higher levels of government in relation to the use of lethal force. Nonetheless, the recourse to set-piece confrontation tactics is of definite significance in evaluating official levels of state backing for lethal force showdowns. This is notably the case because the deployment of specialist units, especially the SAS, is sanctioned at the highest levels of government, dependent on ministerial approval.

III
Bringing the convention home

In reflecting on the influence of supra-national legal standards to a specific state, in this case, the United Kingdom, two motifs emerge. The first is historical and requires consideration of the extent to which the right of individual petition has encouraged the United Kingdom to observe its international and domestic obligations in respect of the right to life. The second is contemporary and contemplates the future relationship of the European Bill of Rights within the British legal system, as the European Convention becomes a part of domestic law.

The United Kingdom was one of the leading proponents in favour of the adoption of a regional charter in Europe after the Second World War. It proposed drafts for many of the rights now incorporated in the convention. Article 2, protecting the right to life, was based on a draft submitted by the United Kingdom,[98] and the United Kingdom was one of the first states to ratify the convention.[99] In practice, however, the state's outlook on the convention has been marked by ambivalence.

The right of individual petition was accepted by the United Kingdom in 1966. Until the recent governmental decision the United Kingdom was one of the few Council of Europe states which had not adopted the European Bill of Rights into domestic law. The decision to incorporate the European Convention now places the United Kingdom in a situation of parity with other European states in respect of its constitutional protection for human rights. The non-adoption of the bill meant that an individual who claimed a human rights violation could only pursue a claim at the European institutes in Strasbourg, not in the United

Kingdom courts. This had a distinct effect on legal culture in the United Kingdom. For many lawyers schooled in domestic legal provisions the convention was viewed as irrelevant and marginal to the notion of a 'successful' outcome for a client. Further, the average citizen experiencing a human rights violation would have had little knowledge of his or her supra-national rights.

While the United Kingdom courts made hesitant steps towards acknowledging an interpretative role for the convention, there was an admitted lack of binding force in its domestic applicability. In cases such as *Malone* the English bench indicated that they were prepared to take note of the applicability of the rights contained in the convention to domestic law.[100] However, they were not prepared to permit the direct invocation or application of the convention in the domestic courts. In *Malone*, the court accepted that the actions of the state could potentially have been in violation of the convention and its case law.[101] The case was concerned with wiretapping and the resultant violation of Article 8 of the convention. Furthermore, in a series of cases concerning immigration, the English courts agreed that the convention followed directly in the tradition of the Magna Carta.[102] Over time, the approach of the judiciary in the United Kingdom became less hostile to the convention, and its influence on domestic legal interpretation increased. This is clearly recognised in the title to the legislation foreshadowing the incorporation of the convention into domestic law – 'An Act To Give Further Effect to Rights and Freedoms Guaranteed Under the European Convention on Human Rights'. The Lord Chancellor explained that the use of the term 'further' rather than 'domestic' was a recognition of the fact that the United Kingdom courts already apply the convention in many circumstances.[103] So while the courts in certain circumstances were prepared to be flexible in using and applying the standards of the convention in judicial decision-making, there has been little evidence to suggest that in the same period government decision-making was influenced to the same degree by its European Convention obligations. Primarily there was an unwillingness to be publicly committed to domestic legal adherence with the convention's standards in day-to-day law-making.

Until 1990 the United Kingdom had the largest number of convention violations alleged against it. It also had the greatest number of cases by any state referred against it to the court.[104] It has a lamentable monopoly of cases concerning a violation of the right to life under the convention. In the first of these cases, *Farrell*, the United Kingdom had agreed a friendly settlement with the applicants after the commission report confirmed violation of Article 2.[105] A requirement of the settlement was the government undertaking that it would endeavour to avoid similar action in the future which might contravene the convention. Clearly, continued violation of the right to life in Northern Ireland has undermined the entrenchment of that commitment in practice. The empirical evidence suggests that even where the United Kingdom has been found in violation of fundamental nonderogable rights, this does not constitute a guarantee that such violation will not occur again.

This is illustrated in the context of ill-treatment directed at those in custody in Northern Ireland. The *Ireland v. United Kingdom* case found that inhuman and degrading treatment had been meted out to persons detained under emergency legislation in Northern Ireland in the early 1970s.[106] Counsel for the United Kingdom, in oral and written arguments, had guaranteed on behalf of the government that the five interrogation techniques under consideration by the commission and court would never be used again in the jurisdiction. In the early 1990s, reports emerged of serious ill-treatment in Northern Ireland's holding centres.[107] Credible and independent evidence was adduced to demonstrate that, though the five techniques were not universally employed, fundamental practices of ill-treatment had not changed.[108] These allegations were seriously considered by the European Commission on Torture and the Human Rights Committee of the United Nations. In short, the broad commitment to end ill-treatment had not been adopted in the day-to-day practices of the state on an ongoing basis. This has also been the experience in respect of protection for the right to life in the jurisdiction. The thrust of the United Kingdom's approach, in respect of violations associated with the conflict in Northern Ireland, reveals a distinct gap between a rhetoric that places a primacy on human rights and a reality that abuses them.

The narrative which the state has told about the use of force faces a great challenge with the incorporation of the European Convention into domestic law. As this chapter has affirmed, given the overall number of controversial lethal force deaths in Northern Ireland, few cases have actually come to the European Court and the European Commission. In creating greater accessibility to positive rights, the incorporation process may signify that larger numbers of victims will seek to utilise their local courts to assert their rights and demand remedy for violations.

Given the traditional hostility of the Northern Ireland courts to claims arising from lethal force deaths, incorporation poses extraordinary judicial challenges. Judges there will have to adapt to entirely new methods of interpretation.[109] The convention is drafted in broad and general terms, and calls to be understood in a generous manner, giving individuals the full measure of the fundamental rights and freedoms contained within it. In addition, domestic legislation does not come in isolation. With it comes a jurisprudence of almost forty years, enhancing and extending the rights of persons at the European Court and European Commission. There are interesting times ahead, as Northern Ireland's judges take on the thinking developed in decisions like Gibraltar and apply it to cases which imply similar circumstances and the application of the European legal standard on the taking of life by the state.[110] The shift to thinking in terms of rights protection in a jurisdiction defined by the systematic denial of rights will be momentous. If, as the Good Friday Agreement portends, Northern Ireland produces its own Bill of Rights, the boundaries may be stretched further, as home-grown solutions to the particular experiences of rights violation in the jurisdiction are transformed into unique protective structures.[111]

5

The interface between the laws of war and the right to life in Northern Ireland

Thus far, this work has assumed that the United Kingdom is operating its domestic law and practice within the framework of, and with reference to, its international human rights treaty obligations. Specifically, this has meant that where the United Kingdom's practices have been examined, both the stated and implicit reference point has been the standards of practice presumed to apply to a state in peacetime. This assumes a point of normalised departure for the state, albeit that the jurisdiction under consideration has been in a state of permanent emergency since its inception in 1921. Indeed, as the historical examination in chapter 1 has pointed out, Northern Ireland has never operated within the liberal democratic model, with the emergency simply a minor aberration in an otherwise functional society. Rather, as a separate political entity within the United Kingdom, it has operated as an undemocratic religio-national ethnocracy where institutional and political structures were operated to the exclusion of the substate's minority.[1] With the imposition of direct rule in 1972, normal political functionality was not created in Northern Ireland. Instead, normality remained suspended in the jurisdiction and the law and politics of the abnormal have regulated political and social life. Thus, at this closing juncture, a more radical examination point is proposed for the characterisation of both lethal force and the conflict itself in the jurisdiction.

This final chapter examines the possibilities for overlap between the laws of war and human rights laws in situations of permanent emergency, specifically in the context of Northern Ireland. Some argue that only one legal regime can apply to a situation of emergency. However, a

THE INTERFACE BETWEEN THE LAWS OF WAR AND THE RIGHT TO LIFE IN NI   219

strong case can be made for the alternative view that in such emergency situations, the human rights regime, if looked at in isolation, may provide an inadequate analysis. This is because it is these very emergencies which effectively manipulate the derogation process to facilitate limited scrutiny on internal armed conflict and perpetuate the legitimacy of the state by the permanent imposition of extraordinary laws. Consequently, this chapter questions whether the conflict in Northern Ireland can be appropriately measured only within the confines of one legal regime. Instead we examine whether the overlapping legal norms of both international humanitarian law and human rights laws should operate simultaneously in such conflicts. Crucial to this analysis is the use of lethal force and section II closely monitors how this controversial practice is an effective yardstick on the status of conflict in emergency situations.

It is important to stress that the status of conflict issue is solely examined in the context of an ongoing armed conflict in Northern Ireland during the 1969–94 period. The applicability of armed conflict standards is necessarily changed by the August 1994 declaration of a complete cessation of military operations by PIRA, followed by the similar declaration by the Combined Loyalist Military Command two months later. The reinstatement of the republican ceasefire following the February 1996 Canary Wharf bombing in London, in tandem with the Good Friday Agreement, has made this discussion a reflective and historical one, rather than one which has a direct effect on the evaluation of current legal events in the jurisdiction. However, there are still areas where the application of the legal regime of international humanitarian law may be relevant. This would include such matters as decommissioning, the issue of truth and reconciliation in the peace-making process, and the contextualising of past human rights abuses within Northern Ireland.

I
De jure belli ac pacis[2]

In order to hone our understanding of the interrelationship between the laws of war and the human rights regime a more detailed understanding of international humanitarian law is needed. Until the Second World War the regulatory scope of the laws of war were firmly aimed at aligning the methods and means of warfare. Hague Law, codified first in 1899 at a meeting initiated by the Russian government to discuss matters of peace and war, sought to positively systematise the 'laws and customs of war on land'.[3] The proposal was based on a text drafted by an earlier international conference at Brussels in 1874, which had been agreed but was never made binding. This, in turn, was premised on the text of instructions prepared by Francis Lieber in 1863, following an order by the United States president, entitled 'Instructions for the Government of Armies of the United States in the Field'.[4] The development of Hague Law was punctuated with bursts of activity on specific areas, but remained piecemeal over the course of the following thirty years. In 1907, another conference adopted Convention (IX) Concerning Bombardment by Naval Forces in Time of War. Two years later, a conference in London succeeded in agreeing a Declaration Concerning the Laws of Naval War.[5]

Alongside the development of Hague Law was the embryonic evolution of Geneva Law, aimed at ensuring protection for those made most vulnerable by war. Drawing its inspiration from the work of Henry Dunant, whose witness of the misery and suffering caused at the Battle of Solferino in 1859 provoked a life-long commitment to assuage suffering in war.[6] Its first positive enunciation came in 1864, when a Diplomatic Conference in Geneva adopted the Convention for the Amelioration of the Condition of the Wounded in Armies in the Field. This convention had the following significant elements: recognition that ambulances and military hospitals were 'neutral' space, protected and respected by belligerents to conflict; that 'wounded and sick' combatants would be cared for; and the identification of the now broadly known Red Cross symbol of a red cross on a white background. As with Hague Law, the development of Geneva Law had a checkered history. Further treaties were signed in 1899 and 1906. The latter was notable, as it was the first document to deal with repression of violations and infractions in a legally binding international document.[7] Following the First World War, the most significant augmentation of Geneva Law came in 1929,[8] which sought to improve the treatment of the wounded and sick on land, and also saw a separate treaty on the treatment of prisoners of war.

Geneva Law has been characterised from its inception as a body of legal regulation focused upon the protection of vulnerable persons in times of conflict. Its greatest failure, during both the First and Second World Wars, was to make meaningful the paper protections for those defenceless persons caught up unwittingly in a conflict not of their making. By the end of the Second World War there was clear cognisance that not only was the existing legal framework regulating the waging of war inadequate to protect humanitarian needs but that the callous disregard for enforcing pre-existing norms was in urgent need of remedy.

The response was agreement for four new conventions at the 1949 Diplomatic Conference – the 1949 Geneva Conventions. It is evident that the experience of the war substantially affected, in the words of one commentator, 'not only the scope, substantive content and procedural safeguards included in the Conventions but also the system for repression of those Conventions'.[9] In short, there was a concerted desire to put in place a system of law that would prevent such violations from occurring at all in situations of war. What was unique about the 1949 conventions was the attempt to add flesh to the bare humanitarian provisions that had been emerging to guard certain classes of protected persons from the end of the nineteenth century. Second, the creation of a 'grave breaches' system[10] was the attempt (ultimately ill-fated) to establish a functioning mechanism of accountability which distinguished between various forms of humanitarian violations when they took place. Finally, the conventions made the first and controversial attempt to express provisions relating to the conduct of parties during civil internal strife, in Common Article 3 to the four conventions.[11]

Common Article 3 is the sole article of the 1949 conventions which specifically addresses the problem of noninternational armed conflicts. It has been variously described as the 'mini-convention' or the 'convention within a convention', providing minimal rules which parties to an internal armed conflict are 'bound to apply as a minimum'. The opening paragraph to the article states:

> In the case of armed conflict not of an international character occurring in the territory of one of the High Contracting Parties, each Party to the conflict shall be bound to apply, as a minimum, the following provisions . . .

The article contains the lowest threshold of both application and standards and is intended to provide a minimum criterion of protection to persons not participating in hostilities during internal armed conflicts.[12] The article protects those classes of people deemed most vulnerable when conflict occurs. Protection is given on the basis of nondiscrimination and nonpartisanship, many of these principles being derived from the then embryonic human rights regimes, and indeed, ahead of them.[13] Its protections are to ensure that violence to life and person is prohibited;[14] that outrages against personal dignity, specifically humiliating and degrading treatment, are forbidden;[15] that legal processes enforcing adverse consequences upon persons are carried out by regularly constituted courts affording recognised due process rights;[16] and finally, that all those wounded and sick in conflict be cared for.[17]

The nature of warfare envisioned and regulated at the 1949 conference drew its inspiration directly from the traumatic and widespread hostilities of the Second World War. War was conceptualised as the privilege of sovereign states, harking back to historical cycles of behaviour when armies marched to distant fields to attack one another. The Second World War, with its technological revolution, brought the monstrosity of war to cities and civilian populations, and forever changed the perception of the ability to distance war. No longer were societies able to remain aloof from the experience of war. Unfortunately, the experience of the Second World War did not change the perception that war was the business of nations and external to them.

The patterns of war from 1949 onwards radically diverged from the concept of 'internationalised' war. A combination of politically aware international liberation movements in countries remaining under colonial domination, the widening of group consciousness on the right to self-determination, and a rights vocabulary with which to confront the practices of racist regimes, gave new authenticity to old cycles of internal revolt and revolution. Post-1950, the empirical reality of the practice of war was entirely removed from the laws that regulated conflict. This meant that protection for victims of internal conflicts was virtually nonexistent, or little applied. It also meant that the laws of war were outdated and irrelevant, unable to structure and limit the excesses that aggression breeds.

In response to fears of irrelevancy and concern for protection of victims, the International Committee of the Red Cross (ICRC)[18] requested the Swiss Federal Council to convene a Diplomatic Conference on the Reaffirmation and Development of International Humanitarian Law Applicable in Armed Conflict. The conference held four sessions between 1974 and 1977 to study two draft Additional Protocols,[19] which had been prepared by the ICRC after several years of private and official consultations with governments and others.[20] The final agreement on two protocols saw the traditionally separate bodies of Hague Law and Geneva Law merge, a recognition that the mode of armed conflict directly affects the conditions of its victims.[21] The creation of two protocols was a testament to the lack of consensus on one instrument which would serve all armed conflicts, on the grounds that humanitarian principles are equally vital and applicable irrespective of the international or noninternational character of the hostilities taking place.

A
PROTOCOL I

Protocol I extends the criteria and status of international armed conflicts to specifically enumerated internal conflicts, deemed 'internationalised' by certain inherent characteristics. Fashioning these 'privileged' conflicts was a direct corollary to the strong advocacy by developing nations for whom 'wars of national liberation' and other forms of internal conflict were a defining feature of state creation and consolidation. Article 1 (4) of the protocol sets out these favoured conflicts as follows:

> The situations referred to in [Common Article 2 of the Geneva Conventions of 1949] include armed conflicts in which people are fighting against colonial domination and alien occupation and against racist regimes in the exercise of their right to self-determination, as enshrined in the Charter of the UN and the Declaration of Principles of International Law concerning Friendly Relations ... among States in accordance with the Charter of the UN.[22]

Once a conflict is deemed to fall within these confines, all the benefits of international conflict status and combatant standing are given.

B
PROTOCOL II

Discussion of Protocol II is a crucial part of any analysis about the regulation of internal conflict. Protocol II was a compromise document: neither its proponents nor adversaries were entirely satisfied with it. The traditional view of Protocol II is that it 'develops and supplements Article 3 common to the Conventions of 1949'.[23] Such a description belies much of the controversy which surrounded its negotiation. The Diplomatic Conferences were split into two camps on the subject of the appropriate field of application for the protocol. One camp, whose approach was embodied in the ICRC draft for Protocol II, favoured that its scope be limited to basic humanitarian provisions and that it should be broadly applicable to a wide variety of armed conflicts.[24] This approach was strongly resisted by a number of governmental delegations which regarded a protocol with such a low threshold as an unacceptable limitation on the sovereignty of states.[25] In the end, the agreed document sets a high threshold of application. Agreement was finally reached to have the protocol apply to all noninternational armed conflicts which take place in the territory of a contracting party between its armed forces and dissident armed forces, which, under responsible command, exercise such control over a part of its territory as to enable them to carry out sustained and concerted military operations and to implement the protocol.[26] It lies somewhere on the continuum between Protocol I requirements and the stipulation of Common Article 3 applicability.

II
Contextualising conflict in Northern Ireland

Northern Ireland has never functioned as an active, pluralistic and participatory democracy. It is a jurisdiction functioning on the normalisation of the politically abnormal; its political life has been defined by an entrenched emergency. The United Kingdom has been in persistent derogation from its human rights obligations under the European Convention and International Covenant on Civil and Political Rights. Extraordinary law has become a norm of legal regulation.

Civil liberties advocates have traditionally viewed the application of conflict rules as a move away from enforceable contractual obligations voluntarily assumed by states when they sign international human rights treaties. They argue that humanitarian law protects fewer rights, that protected rights have less content, and that there are no meaningful enforcement procedures which bring states to task when they fail to comply with humanitarian standards. These are cogent arguments. Nonetheless they ignore some important aspects of the value of humanitarian law. First, that significant aspects of human rights law are drawn from humanitarian standards. Second, that the regulatory laws of conflict impose normative standards that are observed as a matter of convention between states and within states (the latter undoubtedly to a lesser degree). Third, that humanitarian law contains a different conception of the locus of power within and between states. The value and the limitation of human rights law is that the state is presumed legitimate and the sole source of power responsible for enforcing rights commitments. Humanitarian law, seen particularly in its recent developments under the Additional Protocols to the Geneva Conventions,[27] does not assume this straitjacket. The laws of war explicitly recognise that enforcement and violation capacity is individual, both government and opposition based – the insurgent is as bound to adherence as is the lawful government.

The categorisation of the conflict and the use of international humanitarian law do not necessarily oust the jurisdiction of human rights law. In conflicts such as that in Northern Ireland arguably both standards can and do apply. The potential linkage of the two systems of law and policy is most probable in situations of entrenched or permanent emergency, where the dividing lines between a low-intensity conflict and an extended emergency have become blurred. Thus, finding that the minimum standards of the laws of war are potentially applicable should not lead us to the conclusion that the state is not bound by its human rights obligations under international law.[28]

A number of clear legal principles sustain this position. First, the existence of a strong overlap between the 1949 Geneva Conventions (Common Article 3 in particular) and the substantive human rights norms contained in international human rights treaties. That is to say, that the minimal thresholds of each are strongly reflective of one another, rather than exclusionary of one another, and have been recently interpreted as such by international judicial opinion.[29] Second, all the international human rights treaties to which the United Kingdom is bound, and which are applicable to Northern Ireland, hold that measures taken by the state in time of emergency should not be inconsistent with 'a State's other obligations under international legal obligations'. This implies that the application of human rights standards *per se* should not be taken to infer that the state's actions in a situation of emergency cannot be evaluated by the standards of international humanitarian law. Inversely, it also means that applicability of 'other standards', including humanitarian law, does not banish human rights norms and duties.

It is possible that both of these bodies of law can complement and enhance one another in situations of protracted conflict. However, states have remained wary of applying humanitarian law and thus foreclosed any reflection on the possibilities of dual application. This is in large part because of the perceived effect that the importation of humanitarian law might have upon the status and actions of both state and nonstate actors in a low-intensity armed conflict.

The relevance of international humanitarian law to Northern Ireland lies principally in the process of categorising the conflict. That categorisation has an overt political content, as it involves a judgement on the status and internal regulation of the jurisdiction, which is legally determined to be part of a sovereign state, in the period under examination in this book.[30] This is not a problem unique to Northern Ireland; it is a persistent problem encountered by international humanitarian law – the unwillingness of states to accept that the laws of war are applicable to conflicts taking place in their own jurisdiction. The reasons for this are invariably the violation of state sovereignty and the legitimacy problems consequently created for state responses to internal threat. The application of the laws of war to internal conflict can arguably have the effect of legitimising the actions of insurgents, removing the state's ability to deal with them as criminal, and internationalising internal disorder.

Categorising the conflict in Northern Ireland inevitably raises uncomfortable questions about the legitimacy and status of such organisations as PIRA and loyalist paramilitary groups during the 1969–94 period. While humanitarian law provokes discussion of such issues, this is neither its sole nor primary function. Humanitarian law provides rules of behaviour by which one can measure the actions of state and nonstate actors in a situation of conflict, in order to judge whether certain fundamental norms of humane behaviour are being observed. As such, it may provide a valuable mechanism to evaluate the fluid conflict situation which existed in Northern Ireland, where the legal status of the situation was historically fudged by political unwillingness to categorise.

Political ambiguity has fed into judicial evaluation of the appropriate standards by which to judge actions taken by the state in response to conflict. This is illustrated by judicial approaches to the use of lethal force by the security forces. One disturbing aspect of this is seen in the judgments arising from criminal prosecution of members of the security forces. A notable feature has been the misapplication of legal standards and terminology. One manifestation was the use of such phrases in these cases as 'quasi-war situation', 'armed insurrection', and 'hostile territory'. Such military language became a means of contextualising the use of lethal force. However, it has served only to confuse and blur the application of appropriate legal standards. Applying humanitarian law standards to judge the use of force is one method of clarifying the precise nature and context of many lethal force deaths and linking that factual evaluation with the political crisis in Northern Ireland.

Common Article 3 of the Geneva Conventions provides the most likely source of humanitarian law applicability for Northern Ireland. One of the questions to be addressed here is whether the Northern Ireland conflict reaches its threshold of applicability. The Nicaragua judgment by the International Court of Justice makes clear that the existence of a Common Article 3 conflict is not dependent on recognition or confirmation by the state.[31] Very simply, this means that the British government need not have asserted that they recognise the implementation of Common Article 3 for it to be applicable to Northern Ireland. Common Article 3 is applicable without state acquiescence. This is the theory. In reality, there is unlikely to be an adversarial legal context in which such a practical determination is made by a neutral third party, and recognition of status remains reliant on states being prepared to politically acknowledge the existence of armed conflicts within their borders.

Existing guidelines on the applicability of Common Article 3 status are mostly concerned with the concept of conflict threshold. Thus, threshold of violence is central to defining the scale of conflict. In Northern Ireland the intermittent nature of the violence has been a mechanism for declaring that it is inappropriate to invoke international humanitarian law standards. Violence in the conflict peaked in 1972 with a total of 470 deaths, whereas in the 1980s the highest number of conflict-related deaths recorded was 101 in 1981, the year of the republican hunger strikes.[32] Though the numbers of deaths resulting from the conflict seem low in absolute terms, relative to the total population base they are extremely significant. Further, the perception that overall levels of violence, resulting from the conflict, are low correlate to two additional factors. First, the sophisticated level of medical care in the jurisdiction, related to the site of the conflict in a western welfare state with accompanying standards of therapeutic rehabilitation and medical professionalism. By contrast, other internal conflicts in the post-Second World War era have manifested themselves largely in the stagnant political economics of former colonies, with neither the resources nor institutional structures to ameliorate suffering and prevent deaths through refined medical intervention. Thus, fatalities in the Northern Ireland conflict have been curbed by quick access to modern medical supervision, which has had a bearing on the perceptions of the overall levels of violence.

Second, and more controversially, comparative internal conflicts in other jurisdictions have been identified with small scale civil wars where no rules of combatancy at all apply – in short, where claims of ethnic political entitlement have devolved into mass terrorism, as the recent experiences of Bosnia and Rwanda attest. Here, as Hans Magnus Enzensberger explains:

> There is no longer any need to legitimize your actions. Violence has freed itself from ideology ... When they [the combatants] talk about a right to self-determination, they mean their right to determine who will be allowed to survive on their territory, and who will not. Their principle concern is the extermination of the worthless.[33]

The targeting of violence at state agents and their institutional structures has meant that, comparatively, the overall levels of violence for the jurisdiction may appear low.[34] Furthermore, such practices facilitated a containment of the conflict as a political matter and the appearance of relative normality in a highly abnormal situation.

Brendan O'Leary and John McGarry have undertaken groundbreaking empirical work on auditing the conflict in Northern Ireland. As they point out:

> Nearly three thousand dead may seem a relatively small toll in a conflict ... However, scale matters. The population of Northern Ireland in the 1981 census, itself disrupted by violence and abstention, was estimated as 1,488,077. If the equivalent ratio of victims to population had been produced in Great Britain in the same period, some 100,000 people would have died, and if a similar level of political violence had taken place the number of fatalities in the USA would have been over 500,000, or about ten times the number of Americans killed in the Vietnam war.[35]

The authors also undertake a comparative analysis of total deaths from internal political violence in liberal democracies. In this process they reveal the astonishing scale of the conflict in Northern Ireland and conclude:

Northern Ireland was by far the most internally politically violent of the recognizably continuous liberal democracies during the period 1948–77, both in absolute numbers killed and relatively, as indicated by the per capita death-toll.[36]

The scale of conflict is all the more concentrated if one acknowledges that it occurred in the context of largely amicable relations between the relevant neighbouring states, and in the absence of superpower ideological rivalries during the Cold War.[37] In evaluating the loss of life in this matter one is led to the unavoidable conclusion that the threshold tests for the application of international humanitarian law may be appropriate to apply to an analysis of the Northern Ireland conflict in the 1969–94 period. Equally, it may then be difficult to deny the existence of an armed conflict situation based on the threshold of violence test.

Violence has been a persistent feature of daily life in the jurisdiction, aimed both at persons and property, distinguishable from ordinary crime in its targeting and methodology. Security costs indicate the escalation of the violence from 1969. In 1969–70, expenditure on law, order and protective services stood at £15 million; by 1983 this cost had risen to £369 million.[38]

The low-intensity nature of the violence is not *per se* a reason to exclude the applicability of Common Article 3. Consistent low-intensity violence over a sustained period of time, with the nature of armed confrontation aimed at the commercial, economic and political functioning of the state, can factually amount to an armed conflict situation. The peace negotiation in El Salvador, brokered between the insurgent Frente Farabundo Martí para la Liberación (FMLN) and the government and premised on the applicability of Protocol II, aptly demonstrates the point.[39]

One issue to be resolved is whether violence can objectively be defined as amounting to armed conflict, as opposed to merely low-level societal violence. One means to measure this is to reconceptualise the test on threshold of violence. Currently, the examination is based on an evaluation of a conflict having reached the required intensity at a given moment of inspection. This test amounts to a requirement that the numbers of persons killed or the destruction of property on any given day of conflict be absolutely consistent throughout the conflict experience. The reconceptualisation requires a horizontal evaluation, whereby intensity of violence is measured over time by a lateral method. For example, measuring the number of persons killed in relation to the population density over the cumulative twenty-five-year period. Thus, a cumulative measurement of violence over time may indicate that the threshold requirement is being met by the constant disruption to state order by organised political violence.

A

THE ARMED CONFLICT CONCEPT AS IT APPLIES TO NORTHERN IRELAND

The notion of 'armed conflict' is indispensable to the application of international humanitarian law. The concept invokes three elements. First, the necessity of collective as opposed to individual violence. Second, the communal impact of violence on the fabric of society. Finally, the nature of the military campaign waged both by state and nonstate actors. Common Article 3 unequivocally sets out that its provisions are applicable only to parties organisationally capable of imposing military discipline to prevent violations of its provisions.

The policy of criminalisation in Northern Ireland has politically defined the violence of paramilitary organisations as deviant criminal behaviour, to be processed through modified criminal courts. Nonetheless, the political nature of the violence is acknowledged in the Prevention of Terrorism Act, which defines terrorism as 'the use of violence for political ends'. The scheduled offences of the Emergency Provisions Act equally distinguish a certain class of offences from the criminal norm by isolating the trial of their perpetrators to special courts. The isolation of politically motivated offences as a classification matter does not *per se* amount to a recognition of armed conflict. However, inherent in the notion of traditional armed conflict in humanitarian law is a political content or objective to be achieved through the use of military means. Severe modification of the criminal justice system and the constitutional framework is indicative that the violence experienced by society is not simply categorised as merely criminal or a transient escalation of low-level internal disturbances.

Some delegates of the ICRC have argued that the point at which the military extends long-term assistance to the civilian power indicates a threshold point signifying an armed conflict situation.[40] In Northern Ireland the army has been employed for this function since August 1969. The British government would doubtless argue (with other states in chorus) that the right to use the army internally is a constitutional prerogative, used historically as a means of restoring order and having no implications for the status of conflict in Northern Ireland.[41] This argument ignores the long-term nature of the commitment of military forces, the role of specialist units in active counter-insurgency and the militarisation of conflict between PIRA and the armed forces. Yet there is no authoritative statement in which any United Kingdom government has unilaterally and unequivocally declared that Common Article 3 is applicable to the jurisdiction. Such evidence as exists from official practice is disparate and scanty. However, there are a number of factors which may be invoked to indicate that Common Article 3 is a relevant standard within which to evaluate the Northern Ireland conflict in the 1969–94 period.

Prior to the current round of troubles in Northern Ireland, members of the IRA, when engaging in acts of violence against the state, were not consistently charged, as might be expected, with ordinary criminal offences. The case of eight members of the IRA, arrested after a raid on Omagh barracks in 1954, is instructive. They were not indicted under the Special Powers Act, but under section 3 of the Felony Treason Act 1848 with 'compassing and intending to levy war against her Majesty the Queen . . . in order to put ferie [sic] and constraint and to intimidate and overcome both Houses of Parliament of the United Kingdom'.[42] This language and choice of indictment is indicative of a perception of the IRA as insurgents rather than mere criminals. This language was not consistently used, but the tangled approach is illustrative of a possible range of legal classification for the 1950s conflict and thereafter.

More recently, the British army itself has used Common Article 3 as the standard by which to regulate certain actions in Northern Ireland. The Parker Report, which investigated allegations of ill-treatment aimed at detainees during the internment process, found that the basis for interrogations was the 'Joint Military Directive on Military Operations', a document which draws its provisions literally from Common Article 3.[43] Section 5 of the directive specifically states that the broad treatment of persons during the civil disturbances is laid down in Common Article 3 of the Geneva Conventions. The European Court of Human Rights, when examining the merits of *Ireland v. United Kingdom*,[44] and considering whether interrogation practices breached Article 3 of the convention, examined the applicability of the Geneva Conventions. Although it was stated that the 'main provisions' of these conventions did not directly apply to detainees in Northern Ireland, the issue of potential applicability of Common Article 3 was left open. This open-ended approach is balanced by the decision of the European Commission when it examined the merits of a claim by applicant prisoners who were members of PIRA during the dirty protest, which argued that they be exempted from ordinary prison rules.[45] The commission concluded that no right of special treatment accrued to them under international law.

Incarceration, whether post-trial or as a result of detention without trial, plays a significant role in defining conflict status in Northern Ireland. Between 9 August and 14 December 1971, 1,576 persons were interned under the Special Powers Act in Northern Ireland.[46] Internees were allowed to wear their own clothes and were not required to work.[47] These are not unusual provisions, given that those detained were not convicted of any offences and the assumption that internment was a short-term solution to an immediate political problem. What is interesting, as the authors of *Law and State* point out, is that the internees perceived themselves as prisoners of war, and this was a perception shared by the Catholic community as a whole.[48] The Gardiner Committee noted that during the internment phase men in camps were free to organise militarily within prison confines.[49]

In the militarisation phase of the conflict, the 'special category' prisoner emerged. Persons convicted and sentenced to more than nine months' imprisonment for politically motivated crimes enjoyed the privileges of a regime free of work and prison duties. Analysing the status of Irish republican prisoners, Clive Walker notes that their claims to preferential treatment were neither 'consistent nor unambiguous'.[50] At certain times they laid historic claim to the status of prisoners of war; at others, they merely sought a recognition of political status. Primarily they sought to be distinguished from 'ordinary convicted prisoners'.[51] Special category status was phased out from March 1976. Its creation and short tenure was pointed to as *de facto* recognition that prisoners engaged in politically motivated acts were distinguishable from their ordinary criminal counterparts.

Republican prisoners refused to accept the new designation of normal criminal status within the prison system after 1976. This refusal led to the republican hunger strikes of 1981. Since the ending of the hunger strikes the demands of these prisoners have largely been met within the confines of the prison system.[52] Equally, there is no denial in official circles that both republican and loyalist prisoners operate military structures within Northern Ireland prisons. Ongoing negotiations take place between state officials and prisoners to ensure that the prison regime will not become a political flash point. The early release of prisoners almost completed under the terms of the Good Friday Agreement manifests that a unique class of prisoner has been associated with this conflict, and that their position is a critical component of the transitionary process.[53]

Despite this diplomatic agreement and internal resolution to the thorny problem of political standing in prisons, there is no recognition, either in the jurisprudence of domestic courts or international courts, of political or special status.[54] The European Commission has, in fact, upheld the discretionary right to states to impose a stricter prison regime on convicted terrorists on national security grounds.[55] Nevertheless, it should also be noted that the ICRC visits Northern Ireland prisons where paramilitary prisoners are held. This occurs through the United Kingdom accepting the good offices of the organisation. The Red Cross has taken no public position on the status of these visits, or what legal status it attributed to the prisoners being visited. The fact that such visits occur, however, distinguishes the prison population in Northern Ireland from the prison community in the United Kingdom as a whole.

What should be noted as a general matter is that humanitarian law application should not be seen as a fixed undertaking. If one critique of the human rights regime is its limited capacity to acknowledge a certain range of political and legal categories, simply replacing it with another straitjacket will not ease the difficulty of accommodating diverse situations of crisis. It is entirely possible for a situation to fall within the demands of the humanitarian law regime at one point, and to move out of it at a later date. Thus, it might be argued, for example, that in the militarisation phase of the conflict during 1969–74, Northern Ireland was categorically experiencing (as an objective assessment) an armed conflict situation of a Protocol II type, and that in the normalisation phase during 1975–80, the threshold shifted to a Common Article 3 model. What this chapter proposes is a more realistic assessment of the capacity of a crisis situation to move up and down within applicable internal legal frameworks and to move across differing legal regimes. This also inevitably leads to the finding that there will be times when dual regimes are applicable to crisis situations, allowing both humanitarian law and human rights law to apply simultaneously.

A more problematic evaluation is whether or not PIRA or other para-military organisations can structurally and operationally be defined as combatants for the purposes of Common Article 3. A recent develop-ment has been the decision of Amnesty International and Human Rights Watch to use the standards of the laws of war, and specifically Common Article 3, to assess human rights violations perpetrated by these organisations.[56] Unlike Protocol I, which sets out clear guidelines to establish combatancy, there are no such criteria articulated for Common Article 3. In fact, any mention of combatancy status is notice-ably excluded from the language of the provision. PIRA is known to operate in a cellular structure, with defined chains of command and hier-archy.[57] Further, the steady trickle of armaments procured by the orga-nisation from the United States in the 1970s, followed by the procurement of extensive weaponry via Libya in the 1980s, illustrate the extent to which the organisation was capable of sustaining a low-inten-sity conflict with the state for an indefinite time.[58] The organisation moved from the battalion structure of an old-fashioned guerrilla organi-sation, which attempted to emulate the state military apparatus, to a tightly knit cell-based movement in the 1970s. The emergence of the Combined Loyalist Military Command in the early 1990s emphasises the militarisation of parallel organisations. For the purposes of humani-tarian law applicability the most pertinent issue in evaluating such orga-nisations is their capacity to impose and maintain humanitarian standards. Their uniform practices of targeting civilians, persistent atrocities and a failure to apply the rules of distinction differentiating civilians from mili-tary targets, make such claims weak. Nevertheless, the conversation on combatancy status is not closed off because of these transgressions, but rather made more splintered and muddy.

B

SET-PIECE KILLINGS AND HUMANITARIAN LAW

The context of life-taking in Northern Ireland may indicate that a *de facto* situation of armed conflict has existed in the jurisdiction. The emergence of the set-piece confrontation; the lack of emphasis on arrest and due process enforcement; the attitude of many republican families that legal remedies are unnecessary because death on 'active service' connotes military death in a war situation; and the implied combatancy relationship between specialist forces and the paramilitary organisations all emphasise that many lethal force incidents are far removed from the criminalisation model of law enforcement in Northern Ireland. Judicial responses also reflect this anomaly. The trials of soldiers and police officers, charged with offences arising from the use of lethal force, show an ambiguous attitude by members of the judicial branch to the conflict situation. As the gatekeepers of the criminalisation model of conflict control, judges nonetheless have stated that they believe the situation in Northern Ireland to be akin to a war scenario.[59] The actions of state actors when they use force excessively are judged not infrequently by this standard. Judges in other jurisdictions faced with extraditing individuals to Northern Ireland have made the same judgment. In the *Quinn* case, United States prosecutors seeking extradition argued that the British government's failure to follow identification procedures under British law were 'excusable because there was a "war" situation in Northern Ireland in which lives were at stake'.[60] The fraught working-out of the extradition process between the United Kingdom and the Irish Republic reflects similar tensions, as the Irish Supreme Court has continued to invoke the political exception doctrine.[61]

Common Article 3 represents a minimum yardstick to measure the standards by which actors in a conflict treat those uninvolved with the conflict but directly affected by it. Protocols I and II Additional to the Geneva Conventions are two higher standards by which the status of a conflict and those engaged in it can be measured. Are either of these two instruments applicable to Northern Ireland? During 1969–94 neither protocol had been ratified by either the United Kingdom government or the Irish government, so their value in regulating the conflict was limited, aside from those portions that have attained customary status. The British government announced on 22 October 1993 that it would ratify the two protocols;[62] it has now ratified Protocol I but has not substantively moved towards similar progress on Protocol II.[63]

Protocol I is unlikely to be applicable to the Northern Ireland situation. The conflict does not sit easily with any of the three favoured conflict types endorsed by the Diplomatic Conference which created the protocols. While the republican paramilitaries claim to be fighting a war of illegal occupation,[64] mere declaration of occupation does not satisfy the standards of the protocol. The Diplomatic Conference's compromise on privileged conflict status effectively mandates that the insurgent group should be recognised as a liberation movement both regionally and internationally. This has not been the case for any paramilitary organisation in the jurisdiction. There has been a marked lack of external support for the claims of occupation and liberation war. Northern Ireland has no series of United Nations resolutions designating its internal situation to fall within the scope of the protocol by consensus of the international community.

Application of Protocol I depends on a number of prerequisites being satisfied. These include conflict type, control of subordinates within the relevant military structures, and threshold of violence. While control of territory by insurgent parties is not explicitly codified in Protocol I, it has nonetheless been 'read-in' by many observers as a necessary element for concluding armed conflict status. The British government made it clear at the time it signed and entered reservations to the protocols, that it viewed the Northern Ireland situation as outside the scope of Protocol I in particular. Evan Luard MP stated in the House of Commons in December 1977 that:

> Neither in Northern Ireland nor in any other part of the United Kingdom is there a situation which meets the criteria laid down for the application of either Protocol. Nor is there any terrorist organisation operating within the United Kingdom that fulfils the requirements which a national liberation movement must meet in order to be entitled to claim rights under Protocol I, There is, therefore, no question of any of the provisions of either Protocol benefiting the IRA or any others who may carry out terrorist activities in peacetime.[65]

Laying political considerations of territory aside, the key element for combatant status under Protocol I is a factual issue, which is expressed as a command link rather than as a political issue of recognition.[66] Protocol I explicitly demands that insurgents belong to a party involved in the conflict.[67] The *Kassem* case creates the novel possibility that a liberal interpretation of 'belong' allows that insurgents can be granted prisoner of war status, even if the legitimacy of insurgency is unrecognised by the state.[68] This reconfirms the proposition that recognition is not dependent on political will. The command structure of PIRA is well documented, and increasing sophisticated structuring of parallel loyalist organisations is also apparent. On this basis there is a reasonable argument to present these organisations as *prima facie* qualifying for insurgency status, though it is more likely that the republican paramilitaries would ultimately qualify than their loyalist counterparts. However, this isolated prerequisite is not sufficient on its own to qualify the conflict as an armed conflict, without a corresponding territorial evaluation.

Both the Irish and British governments have accepted Northern Ireland as the appropriate unit for the exercise of the right to self-determination based on the principle of consent.[69] As the Good Friday Agreement and subsequent referendums firmly established, there will be no change in the legal status of the jurisdiction unless such changes are premised on a majority democratic vote by referendum.[70] In short, the historical claim of alien occupation, or a *de facto* war of national liberation, is likely to be dismissed in the Northern Ireland context.

Nonextension of Protocol I status is linked to the historical and diplomatic context of the 1974 Diplomatic Conference, where its text was largely agreed.[71] The conference was dominated by Western state demands that the principle of self-determination enunciated in the UN Charter be legitimately exercised through the use of force. That political dynamic was manipulated by newly emerging African states, despite the concerns of Western nations about the conceptual and practical difficulties of superimposing internal conflicts over existing internationalised structures. The political deal to temper both sides was to limit the extension of the international laws of war to three particularly defined contexts. This prevented (in Western eyes) self-serving interpretations of ill-defined criteria, which could be made equally applicable to Western states. This express limitation has the effect, above all others, of precluding the Northern Ireland situation from slipping into the net of Protocol I.

As regards Protocol II, the discussion is a more complex one in respect of Northern Ireland. The primary limiting factor of Protocol II's applicability to the jurisdiction is the requirement that any dissident armed forces exercise such control over a part of the territory as to enable them to carry out sustained military operations, thus activating armed conflict status. In Northern Ireland there has been some argument as to whether such areas as south Armagh were within the 'control' of PIRA.[72] The view has been advanced that the building of numerous watchtowers on the hilltops of the region bordering the Irish Republic throughout the 1980s, to which soldiers were ferried into and out of by military helicopter, was a response to the fear that a claim might be made for loss of ground control, thereby implicating the activation of the laws of war. The army continued to operate in the region, both prior to and after the ceasefire commitments.

A more pertinent question is whether or not effective control was exercised by PIRA in limiting the capacity of the state, by forcing its agents to limit their mode of operation in the area. International humanitarian law has by and large focused on the issue of control of territory in terms of actual physical presence, limitation of access, and influence on the capacity of state civil interaction. It is arguable that in situations such as that in Northern Ireland the focus should be on whether the state exercises *effective control*, This was questionable in certain urban and rural locations in the jurisdiction (Tyrone, west Belfast and south Armagh are the obvious examples), where normal community policing was effectively suspended, alternative mechanisms for social control such as paramilitary punishment shootings replaced law enforcement, and the social order was partially controlled by paramilitary organisations. Furthermore, throughout the 1980s it seems that in south Armagh, the army felt it unsafe for its personnel to travel overland through parts of the county even in armoured vehicles. This may suggest that in parts of Northern Ireland *effective control* was ceded by the military to paramilitary organisations.

Under Protocol II the test for control of territory is not an abstract one. It seems only to require that the insurgent group be capable of carrying out sustained and concerted military operations and enforcing the rules contained in the protocol. Thus, two questions arise. First, can it be amply demonstrated that the military exercised incomplete or partial control of some of the territory of Northern Ireland? Second, during 1969–94, were paramilitary organisations carrying out sustained and concerted military operations relational to their effective control of the areas yielded by the state? If the answers to both questions are positive, then significant consequences arise for the classification of conflict in Northern Ireland during this period.

III
If humanitarian law were applicable, what would be the effect on the right to life?

If international humanitarian law, and more specifically Common

Article 3, were applicable to Northern Ireland there would be a direct effect on the status of the right to life in the jurisdiction, in both legal and practical terms. However, Tom Hadden has argued that, in general, there would be no effect from such application:

> It would appear from this that even if common Article 3 were applicable to some aspects of the conflict in Northern Ireland it would be unlikely to affect the legitimacy of the operations of the security forces or of members of dissident paramilitary groups. Both would remain subject to the relevant domestic law.[73]

There can be no quibbling about the coexistence and continued preeminence of domestic legal standards when Common Article 3 applies. However, there can be disagreement with the assessment that there is no effect on the perceptions of state and insurgent legitimacy arising from its usage. The crux of current interpretations of the consequences for applying this article lies in understanding that it changes both perception and reality of conflict context, the behaviour of the actors to the conflict and the manner in which life is taken and protected.

Common Article 3 requires that those *hors de combat* be protected from unnecessary violence and targeting. In practice this means that no such duty of care is necessarily exercised for combatants. No distinction is made in humanitarian law between the part-time combatant and the full-time combatant. The principle of distinction in humanitarian law requires parties to a conflict to distinguish *only* between civilian population and combatants, and civilian objects (such as hospitals) and military objectives of winning the war, accordingly directing operations only against military objectives. The principle of distinction was the customary basis for the codification of the Hague Law and the Geneva Law, the principle itself becoming part of conventional international law via Article 48 of Protocol I.[74] While some moves have been made towards subdividing the civilian category more minutely,[75] proposals for creating a 'quasi-civilian' population were vigorously opposed by most international legal scholars, most notably Fritz Kalshoven, who warned of the danger of approaching the 'slippery slope'.[76]

In a Common Article 3 armed conflict, the killing of an unarmed combatant, even if not immediately engaged in military activity, is legally unproblematic. The sole proviso is that he should not be killed by the use of perfidy.[77] Perfidy is defined as 'inviting confidence with intent to betray it'. Furthermore, if an insurgent surrenders and is held in the power of the opposing side, he must be treated humanely until his status as prisoner of war or otherwise is decided by due process mechanisms.[78]

Identifying combatants in situations of internal armed conflict presents particular problems. If a civilian opts to take a direct, even minor, part in hostilities, does he lose his civilian status? What exactly counts for the assessment of civilian status? Does throwing a petrol bomb at state forces mean that an individual has revoked his right to be deemed a civilian? Humanitarian law has no direct answers to these questions, particularly significant to the protection of life in internal conflict situation. Conflict law deems all those not combatants as civilians. The civilian is heavily dependent on the combatant to distinguish himself sufficiently from the civilian population in order that civilian status is clearly demonstrated and not subject to any ambiguity. In areas defined as 'hostile territory' a soldier could arguably state that all civilians pose the potential danger to behave as combatants, given a guerrilla, or insurgent, situation.

In a time of civil strife a government may feel itself most threatened by its own civilian population. At the lower end of that spectrum of vulnerability is the political instability faced by the Stormont government in 1968, with a civil rights movement demanding equal inclusion in the structures and governance of the state. At the top end is the waging of low-level warfare against the apparatus of the state as experienced in Northern Ireland since 1969. Sorting out who is the enemy in low-level internal conflict is never a clear-cut enterprise. It gives rise to a demonstrable lowering of life protection for a certain suspect class of citizens. The 'suspect' community, which already bears the brunt of wide powers of scrutiny, arrest and detention, exclusion and investigation, is by extension also the community most likely to be subject to the use of force and military action. Controlling the use of force against civilians is hampered by judicial perceptions of part-time combatancy. This is amply demonstrated by prosecutions for lethal force arising out of incidents which occurred in south Armagh. Judges have readily adopted the notion of a 'bad area' and 'hostile terrain'.[79] This is not only a geographical description but an indictment of the persons who inhabit a particular area. These contextualisations, accepted as valid criteria shaping a soldier's perceptions of an uninvolved civilian, create a lawful context within which force is exercised.

The corollary of this in Northern Ireland is that killing members of paramilitary organisations, if they are recognised as insurgents, is generally unproblematic if carried out in accordance with the laws of war. Additionally, the rules allow that a combatant need not be given a warning before being killed.[80] The problem lies in identifying breaches, such as refusal of quarter in fluid confrontation situations. There still exists disagreement as to whether engaging in 'unprivileged belligerency' (acting as a combatant while not in fact adhering to the standards for combatancy participation) is itself a war crime. However, it is firmly established that the killing of captured insurgents, by military forces of the state, without trial, is murder by humanitarian law standards.[81] If one were to accept that humanitarian law was applicable (dually or singly) in Northern Ireland, some lethal force killings of paramilitary members raise issues of humanitarian breach. An example is the *McElwaine* case,[82] where an inquest jury accepted in their finding of fact that a *coup de grâce* had been administered to the deceased, a member of PIRA on 'active service'.

It is worth noting at this point that the British army's 'Manual of Counter-Insurgency Warfare' recommends that ambushes only be set up where control of territory has been lost. If we reflect on the statistical evidence presented in the historical analysis of chapter 1, we note that from 1981 onwards set-piece killings became the primary context in which individuals were killed by the use of lethal force in Northern Ireland. Of the 50 persons killed in those incidents, 40 were members of paramilitary organisations. The vast majority of these deaths occurred in three geographical locations – Tyrone, Belfast and Armagh. Portions of these geographical locales clearly manifest characteristics of a loss of effective control by the state over territory. Evidently, there is a strong link between the loss of such control, or a tug-of-war over authority, and the prevalence of a certain type of counter-insurgency action leading to fatalities. Hence the intertwining between the manner in which death takes place in such territory and the status of the conflict itself.

The killing of civilians by the use of force can potentially breach humanitarian standards.[83] Some 178 civilians have been killed by the security forces in Northern Ireland between 1969 and 1994. The deaths have frequently occurred in situations where the taking of life was objectively unnecessary, deliberately provocative and not required by the excuse of military or police necessity. Assuming the applicability of humanitarian standards, it is arguable that Common Article 3 (1) (a), disallowing violence to life and person, has been persistently violated (by both state and nonstate actors). The regulation of internal armed conflict has not eroded the distinction between combatants and civilians, and there is no expanded legitimacy for the killing of civilians. The more problematic issue is whether civilian 'participants' in either state or insurgent administrative structures are the proper and lawful objects of attack. Though the question is open to discussion, humanitarian law does not seem to accord different treatment to different categories of noncombatant during the conduct of tactical military operations. The reasons for this are straightforward. The category into which noncombatants fall is not always readily apparent. Categorisation is a complex political judgement which the average soldier may be ill-equipped to make. To erode the civilian classification would be to undermine the humanitarian principles upon which humanitarian law was founded – to maximise protection for civilians.[84] In Northern Ireland, for the state and insurgent groups to adhere to humanitarian standards, their primary duty amounts to enforcing the principle of distinction.

An interesting though minor point illustrates where breach of humanitarian principles has been a consistent problem, arising from the use of force by state agents. During the militarisation phase of the conflict, not infrequently, limitations were placed on medical personnel and ambulances reaching and attending those killed or injured by the use of force.[85] Particular problems in this phase included ambulances being stopped, unnecessarily detained and, on occasion, searched while carrying gravely injured civilians to receive medical attention.

The death of Patrick Elliman on 3 July 1970 is illustrative of the kinds of practices which potentially implicate soldiers in breaches of minimum humanitarian standards. Elliman was aged sixty-two and living in west Belfast at the time of his death. During the day of his death, considerable rioting had been taking place in the area near his home. Witnesses report that he went for a stroll outside his home during a lull in the rioting and was shot at a nearby street corner. The army stated that they had opened fire on a gunman. Family members stated that the ambulance carrying Elliman was stopped and searched by troops several times. Though the family home and the site of the incident was only a few hundred yards from the Royal Victoria Hospital, it took thirty minutes for the ambulance to reach the hospital.[86]

The First Geneva Convention outlines protection for the sick and wounded in conflict situations. Article 12 of the convention provides that the wounded and sick be treated and cared for 'by the Party to the conflict in whose power they may be'. This provision is largely duplicated in Article 8 of Protocol I, and is also echoed in the standards set by Common Article 3 for care of those *hors de combat,* Any restriction on medical care which could not be justified by military necessity would clearly be a breach of humanitarian law. More recently, the practice by specialist military forces of sealing off areas in which set-piece killings have taken place, preventing access to those injured or killed, would seem to contravene the implied promptness required in the provisions made for the care of the wounded by humanitarian law.

It should be made clear that applying Common Article 3 does not mean that stronger implementation of protection exists in humanitarian law to ensure accountability when breach occurs. Generally speaking, the opposite is true. There is no doubt that the implementation procedures of this body of law are weak and rarely enforced. Moreover, lack of recognition by relevant state parties that an armed conflict situation exists further limits the possibilities of meaningful enforcement. The lack of political recognition for even a modicum of an armed conflict situation in Northern Ireland makes these limitations all the more cogent.

A

THE VALUE OF APPLICATION

What is the value of exploring the potential applicability of humanitarian law to this jurisdiction? The following advantages may be gleaned. There is a measure of intellectual and legal honesty in exploring the applicability of alternative legal regimes, even where their content is politically controversial and not divested of internal policy preferences. Second, there is the chance that such exploration leads to meaningful dialogue on the status of conflict. In particular, outstanding legal ambiguities may be clarified by a new viewfinder on conflict status. For example, humanitarian law applicability may help to clarify the legal position of the army in Northern Ireland, which military analysts have indicated is subject to unnecessary confusion, given the combination of a quasi-policing and counter-insurgency role.[87] On one reading, such clarification may augment civilian life protection. Military training is directly based on the practical application of the laws of war. Dealing with the conflict in humanitarian law terms institutes a familiar standard, with which one of the primary conflict controllers are familiar.

The political consequences of applying Common Article 3 should not be underestimated and will be briefly sketched here. No doubt, given the polarisation of the political communities in the jurisdiction, the danger of applying a symbolically validating legal regime is very real – the pitfall being that endorsement is given to one community at the expense of the other. Those military entities who claim to have been engaged in a 'war of liberation' are given a measure of perceived, if not actual, status. One is faced with the certainty that the political differences centred on the status and validity of the state entity are potentially isolated and further entrenched. When significant communities within a fragmented society take the view that the experience of internal collective violence represents nothing more than an organised criminal element which should be denied political status of any kind (by implication or otherwise), humanitarian law manifests within the internal discourse of the state the problems that define it in intra-state discourse.

Thus, the value of humanitarian law should not be oversold. We live in a world of states which must be convinced of the value of applying humanitarian standards to their own crises. This is no easy task – there is a tangible burden to the state in applying humanitarian law standards. Starting with the principle that self-interest is a prime motivator in state conduct, it is contrary to many states' political interests to embrace the applicability of humanitarian law to low-intensity armed conflict situations. This reality must not be ignored or muted in trying to advance the position asserted by this book, which is that human rights and humanitarian law may be dually applicable to situations of low-intensity conflict. Humanitarian law applicability is invested with a meaning and symbolism that goes beyond its protective mandate. This symbolism must be addressed to enable the international community to find ways around the political minefields which are scattered throughout this branch of law.[88]

There are small groupings of states that concede, in the context of their larger political façades, the value of augmenting humanitarian law protections. These are the states endorsing the minimum standards approach, which has garnered the approval of many experts in the field and some institutional backing.[89] The minimum standards mechanism has been seen as a means to facilitate regulation of internal armed conflicts without raising the same kinds of sensitivities for states that arise when the Geneva Conventions are invoked. It has had some effect. There is a growing tendency within the political bodies of the United Nations to rely on humanitarian legal norms while examining internal conflict situations.[90] However welcome this departure, it should not currently be confused with widespread state acquiescence in the general applicability of humanitarian law to internal conflicts. It remains the case that states which seek to widen the net of applicability are small in number and politically outflanked by the larger number, wary of the political consequences of accepting the designation of Common Article 3 or Protocol II to an internal crisis situation.

How is this likely to change? There is no overnight panacea to stripping the laws of war of their inbuilt political symbolism. States are finely tuned to the wavelength of political recognition. There is a language of communication surrounding the provisions of humanitarian law that goes far beyond the minute responsibilities that are laid upon states which accept its relevance to their particular conflict. We need to start by attempting to place a schism between the duties of protection which accrue to this body of law and the political consequences that are seen to follow from them. One of the greatest limitations in this arena is the lack of reference to or reliance upon humanitarian law in the ordinary discourse between states themselves and between states and international oversight bodies. The less the frequency of the language of humanitarian law and the invocation of its standards, the greater the sense of isolation for the state who falls into the limelight of applicability. Thus, the capacity to transform state views of humanitarian law lies firstly in expanding the use of language and standards in the venues where bilateral and institutional discourse occur. If the use of humanitarian standards were to become ordinary, the sacred cow will be divested of some of its divinity. Humanitarian law may thus move from being a politically loaded weapon which undermines a government's legitimacy to a common frame of reference in which discussions about protection and means of enforcement are safe.

It is not suggested that human rights protection should be abandoned entirely in a rush to embrace the applicability of humanitarian law. It may well be that the two regimes must complement and reinforce one another in twilight legal situations where neither is master. In the specific context of Northern Ireland, and similarly placed permanent emergencies, humanitarian law applicability is ignored and partly obscured by the primacy of human rights standards under international law. This, despite the fact that there are clear indicators to suggest that Common Article 3 is directly relevant to assessing the actions of state and nonstate actors. The application of the laws of war offers another narrative on the conflict.

Multiple narratives are required in order to come to terms with the complexity of a prolonged internal conflict. Northern Ireland can be described as existing in a state of legal limbo. Derogations by the United Kingdom government allow the title of 'emergency' to comfortably, if not always accurately, describe the conflict and its regulation. Internally, the criminalisation process stakes a claim to an apparent normality of civil regulation. In short, both descriptive analyses need to be examined more closely. Short of a reinvigoration of the oversight bodies envisaged by the Geneva Conventions, which seems unlikely in the short term, the burden falls to the human rights regimes which regularly come into contact with these 'twilight' situations. Much is expected of these bodies in both jurisprudential and political terms to fulfil a clarification and categorisation role.

Laying claim to a state of emergency alone may, in fact, cover up the extent of the disruption to civil society in Northern Ireland. This book has pointed out the extent to which domestic and European Court jurisprudence has facilitated this concealment and avoided addressing the hard issues raised by long-term crisis, coexisting with low-level insurgency within the state. International courts, which are generally in a better position to do this than national courts, have avoided examining whether derogations are the appropriate framework to judicially endorse, despite the fact that the domestic situation being examined is more extreme than a mere finite emergency. Essentially, the square peg of low threshold armed conflict is being made to fit the round hole of emergency derogation, keeping conflict examination in the human rights framework. Northern Ireland continues to operate in a twilight zone, where there are real divergences between the stated internal legal regime applicable to the conflict and the potential international status of the conflict under humanitarian law standards. More seriously for international law, Northern Ireland represents a wider problem of the expanding gap between the inadequacies of international conflict categorisation and the manipulation of this lacuna by states within the framework of human rights instruments.

What does all this mean for the protection of life within the jurisdiction? The defining feature of legal protection for life by the state in such a situation of low-intensity conflict is ambiguity. Specifically in Northern Ireland, this ambiguity is indisputably related to a lack of successful prosecutions for the taking of life and a reluctance to initiate prosecutions at all. It is illustrated in the patterns in life-taking by agents of the state that point to a *de facto* armed conflict situation on the ground, tacitly acknowledged by the practices of the military and paramilitary organisations themselves. Thus members of organised armed groups like PIRA have regarded and treated members of the security forces as legitimate targets, and have arguably been treated similarly in the set-piece killings of the active counter-insurgency phase of the conflict. This is the most telling manifestation of combatancy rules being applied in the jurisdiction, quite simply, the legitimisation of killing without warning when the target is a combatant.[91] There is much evidence that this has been an unacknowledged rule of the game in Northern Ireland from 1969 to 1994. Despite its nonderogable status under international law, the right to life's actual status is undefined in this confused political situation. The fluidity of the political and military dynamic makes it difficult to infuse the protection of life with a clear penumbra of nonviolation ensuring that it is adequately protected by law.

However, this book has also demonstrated the extent to which the management of the conflict itself is intimately tied into the practices of life protection. Conflict management for any state constitutes a sophisticated interplay of law and politics. When the management rules are underdefined the state has the opportunity to manipulate the terms in which the conflict is defined both internally and internationally. This manipulation inevitably results in lower standards of protection for the human rights of citizens. Until the conflict is sufficiently defined in both legal and political terms, the use of lethal force becomes one means of exercising control over the direction of the conflict itself, with ambiguity facilitating a lack of meaningful control on the exercise of that force by the state. In this equation the use of force and the efforts to control conflict remain undeniably intertwined, bound into one another's embrace as the state struggles to maintain a tight grip on ever-persisting internal crisis.

Appendix

Identification of fatalities which comprise the lethal force database

This appendix contains a full list of all those individuals killed by the use of force whose deaths have formed the basis for the research and analysis contained in this book. All of the personal information listed below is already in the public arena. Nonetheless, it is acknowledged that the listing of this information may again invade the privacy of the bereaved and focus public attention on individual cases. However, given the sensitive nature of the study and the strong empirical conclusions drawn from the data, it was felt that the details of the study should be published in order to ensure transparency and openness of the research method. It should also be noted that in some cases listed below, sufficient information was not available to complete a full descriptive and substantive analysis of death. Furthermore, in a small number of cases conflicting personal information concerning the deceased exists in the public records (newspaper reports, etc.), which will inevitably affect some of the information contained on the database itself.

	NAME	DATE OF INCIDENT	LOCATION	RELIGION
1	Samuel Devenney	19.4.69	Derry city	Catholic
2	Francis McCloskey	14.7.69	Dungiven, Co. Londonderry	Catholic
3	Patrick Gallagher	14.8.69	Armagh city	Catholic
4	Samuel McLarnon	14.8.69	north Belfast	Catholic
5	Michael Lynch	14.8.69	north Belfast	Catholic

	NAME	DATE OF INCIDENT	LOCATION	RELIGION
6	Patrick Rooney	14.8.69	west Belfast	Catholic
7	Hugh McCabe	15.8.69	west Belfast	Catholic
8	Herbert Hawe	12.10.69	west Belfast	Protestant
9	George Dickie	12.10.69	west Belfast	Protestant
10	Patrick Corry	1.12.69	west Belfast	Catholic
11	William Burns	3.7.70	west Belfast	Catholic
12	Zbigniew Uglick	3.7.70	west Belfast	unknown
13	Patrick Elliman	11.7.70	west Belfast	Catholic
14	Daniel O'Hagan	31.7.70	north Belfast	Catholic
15	Bernard Watt	6.2.71	north Belfast	Catholic
16	James Saunders	6.2.71	north Belfast	Catholic
17	John McGuinness	6.2.71	north Belfast	Catholic
18	William Halligan	5.3.71	west Belfast	Catholic
19	Pvt Kenneth Eastaugh	23.3.71	north Belfast	unknown
20	Billy Reid	16.5.71	central Belfast	Catholic
21	Seamus Cusack	8.7.71	Derry city	Catholic
22	Desmond Beattie	8.7.71	Derry city	Catholic
23	Harry Thornton	7.8.71	west Belfast	Catholic
24	Frank McGuinness	9.8.71	west Belfast	Catholic
25	Desmond Healey	9.8.71	west Belfast	Catholic
26	Sarah Worthington	9.8.71	north Belfast	Protestant
27	Leo McGuigan	9.8.71	north Belfast	Catholic
28	Noel Phillips	9.8.71	west Belfast	Catholic
29	Daniel Teggart	9.8.71	west Belfast	Catholic
30	Joan Connolly	9.8.71	west Belfast	Catholic
31	Norman Watson	9.8.71	Armagh city	Protestant
32	Father Hugh Mullan	9.8.71	west Belfast	Catholic
33	Hugh Herron	9.8.71	Derry city	Catholic
34	Patrick McAdorey	9.8.71	north Belfast	Catholic
35	Frank Quinn	9.8.71	west Belfast	Catholic
36	Edward Doherty	10.8.71	west Belfast	Catholic
37	John Beattie	10.8.71	west Belfast	Catholic
38	John Laverty	10.8.71	north Belfast	Catholic
39	Joseph Corr	11.8.71	west Belfast	Catholic
40	Seamus Simpson	11.8.71	west Belfast	Catholic
41	William McKavanagh	11.8.71	south Belfast	Catholic
42	William Ferris	12.8.71	north Belfast	Protestant
43	Eamonn Lafferty	18.8.71	Derry city	Catholic

	NAME	DATE OF INCIDENT	LOCATION	RELIGION
44	Eamonn McDevitt	18.8.71	Strabane, Co. Tyrone	Catholic
45	Joseph Murphy	23.8.71	west Belfast	Catholic
46	Annette McGavigan	6.9.71	Derry city	Catholic
47	William McGreanery	14.9.71	Derry city	Catholic
48	David Thompson	17.10.71	east Belfast	Catholic
49	Dorothy Maguire	23.10.71	west Belfast	Catholic
50	Maura Meehan	23.10.71	west Belfast	Catholic
51	James McLaughlin	23.10.71	Newry, Co. Down	Catholic
52	Sean Ruddy	23.10.71	Newry, Co. Down	Catholic
53	Robert Anderson	23.10.71	Newry, Co. Down	Catholic
54	Martin Forsythe	24.10.71	central Belfast	Catholic
55	Michael McLarnon	28.10.71	north Belfast	Catholic
56	John Copeland	30.10.71	north Belfast	Catholic
57	Christopher Quinn	3.11.71	west Belfast	Catholic
58	Kathleen Thompson	6.11.71	Derry city	Catholic
59	Joseph Parker	12.12.71	north Belfast	Catholic
60	Martin McShane	14.12.71	Coalisland, Co. Tyrone	Catholic
61	Gerald McDade	21.12.71	north Belfast	Catholic
62	Daniel O'Neill	4.1.72	west Belfast	Catholic
63	Joseph Ward	12.1.72	north Belfast	Catholic
64	Pat Joe Doherty	30.1.72	Derry city	Catholic
65	Gerard McKinney	30.1.72	Derry city	Catholic
66	John Young	30.1.72	Derry city	Catholic
67	Michael McDaid	30.1.72	Derry city	Catholic
68	James Wray	30.1.72	Derry city	Catholic
69	Hugh Gilmore	30.1.72	Derry city	Catholic
70	William Nash	30.1.72	Derry city	Catholic
71	William McKinney	30.1.72	Derry city	Catholic
72	Bernard McGuigan	30.1.72	Derry city	Catholic
73	Michael Kelly	30.1.72	Derry city	Catholic
74	Kevin McElhinney	30.1.72	Derry city	Catholic
75	Gerard Donaghy	30.1.72	Derry city	Catholic
76	John Duddy	30.1.72	Derry city	Catholic
77	Thomas McElroy	2.2.72	west Belfast	Catholic
78	Joseph Cunningham	10.2.72	Newtownabbey, Co. Antrim	Catholic
79	Michael Connors	1.3.72	central Belfast	Catholic

	NAME	DATE OF INCIDENT	LOCATION	RELIGION
80	John Maugham	1.3.72	central Belfast	Catholic
81	Albert Kavanagh	4.3.72	south Belfast	Catholic
82	Colm Keenan	14.3.72	Derry city	Catholic
83	Eugene McGillan	14.3.72	Derry city	Catholic
84	Sean O'Riordan	23.3.72	west Belfast	Catholic
85	Joseph McCann	15.4.72	south Belfast	Catholic
86	Patrick Joseph Magee	17.4.72	west Belfast	Catholic
87	Patrick Donaghy	17.4.72	west Belfast	Catholic
88	Francis Rowntree	22.4.72	west Belfast	Catholic
89	Joseph McVeigh	12.5.72	west Belfast	Catholic
90	John Starrs	13.5.72	Derry city	Catholic
91	Manus Deery	19.5.72	Derry city	Catholic
92	Joseph Campbell	11.6.72	north Belfast	Catholic
93	Norman McGrath	11.6.72	north Belfast	Protestant
94	James Bonner	25.6.72	west Belfast	Catholic
95	John Black	26.6.72	east Belfast	Protestant
96	Father Noel Fitzpatrick	9.7.72	west Belfast	Catholic
97	Margaret Gargan	9.7.72	west Belfast	Catholic
98	John Dougal	9.7.72	west Belfast	Catholic
99	Paddy Butler	9.7.72	west Belfast	Catholic
100	David McCafferty	9.7.72	west Belfast	Catholic
101	Gerald Gibson	11.7.72	west Belfast	Catholic
102	Thomas Burns	13.7.72	north Belfast	Catholic
103	Edward Brady	14.7.72	north Belfast	Catholic
104	Lewis Scullion	14.7.72	west Belfast	Catholic
105	James Reid	14.7.72	north Belfast	Catholic
106	Terry Toolan	14.7.72	north Belfast	Catholic
107	Francis McKeown	14.7.72	west Belfast	Catholic
108	John Mooney	15.7.72	north Belfast	Catholic
109	Tobias Molloy	16.7.72	Strabane, Co. Tyrone	Catholic
110	Joseph Downey	22.7.72	south Belfast	Catholic
111	James Casey	24.7.72	Derry city	Catholic
112	Seamus Cassidy	28.7.72	north Belfast	Catholic
113	Daniel Hegarty	31.7.72	Derry city	Catholic
114	Seamus Bradley	31.7.72	Derry city	Catholic
115	Robert McCrudden	3.8.72	north Belfast	Catholic
116	Pvt Anthony Rowe	28.8.72	north Belfast	unknown
117	Gnr Robert Cunning	3.9.72	north Belfast	unknown

	NAME	DATE OF INCIDENT	LOCATION	RELIGION
118	Robert Johnson	7.9.72	west Belfast	Protestant
119	Robert McKinnie	7.9.72	west Belfast	Protestant
120	Robert James Warnock	13.9.72	east Belfast	Protestant
121	Sinclair Johnson	16.9.72	Larne, Co. Antrim	Protestant
122	Michael Quigley	17.9.72	Derry city	Catholic
123	John McComiskey	20.9.72	north Belfast	Catholic
124	Daniel Rooney	27.9.72	west Belfast	Catholic
125	Patricia McKay	29.9.72	west Belfast	Catholic
126	Jimmy Quigley	29.9.72	west Belfast	Catholic
127	John Kelly	30.9.72	west Belfast	Catholic
128	Michael Hayes	1.10.72	north Belfast	Catholic
129	Daniel McAreavey	6.10.72	west Belfast	Catholic
130	Alex Moorehead	7.10.72	Newtownstewart, Co. Tyrone	Protestant
131	Robert Stuart Nicholl	12.10.72	central Belfast	Protestant
132	Hugh Heron	16.10.72	Coagh, Co. Tyrone	Catholic
133	John Mullan	16.10.72	Coagh, Co. Tyrone	Catholic
134	Andrew Murray	24.10.72	Newtownbutler, Co. Fermanagh	Catholic
135	Michael Naan	24.10.72	Newtownbutler, Co. Fermanagh	Catholic
136	Stanislaus Carberry	13.11.72	west Belfast	Catholic
137	Bernard Fox	4.12.72	north Belfast	Catholic
138	William Bell	5.12.72	north Belfast	Protestant
139	James Ward	11.12.72	north Belfast	Catholic
140	Eugene Devlin	27.12.72	Strabane, Co. Tyrone	Catholic
141	James McDaid	29.12.72	Ballyarnett, Co. Londonderry	Catholic
142	Elizabeth McGregor	12.1.73	north Belfast	Protestant
143	Francis Ligget	18.1.73	west Belfast	Catholic
144	Ambrose Hardy	4.2.73	north Belfast	Catholic
145	Anthony Campbell	4.2.73	north Belfast	Catholic
146	Sean Loughran	4.2.73	north Belfast	Catholic
147	Brendan Maguire	4.2.73	north Belfast	Catholic
148	Robert Bennett	7.2.73	east Belfast	Protestant
149	Hugh Connolly	7.2.73	west Belfast	Catholic
150	Andrew Petheridge	7.2.73	east Belfast	Protestant
151	Kevin Heatley	28.2.73	Newry, Co. Down	Catholic

	NAME	DATE OF INCIDENT	LOCATION	RELIGION
152	Jim McGerrigan	7.3.73	Armagh city	Catholic
153	Edward Sharpe	13.3.73	north Belfast	Catholic
154	Samuel Martin	26.3.73	south Armagh	Protestant
155	Patrick McCabe	27.3.73	north Belfast	Catholic
156	John Hughes	9.4.73	Armagh city	Catholic
157	Edward O'Rawe	12.4.73	west Belfast	Catholic
158	Brendan Brian Smith	18.4.73	north Belfast	Catholic
159	Tony McDowell	19.4.73	north Belfast	Catholic
160	Kevin Gerard Fitzpatrick	14.5.73	Coalisland, Co. Tyrone	Catholic
161	Michael Leonard	17.5.73	Belleek, Co. Fermanagh	Catholic
162	Thomas Friel	17.5.73	Derry city	Catholic
163	Joseph McKee	19.5.73	north Belfast	Catholic
164	Anthony Mitchell	12.6.73	west Belfast	Catholic
165	Robert McGuinness	26.6.73	Derry city	Catholic
166	Patrick Mulvenna	1.9.73	north Belfast	Catholic
167	Michael McVerry	15.11.73	south Armagh	Catholic
168	Michael Marley	24.11.73	west Belfast	Catholic
169	Desmond Morgan	27.11.73	Coalisland, Co. Tyrone	Catholic
170	Joseph Walker	3.12.73	Derry city	Catholic
171	Alex Howell	28.12.73	north Belfast	Protestant
172	Matilda Worthington	29.1.74	Newcastle, Co. Down	Protestant
173	Gary Reid	17.2.74	east Belfast	Protestant
174	Kirk Watters	17.2.74	east Belfast	Protestant
175	Pvt Michael Cotton	20.3.74	Mowhan, Co. Armagh	unknown
176	Corp Michael Herbert	20.3.74	Mowhan, Co. Armagh	unknown
177	Daniel Burke	9.4.74	west Belfast	Catholic
178	William McDonald	14.4.74	west Belfast	Protestant
179	Martin McAlinden	15.5.74	Newry, Co. Down	Catholic
180	Colman Rowntree	15.5.74	Newry, Co. Down	Catholic
181	Patrick Cunningham	15.6.74	Benburb, Co. Tyrone	Catholic
182	Hugh Devine	22.6.74	Strabane, Co. Tyrone	Catholic
183	Martin Patrick Skillen	2.8.74	west Belfast	Catholic
184	Patrick McElhone	7.8.74	Pomeroy, Co. Tyrone	Catholic

	NAME	DATE OF INCIDENT	LOCATION	RELIGION
185	Paul Magorrian	14.8.74	Castlewellan, Co. Down	Catholic
186	Michael Hughes	18.10.74	Newry, Co. Down	Catholic
187	Hugh Gerard Coney	6.11.74	Long Kesh prison	Catholic
188	Gerald Fennell	8.11.74	west Belfast	Catholic
189	Kevin Coen	20.1.75	Fermanagh border	Catholic
190	Robert Wadsworth	11.4.75	south Belfast	Protestant
191	Francis Jordan	5.6.75	south Armagh	Catholic
192	Charles Irvine	13.7.75	west Belfast	Catholic
193	Stephen Geddis	30.8.75	west Belfast	Catholic
194	Leo Norney	14.9.75	west Belfast	Catholic
195	David McDowell	25.1.76	Middletown, Co. Armagh	Protestant
196	Hugh Woodside	31.1.76	west Belfast	Protestant
197	James Oliver McGrillen	15.2.76	west Belfast	Catholic
198	Sean Terence McDermott	5.4.76	south Belfast	Catholic
199	Peter Cleary	15.4.76	south Armagh	Catholic
200	Rory Hawkins	26.4.76	east Belfast	Catholic
201	Seamus Ludlow	1.5.76	Culmore, Co. Monaghan	Catholic
202	Anthony Gallagher	17.5.76	Derry city	Catholic
203	Liam Prince	12.6.76	south Armagh	Catholic
204	Edward Walker	12.6.76	north Belfast	Protestant
205	George Edward Johnston	29.7.76	south Armagh	Protestant
206	Daniel Lennon	10.8.76	north Belfast	Catholic
207	Majella O'Hare	14.8.76	south Armagh	Catholic
208	Brian Stewart	4.10.76	west Belfast	Catholic
209	Patrick McGeown	15.12.76	south Armagh	Catholic
210	John Joe Savage	18.12.76	west Belfast	Catholic
211	Paul Kerr	27.12.76	Coalisland, Co. Tyrone	Catholic
212	Seamus Harvey	16.1.77	south Armagh	Catholic
213	Trevor McKibbin	17.4.77	north Belfast	Catholic
214	Brendan O'Callaghan	23.4.77	west Belfast	Catholic
215	Daniel McCooey	20.5.77	central Belfast	Catholic
216	John (Jack) McCartan	4.8.77	west Belfast	Catholic

	NAME	DATE OF INCIDENT	LOCATION	RELIGION
217	Paul McWilliams	9.8.77	west Belfast	Catholic
218	Michael Neill	24.10.77	north Belfast	Catholic
219	Colm NcNutt	12.12.77	Derry city	Catholic
220	Paul Duffy	26.2.78	Carnan, Co. Tyrone	Catholic
221	John Collins	7.5.78	west Belfast	Catholic
222	James McConnell	6.78	Derry city	Catholic
223	Denis Heaney	10.6.78	Derry city	Catholic
224	William Hanna	20.6.78	north Belfast	Protestant
225	Denis Brown	20.6.78	north Belfast	Catholic
226	William John Mailey	20.6.78	north Belfast	Catholic
227	Jim Mulvenna	20.6.78	north Belfast	Catholic
228	John Boyle	11.7.78	Dunloy, Co. Antrim	Catholic
229	James Taylor	30.9.78	Coagh, Co. Tyrone	Protestant
230	William Smyth	25.10.78	north Belfast	Catholic
231	Patrick Duffy	24.11.78	Derry city	Catholic
232	Peadar McElvenna	9.6.79	south Armagh	Catholic
233	Michael Hudson	27.8.79	Co. Down	unknown
234	Lt Simon Bates	1.1.80	south Armagh	unknown
235	Pvt Gerald Hardy	1.1.80	south Armagh	unknown
236	Doreen McGuinness	1.1.80	west Belfast	Catholic
237	Paul Moan	31.3.80	west Belfast	Catholic
238	Theresa Donaghy	12.4.80	Strabane/Lifford border	Catholic
239	Terence O'Neill	1.7.80	west Belfast	Catholic
240	Michael McCartan	23.7.80	south Belfast	Catholic
241	Michael Donnelly	9.8.80	west Belfast	Catholic
242	Jim Bell	14.8.80	west Belfast	Protestant
243	Patrick McNally	20.3.81	west Belfast	Catholic
244	Paul Whitters	15.4.81	Derry city	Catholic
245	Emmanuel McLarnon	12.5.81	west Belfast	Catholic
246	Julie Livingstone	13.5.81	west Belfast	Catholic
247	Carol-Ann Kelly	22.5.81	west Belfast	Catholic
248	Harry Duffy	25.5.81	Derry city	Catholic
249	George McBrearty	28.5.81	Derry city	Catholic
250	Charles Paul Maguire	28.5.81	Derry city	Catholic
251	John Dempsey	9.7.81	west Belfast	Catholic
252	Daniel Barrett	9.7.81	north Belfast	Catholic

	NAME	DATE OF INCIDENT	LOCATION	RELIGION
253	Nora McCabe	9.7.81	west Belfast	Catholic
254	Peter Doherty	31.7.81	west Belfast	Catholic
255	Pvt William Corbett	1.8.81	Belfast	Catholic
256	Peter McGuinness	9.8.81	north Belfast	Catholic
257	Pvt Stephen Humble	26.8.81	Craigavon, Co. Armagh	Catholic
258	Stephen Hamilton	18.10.81	west Belfast	Protestant
259	Tony Harker	24.1.82	Armagh city	Catholic
260	Martin Kyles	7.2.82	west Belfast	Catholic
261	Stephen McConomy	16.4.82	Derry city	Catholic
262	Eamonn John Bradley	25.8.82	Derry city	Catholic
263	Ron Brennan	28.10.82	Mallusk, Co. Antrim	Catholic
264	Gervaise McKerr	11.11.82	Lurgan, Co. Armagh	Catholic
265	Eugene Toman	11.11.82	Lurgan, Co. Armagh	Catholic
266	Sean Burns	11.11.82	Lurgan, Co. Armagh	Catholic
267	Michael Tighe	24.11.82	Lurgan, Co. Armagh	Catholic
268	Seamus Grew	12.12.82	south Armagh	Catholic
269	Roddy Carroll	12.12.82	south Armagh	Catholic
270	Patrick Elliott	27.12.82	west Belfast	Catholic
271	Francis McColgan	19.1.83	west Belfast	Catholic
272	Neil Liam McMonagle	2.2.83	Derry city	Catholic
273	William Millar	16.3.83	south Belfast	Protestant
274	John O'Hare	26.7.83	Lurgan, Co. Armagh	Catholic
275	Martin Malone	30.7.83	Armagh city	Catholic
276	Thomas Reilly	9.8.83	west Belfast	Catholic
277	Brendan Convery	13.8.83	Dungannon, Co. Tyrone	Catholic
278	Gerald Mallon	13.8.83	Dungannon, Co. Tyrone	Catholic
279	Brigid Foster	28.11.83	Pomeroy, Co. Tyrone	Catholic
280	Brian Campbell	4.12.83	Coalisland, Co. Tyrone	Catholic
281	Colm McGirr	4.12.83	Coalisland, Co. Tyrone	Catholic
282	Mark Marron	30.1.84	west Belfast	Catholic
283	Henry Hogan	21.2.84	Dunloy, Co. Antrim	Catholic
284	Declan Martin	21.2.84	Dunloy, Co. Antrim	Catholic
285	Seamus Fitzsimmons	14.4.84	Ballygally, Co. Antrim	Catholic

NAME	DATE OF INCIDENT	LOCATION	RELIGION
286 William Price	13.7.84	Ardboe, Co. Tyrone	Catholic
287 Sean Downes	12.8.84	west Belfast	Catholic
288 Frederick Jackson	19.10.84	Dungannon, Co. Tyrone	Protestant
289 Tony McBride	2.12.84	Kesh, Co. Fermanagh	Catholic
290 Pvt Alistair Slater	2.12.84	Kesh, Co. Fermanagh	unknown
291 Daniel Doherty	6.12.84	Derry city	Catholic
292 William Fleming	6.12.84	Derry city	Catholic
293 Sean McIlvenna	17.12.84	Lisbofin, Co. Tyrone	Catholic
294 Paul Kelly	15.1.85	west Belfast	Catholic
295 Gerard Logue	8.2.85	west Belfast	Catholic
296 Charles Breslin	23.2.85	Strabane, Co. Tyrone	Catholic
297 Michael Devine	23.2.85	Strabane, Co. Tyrone	Catholic
298 David Devine	23.2.85	Strabane, Co. Tyrone	Catholic
299 Francis Bradley	18.2.86	Toomebridge, Co. Antrim	Catholic
300 Tony Gough	23.2.86	Derry city	Catholic
301 Keith White	31.3.86	Portadown, Co. Armagh	Protestant
302 Seamus McElwaine	26.4.86	Rosslea, Co. Fermanagh	Catholic
303 James McKernan	14.9.86	west Belfast	Catholic
304 Patrick Kelly	8.5.87	Loughgall, Co. Armagh	Catholic
305 James Lynagh	8.5.87	Loughgall, Co. Armagh	Catholic
306 Anthony Gormley	8.5.87	Loughgall, Co. Armagh	Catholic
307 Seamus Donnelly	8.5.87	Loughgall, Co. Armagh	Catholic
308 Declan Arthurs	8.5.87	Loughgall, Co. Armagh	Catholic
309 Eugene Kelly	8.5.87	Loughgall, Co. Armagh	Catholic
310 Patrick McKearney	8.5.87	Loughgall, Co. Armagh	Catholic
311 Anthony Hughes	8.5.87	Loughgall, Co. Armagh	Catholic

	NAME	DATE OF INCIDENT	LOCATION	RELIGION
312	Gerard O'Callaghan	8.5.87	Loughgall, Co. Armagh	Catholic
313	Aidan McAnespie	21.2.88	Aughnacloy, Co. Tyrone	Catholic
314	Mairead Farrell	6.3.88	Gibraltar	Catholic
315	Daniel McCann	6.3.88	Gibraltar	Catholic
316	Sean Savage	6.3.88	Gibraltar	Catholic
317	Kevin McCracken	14.3.88	west Belfast	Catholic
318	Kenneth Stronge	4.7.88	Belfast	Protestant
319	James McPhilemy	10.8.88	Clady, Co. Tyrone	Catholic
320	Gerard Harte	30.8.88	Drumnakilly, Co. Tyrone	Catholic
321	Martin Harte	30.8.88	Drumnakilly, Co. Tyrone	Catholic
322	Brian Mullin	30.8.88	Drumnakilly, Co. Tyrone	Catholic
323	Pvt Adam Gilbert	15.6.89	north Belfast	Protestant
324	Seamus Duffy	9.8.89	north Belfast	Catholic
325	Brian Robinson	2.9.89	north Belfast	Protestant
326	Ian Johnston	9.11.89	north Belfast	Protestant
327	Eddie Hale	13.1.90	west Belfast	Catholic
328	John McNeill	13.1.90	west Belfast	Catholic
329	Peter Thompson	13.1.90	west Belfast	Catholic
330	Martin Corrigan	18.4.90	Kinnego, Co. Armagh	Catholic
331	Karen Reilly	30.9.90	west Belfast	Catholic
332	Martin Peake	30.9.90	west Belfast	Catholic
333	Martin McCaughey	9.10.90	Lislasley, Co. Armagh	Catholic
334	Desmond Grew	9.10.90	Lislasley, Co. Armagh	Catholic
335	Alexander Patterson	12.11.90	Victoria Bridge, Co. Tyrone	Catholic
336	Fergal Caraher	30.12.90	Cullyhanna, Co. Armagh	Catholic
337	Colum Marks	10.4.91	Downpatrick, Co. Down	Catholic
338	Michael Ryan	3.6.91	Coagh, Co. Tyrone	Catholic
339	Tony Doris	3.6.91	Coagh, Co. Tyrone	Catholic
340	Lawrence McNally	3.6.91	Coagh, Co. Tyrone	Catholic

NAME	DATE OF INCIDENT	LOCATION	RELIGION
341	Kevin McGovern	29.9.91	Cookstown, Co. Tyrone	Catholic
342	Gerard Maginn	3.11.91	west Belfast	Catholic
343	Patrick Daniel Vincent	16.2.92	Coalisland, Co. Tyrone	Catholic
344	Peter Clancy	16.2.92	Coalisland, Co. Tyrone	Catholic
345	Sean O'Farrell	16.2.92	Coalisland, Co. Tyrone	Catholic
346	Kevin Barry O'Donnell	16.2.92	Coalisland, Co. Tyrone	Catholic
347	Peter McBride	4.9.92	north Belfast	Catholic
348	Pearse Jordan	25.11.92	west Belfast	Catholic
349	David Terence Fenley	18.2.93	Strabane, Co. Tyrone	unknown
350	Robin Maxwell	27.1.94	Donaghadee, Co. Down	Protestant

The human cost

A significant portion of this analysis has been drawn from empirical enquiry and, inevitably, cumulative information and impersonal statistics dominate this book. However, individual narratives of loss are the backdrop to those raw statistics and must be acknowledged, though telling the stories of how 350 individuals were killed by the use of lethal force is not an easy matter. Many of these deaths were controversial, and in numerous instances the circumstances of the deaths are disputed or unclear. Nonetheless, the relevance of each individual death cannot be ignored. First, because these narratives make tangible and give voice to the statistics upon which this study is founded. Second, they explain, in part, the effect of these deaths on the isolated communities in which they occurred, and on wider communities in Northern Ireland.

Reconstructing some of these stories is not unproblematic. One faces the dilemma of invading the private worlds of those who have been bereaved. In this process judgements are made far from the circumscribed world where bereavement is experienced. The danger of voyeurism is apparent. It should also be evident that the narratives charted here are not presumed to determine the legal culpability of the agents defined as causally responsible.

What is most striking about these deaths is the way in which individuals from all walks of life have been victims of the use of lethal force. It is these distinctive characteristics – age, class, gender, religion – remembered by families and communities, that create the power and myth from which cultural consciousness and collective memory about the use of force are located.

The children

The first child killed by the use of lethal force was nine-year-old Patrick Rooney. He died at his home in Divis Flats, west Belfast, on 14 August 1969; the site of his death was his bedroom, where he sustained a gunshot wound to his head when the Divis Flats complex was sprayed with gunfire. The gunfire emanated from a machine gun mounted by police on a Shortland armoured personnel carrier. Witnesses reported that after the armoured carrier had ceased to shoot at the flats it continued to drive in the area. No criminal prosecution was sought by the state in respect of the child's death. In November 1969 an inquest was held in Belfast and the jury returned an open verdict on his death. Subsequently the Scarman Report stated that the child's death was 'not justified'.[1]

In 1971 six children, all under the age of eighteen, were killed by the use of lethal force.[2] They were Desmond Healey, aged 14; Leo McGuigan, aged 16; John Beattie, aged 17; Martin McShane, aged 16; Frank McGuinness, aged 17; and Annette McGavigan, aged 14. Annette was the first girl to be killed by the use of lethal force in the conflict. She and a group of young girls of similar age were caught in crossfire between PIRA and the British army in Derry/Londonderry. The army opened fire after a nail bomb had been thrown at their position. Eyewitnesses reported that gunfire was aimed directly at the group of girls, and Annette was fatally injured. At the inquest proceedings investigating her death the jury returned an open verdict. The McGavigan family was subsequently paid an undisclosed amount of civil compensation.

The death of a child is a particularly traumatic event for any community. It is the children's vulnerability and their lack of choice in the creation of political circumstances that draws such an intense and emotional response to their deaths, which always seems *de facto* disproportionate to the causal reason for their occurrence. In Northern Ireland the use of plastic bullets, notably directed at children and young adults, has provoked a particular sense of victimisation in segments of the nationalist community. These supposedly nonlethal weapons have killed seven children,[3] and maimed numerous others.

The child fatality which has received the widest international attention is the death of thirteen-year-old Brian Stewart on 4 October 1976. Brian was killed by a plastic bullet in the Turf Lodge area of west Belfast. A member of the King's Own Borderers discharged the fatal bullet. Brian's injuries included laceration, bruising and oedema of the brain, associated with fractures of the skull, all of which were caused by a bullet wound to the left side of the head. As with many other lethal force incidents, there was an immense disparity between eyewitness accounts and the army's version of events. The army claimed that the boy was a leading rioter in a group of youths that had set upon the soldiers involved in the incident. Eyewitnesses disputed this. In the local civil proceedings, Lord Justice Jones ruled that the boy had been rioting and refused civil compensation to the family. The family then took legal proceedings outside the jurisdiction at the European Court of Human Rights. Although the European Commission decided that the case was admissible, the European Court accepted the finding of the local civil courts in Northern Ireland that the boy had been rioting, and in October 1984 ruled that there had been no violation of the right to life under the convention.

The most recent death of a minor caused by a plastic bullet occurred on 9 August 1989. Fifteen-year-old Seamus Duffy was killed during internment commemorations which took place in north Belfast on that day. The RUC contended that the young man was rioting at the time of his death. That assertion was strongly disputed by the young man's family and a friend who had been with the boy at the time of the shooting. The inquest proceedings into his death concluded that he had been rioting earlier, but found no conclusive evidence to confirm that he had been rioting when shot. It was also reported that he had been shot in a street some distance from the riot scene. The RUC initially contended that they had in their possession video-tape evidence, demonstrating that the boy was running away from the riot scene.

As with many lethal force incidents, the facts surrounding the context of this fatality remain hotly disputed. In April 1990 the DPP announced there would be no criminal prosecution of the policeman who fired the weapon. In a statement the Duffy family indicated that they were 'very hurt but not surprised' by the decision.[4] An inquest took place in June 1990, where the factual cause of death was confirmed but legal adjustments to the inquest process meant that the inquest jury was no longer empowered to issue a verdict on the death.

During the 1981 hunger strikes scores of individuals were injured by the use of plastic bullets. Children were physically exposed to the harshness of force in an unprecedented way, as the generally ambiguous relationship between militant republicanism and mainstream nationalism was momentarily bridged in an eruption of conflict with the state. In that period 10 hunger-strikers died and 21 young people, whose injuries were recorded, suffered both minor and catastrophic injuries by the use of plastic bullets.[5] In April 1981 eighteen-year-old Alec McLaughlin lost his right eye, suffered head injuries and had facial bones broken. In May four-year-old David Madden required six stitches to a head wound, and nine-year-old Declan Burgoyne was hit in the groin by a baton round. In August eleven-year-old Dermot Gallagher sustained a fractured skull and a broken nose. Twelve-year-old Paul Corr required emergency surgery for a shattered palate and his injuries resulted in part of his nose being permanently disfigured. Equally, permanent injuries were sustained by Conor Campbell in the same month when a plastic baton caused a depression to the left side of his head and speech impairment.

The United Kingdom has signed various international treaties that give a special protection to the rights of children, not least the Convention on the Rights of the Child.[6] Yet these injuries *prima facie* contravene the obligations of the state to prevent children from being subjected to torture, inhuman and degrading treatment,[7] and to ensure the right to health of each child regardless of the child's or its parents' political or other opinion.[8] Notwithstanding the factual disputes over the contexts in which these children were killed or injured, children are placed in a unique position of protection by virtue of their youth. This requires that special protection of the state, even when it is onerous to provide that protection. The Convention on the Rights of the Child requires the state to specifically protect the right to life of the child.[9] Furthermore, the state is required to 'ensure to the maximum extent possible the survival and development of the child'.[10]

The good faith of the United Kingdom to adhere to its duties in this respect is severely undermined by the number of young persons killed and injured by agents of the state since 1969. The state may make the argument that some of these children have engaged in activities and behaviours that undermine their rights to these special protections. But such a position is contrary to the generally recognised standards of international law. The Convention of the Rights of the Child specifically envisages such a situation, and holds that where a child is alleged, accused or recognised to have infringed upon the penal laws of a state that child 'is to be treated in a manner consistent with the promotion of the child's sense of dignity and worth . . . and which takes into account the child's age and the desirability of promoting the child's reintegration and the child's assuming a constructive role in society'.[11]

The women

In relative terms few women have been killed by the use of lethal force in Northern Ireland, yet many of their deaths have provoked notable controversy. In the late twentieth century women remain powerfully symbolic of older values, of motherhood and of family. Their loss strikes a deep psychological chord of victimhood rarely associated with the deaths of men.

On 9 August 1971, the day in which Operation Demetrius heralded the introduction of internment without trial, fifty-year-old Sarah Worthington was killed. That same day eleven other citizens were killed by the use of lethal force.[12] With two exceptions, all were killed in Belfast and by members of the armed forces. Sarah was a Protestant and the first woman to be killed by the use of lethal force. She died of an interabdominal haemorrhage after being shot in her home. Soldiers had entered the building believing it to be empty, and opened fire when they came upon her. During the inquest into her death four months later, army personnel acknowledged that her death had been a mistake. However, neither internal disciplinary proceedings nor criminal sanction were sought against the soldiers responsible for her death.

Equally unresolved was the controversial death of Elizabeth McGregor. Elizabeth was seventy-six years old and was killed by a gunshot wound to her head in the Ardoyne area of north Belfast in January 1973. At the time of her death the army acknowledged that an error had resulted in the fatal discharge of the weapon. Nonetheless, a year later at the inquest proceedings the army claimed that the intended target were four men in the vicinity. In directing the inquest jury, the coroner suggested that if they were dissatisfied with the army's account they should return an open verdict. The jury returned an open verdict.

On 8 July 1981 Joe McDonnell was the fifth prisoner to die while on hunger strike in the Maze prison. It was the presence of the international news media, recording the aftermath of McDonnell's death the next day, which proved crucial to verifying the circumstances of Nora McCabe's last moments. A thirty-three-year-old housewife living in west Belfast, at the time of her death Nora was on her way to her local shops. She was killed by the discharge of a plastic bullet fired at close range. The bullet was fired by an RUC officer, who claimed that rioting had been taking place in the vicinity of the incident.[13] Eyewitnesses keenly disputed this assertion and, ultimately, it was film taken by a Canadian cameraman that was used to firmly dispose of the RUC claim. A file on the case was submitted to the DPP but no criminal prosecution took place. An out-of-court civil settlement was reached with Nora McCabe's family in December 1984.[14]

Two cases involving the deaths of women have resulted in criminal prosecutions. A successful prosecution for the use of lethal force resulted from the conviction of Private Robert Davidson for the manslaughter of Theresa Donaghy in 1981.[15] Theresa was shot at a checkpoint at the Strabane/Lifford border crossing on 12 April 1980. When convicted, Private Davidson was sentenced to twelve months in a Young Offenders' Centre and his sentence was suspended for two years. On 4 June 1993 in the Belfast High Court Private Lee Clegg was convicted of the murder of eighteen-year-old Karen Reilly.[16] Karen had been a passenger in a stolen car driven by Martin Peake who was also killed in the incident. The *Clegg* case wound its way through the appellate judicial process. The Northern Ireland Court of Appeal sustained his conviction, while giving leave of appeal to the House of Lords. At the Appeal Court, Lord Chief Justice Hutton recommended that 'Parliament should consider a change in the existing law', referring to the nonavailability of the charge of manslaughter in the circumstances to the prosecuting authorities. The House of Lords upheld the conviction of the soldier. However, the judicial saga continued when Clegg was granted a retrial on the basis of new forensic evidence, and in March 1999 he was acquitted of the murder of the young woman, though a conviction for attempting to wound the car's driver was sustained. On appeal Clegg's conviction on the minor charge was overturned on the basis of forensic evidence gathered by his legal team.

Though most women killed by the use of lethal force were civilians, uninvolved in the violence around them, a small number were members of paramilitary organisations at the time of their deaths. It remains unclear from the scant information available about some of these lethal force incidents whether knowledge of their paramilitary affiliations was available to the security forces prior to the fatal shootings.[17]

On 23 October 1971 two sisters were killed while travelling in a car in west Belfast. Dorothy Maguire was nineteen years old and her sister Maura Meehan was thirty-one. Dorothy was a member of Cumann na mBan, the women's section of PIRA, and there are conflicting accounts as to Maura's membership of the same organisation. When they were shot they were sounding the car's horn to alert passersby and the local neighbourhood of the presence of the army. Dorothy died as a result of a fracture to her skull, caused by a gunshot wound; Maura's death resulted from a transection of her spinal chord caused by a gunshot wound to her neck. After the incident the army released a series of conflicting public statements.[18] First, that the two women were dressed as terrorists and had thrown two nail bombs from the car. Second, that only one nail bomb had been thrown. Finally, another statement claimed that the army had been fired upon from the vehicle in which the two women were travelling. At the inquest members of the Queen's Regiment reiterated that they had been fired upon, although no direct evidence was produced to verify this. Eyewitnesses denied that any shots were fired from the vehicle. The inquest jury returned an open verdict on both deaths. The case was forwarded to the DPP, but no criminal prosecution was sought.

Undoubtedly, the most controversial death of a woman killed by the use of lethal force is that of Mairead Farrell, who was killed by the SAS in Gibraltar in March 1988. From a middle-class Catholic background and an apolitical upbringing, she was thirty-one years old at the time of her death and a mature student in the Department of Politics at Queen's University Belfast. She had previously been convicted and sentenced to fourteen years' imprisonment for explosives offences. During her time in Armagh women's jail, she was the PIRA officer in command.

Her death, and the deaths of her two companions, Daniel McCann and Sean Savage, received saturation publicity. At the inquest proceedings, which were controversial in their own right, being constrained by the imposition of Public Interest Immunity Certificates and held in a blitz of media attention, the jury returned a verdict of 'lawful killing' in respect of the three deaths. The case was submitted to the European Court and European Commission in August 1991, on the grounds of a breach of the right to life protected by the convention.[19] The commission found no breach, but the court, in a majority decision, held that the right to life of the three deceased had been breached by the United Kingdom government.

The security forces

The common usage of the term 'lethal force' is taken to imply the death of citizens by agents of the state. For the most part, in practice, that definition holds true. However, this study includes thirteen members of the police and army who have been killed by their colleagues in situations of excessive or mistaken use of force. Their deaths raise the same concerns about unnecessary use of force, a lack of openness about the circumstances of death, and an abject lack of accountability.

The first soldier killed by a so-called friendly-fire incident in Northern Ireland was Private Kenneth Eastaugh, who died in Belfast on 23 March 1971. He was shot when a bomb exploded in a parked van near the position he and his colleagues were holding. The inquest jury recorded a verdict of death by misadventure.[20] No disciplinary or criminal proceedings were taken against the soldier who caused his death.

In 1972 two soldiers were killed by army personnel while undertaking their day-to-day duties. Private Anthony Rowe died on 28 August, a little over a year after the introduction of internment. He was shot by another soldier as they jointly undertook a patrol of the Ardoyne area of Belfast. Six days later, eighteen-year-old Gunner Robert Cunning was also killed by a fellow soldier in the New Lodge area of north Belfast. Army press statements confirmed that the soldier mistook him for a sniper and opened fire.[21] There are no inquest details available for either of these fatalities, nor did any official investigation or legal process take place. Consequently, it is difficult to piece together a comprehensive picture of fatal events and therefore the question of legal culpability, if any, is unresolved.

The most striking aspect of fatalities which concern members of the armed forces is the lack of transparency and openness about the circumstances of death. Military unwillingness to candidly investigate these deaths may stem from a perception that to do so would weaken the cohesiveness of military structures in Northern Ireland. Equally, the perception may have been that overt investigation of military deaths without corresponding investigation of civilian deaths would be politically problematic. This seems to have created a rationale for avoiding all public scrutiny.

This study has also identified two incidents involving multiple deaths of members of the security forces by other law-enforcers. The first occurred at Mowhan, County Armagh, in March 1974. In this incident Private Michael Cotton and Corporal Michael Herbert, two members of the King's Hussars, were killed by the RUC on an isolated country road. Scant information was provided by the authorities about the circumstances of their deaths. This was one of the few cases involving intra-security-force deaths in which some public debate arose over the lack of information. The Secretary of State, Merlyn Rees, issued a public statement on the fatalities. He claimed that the two soldiers were returning from leave at the time of their deaths and strongly denied speculation that they were part of a botched undercover operation. The strength of his protests added to the conspiracy theories which abounded about the soldiers' precise activities prior to their deaths.

The deaths of Private Gerald Hardy and his companion Lieutenant Simon Bates in January 1980 gave rise to similar speculation. Following the incident, official statements claimed that Lieutenant Bates had been leading a patrol in the vicinity of Forkhill, County Armagh. For an unspecified reason, at least publicly, the patrol divided into two groups. When it regrouped later that day, one division was lying in wait and fired on the second. The two soldiers were killed in the ensuing fracas.

Unfailingly these intra-security-force deaths are characterised by a lack of information and public commentary.[22] The fact that the deceased were members of the security forces does not lessen the state's obligation under both domestic and international law to investigate and fully account for the manner of their deaths. Members of the security forces and their families require the same levels of protection for their rights as ordinary citizens. The lethal force incidents involving such personnel ultimately reveal some of the broader issues of accountability that are thrown into sharp relief when civilian deaths are at issue.

Republican paramilitary deaths

While many deaths examined in this book have been controversial, one particular subcategory stands out above others. These are the republican paramilitary deaths which have created a mythology of their own, and have been politicised above others, symbolising many of the most difficult facets of the relationship between the minority community and the state. As the statistical evidence reveals (see figure 13, p. 63) republican paramilitary deaths constitute the majority of deaths in the paramilitary category, and contribute to the perception that the experience of lethal force killings is predominantly confined to the nationalist community. The use of force against republican paramilitaries has the aura of sanction from a significant segment of civil society in Northern Ireland, endorsed as an exercise of military might and the destruction of paramilitary actors within the state. By contrast, the response to these deaths in the nationalist community has been a curious mixture of triumphalism and ceremonial grief.

The killing of eight members of PIRA and one innocent civilian in Loughgall, County Armagh, is a clear example of this curious political cocktail. The incident in May 1987 was centred on an attempt by an active service unit of PIRA to completely destroy an RUC station in the heart of the small village. A heavily armed group of paramilitaries assaulted the police station which was being staked out by the SAS awaiting their arrival.[23] The operational planning by the state agents seems to have been meticulous and the PIRA unit was clearly not expecting the police station to be occupied. The result of the operation was that all eight PIRA members were killed. They were Anthony Gormley (aged 25), Eugene Kelly (25), Gerard O'Callaghan (29), Patrick Kelly (32), James Lynagh (32), Seamus Donnelly (19), Declan Arthurs (21) and Patrick McKearney (32). In addition, Anthony Hughes, an entirely uninvolved civilian, was killed, and his brother Oliver was seriously injured. Both had been driving through the village at the time of the attack, and the SAS opened fire on their car. The death of this civilian raises serious questions about the manner in which the military operation was conducted. The SAS also fired on another civilian car being driven through the village by a woman, with her young daughter in the passenger seat. Both escaped serious injury.

The operation in Loughgall was a huge propaganda coup for the military and for those in the political arena advocating a hard-line response to terrorist action. There was the feeling in some official circles that the 'score' was being evened out with the republican paramilitaries. The London *Times* editorial set the tone by stating: 'Occasions on which the security forces strike back and be seen to do so help boost the confidence which must have been eroded in many law-abiding minds in Northern Ireland.'[24]

Despite this immediate validation for state action, the exercise of military force at Loughgall remains a matter of local political debate and international legal scrutiny. The case has been deemed admissible by the European Commission on Human Rights.[25] The controversial circumstances of the incident, the lack of meaningful domestic inquiry, and the relationship between counter-insurgency and protection for the right to life will make for interesting review by the European Court and Commission and the reawakening of a continuing debate domestically.

Another incident that raises many similar questions concerning the use of lethal force against republican paramilitary actors took place on 11 November 1982. Three unarmed members of PIRA were shot dead by members of RUC specialist units,[26] on the Tullygally East Road near Lurgan, County Armagh. Following the incident, speculation was rife as to the intention of the police officers and the operational orders they were following in respect of their law-enforcement duties. This incident, combined with two others in the November–December period of 1982, led to six deaths, all caused by specialist RUC units. Five of those killed were republican paramilitaries,[27] and one was a young man, Michael Tighe, with no involvement in any paramilitary organisation.

In isolation the shooting on 11 November 1982 might have created a small storm about policing methods and excessive use of force. However, in tandem with two subsequent and similar incidents, a public relations disaster ensued for the RUC, The controversy about these deaths was heightened when it became apparent that a number of police officers had, on the advice of their senior officers, given misleading and false evidence about the incident to CID investigators. An internal RUC investigation followed, which did little to assuage public concern. Ultimately, the DPP decided to bring charges against the three officers involved in the killings.[28] The murder charges related solely to the death of Eugene Toman, possibly premised on the compelling forensic evidence which indicated that his body had been tampered with at the vehicle site.

The criminal proceedings were wrought with controversy. Lord Justice Gibson acceded to the defence contention that the three police officers had no case to answer and they were acquitted of all charges. He concluded infamously that there was never 'the slightest chance of sustaining a conviction', and commended the three officers for their 'courage and determination in bringing the three deceased men to justice; in this case, to the final court of justice'.[29]

The controversy surrounding these deaths did not subside with the conclusion of the criminal trial. Self-evidently the trial had failed to provide satisfactory explanations for the manner in which the three men were killed. An official inquiry conducted by an English policeman, John Stalker, followed. The abortive ending of that investigation fuelled the belief that an undeclared shoot-to-kill policy had been effected by the RUC in the early 1980s.[30] Stalker had concluded that there were grounds for charging a number of police officers, and the Sampson inquiry which followed was eventually referred to the DPP, In January 1988 the Attorney-General, Sir Patrick Mayhew, announced that eight RUC officers involved in a conspiracy to prevent the course of justice would not be prosecuted for reasons of national security. Inquest proceedings dragged on until 1995, when the Belfast Coroner John Leckey was forced to concede that official obstruction and legal delays prevented the inquest process being completed.

Loyalist paramilitary deaths

The deaths of Protestant paramilitaries constitute a tiny percentage of total fatalities in the paramilitary category. Nonetheless, examining these deaths provides a comprehensive framework within which to analyse all paramilitary fatalities in Northern Ireland. While the deaths of loyalist paramilitary members bear some similarities with their republican counterparts, overall, the patterns of state response to these paramilitary actors is very different. One similarity between loyalist and republican deaths is a lack of openness and the nonresponsiveness of the state to external inquiry. What notably differentiates loyalist deaths from republican deaths is the scant publicity and condemnation for the state from the victim's own community. This may be explained by a broader lack of rights consciousness in the Protestant community, coupled with an unwillingness to criticise the state and its agents and a traditional lack of sympathy for violence exercised by nonstate actors.

In May 1972 John Black was shot by the army in east Belfast. A member of the Ulster Defence Association (UDA/UFF), he died five weeks later from his injuries. His death occurred as army personnel were dismantling and removing barricades placed on roads in the city. (The barricades served as structures to control the flow of persons and traffic into particular districts, prevented military and police access, and were gathering points for rioters and others seeking to taunt and attack the security forces. These structures were to become a common feature in Protestant neighbourhoods in the month of July, in part as a response to the creation of republican no-go areas in the city. At that time the barricades were a product of fears that the British government was about to make significant concessions to PIRA following their 22 June ceasefire statement.) As with many other fatalities in this period, information on John Black's death is scarce. There were no criminal legal proceedings following his death and he was given a funeral with full paramilitary-style trappings.

In September of the same year Sinclair Johnson, a member of the Ulster Volunteer Force (UVF), was shot by police during loyalist riots in Larne, County Antrim. Again, this death is marked by a lack of publicly available information and official investigation. Also in that month, eighteen-year-old Robert Warnock was killed. He was a member of the Ulster Freedom Fighters (UFF) and was killed in the Castlereagh area of east Belfast. He was attempting an armed robbery at the Hillfoot bar when he was shot by police. In a number of cases the deaths of loyalist paramilitaries are distinguished by reports of illegal activity occurring around the time that force was exercised. That is to say, many of these deaths occur in the context of so-called 'ordinary' crime, particularly property crime, such as theft and burglary. In some of these cases, it seems unlikely that the security forces were aware of the paramilitary affiliations of the victim, or that victims were targeted as a result of informer information specific to paramilitary activity. As no further information about Warnock's death was made public, it is difficult to ascertain whether he could have been arrested rather than killed. Similar concerns are raised by the death of nineteen-year-old Kirk Watters in February 1974. A member of the UFF, he was shot by the army in east Belfast during rioting, which had flared up after the security forces sought to quell celebrations resulting from the acquittal of seven UDA members on murder charges.

In June 1976, nineteen-year-old UDA member Edward Walker was shot by the RUC at a checkpoint on the Shore Road in north Belfast. Press statements issued by the police after the incident and the inquest report indicated that the checkpoint was set up following the report of a stolen vehicle. Police statements claimed that when the identified stolen vehicle approached the checkpoint it sped through, knocking one police officer to the ground. Police fired shots as the vehicle passed the centre of the checkpoint, the car subsequently halted, and four men were taken from it, including Edward Walker who later died from a gunshot wound to his head.[31] The inquest jury returned an open verdict on his death and there were no further legal proceedings.

One of the most controversial loyalist paramilitary deaths was that of Brian Robinson in September 1989. A member of the UVF, he and another man were escaping on a motorbike, having just committed a sectarian murder in north Belfast. The motorbike was travelling at high speed when it was rammed by a car carrying an undercover unit from the 14th Intelligence Company. The inquest into the death established that Robinson was armed while the motorcycle was moving but was without a weapon when he was shot. It determined that Robinson had been thrown from the bike and was lying in a crouched position when he was shot.[32]

The presence of the undercover surveillance unit in this case raises some uncomfortable and unresolved issues. First, was the sectarian murder carried out by Robinson preventable? Had the unit been following Robinson for an extended period or did they simply happen upon him while he was escaping from the murder he had just committed? Second, what precise activity was being carried out by the surveillance unit in the area? Finally, why was Robinson killed rather than arrested, given that he was unarmed and unresisting at the moment of his death?

Following the inquest the DPP decided to reopen its examination of the case. In November 1992, the DPP confirmed its decision not to prosecute any military personnel in respect of Robinson's death. One commentator has suggested that the empirical evidence suggests the death resulted from a spur of the moment decision by surveillance operators, rather than constituting a preplanned ambush.[33] Nevertheless, the lack of comprehensive investigation into this case leaves many issues unresolved.

Responding to individual stories

The deaths described in this appendix represent only a fraction of the fatalities which constitute the foundation for this work. Choosing to discuss a small number of them in detail was intended to illustrate the finality of each death for the family and community within which the loss was suffered. The immediacy of loss is self-evident and is played out publicly in the rituals of grief and mourning. But there is a deeper wound inflicted when death does not come naturally, and is the result of acts by third parties. When death is caused by the state itself, there are expectations of transparency, accountability and remedy by the state.

Since 1969 there have been a great many victims of violent conflict in Northern Ireland. Over three thousand people have been killed, the vast majority by paramilitary organisations. This study has focused its attention on the smaller subset of 350 deaths caused by agents of the state. Over time, as with many entrenched conflict situations, memories of these deaths fade for those fortunate enough not to have been directly affected by them. Telling individual stories of loss is crucial in the process of reclaiming those persons who have lost their lives in controversial or unresolved circumstances. The simplicity of placing forgotten names in the public view has an instrumental value. It is a reminder of things that remain unresolved and which require attention if societal change is to be meaningful.

Trust is the mechanism that connects state and citizen in a mutual contract. When that mechanism is constantly beleaguered, faith is destroyed between state and community. The use of lethal force, in particular, has splintered the relationship between the nationalist community and the apparatus of the state. Equally, segments of the loyalist community have been profoundly alienated by loss of life caused and unresolved by the state. There are some who might argue that these communities make up small and peripheral entities which are marginal to the state and its interests. This is a shortsighted view. In deeply divided societies, re-establishing trust with communities who have been disaffected is a necessary component of bridging conflict for all. For many, lethal force deaths in Northern Ireland are a collective symbol of the need for the renewal of relationships between the state and the multifarious communities it serves. In the new post-conflict Northern Ireland there is a pressing need to revisit and reinvent that symbolism and to create bridges of inclusion to all communities whatever their past relationship with the state. Such bridging constitutes the key to successful conflict resolution in the jurisdiction.

List of journal abbreviations

A.B.A.J.	American Bar Association Journal
Albany L. Rev.	Albany Law Review
Am. J. Int'l L.	American Journal of International Law
Am. J. Int'l L. and Pol'y	American Journal of International Law and Policy
Am. U. L. Rev.	American University Law Review
Anglo-Am L. Rev.	Anglo-American Law Review
Brit. Y. B. Int'l L.	British Year Book of International Law
Buff. L. Rev.	Buffalo Law Review
Camb, L. J.	Cambridge Law Journal
Can. Y. B. Int'l L.	Canadian Year Book of International Law
Case W. Res. J. Int'l L.	Case Western Reserve Journal of International Law
CLR	Common Law Review
Colum. Hum. Rts Rev.	Columbia Human Rights Review
Colum. L. Rev.	Columbia Law Review
Conn, J. Int'l L.	Connecticut Journal of International Law
Crim. L. J.	Criminal Law Journal
Crim. L. Rev.	Criminal Law Review
De Paul L. Rev.	De Paul Law Review
EHRR	European Human Rights Reports
E. H. Rts L. Rev.	European Human Rights Law Review
Fordham Int'l L. J.	Fordham International Law Journal
Ga. J. Int'l and Comp. L.	Georgia Journal of International and Comparative Law
Harv. Hum. Rts J.	Harvard Human Rights Journal
Harv. Int'l L. J.	Harvard International Law Journal
Harv. L. Rev.	Harvard Law Review
Hastings L. J.	Hastings Law Journal
Hum. Rts	Human Rights
Hum. Rts L. J.	Human Rights Law Journal
Hum. Rts Q.	Human Rights Quarterly
ICJ Rev.	International Commission of Jurists Review
Int'l and Comp. L. Q.	International and Comparative Law Quarterly
Int'l J. L. Lib	International Journal of Law Libraries
Int'l J. Sociology of Law	International Journal of the Sociology of Law
Int'l L. and Politics	International Law and Politics
Int'l Rev. Red Cross	International Review of the Red Cross
Ir. Jur.	Irish Jurist
Isr. Y. B. Hum. Rts	Israel Year Book of Human Rights
Israel L. Rev.	Israel Law Review
J. Crim. L. C. and P. S.	Journal of Criminal Law, Criminology and Police Science
J. Int'l Aff.	Journal of International Affairs
J. Int'l L. and Econ.	Journal of International Law and Economics
Loy. L. A. L. Rev.	Loyola of Los Angeles Law Review
L. Q. Rev.	Law Quarterly Review
Maastricht J. Eur. and Comp. L.	Maastricht Journal of European and Comparative Law

Md. L. Rev.	Modern Law Review
Mich. J. Int'l L.	Michigan Journal of International Law
Mil. L. Rev.	Military Law Review
Neth. Hum Rts Q.	Netherlands Human Rights Quarterly
Neth. Y. B. Int'l L.	Netherlands Year Book of International Law
New Law J.	New Law Journal
NILQ	Northern Ireland Legal Quarterly
Nordic J. Int'l Law	Nordic Journal of International Law
Notre Dame L. Rev.	Notre Dame Law Review
Nw. J. Crim. L. and Criminology	New Journal of Criminal Law and Criminology
N. Y. L. Sch. J. Int'l and Comp. L.	New York Law School Journal of International and Comparative Law
N. Y. U. L. Rev.	New York University Law Review
O. J. L. S.	Oxford Journal of Legal Studies
Oxford J. Legal Studies	Oxford Journal of Legal Studies
Penn. L. Rev.	Pennsylvania Law Review
Rev. Int'l Comm'n. Jurists	Review of the International Commission of Jurists
Review of Int'l Studies	Review of International Studies
Stan. L. Rev.	Stanford Law Review
Temple L. Rev.	Temple Law Review
Tex. Int'l L. J.	Texas International Law Journal
Tex. L. Rev.	Texas Law Review
UCLA Law Rev.	University of California at Los Angeles Law Review
U. Det. L. Rev.	University of Detroit Law Review
Va. J. Int'l L.	Vanderbilt Journal of International Law
Vand. J. Transnt'l L.	Vanderbilt Journal of Transnational Law
Wash. and Lee L. Rev.	Washington and Lee Law Review
Will. and Mary L. Rev.	William and Mary Law Review
Yale J. World Pub. Ord.	Yale Journal of World Public Order
Yale L. J.	Yale Law Journal
Y. B. World Aff.	Year Book of World Affairs

Notes

Preface and acknowledgements

1 Note that off-duty deaths are specifically excluded from the study.
2 The following law-enforcement agencies fall within this category: the Royal Ulster Constabulary (RUC), the B Specials, HM Armed Forces, the Royal Irish Regiment (RIR) and the Ulster Defence Regiment (UDR). For completeness, the following specialist units of the military are also authorised as state agents for the purposes of this study: the Special Air Service (SAS) and the 14th Intelligence Company.
3 Such deaths include Charles O'Neill, a former British soldier killed on 3 July 1970 by an army armoured car that ran over him; Denise Ann Dickson, knocked over while playing near her home by a military scout car on 8 February 1971; Garry Gormley, a three-year-old killed by a speeding army armoured car that failed to stop on 9 September 1971; John Clarke, killed when an army Saracen went out of control on 16 October 1972; James Brown and Gary English, both teenagers, killed when an army Land Rover ploughed into a crowd on 19 April 1981; Joseph Lynch, killed by an RUC vehicle driving away from a stone-throwing crowd on 23 May 1981; Private Tony Anderson, a soldier crushed under an armoured vehicle on 24 May 1982; Alan McCormick, killed by a police Land Rover on 15 November 1986.
4 Such deaths would include, for example, Henry McIlhone, killed on 29 June 1970, where there are lingering doubts about state involvement in the gun battles and rioting which were the context to his death; John Johnston, who died on 16 June 1972, was one of the first people hit by gunfire on Bloody Sunday, 30 January 1972. He was admitted to hospital, apparently recovered from his injuries, but was later readmitted suffering from a brain tumour. It is unclear if the Bloody Sunday injuries were causal or marginal to his death. Both these deaths are excluded from the data base.

Introduction

1 Simultaneous referenda took place in both parts of Ireland on 22 May 1998. In the South 94 per cent voted in support of the Good Friday Agreement, in the North the agreement was supported by 71 per cent. The question put forward in the Northern Ireland referendum was '[d]o you support the agreement reached in the multiparty talks on Northern Ireland and set out in Command Paper 3883?'
2 For an extended discussion on the role of law and legality in this process *see* Mark Osiel, *Mass Atrocity, Collective Memory and the Law* (1997)
3 *See* Steven R. Rathner and Jason S. Abrams, *Accountability for Human Rights Atrocities in International Law* (1997)
4 *See* Kader Asmal *et al*, *Reconciliation Through Truth – A Reckoning of Apartheid's Criminal Governance* (1996); José Zalaquett, *Balancing Ethical Imperatives and Political Constraints: The Dilemma of New Democracies Confronting Past Human Rights Violations*, 43 Hastings L. J. 1,432 (1992); *Report of the Argentinean National Commission of the Disappeared* (1986)
5 Universal Declaration of Human Rights, G.A. Res. 217 (1948), adopted by the UN General Assembly on 10 December 1948. *See also* International Covenant on Civil and Political Rights, 999 UNTS 171, 6 ILM 368 (1967).

1 A brief historical overview

1 The Government of Ireland Act 1920 came into effect in Northern Ireland in 1921 by the May elections provided for under the Act, creating a Northern Ireland parliament with 40 out of the 52 seats going to the Ulster Unionist Party of Sir James Craig. The new parliament in the North was opened by George V in Belfast on 22 June 1921,

confirming the political partition of the island of Ireland. The treaty which created the Irish Free State giving dominion status to the twenty-six-county south was signed on 6 December 1921 and ratified by Dáil Éireann (Irish parliament) on 7 January 1922.

2 'Ulster' is the name given to the nine-county province, which is geographically located in the northern part of the island of Ireland. However, the description is frequently used to refer to the political entity of the six-county Northern Ireland substate. The colonial settlements, or plantations of English and Scottish (Protestant) settlers, began in the seventeenth century.

3 A number of different terms are used to describe Protestants and Catholics in Northern Ireland. The terms 'unionist' and 'loyalist' are both used to describe Protestant political affiliation – 'unionist' being synonymous with the political regime in Northern Ireland from 1921 onwards; 'loyalist' with militaristic responses to maintain the constitutional link with the United Kingdom. The terms 'nationalist' and 'republican' describe political affiliation for Catholics. Both are associated with a belief in the legitimacy of a thirty-two-county all-Ireland state. The term 'republican' is largely used to refer to those who believe that only military responses can facilitate the creation of a thirty-two-county state.

4 The Northern Ireland parliament sat in Belfast City Hall and the Presbyterian Assembly College until 1932, but thereafter at Stormont, which led to the colloquial practice of naming the regime after its geographical location.

5 See F.S.L. Lyons, *Ireland Since the Famine* (2nd ed., 1974), chapter 4

6 *Ibid.*, pp. 421–39

7 The state remained neutral during the Second World War, despite British and American pressure to join the war effort on the side of the allies. *See* Robert Fisk, *In Time of War – Ireland, Ulster and the Price of Neutrality, 1935–45* (1983).

8 *See* F.S.L. Lyons, *Culture and Anarchy in Ireland, 1890–1939* (1982)

9 Taoiseach of Ireland, February 1996, *Northern Ireland Peace Process: Statements, Debates,* Official Report Unrevised, vol. 461, n. 6 at 1,739 (1996)

10 Bursts of republican paramilitary activity between 1922 and 1969 reinforced this political psychosis. In 1938 a plot against the government was uncovered and 827 men were interned. A brief IRA campaign in 1956–62 was unsuccessful in large measure for a lack of popular support from the nationalist community.

11 Bunreacht na hÉireann (Irish Constitution) 1937, Articles 2 and 3. Article 2 holds that: 'The national territory consists of the whole island of Ireland, its islands and the territorial seas.' Article 3 provides that: 'Pending the re-integration of the national territory, and without prejudice to the right of the Parliament and Government established by this Constitution to exercise jurisdiction over the whole of that territory, the laws enacted by that Parliament shall have the like area and extent of application as the laws of Saorstát Éireann and the like extra-territorial effect.' Under the terms of the Good Friday Agreement, the Irish government undertook to review and reformulate Articles 2 and 3 of the constitution. This resulted in removing the explicit territorial claim and replacing it with a consent-based claim whose activation would be premised by all other strands of the agreement coming into force.

12 *See* Fionnuala O Connor, *In Search of a State: Catholics in Northern Ireland* (1993)

13 The Education Act 1923, which followed the report of the Lynn Committee, underlined the lack of political power exercised by nationalists in the Northern Ireland parliament. Despite an amending Act negotiated with the Prime Minister in 1925, schools were secularised and Catholic schools were only partly maintained by the state.

14 Less than 10 per cent of the police force (RUC) are Catholic. *Chief Constable's Report* (1998).

15 *See* Colm Campbell, *Emergency Law in*

Ireland, 1918–1925 9–10, 27–8 (1994)

16 *See* Kevin Boyle *et al, Law and State: The Case of Northern Ireland* (1975)

17 *See* Subrata Roy Chowdhury, *Rule of Law in a State of Emergency* (1989); *Study on the Implications for Human Rights of Recent Developments Concerning Situations Known as States of Siege or Emergency*, UN Commission on Human Rights, 35th Sess., Agenda Item 10, UN Doc. E/CN.4/Sub.2/15 (1982) (Questiaux Report); Joan Fitzpatrick, *Human Rights in Crisis: The International System for Protecting Rights During States of Emergency* (1994)

18 European Convention on Human Rights, 4 November 1950, 213 UNTS 221, Europ. TS No. 5 Article 15; American Convention on Human Rights, *opened for signature*, 22 November 1969, OASTS No. 36, 9 ILM 673 (entered into force 18 July 1978) Article 27; International Covenant on Civil and Political Rights, 16 December 1966, 999 UNTS 171, 1977 Gr. Brit. TS No. 6 (Cmnd. 6702) Article 4

19 *See* Human Rights Watch, *Justice For All? An Analysis of the Human Rights Provisions of the 1998 Northern Ireland Peace Agreement* (1998)

20 Questiaux Report, *supra* note 17, § 63

21 *Disturbances in Northern Ireland: Report of the Commission Appointed by the Governor of Northern Ireland* (Cmnd. 532) 1969 (Cameron Report)

22 *Report of the Advisory Committee on Police in Northern Ireland* (Cmnd. 535) 1969 (Hunt Report). Though perceptions of police bias pervaded the cultural consciousness of the nationalist community, there was nonetheless an expectation by the reformist element of the civil rights movement that the RUC would not ally as squarely as it did with the sectarian response of the Protestant loyalists.

23 The Police Act (Northern Ireland) 1970 reorganised and disarmed the RUC; the B Specials were abolished and local government franchise was reformed.

24 *See* Keith Jeffery, *Military Aid to the Civil Power in the United Kingdom – An Historical Perspective*, in P. Rowe and C. Whelan (eds), *Military Intervention in Democratic Societies* (1985)

25 *See generally*, David Lowry, *Internment: Detention Without Trial in Northern Ireland*, 6 Hum. Rts 261 (1975–6). Those interned in 1922 were held for up to two years. The group interned in 1938 were held until the outbreak of war in 1939, and thereafter many were to remain in state custody until the ending of the war in 1945. *See generally*, John McGuffin, *Internment* (1974).

26 *Lawless v. Ireland*, 1 E.Ct.H.R. (ser. A) at 56 (1961)

27 It should be noted that while there were incidents of covert counter-insurgency taking place in Northern Ireland from 1969 onwards, most notably during 1978, the post-hunger-strike period marks a point at which an organised covert response can be pinpointed as emerging from the state.

28 The Criminal Evidence (Northern Ireland) Order 1987. § 34 of the Criminal Justice and Public Order Act 1994 extends the same provisions to England and Wales.

29 Examples of this include the Bombay Street incident in Belfast on 15 August 1969. The army response to the siege of the Bogside in Derry/Londonderry, which had been sparked by the Apprentice Boys parade on 12 August 1969, was equally problematic. In Belfast's Lower Falls Road area on 3 July 1970 the army commenced a search for arms. In response to stoning incidents the army initially used tear gas and refused to negotiate with local priests who offered to mediate to calm the situation. The lack of mediation ultimately led to an official curfew being imposed on the area. An equally insensitive operation was Operation Motorman in July 1971, where a motorised, high profile thrust into the no-go areas in Derry/Londonderry and Belfast to bring down barricades, failed to root out members of the IRA and incensed local opinion.

30 *See* Claire Palley, *The Evolution, Disintegration and Possible Reconstruction of the Northern Ireland Constitution*, Anglo-Am. L. Rev. 368, 412 (1973)

31 *See, Thomas v. Sawkins* (1935) 2 KB 249; *Coyne v. Tweedy* (1898) 2 IR 167; *Phillips v. Eyre* (1870) LR 1; *Hughes v. Caseres* (1967) 111 Sol. Jo. 637

32 *See, Reference under* § *48 of the Criminal Appeal (Northern Ireland) Act 1968* (No. 1 of 1975), 937

33 *Hume v. Londonderry Justices* NI 1 (1972)

34 Government of Ireland Act § 10 and 11 Geo. 5, 5 (4)

35 As cited in Tony Geraghty, *The Irish War* 92–3 (1998)

36 *Reference under* § *48 of the Criminal Appeal (Northern Ireland) Act 1968* at 946

37 *See, Sunday Times* Insight Team, *Ulster* 141 (1972)

38 A soldier was charged following the death of Seamus Cusack (8 July 1971) in the Bogside, Derry/Londonderry. The circumstances of death were disputed and Cusack died following the incident in hospital in Letterkenny, Co. Donegal. David McKittrick reports that 'the soldier was acquitted in a subsequent court case . . . The judge, Lord Justice Gibson, later killed by the IRA, apportioned blame equally between the victim and the soldier who shot him.' *See* David McKittrick *et al, Lost Lives* 75–6 (1999).

39 The categories here are 17 in total. They derive from three overriding framework contexts in which deaths take place in the emergency situation of Northern Ireland. These are, security-linked deaths, public-order-related deaths and a miscellaneous category which includes such incidents as accidental discharge of a weapon.

40 The terms of the legislation stipulated the jail terms for 'riotous behaviour', 'disorderly behaviour' or 'behaviour likely to cause a breach of the peace'.

41 Geraghty, *supra* note 35, at 37. Similar issues concerning the relevant legal standards to apply also concern Operation Motorman, which took place in Derry/Londonderry and Belfast in 1972. In November 1998 the former British Prime Minister Edward Heath stated that in July 1972 the Royal Navy and the Royal Air Force were placed on standby at the beginning of the operation to clear the no-go areas of the two cities. *See, Civil Liberties Diary,* 13 Just News, November 1998 at 8.

42 Palley, *supra* note 30. *See also* Michael P. O'Boyle, *Emergency Situations and the Protection of Human Rights: A Model*

Derogation Provision for a Northern Ireland Bill of Rights, 28 NILQ 166 (1977).

43 'Newsman in Curfew Case Cleared', *Irish News,* 28 July 1970; 'Freeland Right in Imposing Curfew, Magistrate Rules', *Irish News,* 9 September 1970

44 Wade and Phillips, *Constitutional Law* 402 (7th ed. 1965)

45 *See, Tilonko v. A.G. of Natal* (1907) AC 93. *See generally,* F.K.M.A. Munim, *Legal Aspects of Martial Law* (1989); Charles Fairman, *The Law of Martial Rule* (2nd ed. 1943).

46 (1972) NI 1. The case established that the Stormont government was acting *ultra vires* the Government of Ireland Act by regulating under the Special Powers Act for the use and deployment of the army.

47 Two Electoral Law Acts had brought the franchise in Northern Ireland in line with the rest of the United Kingdom. An ombudsman was created to look into grievances against central government. Minor reform of housing and local government was initiated. However, no independent prosecutor separate from the police was created. No antidiscrimination clause was placed in governmental contracts. The Special Powers Act was withdrawn.

48 The *Sunday Times* Insight Team indicates that the army under the command of General Harry Tuzo were highly sceptical of the 'Unionists' panacea', as he termed internment. The days leading up to the final decision to activate internment were characterised by the army seeking an alternative, convinced that the failure of Jack Lynch's government in the Republic of Ireland to collaborate with simultaneous introduction doomed the exercise to failure. *Ulster, supra* note 37, chapter 15.

49 *See* Don Mullan (ed.) *Eyewitness, Bloody Sunday* (1997). Following the publication of the book, *Channel 4 News* (United Kingdom) published interviews with soldiers who were present the day of the incident, which supported the accounts of witnesses.

50 The tribunal started its inquiry in the Guildhall in Derry/Londonderry in February 1999.

51 *See, The Events on Sunday 30th January*

1972 which Led to Loss of Life in Connection With the Procession in Londonderry on that Day, HC 220 (1972) § 34 (Widgery Report)

52 The deaths and the lack of state acknowledgment of responsibility created ongoing contention within the nationalist community. Families of the deceased continued to seek legal redress both domestically and internationally. For example, in March 1994 the relatives of those killed announced their decision to take their case to the European Court of Human Rights, following a governmental refusal to reopen the inquiries into the 13 deaths. *See* Committee on the Administration of Justice, 9 Just News (1994). The European Commission declared the application inadmissible on the grounds that the case failed to comply with the procedural requirements of admissibility as set out in Article 26 of the convention.

53 Helsinki Watch, *Human Rights in Northern Ireland* 45 (1993)

54 *See* Paul Bew and Gordon Gillespie, *Northern Ireland: A Chronology of the Troubles, 1968–1993* 57 (1993)

55 *See* Schedule 1 to the Northern Ireland (Emergency Provisions) Act 1973, where the term 'internment' was also replaced by 'detention'.

56 *See, Report of the Commission to Consider Legal Procedures to Deal with Terrorist Activities in Northern Ireland* (Cmnd. 5185) (1972) (Diplock Report)

57 *See* William Twining, *Emergency Powers and Criminal Process: The Diplock Report*, Crim. L. Rev. 406, 415 (1973)

58 *Report of a Committee to Consider, in the Context of Civil Liberties and Human Rights, Measures to Deal with Terrorism in Northern Ireland* (Cmnd. 5847) (1975) (Gardiner Report) states that on 30 November 1974 there were 1,119 special category prisoners in Northern Ireland. *Ibid.* at Appendix E.

59 Convention Relative to the Treatment of Prisoners of War, 6 UST 3316, 75 UNTS 135

60 This model has been contrasted with the due process model, dominant in common law legal process in the 1960s. Walsh admirably outlines the tension between the two in the Irish Republic since the re-emergence of conflict in Northern Ireland. *See* Dermot P.J. Walsh, *The Impact of Anti-Subversive Laws on Police Powers and Practice in Ireland: The Silent Erosion of Individual Freedom*, 62 Temple L. Rev. 1099 (1989).

61 *See generally*, Dermot P.J. Walsh, *The Use and Abuse of Emergency Legislation in Northern Ireland* (1983)

62 Civil Authorities (Special Powers) Act 1922

63 *See* Lawyers Committee for Human Rights, *Human Rights and Legal Defense in Northern Ireland: The Intimidation of Defense Lawyers, The Murder of Patrick Finucane* 1 (1993)

64 *See* Walsh, *supra* note 61

65 *See* Paddy Hillyard, *Suspect Community: People's Experience of the Prevention of Terrorism Acts in Britain* 1 (1993)

66 Northern Ireland (Emergency Provisions) Act 1973, *ch* 53 (Eng)

67 Prevention of Violence (Temporary Provisions) Act 1939, 2 and 3 Geo. 6, *ch* 50 (Eng)

68 Prevention of Terrorism (Temporary Provisions) Act 1976, *ch* 8 (Eng)

69 Prevention of Terrorism (Temporary Provisions) Act 1984, *ch* 8 (Eng)

70 Prevention of Terrorism (Temporary Provisions) Act 1989, *ch* 4 (Eng)

71 *See* for example, Gardiner Report, *supra* note 58. *Review of the Operation of the Northern Ireland (Emergency Provisions) Act 1973* (1984) (Baker Report). *Report of the Operation of the Prevention of Terrorism (Temporary Provisions) Acts 1976* (1983) (Jellicoe Report). *Review of the Operation of the Prevention of Terrorism (Temporary Provisions) Act 1974 & 1976* (1978) (Shackelton Report). *Report of the Operation in 1991 of the Northern Ireland (Emergency Provisions) Act 1991* (1992) (Colville EPA Report). *Review of the Northern Ireland (Emergency Provisions) Act 1991* (1995) (J.J. Rowe QC EPA Report). *Report on the Operation in 1994 of the Prevention of Terrorism (Temporary Provisions) Act 1989* by J.J. Rowe QC, published 17 February 1995. *See* Hillyard, *supra* note 65.

72 *Fourth Periodic Report by the United Kingdom of Great Britain and Northern Ireland to the Human Rights Committee*

Under Article 40 of the International Covenant on Civil and Political Rights (1994); Mary Ann Dadisman, *The Irish Question: Into the Lion's Den, Britain Grilled on Human Rights Issues of Northern Ireland*, Hum. Rts (summer 1994) (outlining how the Right. Hon. Sir Patrick Mayhew, Secretary of State for Northern Ireland, at the spring meeting of the IR & R Section in Washington, DC set out the value of these reviews).

73   For an outline of the South African emergency response during the apartheid regime, *see* Anthony Mathews, *Freedom, State Security, and the Rule of Law* 192–215 (2nd ed. 1988); John Quigley, *Israel's Forty-Five-Year Emergency: Are There Time Limits to Derogations to Human Rights Violations?*, 15 Mich. J. Int'l. L. 491, 492 (1994); B'tselem, *Activity of the Undercover Units in the Occupied Territories* 7–9, 13–33, 75–89 (1992); B'tselem, *The Use of Firearms by the Security Forces in the Occupied Territories* (1990).

74   *See* Mark Urban, *Big Boys' Rules: The Secret Struggle Against the IRA* xvii (1992); Kader Asmal, *Shoot to Kill? International Lawyers' Inquiry into the Lethal Use of Firearms by the Security Forces in Northern Ireland* 10 (1985)

75   *See generally*, Walsh, *supra* note 61

76   *Committee on the Prevention of Torture (CPA) Report*, CPA/Inf (94) 17 at 34, cif.104

77   UN Human Rights Commission, *Consideration of Reports Submitted by State Parties under Article 40 of the Covenant, United Kingdom of Great Britain and Northern Ireland* §§ 11, UN Doc CCPR/C/79 Add.55 (1995)

78   *Ibid.*, § 22, 27 July 1995. On 10 December 1999 RUC Chief Constable Ronnie Flanagan announced the closure of Castlereagh Detention Centre.

79   E/CN.4/Sub.2/1994/24

80   *Brogan and Others v. United Kingdom*, 145B E.Ct.H.R. (ser. A) (29 November 1988)

81   Note the statement of Douglas Hogg to the House of Commons on 13 December 1988: 'The Case of Brogan and Others has rightly exercised Hon. Members' minds. The Committee will recall that my Right Hon. Friend the Home Secretary told the House on 6 December that we shall bring forward our proposals for responding to the judgment in the Brogan case as soon as possible and before the Bill leaves the House. The matter is complex, and whether *we opt for derogation* or some sort of judicial control, the implications are obviously far reaching [emphasis added].' The European Court recognised in the *Brannigan and McBride* case that the *Brogan* judgment may have 'triggered off' the derogation. *See, Brannigan and McBride*, 258 E.Ct.H.R. (ser. A) at 51.

82   *See* Stephen Greer, *Supergrasses: A Study in Anti-Terrorist Law Enforcement in Northern Ireland* 35–49 (1995). *See also* Walsh, *supra* note 60, who notes that the Diplock Courts blurred the line between ordinary criminal activity and proscribed paramilitary activity. The Diplock Courts now exist under § 11 of the 1996 Emergency Provisions Act.

83   *See* Amnesty International, *United Kingdom Summary of Human Rights Concerns* (1995), A1/ Eur/45/06/95 at 22–3

84   Under the EPA any written or oral statement by the accused may be admitted as evidence provided that the defence does not bring forward *prima facie* evidence to show that the accused was subject to 'torture or to inhuman or degrading treatment or to any violence or threat of violence in order to induce him to make a statement'. The test is a much lower one than that imposed by the PACE legislation which governs the ordinary criminal law. *See, R v. Flynn and Leonard*, NIJB (1972).

85   *See* for example, *McEldowney v. Forde* (1969) 2 ALL ER 1039 and *In re Keenan and Another* (1972) NI 118 (QBD)

86   *Reform of the Judiciary*, 2 Common Ground (1995)

87   National Council for Civil Liberties, *Report of a Commission of Inquiry Appointed to Examine the Purpose and Effect of the Civil Authorities (Special Powers) Act (Northern Ireland) 1922 and 1933* (1936)

88   *See* Alejandro Garro, *The Role of the Argentine Judiciary in Controlling Governmental Action Under a State of*

Siege, 4 Hum. Rts L.J. 311 (1983)

89 Walsh identifies three particular problems with this strategy. First, that criminalisation diverts attention away from the essentially political nature of the problem. Second, extensive police powers will become the norm for dealing with both terrorist and ordinary crime. Finally, that it may be difficult to exercise control over the oppressive exercise of such powers as they are so broadly defined. Walsh, *supra* note 60 at 13.

90 Urban also makes the claim that the SAS was reined in between 1979 and 1983, in part as a result of changes in the personalities directing the security force apparatus. *See* Urban, *supra* note 74 at 82.

91 *Donnelly v. United Kingdom* (No. 1) Application Nos 5577/72, 5533/72 43 *Collected Decisions* (1973) 122; *Ireland v. United Kingdom*, 1976 Y.B. ECHR 512. These cases are discussed in depth in chapter 4.

92 *See* Amnesty International, *Report of an Amnesty International Mission to Northern Ireland* 55, 67 (1978) A1 Index Eur 45/01/78; *Ireland v. United Kingdom*, 1976 Y.B. ECHR 512

93 *See* Boyle *et al*, *Ten Years on in Northern Ireland* 44–6 (1980)

94 *Report of the Committee of Inquiry into Police Interrogation Procedures in Northern Ireland* (Cmnd. 7497) (1979) (Bennett Report)

95 On 19 June 1980 a report from the European Commission on Human Rights rejected a case brought by Kieran Nugent and three other prisoners, alleging violations of the ECHR by the United Kingdom government. The context of the application resulted from the failure of the government to recognise them as political prisoners, thus the applicants had refused to comply with certain prison regulations, including the requirement to wear a uniform. The commission had to consider to what extent the inhuman and degrading treatment was a consequence of the applicants' own acts; for example, their refusal to leave their cells to use the dining room, toilets or washroom or to take exercise. *See, McFeeley v. United*

Kingdom 38 D & R 11 (1984). The commission observed 'that the applicants are seeking to achieve a status of political prisoner which they are not entitled to under national law or under the Convention. Furthermore . . . the Commission does not consider that such an entitlement in the present context can be derived from the existing norms of international law'. *Ibid.*, at paragraph 43. One of the grounds for rejecting the claims was that the inhuman treatment alleged was self-inflicted by the prisoners. The commission stated, 'The protest campaign was designed and coordinated by the prisoners to create the maximum publicity and to enlist public sympathy and support for their political aims. That such a strategy involved self-inflicted debasement and humiliation to an almost sub-human degree must be taken into account.' *Ibid.* at paragraph 45. *See generally*, Padraig O'Malley, *Biting at the Grave: The Irish Hunger Strikes and the Politics of Despair* (1990).

96 *See* Colin Crawford, *Defenders or Criminals? Loyalist Prisoners and Criminalisation* 56–61 (1999)

97 *See* Bew and Gillespie, *supra* note 54 at 156

98 *See* Richard Kearney, *Myth and Motherland* 5 Field Day Pamphlet (1984)

99 *See* Urban, *supra* note 74 at 151

100 Inquest transcript (unofficial) May 1993, on file with author

101 *R v. Robinson, Montgomery and Brannigan* (1984) unreported

102 *R v. Robinson* (1984) unreported

103 *See* Greer, *supra* note 82

104 *Ibid.*

105 Amnesty International, *Northern Ireland Killings by the Security Forces and 'Supergrass' Trials* 61 (1988) A1 Index: Eur 45/08/88

106 *See* Anthony Jennings (ed.), *Justice Under Fire: The Abuse of Civil Liberties in Northern Ireland* (1988)

107 The choice of the SAS was no mere chance. The unit has a long history of involvement in situations of counter-insurgency, particularly in post-colonial management. *See generally* Bowen, *Report on Interrogation of*

Suspected Suspects in Aden (Cmnd. 3165). Hansard H.C. Deb, vol 78 col 1005–1008; and Tony Geraghty, *Who Dares Wins* (1983).

108 Criminal Law Act (Northern Ireland) 1967, § 3

109 *See* Oren Gross, 'Theoretical Models of Emergency Powers', unpublished SJD thesis, Harvard Law School, 1997

110 May 1995. Officials indicated that the review would be 'along the lines of past reviews'. Interview with Northern Ireland officials, on file with author (19 June 1995).

111 Lord Lloyd and Mr Justice Kerr were invited to 'consider the future need for specific counter terrorism legislation in the United Kingdom, if the cessation of violence connected with the affairs of Northern Ireland leads to a lasting peace, taking into account the threat from other kinds of terrorism, and the United Kingdom's obligations under international law'. The Secretary of State has made clear from the outset in parliament what his preference for the outcome would be: 'Mr. Rowe recommends that the Northern Ireland (Emergency Provisions) Act, which applies only to Northern Ireland, and the Prevention of Terrorism (Temporary Provisions) Act 1989, which applies in the main to the United Kingdom as a whole, should be consolidated in one comprehensive statute, providing all that is needed to cope with the perceived threat of terrorism anywhere in the United Kingdom . . . I believe that there is much merit in that.' *See, Inquiry into Legislation against Terrorism* (1996): Paragraph 5.15 concludes that 'when lasting peace is established in Northern Ireland, there will continue to be a need for permanent anti-terrorist legislation'. Paragraph 5.21 finds that 'the new Act should apply throughout the UK and should cover domestic as well as international terrorism'.

112 *Ibid.*, paragraph 5.10

113 *Ibid.*, paragraphs 5.11 and 5.12

114 *See* Urban, *supra* note 74 at 227–37

115 *Ibid.*, at 230

116 This account is heavily reliant on Mark Urban's account, which is based on interviews with the army personnel

involved. As there has been no inquest, and press reporting was limited by lack of access to the site, it is difficult to be entirely certain of the sequence of events.

117 Application no. 30054/96

118 *See generally*, Tom Hadden and Kevin Boyle, *The Anglo-Irish Agreement: Commentary, Text and Official Review* (1989)

119 *See* Paul H. Robinson, *Criminal Law Defences: A Systematic Analysis*, 82 Colum. L. Rev. 199 (1982); Kent Greenawalt, *The Perplexing Borders of Justification and Excuse*, 84 Colum. L. Rev. 1,987 (1984); J.C. Smith, *Justification and Excuse in the Criminal Law*, Hamlyn Lectures (1989)

2 Patterns in the use of force and the response of the criminal justice system

1 *See* David McKittrick *et al*, *Lost Lives* (1999). A soldier was charged following the death of Seamus Cusack (8 July 1971). The soldier was acquitted of all charges. *Ibid.*, at 75–6. A soldier was convicted in June 1974 of manslaughter. The twenty-year-old private from the Queen's Lancashire Regiment was jailed for a year, resulting from his shooting of James Ward (11 December 1972). *Ibid.* at 304–5. The deaths of Michael Naan and Andrew Murray (23 October 1972) were belatedly reviewed by the criminal courts. In 1981 two soldiers who were former members of the Argyll and Sutherland Highlanders were given life sentences for murder. *Ibid.*, at 286–7.

2 These recently included the conviction of two Scots Guards for the murder of Belfast teenager Peter Paul McBride in February 1995. *See* 'Judge Queries Mandatory Life Term for Murder as He Jails Two Soldiers in the North', *Irish Times*, 11 February 1995. This case has again created recent controversy, following the release of the two convicted soldiers on licence in 1998. The mother of Peter McBride has taken legal action to prevent the two

soldiers serving in the army again. *See* 'Mother's Case for Review of Army Move Questioned', *Irish Times*, 2 June 1999 at 7.

3 It should be noted that other commentators have recognised that the use of lethal force occurs in a number of different but clearly identifiable situations in Northern Ireland. Tom Hadden has identified three broad categories in which such incidents occur. These are (1) accidental shootings (2) spur of the moment shootings and (3) planned confrontations. *See* Tom Hadden, *Legal Controls on the Use of Lethal Force: Options for Reform*, in Standing Advisory Commission on Human Rights, 18th Annual Report 5 (1992–3).

4 Detailed information on the process of categorisation is included in the Preface.

5 The 14th Intelligence Company was known during the 1970s as the Reconnaissance Force.

6 *R v. Bohan and Temperley* (1979) NIJB 1

7 *See*, for example, Bowen, *Report on Interrogation of Suspected Terrorists in Aden* (Cmnd. 3165) Hansard H.C. Deb, vol 78. col 1005–1008

8 *See* Tony Geraghty, *Who Dares Wins* (1983)

9 Those are the killings in January 1990 of three men at a bookmaker's shop in west Belfast and the shooting of Brian Robinson in 1989.

10 *See* Mark Urban, *Big Boys' Rules* (1992). Appendix includes the deaths of Denis Heaney (June 1978), Charles Maguire and George McBrearty (May 1981), Henry Hogan and Declan Martin (February 1984) and Neil Liam McMonagle (February 1983).

11 Evidence by Deputy Chief Constable Michael McAtamney at the trial of three RUC officers charged with the death of Eugene Toman, describing the key elements of the police training in these specialist units.

12 In 1977 Special Branch formed a surveillance squad which became part of its Operations Division. This unit was E4A, which became the focus of controversy during the Stalker investigation into the alleged RUC

shoot-to-kill policy in 1984. The centralisation of intelligence information in the RUC from the late 1970s onwards precipitated the move by the police to active counter-insurgency.

13 Paragraph 81 of the Hunt Report went further in stating that the military character of the police force made it 'less acceptable to the public and moderate opinion'.

14 This method of security is known as 'jarking'. It is the Weapons Intelligence Unit (WIU) which generally has responsibility for ballistics and arms finds.

15 Informer information has been consistently excluded from consideration by inquests and criminal proceedings by Public Interest Immunity Certificates. *See, R v. Robinson* (1984) NIJB 1; *R v. Robinson, Montgomery and Brannigan* (1984).

16 Gibraltar Inquest transcript at 39, copy on file with author

17 *See, Land Operations* volume 3 – *Counter Revolutionary Operations* as cited in Urban *supra* note 10 at 19

18 *See* George Fletcher, *The Right and the Reasonable*, 98 Harvard L. Rev. 949 (1985); Eric Colvin, *Exculpatory Defences in Criminal Law*, 10 Oxford J. L. S. 381 (1990)

19 Those cases which have include *R v. Bohan and Temperley* (1979), *R v. Robinson* (1984) and *R v. Robinson, Montgomery and Brannigan* (1984).

20 *See* Urban *supra* note 10 at 164. Based on interviews with military sources in Britain and Northern Ireland he applies this principle to mean that there is no shoot-to-kill policy in the sense of a blanket order to shoot IRA terrorists on sight in Northern Ireland. However, there was a clear desire to create or utilise the circumstances in which known and active members of the IRA were apprehended carrying and appearing potentially capable of using weapons. The death of a member of an illegal organisation in these circumstances was a clean kill as 'lethal force [is] being used in such a way as to appear fair and within the law'.

21 'Instructions for Opening Fire in Northern Ireland' (Army Code no.

70771) commonly known as the 'Yellow Card'. Paragraph 5 provides: 'You may only open fire against a person: a. if he is committing or about to commit an act likely to endanger life, and there is no other way to prevent the danger. The following are some examples of acts where life could be endangered, dependent always on the circumstances: (1) firing or about to fire a weapon, planting, detonating or throwing an explosive device (including a petrol bomb) (2) deliberately driving a vehicle at a person and there is no other way of stopping him.' Cited by the Northern Ireland Court of Appeal in *R v. Lee William Clegg and Barry Wayne Aindow* at 24.

22 1972 version

23 *See, R v. Davidson*, Convicted of manslaughter in 1981.

24 *See, R v. Lee William Clegg and Barry Wayne Aindow*, Court of Appeal, 30 March 1994 at 59

25 On this point *see* Anthony Jennings, *Justice Under Fire: The Abuse of Civil Liberties in Northern Ireland* 104 (1988)

26 On this point *see* P.A.J. Waddington, *Arming an Unarmed Police* (1988)

27 *See* European Parliament Press Release, 30 August 1995, 'Green MEP Urges Ban on Plastic Bullets'; *Irish Times*, 14 September 1995, 'RUC Holds Inquiry after Protester Hit by Plastic Bullet'; *Irish News*, 22 March 1995, 'Plastic Bullets Fired at "Hooligans" after Cup Clash'; *Irish Times*, 28 September 1995, 'Plastic Bullets Fired by RUC in Castlederg Riot'.

28 *See, R v. Hegarty* (1986) 12 NIJB 25. The prosecution of a policeman for the murder of Sean Downes, who was killed during an anti-internment rally in 1984, was unsuccessful.

29 *See* 'No Weapon which Deters Rioters is Free From Risk', *New Society*, 21 July 1983 at 3

30 *See* 'Plastic Bullet Victim Claims Court Victory', *Irish News*, 11 November 1998

31 *See* 'Pinochet, Plastic Bullets and the RUC', 13 Just News 1 (December 1998)

32 In terms of raw data, 331 victims were male and only 19 were female.

33 *See* Committee on the Administration of Justice, *Plastic Bullets and the Law*; Jeanne E. Bishop, *The Right to be Arrested: British Government Summary Executions* 11 N.Y.U. Sch.Int'l and Comp. L. 207 (1990); Committee on the Administration of Justice, *Inquests and Disputed Killings in Northern Ireland* (1992); Anthony Jennings, *Justice Under Fire* (1988); Sean Doran, *The Use of Lethal Force by the Security Forces in Northern Ireland: A Legal Perspective* 17 Legal Studies 291 (1987); R.J. Spjut, *The 'Official' Use of Deadly Force Against Suspected Terrorists: Some Lessons From Northern Ireland* Public Law 38 (1986).

34 They include *R v. Foxford* (1974) outcome conviction of manslaughter quashed on appeal; *R v. Ross* (1974) outcome acquitted; *R v. Spencer* (1974), outcome acquitted of manslaughter; *R v. Nicholl* (1975) outcome acquitted of manslaughter; *R v. Jones* (1975) outcome acquitted; *R v. Fury* (1975) outcome acquitted; *R v. Scott* (1976) outcome acquitted; *R v. Williams* (1977) outcome acquitted; *R v. Bohan and Temperley* (1979) outcome acquitted; *R v. Davidson* (1981) outcome acquitted of manslaughter; *R v. McKeown* (1981) outcome acquitted; *R v. Bailey* (1982) outcome acquitted; *R v Robinson* (1984) outcome acquitted; *R v. Robinson, Montgomery and Brannigan* (1984) outcome acquitted; *R v. Thain* (1984) outcome convicted of murder (released after two years); *R v. Baird* (1984) outcome acquitted of manslaughter; *R v. Heggarty* (1987) outcome acquitted of manslaughter; *R v. Holden* (1988) outcome manslaughter charge withdrawn; *R v. Elkington and Callaghan* (1993) outcome acquitted; *R v. Clegg* (1999) acquitted on retrial for murder, convicted of attempting to wound, acquitted on appeal on latter charge.

35 *See* Lawyers Committee for Human Rights, *At the Crossroads: Human Rights and the Northern Ireland Peace Process* 74 (1996)

36 Cmnd. 2659

37 *See, R v. Bohan and Temperley* (1979) 5 NIJB; *R v. Jones* (1975) 2 NIJB; *R v. Hegarty* (1986) 12 NIJB 25

38 *See, Rose* (1884) Cox CC 540 (established that the common law defence covers not only defence of oneself but defence of others)
39 Smith and Hogan maintain that section 3 'may be taken to have clarified the common law'. *See* John Smith and Brian Hogan, *Criminal Law* 326 (5th ed., 1983).
40 *See* Glanville Williams, *The Evil Choice* CLR 4, 6–7 (1975). Some commentators have argued that self-defence should not be available to members of the security forces. Stannard states: 'The police, or any branch of the security forces for that matter, do not act to save themselves. Their aim is to prevent crime. Where they find it necessary to kill in the course of their duty, any defence or justification should be based fairly and squarely where it belongs, which is section 3 of the Criminal Law Act (Northern Ireland) 1967.' *See* John Stannard, *Lethal Force in Self-Defence* NILQ 173, 176 (1980). Recent cases such as *R v. Hanley* (unreported), 27 January 1994, illustrate the unavailability of the defence in certain circumstances to law-enforcers. However, I would maintain that to unilaterally deny members of the security forces the right to legal reliance on the doctrine of self-defence would be an unfair limitation on their rights.
41 *See, R v. Julien* (1969) Cr. App.R. 407
42 *See, R v. Roy Alun Jones* (1975) 2 NIJB 1 at 16
43 *See* 2 East PC 297
44 *See* Criminal Law Revision Committee, *supra* note 36 at paragraphs 22 and 23
45 *See* Doran, *supra* note 33 at 294
46 *See generally*, Glanville Williams, *Textbook on Criminal Law* 500 (2nd ed., 1983); Smith and Hogan, *supra* note 39 at 325
47 Report of the Criminal Code Commission 11 (1879)
48 *R v. Jones* (1975) 2 NIJB
49 Williams, *supra* note 46 at 494
50 *See, R v. Jones* (1975) confirmed by the reference case brought by the Attorney-General, the *Attorney-General for Northern Ireland's Reference* (No. 1 of 1975) (1977) A.C. 105
51 *Ibid.*, at 135
52 *Ibid.*
53 *R v. Heggarty* (1987) at 347 per Lord Chief Justice Hutton
54 Attorney-General's Reference, *supra* note 50 at 138
55 Lord Diplock, *supra* note 50 at 138
56 Lord Hutton approved this principle citing *R v. Gladstone Williams* (1984) 78 Cr. App. R. 276 at 281. *See, R v. James Fisher and Mark Douglas Wright,* Judgment, 21 December 1995 at 5
57 *Beckford v. R* as approved by Lord Chief Justice Hutton in *R v. Richard Elkington and Andrew Callaghan*, Belfast Crown Court, Judgment, 23 December 1993 at 61
58 *R v. Williams* as approved by Lord Chief Justice Hutton in *R v. Richard Elkington and Andrew Callaghan*, Belfast Crown Court, Judgment, 23 December 1993 at 60
59 *R v. Robinson* (1984) NIJB 19
60 *McCann, Farrell and Savage v. United Kingdom*, Application no. 18984/91
61 Report of the European Commission on Human Rights (adopted 4 March 1994)
62 *Ibid.*, at paragraph 33 (a)
63 *Ibid.*, at paragraph 33 (b)
64 *Ibid.*, at paragraph 34
65 *Ibid.*, at paragraph 37
66 *See, R v. Richard Elkington and Andrew Callaghan* (Belfast Crown Court) 23 December 1993 at 1–2
67 *See* David Lanham, *Killing the Fleeing Offender* Crim.L.J. 16 (1975)
68 Attorney-General's Reference, *supra* note 50 at 138
69 (1976) NI 169 at 180
70 *See, R v. Jones* (1975) 2 NIJB 1 at 18
71 *See* Committee on the Administration of Justice, *The Casement Trials: A Case Study on the Right to Fair Trial in Northern Ireland* (1992)
72 Mrs Farrell, the wife of one of the three deceased, brought a civil action for negligence, assault and battery against the four soldiers. At first instance, the trial judge withdrew the issue of negligence from the jury, leaving them to consider the allegations of battery and assault alone. *See McLaughlin v.*

Ministry of Defence (1977) unreported. The jury found for the soldiers. On appeal the Court of Appeal ordered a new trial. *See* NIJB (1978). However, before the jury could retry the case the Ministry of Defence appealed to the House of Lords which overturned the Appeal Court's decision.

73 *See, Farrell v. Ministry of Defence* (1980) 1 All ER. 166

74 On the ideological role of judges, *see generally*, Raymond Suttner, *The Judiciary: Its Ideological Role in South Africa*, 14 Int'l. J. Sociology of Law 67 (1986)

75 Interviews with ten Northern Ireland solicitors, on file with author

76 *See, At the Crossroads, supra* note 35 at 117. This is facilitated by § 14 of the Prevention of Terrorism Act (1989) where the Secretary of State may extend the arrest period 'but any further such period or periods shall not exceed five days in all'.

77 *See, McKenna* Application, Queen's Bench Division (transcript of judgment by Hutton LCJ) 10 February 1992

78 *Ibid.*, at 36–7

79 *See generally*, Kader Asmal, *Shoot to Kill? International Lawyers' Inquiry into the Lethal Use of Firearms by the Security Forces in Northern Ireland* (1985). Although this report is over a decade old, it remains one of the most authoritative sources on the issue of the right to life in Northern Ireland and its findings have not been substantially refuted by the state.

80 Interviews with legal representatives of the next of kin, on file with author

81 *Elkington and Callaghan, supra* note 66 at 23

82 *Ibid.*, at 47–9

83 *See, R v. Bohan and Temperley supra* note 6 at 14. It should also be noted that there were gaps in the forensic evidence presented to the court. The army failed to present the serial numbers and other relevant details pertaining to the weapons used by the soldiers at trial.

84 *See* Spjut, *supra* note 33; Anthony Jennings, 'Shoot-to-Kill; The Final Courts of Justice' in *Justice Under Fire*, *supra* note 25 at 104–23; comments by the Irish Taoiseach, Garret FitzGerald,

The Times, 11 June 1984; comments of Cardinal O Fiaich, *Guardian*, 18 June 1984.

85 *R v. Robinson, Montgomery and Brannigan*, Belfast Crown Court, 5 June 1984 at 16–17

86 *Bohan and Temperley*, *supra* note 6

87 *Ibid.*, at 9

88 *R v. Clegg and Others* (Belfast Crown Court), 17 June 1993. Clegg was released by the Secretary of State on licence in 1995. He has since been retried and acquitted of the murder of Karen Reilly. In January 2000 he was acquitted on appeal of attempting to wound Martin Peake.

89 *See* '"Untruthful" Clegg Acquitted of Murder', *Irish Times*, 12 March 1999

90 *Clegg*, *supra* note 88, at 60–1

91 *Ibid.*, at 12 and 27

92 *Ibid.*, at 14

93 *Ibid.*, at 14 and 16

94 *Ibid.*, at 20

95 *Ibid.*, at 22

96 *Ibid.*, at 22–3

97 *Ibid.*, at 27

98 *McLaughlin v. Ministry of Defence* (1977), unreported, transcript on file with author

99 *R v. Robinson, Montgomery and Brannigan, supra* note 19

100 *The Times*, 12 June 1984

101 *Attorney-General for Northern Ireland's Reference* (No. 1 of 1975) (1977) as per Michael Eastham QC, J.A. Creaney QC and S.B. Crossey (for the respondent soldier) at 115

102 *See* Hadden, *supra* note 3, Annex E at 137

103 Though the doctrine was rejected in *Palmer v. R* (1971) AC 814, the approach of the court is difficult to distinguish from the Australian case of *Howe* (1958) 100 CLR 448, where the proposition was accepted. *Palmer* is not entirely dismissive of the excessive defence doctrine. *See* Sean Doran, *The Doctrine of Excessive Defence: Developments Past, Present and Potential* 36 NILQ 314, 320 (1986).

104 *See, The People v. O'Dwyer* (1972) IR 416; *R v. McKay* (1957) VR 560 and Howe *ibid,*

105 *See, Zecevic v. Director of Public Prosecutions* (1987) 61 ALJR 357. Abandoned the rule that a defendant

NOTES TO PAGES 102–15   289

could be convicted of manslaughter where he lacked reasonable grounds for his belief that the degree of force used in self-defence was necessary to the danger. Found that the law as expressed in *Palmer v. R* should be followed.

106   *R v Clegg, supra* note 88 at 60–1
107   *See* Committee on the Administration of Justice, *Inquests and Disputed Killings in Northern Ireland* (1992); Committee on the Administration of Justice, *The States We Are In* (1993); Committee on the Administration of Justice, *Human Rights: The Agenda for Change* 12 (1995).
108   *See* Hadden, *supra* note 3, Annex E
109   For a United States comparison on this matter, *see* Gerald F. Uelman, *Varieties of Police Policy: A Study of Police Policy Regulations Regarding the Use of Force in LA County*, 6 Loyola of Los Angeles Rev. 1, 40 (1973)
110   Internal guidelines are not a new concept for army operations on the island of Ireland. In 1914 the Irish command issued a special pamphlet to the army on keeping the peace in Ireland. It stands as an interesting historical precursor to the Yellow Card. *See* 'Orders for the Guidance of Troops in Affording Aid to the Civil Power in Ireland' (1914).
111   *R v. Jones, supra* note 70, at 22
112   *R v. McNaughton* (1975) NI 203
113   *Ibid.*, at 206
114   *R v. Timothy Hanley*, unreported, transcript of judgment at 43
115   *See* Hadden, *supra* note 3, Annex E at 142
116   *See* for example, Liberty, *Broken Covenants* (1993)
117   *See* Labour Party amendment to the Northern Ireland (Emergency Provisions) Bill 1987. Legal overhaul of section 3 of the 1967 Act has also been proposed by the Law Commission.
118   SACHR has now been replaced by a new Northern Ireland Human Rights Commission under Strand Three of the Good Friday Agreement; paragraph 5 states: 'A new Northern Ireland Human Rights Commission, with membership from Northern Ireland reflecting the community balance, will be established by Westminster legislation, independent of Government, with an extended and

enhanced role beyond that currently exercised by the Standing Advisory Commission on Human Rights, to include keeping under review the adequacy and effectiveness of laws and practices, making recommendations to Governments as necessary; providing information and promoting awareness of human rights; considering draft legislation referred to them by the new Assembly; and, in appropriate cases, bring court proceedings or providing assistance to individuals doing so.'

3   Other mechanisms of accountability – the inquest procedure

1   For the most recent and comprehensive account of inquests in Northern Ireland generally, *see* John Leckey and Desmond Greer, *Coroner's Law and Practice in Northern Ireland* (1998). *See also* 'Inquests on Controversial Killings in North Criticised', *Irish Times*, 10 January 1991.
2   On limited financial compensation *see*, *W v. Ministry of Defence* (1983) 2 BNIL 85. Here a fourteen-year-old schoolgirl was struck on the head and chest by a plastic baton round in a neighbour's house. Damages of £1,500 were awarded. *Doherty v. Ministry of Defence* (1978) 6 NIJB; the plaintiff was shot by an army patrol in 1972. He was awarded £15,000. On the exclusion of civil liability *see*, *Kelly and Others v. Ministry of Defence* (1989) NI 341; *Lynch v. Ministry of Defence* (1983) 7 BNIL 101. In *Lynch*, Justice Hutton held that since it was evident that the plaintiff had deliberately decided to disobey a clear signal from the soldiers who sought to stop his vehicle, and the soldiers reasonably believed that Lynch was a terrorist, opening fire amounted to reasonable force in the circumstances. He held obiter that even if the use of force by the soldiers had been unreasonable, the defendant could not rely upon *volenti nonfit injuria*, since he could be said to have waived any claim that he might have against the Ministry of Defence. In addition, in the

Gibraltar deaths, the Foreign Secretary issued certificates under the Crown Proceedings Act 1947, exempting the government from any liability in respect of the deaths. Such certificates are conclusive and cannot be legally appealed. Generally, relatives of persons killed as a result of the use of force by the security forces can claim compensation under the Criminal Injuries (Compensation) (Northern Ireland) Order 1988. However, no compensation is payable to anyone who was at any time engaged in terrorism or who had been a member of an organisation which engages in terrorism, proscribed or not. Compensation can also be reduced if the deceased had a criminal record of any description, or is deemed by the Secretary of State to have provoked or contributed to the injury received.

3 *See* Mike Morrissey and John Ditch, *Social Policy Implications of Emergency Legislation in Northern Ireland*, 1 Critical Social Policy 19 (1981–2)

4 Coroner's duties are described in the statute De Officio Coronatoris (1275)

5 *See* R. Hunnisett, *The Medieval Coroner* (1961)

6 Select Coroner's Rolls (Selden Soc.) XX

7 A deodand was any object which was causal in the death of a person, and forfeited initially to the kindred of the deceased. By the thirteenth century it was taken by the sheriff or coroner and sold. Deodands were abolished in 1846. *See* A.T. Carter, *A History of the English Courts* (1944).

8 In 1170, owing to the abuse by the sheriffs of their authority, Henry II appointed an inquest of sheriffs to carry out a general inquiry into their conduct.

9 *See* Criminal Law Act 1977, § 56

10 *Ibid.*, at schedule 10

11 Coroner's Rules 1984, rule 12

12 *Ibid.*, rules 26 and 27, and Coroner's (Practice and Procedure) Rules (Northern Ireland) 1963, rule 12 (1) (as amended to 31 December 1997)

13 *See* Celia Wells, *Inquests, Inquiries and Indictments: The Official Reception of Death by Disaster* 70 Legal Studies 73

14 *Report of the Departmental Committee on Coroners* (1936) (Cmnd. 5070) (Wright Report), *Report of the Committee on Death Certification and Coroners* (1971) (Cmnd. 4810) (Brodrick Report)

15 In addition, the statute specifies the following causal reasons for an inquest: deaths where the cause is unknown, sudden death, and deaths in prison or similar establishment. *See* Coroner's Act 1988, § 8 (1).

16 *Ibid.*, § 8 (3) (b). The extension of the inquest's mandate to deaths in police custody, or at the hands of police officers, was effected by the Administration of Justice Act 1982, § 62.

17 *Report of the Committee on Death Certification and Coroners* (1971) (Cmnd. 4810)

18 Coroner's Rules 1984, schedule 4, form 22, note 4

19 *Ibid.*, rule 36 (2)

20 Coroner's (Practice and Procedure) Rules (Northern Ireland) 1963, Coroner's Rules 1984, rule 23 (2) as amended. Note that the coroner presiding over the inquest into the death of Aidan McAnespie who was killed in February 1988 wrote to the army authorities in respect of the incident. He drew their attention to a defect in the design of the gun that had fired the fatal bullet. He stated that the death was 'totally avoidable'.

21 *See* Tom Hadden, *The Law on Inquests in Northern Ireland – Proposals for Reform*, Standing Advisory Commission on Human Rights 248 (1991–2)

22 *See* Coroner's Act (Northern Ireland) 1959; Coroner's (Practice and Procedure) Rules 1963 (as amended to 31 December 1997)

23 Civil Authorities (Special Powers) Act (Northern Ireland) 1922 § 10

24 Letter from the Secretary of the Cabinet to Major-General J. Dalrymple, 16 May 1922, on file with author

25 This is confirmed in a letter written to Major-General J. Dalrymple by the Secretary of the Cabinet, 23 May 1922, on file with author.

26 *Report of the Committee on Death Certification and Coroners* (1971) (Cmnd. 4810). Brodrick *supra* note 14.

27 Coroner's (Practice and Procedure)

Rules (Northern Ireland) 1963, rule 15, 22, 23 and Third Schedule. Form 22 as amended.

28 *Ibid.* Juries were reduced to the choice of 'natural causes', 'accident', 'misadventure', 'by his own act', 'execution', and 'open verdict'.

29 Wright Report, *supra* note 14. Wright also recommended that juries should not be permitted to add riders to their verdicts, either censuring an individual or exonerating him from blame, and that the coroner should have the power to dispense with an inquest that he did not consider necessary.

30 Criminal Law Act 1977, § 56

31 Charles Breslin was killed with two others at Strabane in February 1985 by an undercover army unit.

32 Coroner's (Practice and Procedure) Rules 1963, rule 9 (2)

33 *McKerr v. Armagh Coroner* (1990) 1 All ER 865

34 In stating the position the court relied heavily on earlier precedents, *Wakely v. Cooke* (1849) Exch. 511, and *Boyle v. Wiseman* (1855) 10 Exch. 360.

35 *McKerr, supra* note 33

36 *Wakely v. Cooke* (1849) Exch. 511; *Boyle v. Wiseman* (1855) 10 Exch. 360

37 *See* Hadden, *supra* note 21 at 7

38 *Robinson* inquest, 27 April 1992; *McKerr* inquest, May 1992; *McElwaine* inquest, March 1993

39 High Court, 9 September 1988 (unreported); Northern Ireland Court of Appeal, 6 December 1990. They also asserted that the admissibility of such statements was a breach of the rules of natural justice.

40 Coroner's (Practice and Procedure) Rules 1963, rule 17 (1)

41 *R v. Greater Manchester Coroner*, ex parte Tal (1985) QB 67, 84–5; *R v. Divine*, ex parte Walton (1930) 2 KB 29, 36

42 *R v. Attorney-General for Northern Ireland*, ex parte Devine and Breslin, 6 February 1992

43 Application no. 20464/92, *Breslin v. United Kingdom*

44 Coroner's Rules 1984, rule 37 (3)

45 *See, Thurston's Coronership*, paragraph 19.30 (3rd ed., 1985)

46 Tony Harker was killed in January 1982. He was unarmed and about to participate in a break-in at the time of

the shooting. The inquest into his death was adjourned eight times, and finally took place in May 1983.

47 The Committee on the Administration of Justice estimated in 1992 that there were over thirty-five cases involving the use of lethal force which had been outstanding since 1982. *See* Committee on the Administration of Justice, *Inquests and Disputed Killings in Northern Ireland* (1992), Appendix A.

48 The decision of the Belfast Coroner John Leckey to abandon the *McKerr, Toman and Burns* inquests in early 1995 means that there has been no full inquest into these deaths which occurred in November 1982. The deaths of Michael Tighe (24 November 1982) and those of Seamus Grew and Roddy Carroll (12 December 1982) still await inquest proceedings.

49 Coroner's (Practice and Procedure) Rules (Northern Ireland) 1963, rule 3

50 *See* Hadden, *supra* note 21

51 *See* Peter Taylor, *Stalker, The Search for Truth* 90 (1987)

52 Coroner's Rules 1984, rule 27. Coroner's (Practice and Procedure) Rules (Northern Ireland) 1963, rule 12

53 *See* Hadden, *supra* note 21

54 *See, McKerr v. Armagh Coroner* (1990) 1 WLR 649; *R v. Attorney-General for Northern Ireland*, ex parte Devine and Breslin, 6 February 1992. *See* J. Hunter, *Northern Ireland Inquest Rules* 138 NLJ 924.

55 *See* Brodrick Report, *supra* note 14

56 Annex to the United Nations Economic and Social Council Resolution 1989/65 of 24 May 1989, Principle 1

57 Interviews with solicitors representing families concerned with lethal force deaths, on file with author

58 Home Office circular 20/1999. The circular arose from recommendations after the investigation into the racist killing of London teenager Stephen Lawrence in February 1997.

59 The medical doctor of the deceased is entitled to an abstract of the entire postmortem report. Interested persons can purchase a copy if both the Lord Chancellor and the coroner agree. Coroner's (Practice and Procedure) Rules (Northern Ireland) 1963, rules 37

and 38.

60 Interview with family members, on file with author

61 The inquest commenced in 1987.

62 *See, in re Breslin* Application (1987) 10 NIJB 18

63 Additionally, one of the solicitors had been charged with assaulting RUC officers when he attempted to remove an album of photographs from the courthouse.

64 *See, Matter v. Eastern Midlands* R y. Co 38 Ch.D. 92; *Nelson v. Anglo-American Land Mortgage Agency Company* (1897) 1 Ch 130

65 *See* Home Office circular, *supra* note 58, Annex A, section B. Enumerated categories of application include: deaths which result when persons are attempting to evade arrest; deaths which result when persons are stopped and searched or questioned by the police; deaths which result when there is a siege or an ambush; and death which arises from a fatal road crash involving the police.

66 *See* Home Office circular, *supra* note 58, paragraph 4

67 Interview with Belfast coroner, John Leckey, December 1999, on file with author

68 *See, in re Mailey and Others* (1980) Northern Ireland 102

69 Coroner's (Practice and Procedure) Rules (Northern Ireland) 1963, rule 8 (1)

70 *Devine and Breslin, supra* note 54

71 *R v. HH Coroner at Hammersmith,* ex parte Peach (1980) Q.B. 211

72 *See, Garnett v. Ferrand* 108 Eng. Rep 576 (1827); *Barcless* case, 82 Eng. Rep 1273 (1658); 7 Halsbury, *Laws of England* 652–3 (2nd ed., 1932). Both relied upon the Californian Supreme Court decision of *The People v. Devine* 44 Cal. 452, 459 (1972). *See also, Agnew v. Stewart,* an early Canadian case confirming full rights to participate at inquests, 21 USQB 396 (1962).

73 Sol. Journal 414–15 (1926)

74 *See generally,* Justice Frankfurter opinion in *Joint Anti-Fascist Refugee Committee v. McGrath* 341 U.S. 123, 170–1 (1950)

75 On file with author

76 Examples include arrests following the death of Peter Doherty, killed on 24 July 1981, and the arrests of four youths travelling with Paul Kelly when he was killed on 15 January 1985. Further, following the Breslin and Devine deaths on 23 February 1985, local houses were searched by the RUC, This hardly made the occupants disposed to part with any information they may have had.

77 *See* Halsbury, *Laws of England,* paragraph 89

78 *See* I. H. Dennis, *The Law of Evidence* (1999)

79 *See* letter from the Attorney-General to *The Times,* 13 November 1992

80 The Gibraltar inquest took place in September 1988, *McKerr* in April 1988, and *McElwaine* in March 1993.

81 *See, R v. Lewes Justices,* ex parte Home Secretary (1973) AC 388

82 *See, Conway v. Rimmer* (1968) AC 910 at 952

83 *See, R v. Henderson, Allen and Abraham,* Central Criminal Court, 5 October 1992 (unreported)

84 *See* F. Doherty, *The Stalker Affair* (1986); Peter Taylor, *Stalker, The Search for Truth,* (1987); John Stalker, *Stalker* (1988); *Stalker and Paramilitary Policing,* Irish Political Review (1986)

85 *See, In re Toman* (unreported judgment)

86 *See* Brice Dickson, *Judicial Review and National Security,* in Brigid Hadfield (ed.), *Judicial Review: A Thematic Approach* 187, 218 (1995)

87 *See* ex parte *McNeill,* 17 June 1994

88 The state has previously sought permission to screen military witnesses in Northern Ireland. *See, Miller, McFadden and McMonagle* (1992) (unreported). In this case the court engaged in a balancing exercise, weighing the instances in which undercover soldiers had previously given evidence without screening, against the issues before the court in the particular case. Justice Haste decided that screening was not warranted.

89 Decision of HM Coroner for Greater Belfast, 22 April 1993 (unreported)

90 *See* (1991) NIJB 68

91 Sir Brian Hutton was quoting his words from an earlier case, *Doherty v. Ministry of Defence* (1991) 1 NIJB at 34.

92 *See* Dickson, *supra* note 86 at 216

93   *See* Legal Aid, Advice and Assistance (Northern Ireland) Order 1981, Schedule 1, Part 1, paragraph 5 (never brought into force)

94   Coroner's (Practice and Procedure) Rules (Northern Ireland) 1963, rule 7 (1)

95   *See* Hilary Kitchin, *The Gibraltar Report, Inquest into the Deaths of Mairead Farrell, Daniel McCann and Sean Savage* 8 (1988). At the Gibraltar inquest a total of eighteen witnesses gave their evidence from behind a screen. Initially, the coroner rejected the Crown's request for screening but when the Crown then indicated to the coroner that unless secrecy requirements were met, witnesses would not attend, felt compelled, albeit reluctantly, to acquiesce.

96   *See, Attorney-General v. Leveller Magazine* (1979) AC 440, 449

97   Coroner's (Practice and Procedure) Rules (Northern Ireland) 1963, rule 5

98   *See, Breslin and Devine* Application, Judgment of Justice Carswell, 5 September 1988

99   Legal Aid, Advice and Assistance (Northern Ireland) Order 1981, *supra* note 93

100 Registration of Births, Deaths and Marriages Regulations (1968)

101 This does not mean that ordinary inquests have escaped all scrutiny. In the inquest into the death of William Smith, a thirteen-year-old from County Antrim who died in 1980, the family sought judicial review of the jury's findings. *See, R v. Coroner for the County of Antrim* (1980) NI 123. The court quashed the finding. Justice Kelly stated: 'It may well be that another Coroner's jury hearing the same evidence assisted by a proper and adequate summing up of it by the Coroner will come to exactly the same verdict but I think that the next-of-kin, at least, are entitled to have their unhappiness tempered by the knowledge that such a verdict was reached by considered and regular inquiry.' *Ibid.*, at 125.

102 An organisation called INQUEST was launched in 1981 to campaign against deaths in custody and to advocate for changes to the Coroner's Court system.

103 *See* Committee on the Administration of Justice, *Inquests and Disputed Killings in Northern Ireland* 53 (1992)

104 *See, In the Matter of an Application by Eleanor McKerr for Judicial Review*, 21 December 1992

105 *See* for example, *R v. Coroner for Western District of East Sussex*, ex parte Homberg, 26 January 1994 (unreported)

106 *See, R v. North Humberside and Scunthorpe Coroner*, ex parte Jamieson, April 1994 at 27 (unreported)

107 *See* Scarman Report (1969) Cmnd. 566; Widgery Tribunal (1972). The terms of reference for the Widgery Tribunal were that it was to inquire into: 'a definite matter of urgent public importance, namely the events on Sunday 30 January which led to the loss of life in connection with the procession in Londonderry on that day'.

108 Others have included the *Gifford* inquiry (1971), investigating the deaths of Desmond Beattie and Seamus Cusack killed in July 1971 in Derry/Londonderry; the *Downes* inquiry into the death of Sean Downes on 12 August 1984 in Andersonstown, west Belfast, and the *Thompson* inquiry into the death of Paul Thompson in 1994. The *Caraher* inquiry took place in July 1991 in Cullyhanna, County Armagh. An international panel of jurists presided; they included Michael Mansfield QC, Hon. Judge Andrew L. Somers Jnr, Ann-Carinne Jacoby, Hon. Kevin Burke, and Veronika Arendt-Rojahn.

109 *See* Dermot Walsh, *The Bloody Sunday Tribunal of Inquiry* (1997)

110 *Ibid.*

111 *Ibid.*

112 *See* further rulings by Lord Saville, Mr William L. Hoyt and Sir Edward Somers, *Applications for Anonymity*, 5 May 1999, paragraph 11

113 *See, R v. Lord Saville*, ex parte 'B', 'O', 'U', and 'V', Decision of the Queen's Bench Division, 16 March 1999 at 25

114 *See, R v. Lord Saville*, ex parte 'B', 'O', 'U', and 'V', Decision of the Court of Appeal, 30 March 1999

115 Saville, *supra* note 113 at 23

116 *See generally*, Adler, *Coroner's Inquests: The Impact of Watts* 15 UCLA Law Rev. 97 (1968); Affleck, *Coroner's Inquests* 7 Criminal Law Quarterly 459 (1968); Flynn, *The Office of the Coroner vs. The Medical Examiner* 46 J. Crim. L.C. and P.S. 232 (1955)
117 *See* Hills, *Coroners under Fire* 114 New Law J. (1964)
118 *Ibid.*, at 567

4 International law and the use of lethal force

1 Article 2, European Convention on Human Rights; Article 6, International Covenant on Civil and Political Rights; Article 4, American Convention on Human Rights. The right is also protected by international humanitarian law. Common Article 3, the Geneva Conventions; Article 4 (2) Protocol II.
2 The work of the Austrian philosopher Josef Popper-Lynkeus develops this principle. Paul Edwards paraphrases him as follows: 'Let us suppose that the angel of death were to allow Shakespeare and Newton, in the most creative periods of their lives, to go on living only on the condition that we surrender to him "two stupid day-labourers or even two incorrigible thieves". As moral beings we must not so much as consider an exchange of this kind. It would be far better if Shakespeare and Newton were to die. One may call attention, as much as one wishes, to the pleasure produced in countless future ages by Shakespeare's plays; one may point to the immense progress of science which would be in the consequence of the prolongation of Newton's life – by comparison with the sacrifice of a human being, these are mere "luxury" values.' Paul Edwards (ed.), 6 *The Encyclopedia of Philosophy* 403 (1967).
3 *See* Rosalyn Higgins, *Problems and Process, International Law and How to Use It* 21 (1994)
4 *See* Kevin Boyle, *The Concept of the Arbitrary Deprivation of Life*, in B.G. Ramcharan (ed.), *The Right to Life in International Law* 221, 223 (1985) (emphasis in the original)

5 On taxonomies and hierarchies of rights generally, *see* Theodor Meron, *On a Hierarchy of International Human Rights*, 80 Am. J. Int'l L. 1 (1986)
6 *Farrell*, Application no. 9013/80; *Stewart*, Application no. 10044/82; *Kelly*, Application no. 17579/90; Gibraltar, Admissibility Decision 3 September 1993. Seven cases have recently been lodged with the European Commission, that of Pearse Jordan, killed in November 1992, Application no. 24746/94; *McKerr*, Application no. 28883/95; *Kelly and Others*, Application no. 30054/96 (pending oral hearing before the European Court); *Shanaghan*, Application no. 37715/97; Fergal Caraher, killed in December 1990; and the Loughgall deaths (eight members of PIRA and one civilian bystander) killed on 8 May 1987, Application no. 30054/96 (this case has been deemed admissible by the commission). The death of Dermot McShane killed by a police plastic baton round in August 1997 has also been submitted for review to the commission.
7 *See* Brian Walsh, *The European Court of Human Rights*, 2 Conn. J. Int'l L. 271 (1987)
8 G.A. Res. 217 (1948). Forty-eight states voted in favour of the Declaration, none against.
9 Boyle, *supra* note 4. He argues, 'By isolating out from the continuum of lawful force the possibility of deadly force, the European formulation arguably results in the wrong emphasis.'
10 *See* J.E.C. Fawcett, *The Application of the European Convention on Human Rights* 37 (1987)
11 Article 6 (1) establishes that: 'In determination of his civil rights and obligations or of any criminal charges against him, everyone is entitled to fair and public trial within a reasonable time by an independent and impartial tribunal established by law.'
12 *See* Application 5207/71, *X v. Federal Republic of Germany*, 14 Yearbook 698 (1971). The complaint was based on Article 2 following from an order of the national court to evict a person in poor health from her house. The

commission found the complaint admissible and not manifestly ill-founded.

13 Application 6040/73, *X v. Ireland* 16 Yearbook 388 (1973)

14 *Ibid.*, at § 103

15 The commission found that the applicant had not suggested that there were 'no laws in Ireland protecting the right to life', and interpretation fell under the second heading. *Ibid.*, paragraph 102. The decision on Application 9348/81 follows in the same vein. The applicant alleged that the failure of the United Kingdom to prevent the killing of her family members was in violation of Articles 1, 2, 8, 9, 10, 11 and 13 of the convention. The complaint concerned the death of the applicant's husband, killed while attending a cattle auction in the Republic of Ireland in June 1980 and her brother, murdered in a village bar in County Tyrone while having a drink in April 1981. The complaint was rejected. *See Mrs W v. United Kingdom*, 32 D & G at 190. The commission emphasised that while Article 2 created positive obligations for the state, it did not create a 'positive obligation to exclude any possible violence'. *Ibid.*, at § 12. The decision also stressed that it was not the commission's task to consider the appropriateness and the efficiency of the measures taken by the United Kingdom government in respect of terrorism in Northern Ireland. *Ibid.*, at § 14. There was a finding that the commission would not expect the United Kingdom to go beyond the measures actually taken in respect of the death of the applicant's brother. *Ibid.*, at § 15.

16 *See* Ralph Beddard, *Human Rights in Europe* 75 (3rd ed., 1993)

17 *See, Mulkiye Osman and Ahmed Osman v. United Kingdom* (Application no. 23452/94) E. Comm. H. R., July 98, 1997 (Merits), Judgment of the Court, 28 October 1998. *See* Decision on Admissibility 17 May 1996. *See also, Susan Keenan v. United Kingdom* (Application no. 27229/95), declared admissible in the 278th session of the commission, 18–29 May 1998; application concerned the suicide of the

applicant's son, who had a history of mental illness while in prison.

18 *See, Osman and Osman, supra* note 17, at § 115

19 In this context, if there was a recognised danger to an identifiable person or group of persons, failure by the state to protect them might disclose a violation of the right to protection of life by law. Further, while as a general rule there has to be loss of life to activate Article 2, it was not excluded that acts of a life-threatening character could also be dealt with under the article. Commission's Report. *Ibid.* This holding makes for interesting application in Northern Ireland, in the context of persons whose identity and personal information was made available to paramilitary organisations from police or military sources.

20 *Ibid.*, at § 116. This view was strongly articulated in terms of the difficulties which police forces face in modern societies, the unpredictability of human conduct and the operational choices which the forces of law must make within the restriction of priorities and budgets.

21 *Ibid.*, at § 116

22 *Ibid.*, at § 141–54. A domestic precedent, the House of Lords decision in *Hill* provided the police with immunity from civil suit for the acts and omissions in the context of the investigation and suppression of crime. While the government had argued that the exclusionary rule was not absolute, the domestic Court of Appeal had proceeded on the basis that it provided a watertight defence to the police. *Ibid.*, at § 150. The court found that the rule operated to provide the police with automatic immunity, regardless of the degree of their alleged negligence or harm suffered as a result.

23 For example, Amnesty International in its report *Political Killings in Northern Ireland* (1994) identifies concerns about collusion between the security forces and loyalist paramilitary 'death squads'. The lack of wide-ranging and independent investigation into these allegations are tantamount to failure by the state to protect the right to life.

24 *See* Torkel Opsahl, *The Right to Life*, in

R. St. J. Macdonald *et al* (eds), *The European System for the Protection of Human Rights* 207, 211 (1993)

25 These exceptions have been described as the 'law-enforcement exceptions' to the right to life. *See* Sarah Joseph, *Denouement of the Deaths on the Rock: The Right to Life of Terrorists*, 14 Neth. Hum. Rts Q. 5, 7 (1996).

26 Article 2 (2) (a)

27 Article 2 (2) (b)

28 Article 2 (2) (c)

29 *McCann, Farrell and Savage v. United Kingdom*, Case 17/1994/464/545, Application no. 18984/91, series A, no. 324, judgment of 27 September 1995 ('Gibraltar')

30 Article 24 of the convention facilitates the interstate complaint procedure.

31 Application no. 5310/71. Judgment of 18 January 1978, *Ireland v. United Kingdom*, series A, vol. 25.

32 Applications 6780/74 and 6950/75

33 *Cyprus v. Turkey*, 4 EHRR 482, the commission found that twelve Greek Cypriot civilians had been killed by Turkish soldiers during the 1974 invasion of north Cyprus by Turkey.

34 *Bruggeman and Scheusten*, 12 July 1977, D & R 10 (1978) 116. The point at issue here being whether the concept of 'everyone' in Article 2 (1) included the unborn foetus. The commission held that Germany was not in violation of Article 8 of the European Convention, because German women were not free to have an abortion on the grounds of unwanted pregnancy. The commission stated that the private life of the woman is closely connected with the developing foetus. The commission did not determine whether the foetus should be protected as 'life' under Article 2, or whether it could justify an interference with the right to private life 'for the protection of others' under Article 8 (2). Application 8416/79, *X v. United Kingdom*, D & R 19 (1980) 244 (249–50), again addressing whether the term 'everyone' included the foetus. *See also, X v. Ireland* Application 6040/73. The duty of the state to take additional and onerous steps to safeguard life. *X v. United Kingdom*, Application 9348/81 5 EHRR. The duty of the state to prevent terrorism

for the protection of life. It is again emphasised that this analysis is not examining the 'moral' right to life debate, specifically excluding discussion of abortion and euthanasia, thus case law on these matters are not included in the substantive discussion.

35 *Paton v. United Kingdom* (1980) 3 EHRR 408

36 *D v. United Kingdom*, Judgment of the E. Ct. H. R., 2 May 1997. *See also, Jilali El Guarti v. France*, Application no. 37681/97, Admissibility Decision by the commission (227th session), 14–24 April 1998. This case concerned the threatened expulsion of the applicant, who was suffering from kidney failure and diabetes, to Morocco. The applicant claimed that the medical care he required would not be available there.

37 *Soering v. United Kingdom*, Series A. No. 161; 11 EHRR 439 (1989)

38 Other recent cases in the same vein include *Launder v. United Kingdom* (Application no. 272729/95) E. Comm. H. R., 8 December 1997 (Decision on Admissibility); *Bahaddar v. the Netherlands*, E. Comm. H. R., 13 September 1996 (Merits).

39 Decision of the commission on admissibility No. 9013/80, *Farrell v. United Kingdom* (December 1982) 30 D & R 96 (1982)

40 *See* Boyle, *supra* note 4

41 The phrase used by the government to describe the parity of the two provisions was 'co-terminous'.

42 *Stewart v. United Kingdom* (Application no. 10044/82) 39 D & R 162 (1984)

43 *Ibid.*, at 171

44 *The Sunday Times v. United Kingdom*, 30 E. Ct. H.R. (ser. A) (1979)

45 This synopsis draws heavily on Joseph, *supra* note 25 at 8.

46 *Stewart*, *supra* note 42 at 8

47 *See* Article 19 of the Convention and the *Greek* case. The recent exceptions are the decisions to send independent fact-finding missions to Turkey to evaluate the situation on the ground there, in the context of a number of cases arising out of the individual complaint procedure.

48 *Reform of the Control Machinery Under the European Convention on Human Rights: Protocol No. 11* 89 Am. J. Int'l L. 145 (1995)

49 *Kelly v. United Kingdom* (No. 17579/90), 74 D & R 139 (1993)

50 In fact, Paul Kelly had fifty wounds on his body, all of them caused by bullet fragments. *See* 'Teenage Joyrider Had Fifty Wounds', *Irish Times*, 20 February 1987.

51 *Kelly, supra* note 49 at 147

52 *See* David J. Harris, *The Right to Life under the European Convention on Human Rights*, 1 Maastricht J. Eur. and Comp. L. 122, 136 (1994)

53 *See* J.C. Smith, *The Right to Life and the Right to Kill in Law Enforcement*, 144 New Law J. 354, 356 (1994)

54 Joseph, *supra* note 25 at 9. Note that this position echoes the current domestic arrangement under United Kingdom law, which remains hotly contested by academic commentators and civil libertarians. *See, Attorney-General for Northern Ireland's Reference* (1977) A.C. 105 (per Lord Diplock).

55 Gibraltar, *supra* note 29

56 Decision of the commission as to admissibility, 14 January 1993. Application no. 18984/91. *See also* E. Comm. H. R., Application no. 18984/91, *McCann and Others v. United Kingdom, Report of the Commission* (adopted 4 March 1994).

57 *Ibid.*, § 148

58 *Ibid.*, § 149

59 On the matter of a hierarchy of human rights norms generally see Meron, *supra* note 5.

60 Gibraltar, *supra* note 29, § 150

61 Memorial of the Applicants to the Court of Human Rights, on file with author

62 Gibraltar, *supra* note 29, § 153

63 *Ibid.*, § 154. *See also* Memorial of the Government and Annexes B–F (admitted to the registry on 3 and 4 November 1994), on file with the author.

64 Gibraltar, *supra* note 29, § 200

65 *Ibid.*, § 201

66 *Ibid.*, § 205

67 Joseph, *supra* note 25 at 17

68 These assumptions included that the suspects would not use a blocking car; the Renault car they crossed into Gibraltar with was a car bomb; that this bomb would be detonated by a remote control 'button job'; that the suspects would be armed; and that upon confrontation they would seek to detonate a bomb and/or use their weapons.

69 Gibraltar, *supra* note 29, § 208

70 This concept of rigid scrutiny has its origins in United States Supreme Court doctrine of heightened scrutiny, where in certain circumstances (notably in relation to racial classifications) governmental action has been subject to a form of more rigorous review. *See, Korematsu v. United States*, 323 US 214 (1944).

71 The basis for this doctrine in United States constitutional jurisprudence is found in the *Carolene Products* case, and Justice Stone's famous footnote 4. *United States v. Carolene Products Co,*, 304 US 144 (1938).

72 Gibraltar, *supra* note 29, § 212

73 For a scathing account of the inquest process following the deaths of McCann, Farrell and Savage *see* Hilary Kitchin, *The Gibraltar Report* (1989).

74 Gibraltar, *supra* note 29, § 157

75 *Ibid.*, § 61

76 For a strong critique of the approach of the court to substantive rights in certain respects *see* Conor Gearty, *The European Court of Human Rights and the Protection of Civil Liberties: An Overview*, 89 Camb. L.J. 122 (1993).

77 Cyprus case, 1958 Y.B. ECHR 174–6 (E. Comm. H.R.)

78 *Andronicou and Constantinou v. Cyprus*, Application nos. 86/1996/705/302. E. Ct. H. R., Judgment of 9 October 1997

79 It was established that Andronicou had a double-barrelled shotgun and possibly other weapons as well.

80 *Kaya v. Turkey*, E. Ct. H. R., Judgment of 19 February 1998. *See, Human Rights News* 16 Neth. Hum. Rts Q. 201 (1998).

81 Note also the recent admissibility decision of *Andreas and Giorghoulla Varnava and Others v. Turkey*, Application nos. 16064–66/90 and 16068–73/90, which touches on this general matter also. The nine applications concern the fate of missing persons in Cyprus.

82 For further information on the use of force in south-eastern Turkey *see generally*, Amnesty International,

Turkey: No Security Without Human Rights (1996); Amnesty International, *Turkey: A Policy of Denial* (1995).

83 I. A. Ct. of Human Rights, Ser. C, No. 4, 9 Hum. Rts L. J. 212 (1988). The Inter-American Court found that Honduras was in violation of the convention, based on its failure to carry out an effective and meaningful investigation into the circumstances of Rodriguez's disappearance. The duty to investigate was held applicable even where the state contended that nonstate actors were responsible for the disappearance.

84 General Assembly Resolution, 34/169 of 17 December 1979

85 While it is fair to say that domestic minorities have been protected as individuals by efficient use of procedural guarantees, there is no coherent theory of 'the group' emerging from the court. *See generally, Golder v. United Kingdom* (1975) 1 EHRR 524, *Schonenberger and Durmaz v. Switzerland* (1988) 11 EHRR 202. Nor has there been a carving out of special status for minorities and identifiable groups within member states' political structures arising from any such duty identified under the convention.

86 *See* Fionnuala Ní Aoláin, *The Emergence of Diversity: Differences in Human Rights Jurisprudence* 19 Fordham Int'l L. J. 101 (1995)

87 *See generally,* Thomas M. Franck, *Legitimacy in the International System* 82 Am. J. Int'l L.705 (1988)

88 *Ireland v. United Kingdom,* 25 E. Ct. H. R. (ser. A) (1978) (*'Ireland v. United Kingdom'*)

89 *See* Aisling Reidy *et al, Gross Violations of Human Rights: Invoking the European Convention on Human Rights in the Case of Turkey,* 15 Neth. Hum. Rts Q. 161, 165 (1997)

90 The *Greek* case, Report of the Commission, 12 Yearbook 194 (1969)

91 *Ibid.*

92 *Donnelly v. United Kingdom,* Application nos. 5577/72–5533/72, Collection of Decisions 122 (1973). Decision on admissibility, 5 April 1973.

93 *Ibid.,* at 262

94 *Ibid.* Final decision of the commission

taken under Articles 26, 27 and 29 of the convention, 15 December 1975.

95 Hurst Hannum and Kevin Boyle, *The Donnelly Case, Administrative Practice and Domestic Remedies under the European Convention: One Step Forward and Two Steps Back,* 71 Am. J. Int'l L. 319 (1975)

96 *Ibid.*

97 *See* John Stalker, *Stalker* (1988)

98 *See* B.G. Ramcharan, *The Drafting History of Article 2 of the European Convention on Human Rights,* in *The Right to Life in International Law, supra* note 4 at 59

99 The United Kingdom ratified the convention on 9 September 1953.

100 *Malone v. Metropolitan Police Commissioner* (1979) 2 W.L.R. 700

101 *Klass v. Germany,* ECHR 622 (1978) (E. Ct. H. R.)

102 *See* (1974) 2 All E.R. 377. (Reliance by the House of Lords on Article 7 of the ECHR, to reject the Crown's arguments regarding the credibility of retrospective legislation); *Birdi v. Secretary of State for the Home Office* (unreported) and *R v. Secretary of State; ex parte Bhajan Singh* (1975) 2 All E.R. 1081. In *R v. Secretary of State, ex parte Begum* (1975) 3 All E.R. 510–11, Lord Scarman stated: 'we will not deny or defer to any man either justice or right. This hallowed principle of our law is now reinforced by the European Convention of Human Rights 1950, to which it is now the duty of our public authorities ... to have regard.' *See generally,* Cary S. Watson, *The European Convention on Human Rights and the British Courts,* 12 Tex. Int'l L. R. 12 (1977).

103 *See* Editorial, *Parliamentary Debates on the Human Rights Bill,* 1, 4 E. H. Rts L. Rev. 1 (1998)

104 As at 31 December 1990 the United Kingdom had appeared as a defendant in forty-one cases before the court. Breach had been found in twenty-seven of those cases. *See* Vincent Berger, 11 *Case Law of the European Court of Human Rights* 265 (1988–90).

105 *Farrell v. United Kingdom* (December 1982) 30 D & R 96 (1982)

106 *See, Ireland v. United Kingdom, supra* note 31 at § 167

107 *See* Helsinki Watch, *Human Rights in*

Northern Ireland 36–40 (1991), which records numerous specific allegations of abuse and brutality in holding centres.

108 *See* Amnesty International, *United Kingdom: Allegations of Ill-treatment in Northern Ireland* (1991); British–Irish Rights Watch, *Intimidation of Defence Lawyers in Northern Ireland* (1992); Haldane Society, *Criminal Justice Under the 'Emergency Powers' in the 1990s* 13–20 (1992)

109 *See* Lord Steyn, *Incorporation and Devolution – A Few Reflections on the Changing Scene* 2 E. H. Rts L. Rev. 153, 155 (1988)

110 Further clause 3 (1) of the Human Rights Bill imposes an interpretative obligation on the courts. It requires courts to interpret all legislation, primary and subordinate, 'so far as is possible' as compatible with convention rights.

111 *See* Good Friday Agreement, Strand 3, Human Rights and Equal Opportunities § 4

5   The interface between the laws of war and the right to life in Northern Ireland

1 On the concept of ethnocracy *see* Oren Yiftachel, *Israel Society and Jewish–Palestinian Reconciliation: 'Ethnocracy' and its Territorial Contradictions*, 51 Middle East Journal 505–19 (1997).

2 Meaning the law of war and peace, from Hugo Grotius, *De Jure Belli ac Pacis*, Book III.

3 *See* Fritz Kalshoven, *Constraints on the Waging of War* 13 (1987)

4 *Ibid.*, at 11

5 *Ibid.*, at 16

6 Henry Dunant, *Un Souvenir de Solferino* (1862)

7 Convention for the Amelioration of the Condition of the Wounded and Sick in Armies in the Field, 6 July 1906, reprinted in Dietrich Schindler and Jiri Toman, *The Laws of Armed Conflicts*, 279, 3rd ed. (1988)

8 Geneva Convention for the Amelioration of the Condition of the Wounded and Sick in the Field, 27 July 1929, 118 LNTS 303

9 *See* Oren Gross, *The Grave Breaches System and the Armed Conflict in the Former Yugoslavia*, 16 Mich. J. Int'l L. 783, 791 (1995)

10 The basis of the grave breaches system is elaborated in Common Articles 49/50/129/146 of the four conventions, where a distinction is drawn between 'grave breaches' and all other breaches of the conventions.

11 G.I.A.D. Draper attests to the negotiation difficulties this provoked at the Diplomatic Conference. *See* G.I.A.D. Draper, *Humanitarian Law and Internal Armed Conflicts*, 13 Ga. J. Int'l and Comp. L. 253, 261 (1983).

12 The norms stated in Common Article 3 may be viewed as applicable to all conflicts, even those of an international character. *See* Theodor Meron, *International Criminalization of Internal Atrocities*, 89 Am. J. Int'l L. 554, 560 (1995). (Noting the US adherence to this position regarding the application of law to the international conflict in the former Yugoslavia.)

13 *See* Draper, *supra* note 11 at 269

14 Common Article 3 §§ 3 (1) (a)

15 *Ibid.*, §§ 3 (1) (c)

16 *Ibid.*, §§ 3 (1) (d)

17 *Ibid.*, §§ 3 (2)

18 The ICRC is responsible for carrying out the humanitarian work of the Red Cross in time of war. For a discussion of the role of the ICRC in overseeing the implementation of Geneva Law, *see* Jean Pictet, *The Principles of International Humanitarian Law* (1966).

19 The sessions were held from 20 February to 29 March 1974; from 3 February to 28 April 1975; from 21 April to 11 June 1976; and from 17 March to 10 June 1977. 1 *Official Records of the Diplomatic Conference on the Reaffirmation and Development of International Humanitarian Law* (1976). *See generally*, David E. Graham, *The 1974 Diplomatic Conference in the Law of War: A Victory for Political Causes and a Return to the 'Just War' Concept of the Eleventh Century*, 32 Wash. and Lee L. Rev. 25 (1975); Fritz Kalshoven, *Reaffirmation and Development of International Humanitarian Law Applicable in Armed Conflicts: The*

Diplomatic Conference, Geneva, 1974–77, 8 Neth. Y.B. Int'l L. 107 (1977); David P. Forsythe, *The 1974 Diplomatic Conference on Humanitarian Law: Some Observations* 69 Am. J. Int'l L. 77 (1975).

20 The beginning of this process came with the XIXth International Red Cross Conference in New Delhi in 1957, which considered 'Draft Rules for the Limitation of the Dangers Incurred by the *Civilian* Population in Time of War [my emphasis]'. The draft received little attention from governments but a way forward had been indicated on the expansion of the laws of war. The next international Red Cross conferences in Vienna (1965), Istanbul (1969) and Tehran (1973) all dealt with this subject. The culmination of the ICRC's efforts was seen when the Swiss Federal Council invited all states to another Diplomatic Conference to begin on 20 February 1974. *See* 3 *Encyclopedia of Public International Law* 184, Rudolf Bernhardt (ed.) (1982).

21 *See* Richard J. Erickson, *Protocol I: A Merging of the Hague and Geneva Law of Armed Conflict*, 19 Va. J. Int'l. L. 557, 559 (1979). *See also* George Aldrich, *New Life for the Laws of War*, 75 Am. J. Int'l. L. 764, 778 (1981).

22 Protocol Relating to the Protection of Victims of International Armed Conflicts, opened for signature 12 December 1977, U.N. Doc A/32/144 (1977) (Protocol I)

23 *See* Kalshoven, *supra* note 3 at 137

24 *See* Waldemar A. Solf and W.George Grandison, *International Humanitarian Law Applicable in Armed Conflict*, 10 J. Int'l L. and Econ. 567, 578 (1975)

25 *Ibid.*, at 579

26 This scope of application is outlined in Article 1 of the protocol.

27 Additional Protocols, *supra* note 22

28 *See* IACHR Report No. 55/97, Case No. 11.137, Argentina, OEA/Ser./L/V/ II.97, Doc. 38, 30 October 1997

29 *Ibid.* Here, the Inter-American Commission on Human Rights has recently adopted a report related to the *Tablada* case concerning the death of persons involved in an attack upon La Tablada military base in Argentina.

The complaint alleged violation by the state of both international humanitarian law and the American Convention on Human Rights. The commission held that it was competent to apply international humanitarian law.

30 Northern Ireland Constitution Act 1973. Good Friday Agreement, signed Friday 10 April 1998, Strand 1, Constitutional Issues §1 (i) and (ii)

31 Military and Paramilitary Activities in and against Nicaragua (Merits), ICJ Reports 14 (1986) (*Nicaragua v. United States*). This principle can be derived in two ways from the Nicaragua decision. First, that Common Article 3 encapsulates minimum standards to be applied whether a particular armed conflict is categorised as international or noninternational. Second, that Common Article 3 represents minimum humanitarian standards applicable in all situations, whether or not formal legal applicability of the article has been reached. *See also* Theodor Meron, *The Geneva Conventions as Customary Law*, 81 Am. J. Int'l L. 348 (1987).

32 *See* Paul Bew and Gordon Gillespie, *Northern Ireland: A Chronology of the Troubles 1968–93* (1993)

33 *See* Hans Magnus Enzensberger, *Civil Wars: From L.A. to Bosnia*, 20, 22 (1994)

34 *See* M.L.R. Smith, *Fighting for Ireland? The Military Strategy of the Irish Republican Movement* (1995)

35 *See* Brendan O'Leary and John McGarry, *The Politics of Antagonism: Understanding Northern Ireland* 11–12 (1993). The work also points out the fallacy of comparing such statistics as road traffic deaths in Northern Ireland with those that occur as a result of politically motivated violence. Whilst the former have generally exceeded the latter in the jurisdiction, comparison between the two is described as 'grossly inappropriate' in a liberal democracy, where states do not generally accept built-in risks of death from political violence when they make and enforce public policy. *Ibid.*, at 12–13.

36 *Ibid.*, at 13. O'Leary and McGarry also confirm that the numbers killed in the

Northern Ireland conflict in its late-twentieth-century phase are 'proportionately greater than the number killed in the whole of Ireland in each episode of extended political violence in the first six decades of this century'. *Ibid.*, at 20.

37 *Ibid.*, at 20

38 New Ireland Forum, *The Cost of Violence Arising from the Northern Ireland Crisis Since 1969* 3 (1984). Mike Tomlinson from Queen's University Belfast has estimated that £1,500,000,000 was paid by the United Kingdom in compensation for death, injury and damage to property between 1969 and 1993. *See, 25 Years On: The Costs of War and the Dividends of Peace*, West Belfast Economic Forum (1994).

39 *See* Bob Goldman, *International Humanitarian Law and the Armed Conflicts in El Salvador and Nicaragua*, 2 Am. J. Int'l L. and Pol'y 539 (1987). *See also, Report of the Secretary-General on the United Nations Observer Mission in El Salvador*, S/1994/375, 31 March 1994.

40 Interview with Hans Peter Gasser, legal adviser to the ICRC, International Red Cross Conference, Warsaw: lecture on file with author (August 1992)

41 *See, Phillips v. Eyre* (1870) LR 6 QB 1; *Hughes v. Casares* (1967) 111 Sol Jo 637

42 *See* J.L.J. Edwards, *Special Powers in Northern Ireland*, Crim. L. Rev. 7 (1956). For an interesting account of one of the personalities involved in this raid *see* Christle 'Charisma Shone Through in Sport, Politics and Trade Unionism', *Irish Times*, 1 June 1998 at 6.

43 *Report of a Committee of Privy Counsellors Appointed to Consider Authorized Procedures for the Interrogation of Persons Suspected of Terrorism* (Cmnd. 4901) (Parker Report)

44 *Ireland v. United Kingdom*, 25 E. Ct. H. R. (ser. A) (1978)

45 *See, McFeeley and Others v. United Kingdom*, Application 8317/78 (1980) 3 EHRR 161

46 *See generally*, John McGuffin, *Internment* (1976)

47 Special treatment was allowed to both republican and loyalist prisoners. H.C. Debs., vol. 840, col. 741, 6 July 1972.

48 *See* Kevin Boyle *et al*, *Law and State: The Case of Northern Ireland* 27–36 (1975)

49 *See, Report of a Committee to Consider, in the Context of Civil Liberties and Human Rights, Measures to Deal with Terrorism in Northern Ireland* (1975) (Gardiner Report)

50 *See* Clive P. Walker, *Irish Republican Prisoners – Political Detainees, Prisoners of War or Common Criminals?*, Irish Jurist 189, 199 (1984)

51 *Ibid.*

52 *See* Brian Gormally and Kieran McEvoy, *Release and Reintegration of Politically Motivated Prisoners in Northern Ireland* (1995)

53 Good Friday Agreement, *supra* note 30, Strand 3, Prisoners

54 *See generally, Badder, Menis, Meinhof and Grundman v. The Federal Republic of Germany*, Application no. 6166/73, D.R. 2 at 58, 18. Y.B.E.C. 132 (1975)

55 *Ensslin, Badder and Raspe v. The Federal Republic of Germany*, Application nos. 7572/76, 7586/76 and 7587/76

56 *See* Helsinki Watch, *Human Rights in Northern Ireland* 109–16 (1991)

57 *See generally*, J. Bowyer Bell, *The Secret Army, The IRA 1916–1979* (1983); Tim Pat Coogan, *The IRA* (1993); J. Bowyer Bell, *IRA Tactics and Targets – An Analysis of Tactical Aspects of the Armed Struggle 1969–88* (1995)

58 *See* J. Bowyer Bell, *The Secret Army, The IRA 1916–1979* 438–45 (1995); David McKittrick, 'Voyage into the Business of Terror', in *Endgame* 80–6 (1994).

59 *See, McLaughlin v. Ministry of Defence* (unreported) (1977). This case gave rise to Justice Gibson's famous 'posse' direction. Directing a jury in a civil action for compensation to the widow of an unarmed man shot during a bank robbery in Newry the judge stated: 'If you watch wild west films, the posse go ready to shoot their men if need be, if they don't bring them back peaceably they shoot them. And in the ultimate result if there isn't any other way to open up to a man it's reasonable to do it in the circumstances.'

60 *See, Quinn v. Robinson*, 783 F2d 776 (9th Cir. 1986)

61 *See, McGlinchey v. Wren* (1982) I.R.

154; *Shannon v. Fanning* (1984) 8
B.N.I.L. 43.

62 Hansard, H.C. Debs., vol 230, col 371
(written answers) (22 October 1993).
See generally, Peter Rowe and Michael
A. Mayer, *Ratification by the United
Kingdom of the 1977 Protocols Additional to
the Geneva Conventions of 1949: Selected
Problems of Implementation* 45 NILQ 343
(1994). Notably, the Irish government
have made similar undertakings in the
form of the Geneva Conventions
(Amendment) Bill 1997.

63 *See* 322 *International Review of the Red
Cross* 186–91 (1998)

64 'The Green Book', a PIRA training
manual, claims that the organisation
speaks as the lawful government of the
Irish Republic. *See* Helsinki Watch
report, *supra* note 56 at 106.

65 Hansard, H.C. Debs., vol 941, col 237
(written answers) (14 December 1977),
as cited in Wortley, *Observations on the
Revision of the 1949 Geneva Conventions*,
at 152. The British government also
made clear at the time that it viewed the
threshold of Protocol II (that is, actual
control of territory) to be 'read into'
the application of Protocol I,

66 Protocol I, Articles 43 and 47

67 Protocol I, Article 43 (1)

68 *See, Military Prosecutor v. Kassem*, as
reviewed in 65 Am. J. Int'l. L. 409
(1971). *See generally*, Georg
Schwarzenberger, *Human Rights and
Guerrilla Warfare*, 1 Isr. Y.B. Hum. Rts
246 (1977).

69 *See* Anglo–Irish Agreement, Article 1.
Also, Principle 5 of the Joint
Declaration of the Irish and British
Prime Ministers, December 1993. *See
also* Good Friday Agreement,
Constitutional Issues § (1) (i) *supra* note
30.

70 Such a poll could be initiated under
section 1 of the Northern Ireland
Constitution Act 1973.

71 *See* John de Pue, *The Amended First
Article to the 1st Draft Protocol Additional to
the Geneva Conventions of 1949*, 75 Mil.
L. Rev. 71 (1977)

72 *See* R. Hull, *The Irish Triangle, Conflict
in Northern Ireland* 152 (1976)

73 *See* Tom Hadden, *Legal Controls on the
Use of Lethal Force: Options for Reform*, in
Standing Advisory Commission on

Human Rights, 18th Annual Report
129, 152 (1992–3)

74 The article states: 'In order to ensure
respect for the protection of the civilian
population and civilian objects, the
parties to the conflict shall at all times
distinguish between the civilian
population and combatants and
between civilian objects and military
objectives and accordingly direct their
operations only against military
objects.'

75 *See*, ICRC *1956 Draft Rules for the
Limitation of the Dangers Incurred by the
Civilian Population in Time of War*, The
proposed categories were: (a) 'pure'
civilians, those with absolutely no
association with the military or war
industries (b) civilians engaged in the
war effort (c) those engaged in the
military effort, commonly referred to
as combat service support units and (d)
those involved in military operations.

76 *See* W. Hays Parks, *The Protection of
Civilians from Air Warfare*, prepared for
the Howard Gilman International
Colloquium on Air and Missile
Warfare (11–13 March 1997). On file
with author.

77 Protocol I, Article 37. *See generally*, P.J.
Erikson, *Protocol I: A Merging of the
Hague and Geneva Law of Armed Conflict*,
19 Va. J. Int'l. L. 557 (1977).

78 Common Article 3 (1). Further Article
23 of the Hague Regulations prohibits
'the killing or wounding of an enemy
. . . who having laid down his arms, or
having no longer means of defence, has
surrendered at discretion. . . .'

79 *See, Attorney-General for Northern
Ireland's Reference* (No. 1 of 1975)
(1977) A.C. 105 at 138. Lord Diplock
stated in his judgment: 'In the other
scale of the balance it would be open
to the jury to take the view that it
would not be unreasonable to assess the
kind of harm to be averted by
preventing the [deceased] escape as
even graver – the killing or wounding
of members of the patrol by terrorists
in an ambush, and the effect that this
kind of success by members of the
Provisional IRA in encouraging the
continuance of the armed insurrection
and all the misery and destruction of
life and property that terrorist activity

in Northern Ireland has entailed.' *Ibid.*, at 247.

80 This is a point made by Tom Hadden in his evaluation of the applicability of humanitarian law to Northern Ireland. *See* Hadden, *supra* note 73 at 150.

81 *See, United States v. List*, 11 *Trials of War Criminals* 757 (1948); *Mohamed Ali and Another v. Public Prosecutor* (1986) 3 All ER 488; *see generally*, Jonathan Paust, *Law in a Guerrilla Conflict: Myths, Norms and Human Rights*, Isr. Y.B. Hum. Rts 3 (1973).

82 *McElwaine* inquest finding (unreported), Belfast, January 1993. Transcript on file with author.

83 *See* Protocol I, Article 85

84 *See generally*, James E. Bond, *Protection of Non-Combatants in Guerrilla Wars*, 12 Will. and Mary L. Rev. 787 (1971)

85 This conclusion is based on evidence gathered to facilitate the database on lethal force deaths upon which a significant portion of the discussion of chapter 3 in particular is based. Much of that evidence is anecdotal, based on conversations with surviving family members of the deceased or persons who witnessed the removal and passage of injured persons. The existing inquest records for the period are incomplete, thus no complete picture can be built of the extent to which this was current practice at the time. All interviews on file with author.

86 The inquest found that Elliman died from a gunshot wound to the head. Another case, that of Joseph Corr, illustrates another intrusion on the provision of medical services to the wounded. Corr was aged forty-three and was shot in Ballymurphy, west Belfast, on 27 August 1971. Details of the context of death remain sketchy, although a file on the incident was sent to the DPP at the time. He was taken immediately to Musgrave Park Hospital's military wing. Family members report that he was questioned on arrival and while gravely ill. He died of gunshot wounds and an open verdict was returned at his inquest. He was not a member of any paramilitary organisation.

87 *See* Robin Everleigh, *Peacekeeping in a Democratic Society* (1978)

88 *See* David Weissbrodt, *The Role of International Organizations in the Implementation of Human Rights and Humanitarian Law in Situations of Armed Conflict*, 21 Vand. J. Trans'ntl. L. 313 (1988). An example of these minefields is the criticism directed at nongovernmental organisations by governments for failing to detail and publicise abuses by terrorists, yet, when they do address these groups, they are accused by the same governments of encouraging the international recognition of insurgents.

89 Such standards include the Minimum Humanitarian Standards, adopted by a meeting of experts convened by the Institute for Human Rights, Abo Akademi University, Turku, Finland, 30 November to 2 December 1990. This was submitted as a working paper to the UN Sub-Commission at its 43rd session, UN Doc. E/CN.4/Sub.2/199/55.

90 *See* Theo van Boven, *Reliance on Norms of Humanitarian Law by United Nations' Organs*, in G. Tanja and A. Delissen (eds), *Humanitarian Law of Armed Conflict: Challenges Ahead* 502 (1991). Van Boven states that 'UN political bodies are on perfectly good ground in invoking Common Article 3 to the Geneva Conventions of 1949 as a minimum standard of humanitarian law to be respected under all circumstances'.

91 *See* Hadden, *supra* note 73

Appendix

1 Violence and Civil Disturbance in Northern Ireland (1969) Cmnd. 566 (1970)

2 Children are defined by the Convention on the Rights of the Child as 'every human being below the age of 18 years unless, under the law applicable to the child, majority is attained earlier'. Article 1.G.A. Res. 44/25, 20 November 1989; entered into force 2 September 1990.

3 The minors killed by the use of plastic bullets are: Stephen Geddis (10), died 29 August 1975; Brian Stewart (13),

died 4 October 1976; Paul Whitters
(15), died 25 April 1981; Julie
Livingstone (14), died 13 May 1981;
Carol-Ann Kelly (12), died 22 May
1981; Stephen McConomy (11), died
19 April 1982; and Seamus Duffy (15),
died 9 August 1989.

4   Cited in Committee on the
Administration of Justice, *Plastic Bullets and the Law* (1990)

5   Alec McLaughlin (18); Martin Hamill
(15); George O'Neill (10); Colin Deery
(14); David Madden (4); Christine
McGuinness (16); Michael Irvine (16);
Dermot Gallagher (11); Steven
McFarlane (16); Martin O'Neill (9);
Paul Corr (12); Conor Campbell (18);
Paul Lavelle (15); Kevin McLaughlin
(14); Declan Burgoyne (9); Margaret
McElorum (15); Marie McKernan
(15); Paul Blaney (9); Thomas Torney
(17); Philomena Whelan (12); Martin
Tumelty (14). *Ibid.*

6   G.A. Res. 44/25 1989; entered into
force 2 September 1990

7   Article 37, Convention on the Rights
of the Child

8   Article 24, Convention on the Rights
of the Child

9   Article 6 (1), Convention on the
Rights of the Child

10   Article 6 (2), Convention on the Rights
of the Child

11   Article 40 (1), Convention on the
Rights of the Child

12   Frank McGuinness (17); Desmond
Healey (14); Leo McGuigan (16); Noel
Phillips (20); Daniel Teggart (44); Joan
Connolly (50); Norman Watson (53);
Fr Hugh Mullan (40); Hugh Herron
(31); Patrick McAdorey (24); Frank
Quinn (19).

13   The first inquest took place into Nora
McCabe's death in November 1982. It
was subsequently adjourned to
November 1983. On 4 November,
findings were issued by the jury which
established that Mrs McCabe had died
of a 'comminuted fracture of the skull'.

14   Source, family solicitor; interview on
file with author.

15   *R v. Davidson* (1981)

16   *R v. Lee William Clegg and Barry Wayne
Aindow* (1993) (unreported) at 65

17   A good example of this is evidenced by
the death of Patricia McKay, killed on
29 September 1972. The little
information available on her death
establishes her as a member of OIRA,
and confirms that the British army was
responsible for her death. It is unclear
whether the army had knowledge of
her political affiliations.

18   *See* Kadar Asmal, *Shoot to Kill?
International Lawyers' Inquiry into the
Lethal Use of Firearms by the Security
Forces in Northern Ireland* 59 (1985)

19   The application was introduced on 14
August 1991 and registered on 24
October 1991.

20   The inquest took place on 27 May
1971. The soldier died of a
haemorrhage and shock caused by
lacerations of the aorta.

21   On file with author

22   Other deaths in this category include:
William Corbett, 1 August 1981;
Stephen Humble, 26 August 1981;
Alistair Slater (SAS), 2 December 1984;
Ian Johnston (undercover military), 9
November 1989; David Fenley, 18
February 1993.

23   *See* Mark Urban, *Big Boys' Rules* 227–37
(1992)

24   *The Times*, 9 May 1987

25   Application no. 30054/96

26   The *Irish Times* reported that members
of the E4A and one member of the 'H'
division's HMSUs were responsible for
the deaths. *Irish Times*, 23 January 1985.

27   The five were Gervaise McKerr,
Eugene Toman, Sean Burns, Seamus
Grew and Roddy Carroll.

28   *R v. Robinson, Montgomery and Brannigan*
(1984) (unreported)

29   *See, R v. William James Montgomery,
David Brannigan and Frederick Nigel
Robinson*, 5 June 1984 (Belfast Crown
Court) at 18

30   *See* Peter Taylor, *Stalker: The Search for
Truth* (1987); John Stalker, *Stalker*
(1988)

31   The inquest took place six months later
on 16 December 1976. It concluded
that Walker had a laceration of the
brain and spinal chord due to gunshot
wounds to the head and neck.

32   The inquest took place on 27 April
1992, after a delay of 2 years and 7
months.

33   Urban, *supra* note 23 at 243

Select bibliography

Books

Allen, Michael J., *Textbook on Criminal Law*, London, 1991

Aquinas, Saint Thomas, *Summa Theologiae*, translated by T. Heath, 1972

Aristotle, *Ethics*, translated by J.A.K. Thompson, rev. ed., New York, 1976

Asmal, Kader, *Shoot to Kill? International Lawyers' Inquiry into the Lethal Use of Firearms by the Security Forces in Northern Ireland*, Dublin, 1985

Baxter, J. and L. Koffman (eds), *Police: The Constitution and the Community*, Abingdon, 1985

Beddard, Ralph, *Human Rights and Europe*, 3rd ed., Cambridge, 1993

Bell, J. Bowyer, *The Secret Army: The IRA 1916–77*, rev. ed., Cambridge, Mass., 1983

———— *The Secret Army*, Dublin, 1989

———— *IRA Tactics and Targets: An Analysis of Tactical Aspects of the Armed Struggle 1969–89*, Dublin, 1990

Bernhardt, Rudolf (ed.), *Encyclopaedia of Public International Law*, Amsterdam, 1982

Best, Geoffrey, *Humanity in Warfare: The Modern Development of the International Law of Armed Conflicts*, rev. ed., London, 1983

Bew, Paul and Gordon Gillespie, *Northern Ireland: A Chronology of the Troubles 1968–1993*, Dublin, 1994

Bindman, Geoffrey, *South Africa and the Rule of Law*, London, 1988

Bishop, Patrick and Eamonn Mallie, *The Provisional IRA*, London, 1988

Bonner, David, *Emergency Powers in Peacetime*, London, 1985

Boyle, Kevin and Tom Hadden, *Ireland: A Positive Proposal*, London, 1985

Boyle, Kevin and Paddy Hillyard, *Law and State: The Case of Northern Ireland*, London, 1975

———— *Ten Years on in Northern Ireland: The Legal Control of Political Violence*, London, 1980

Brazilay, David, *The British Army in Ulster*, vol. 2, Belfast, 1975

Brownlie, Ian, *Principles of Public International Law*, New York, 1990

Buergenthal, Thomas, *Contemporary Issues in International Law: Essays in Honor of Louis B. Sohn*, Arlington, 1984

Campbell, Colm, *Emergency Law in Ireland 1918–1925*, Oxford, 1994

Cassese, Antonio, *International Law in a Divided World*, Oxford, 1986

———— (ed.), *The New Humanitarian Law of Armed Conflict*, Oxford, 1979

Chowdhury, Subrata Roy, *Rule of Law in a State of Emergency*, Oxford, 1989

Clapham, Andrew, *Human Rights in the Private Sphere*, Oxford, 1994

Clements, Luke J., *European Human Rights: Taking a Case Under the Convention*, 1994

Coogan, Tim Pat, *The IRA*, Niwot, Colorado, 1993

Cooney, John, *The Crozier and the Dáil: Church and State 1922–1986*, Cork, 1986

Crozier, Maurna, *Cultural Traditions in Northern Ireland: Varieties of Brightness*, Belfast, 1989

———— (ed.), *Cultural Traditions in Northern Ireland: Varieties of Irishness*, Belfast, 1989

Damrosch, Lori, *Enforcing Restraint: Collective Intervention in Internal Conflicts*, New York, 1993

Delmas, Marty M., *The European Convention for the Protection of Human Rights: International Protection Versus National Restrictions*, Dordrecht, 1991

Devlin, Bernadette, *The Price of My Soul*, New York, 1969

Dewar, Rev. M.W., Rev. John Brown and Rev. S.E. Long, *Orangeism*, Belfast, 1967

Dillon, Martin, *The Dirty War*, London, 1991

Donnelly, J., *International Human Rights*, Boulder, 1993

Draper, G.I.A.D., *The Geneva Conventions of 1949*, London, 1965

Dunant, Henry, *Un Souvenir de Solferino*, Geneva, 1862

Dworkin, Ronald, *Taking Rights Seriously*, London, 1978

————*Law's Empire*, Cambridge, Mass., 1986

————*Life's Dominion*, New York, 1994

Edwards, John U.J., *The Attorney-General, Politics and Public Interest*, London, 1984

Edwards, P. (ed.), *The Encyclopedia of Philosophy*, vol. 6, New York, 1967

Ely, John Hart, *War and Responsibility: Constitutional Lessons of Vietnam and Its Aftermath*, Princeton, 1993

Ewing, K.D. and C.A. Gearty, *Freedom Under Thatcher*, Oxford, 1990

Farrell, Michael, *Northern Ireland: The Orange State*, London, 1980

Fawcett, J.E.C., *The Application of the European Convention on Human Rights*, 2nd ed., Oxford, 1987

Feldman, David, *Civil Liberties and Human Rights in England and Wales*, Oxford, 1993

Fine, B. and R. Millar (eds), *Policing the Miners' Strike*, London, 1985

Finn, John E., *Constitutions in Crisis: Political Violence and the Rule of Law*, Oxford, 1991

Fitzpatrick, Joan, *Human Rights in Crisis: The International System for Protecting Rights During States of Emergency*, Philadelphia, 1994

Franck, Thomas M., *The Power of Legitimacy Among Nations*, New York, 1990

————*Political Questions, Judicial Answers*, Princeton, 1992

Geraghty, Tony, *Who Dares Wins*, London, 1983

Greenwood, Christopher, *Police Tactics in Armed Operation*, Colorado, 1979

Greer, Stephen, *Supergrasses: A Study in Anti-Terrorist Law Enforcement in Northern Ireland*, Oxford, 1995

Greer, Stephen and A. White, *Abolishing the Diplock Courts: The Case for Restoring Jury Trial to Scheduled Offences in Northern Ireland*, London, 1986

Grotius, Hugo, *De Jure Belli ac Pacis*, translated by Francis G. Kelsey, Oxford, 1925

Hadden, Tom and Kevin Boyle, *The Anglo-Irish Agreement: Commentary, Text and Official Review*, Dublin, 1989

Hamill, Desmond, *Pig in the Middle: The Army in Northern Ireland*, London, 1985

Harding, Richard W., *Police Killings in Australia*, Ringwood, Australia, 1970

Hart, H.L.A., *The Concept of Law*, Oxford, 1961

Hellerstein, William E. *et al*, *Criminal Justice and Human Rights in Northern Ireland: A Report to the Association of the Bar of the City of New York*, New York, 1988

Henkin, Louis, *The Rights of Man Today*, New York, 1978

————*How Nations Behave: Law and Foreign Policy*, 2nd ed., New York, 1979

———— *The Age of Rights*, New York, 1990

————(ed.), *The International Bill of Rights: The Covenant on Civil and Political Rights*, New York, 1981

Hillyard, Paddy, *Suspect Community: People's Experience of the Prevention of Terrorism Acts in Britain*, London, 1993

Hobbes, Thomas, *Leviathan*, Glasgow, 1962

————*Man and Citizen*, B. Gert ed., 1972

Hogan, Gerard and Clive Walker, *Political Violence and the Law in Ireland*, Manchester, 1989

Hull, Roger H., *The Irish Triangle: Conflict in Northern Ireland*, Princeton, 1976

Huntington, Samuel P., *The Soldier and the State*, Cambridge, Mass., 1957

Hyde, H. Montgomery, *The Life of Edward Carson, Lord Carson of Duncairn*, 1987

Jacobs, Francis G., *The European Convention on Human Rights*, London, 1975

Jennings, Anthony (ed.), *Justice Under Fire: The Abuse of Civil Liberties in Northern Ireland*, London, 1988

Juviler, Peter and Bertram Gross, *Human Rights for the 21st Century: Foundations for Responsible Hope*, Armonk, NY, 1993

Kalshoven, Fritz, *Constraints on the Waging of War*, Geneva, 1987

Kelly, Kevin, *The Longest War: Northern Ireland and the IRA*, Dingle, 1982

Kitson, Frank, *Low Intensity Operations*, London, 1978

Llewellyn, Karl, *Cases and Materials on the Law of Sales*, Chicago, 1930
————— *The Bramble Bush: On Our Law and Its Study*, 2nd ed., New York, 1951
Locke, John, *Of Civil Government, Second Treatise*, Russell Kirk ed., 1955
Luard, Evan (ed.), *Historical Foundations of Human Rights and Subsequent Developments*, London
Lundman, Richard J., *Police and Policing: An Introduction*, New York, 1980
Lyons, F.S.L., *Ireland Since the Famine*, 2nd ed., London, 1974
————— *Culture and Anarchy in Ireland 1890–1939*, New York, 1982
MacDonald, R. St. J. *et al*, (eds), *The European System for the Protection of Human Rights*, Dordrecht, 1993
McArdle, Patsy, *The Secret War*, Cork, 1984
McDougall, Myers, Harold Lasswell and Lung Chen, *Human Rights and World Public Order*, New Haven, 1980
McGoldrick, Dominic, *The Human Rights Committee*, Oxford, 1991
McGuffin, John, *Internment*, Tralee, 1973
McKittrick, David, *Endgame*, Belfast, 1994
Mathews, Anthony, *Freedom, State Security and the Rule of Law*, 2nd ed., London, 1988
Meron, Theodor, *Human Rights in Internal Strife: Their International Protection*, Cambridge, 1987
————— *Human Rights and Humanitarian Law as Customary Law*, Oxford, 1989
————— (ed.), *Human Rights in International Law: Legal and Policy Issues*, Oxford, 1975
Millar, Richard I., *The Law of War*, New York, 1975
Morten, Peter, *Emergency Tour*, London, 1989
Moxon-Browne, Edward, *Nation, Class and Creed in Northern Ireland*, Aldershot, 1983
Mullin, Chris, *Error of Judgement*, London, 1986
Murray, Raymond, *The SAS in Ireland*, Cork, 1990
Nardin, Terry and David R. Mapel (eds), *Traditions of International Ethics*, Cambridge, 1992
Newman, Frank and David Weissbrodt, *International Human Rights: Law, Policy, and Process*, 2nd ed., Cincinnati, 1996
O'Brien, Conor Cruise, *States of Ireland*, London, 1972
O Connor, Fionnuala, *In Search of a State: Catholics in Northern Ireland*, Belfast, 1993
O'Leary, Brendan and John McGarry, *The Politics of Antagonism: Understanding Northern Ireland*, London, 1993
O'Malley, Padraig, *Biting at the Grave: The Irish Hunger Strikes and the Politics of Despair*, Boston, 1990
Oraá, Jaime, *Human Rights in States of Emergency in International Law*, Oxford, 1992

Patterson, Dennis, *A Companion to Philosophy of Law and Legal Theory*, Oxford, 1996

Pictet, Jean S., *Commentary – I Geneva Convention*, Geneva, 1958

————— *The Principles of International Humanitarian Law*, Geneva, 1966

Probert, Belinda, *Beyond Orange and Green: The Political Economy of the Northern Ireland Crisis*, Westport, Conn., 1978

Ramcharan, B.G. (ed.), *The Right to Life in International Law*, The Hague, 1985

Roberts, Adam and Richard Guelff (eds), *Documents on the Laws of War*, London, 1979

Robertson, A.H., *Human Rights in Europe*, 2nd ed., Manchester, 1977

Robinson, Mary, *The Special Criminal Court*, Dublin, 1974

Rodley, Nigel S., *The Treatment of Prisoners Under International Law*, Oxford, 1987

Rose, Richard, *Governing Without Consensus: An Irish Perspective*, Boston, 1971

Rossiter, Clinton, *Constitutional Dictatorship*, Westport, Conn., 1948

Rousseau, Jean Jacques, *The Social Contract*, translated by W. Kendall, Chicago, 1954

Rowe, P. and C.J. Whelan (eds), *Military Intervention in Democratic Societies: Law, Policy, and Practice in Great Britain and the United States*, London, 1985

Ryder, Chris, *The RUC: A Force Under Fire*, 2nd ed., London, 1992

Schachter, Oscar, *International Law in Theory and Practice*, Dordrecht, 1991

Schindler, Dietrich and Jiri Toman, *The Laws of Armed Conflicts*, 3rd ed., 1988

Schmid, Alex P. and Ronald D. Crelinsten (eds), *Western Responses to Terrorism*, Portland, Oregon, 1993

Schwarzenberger, Georg and E.D. Brown, *A Manual of International Law*, 6th ed., 1976

Senior, Hereward, *Orangeism in Ireland and Britain, 1795–1836*, London, 1966

Shaw, Malcolm N., *International Law*, 3rd ed., Cambridge, 1991

Sibner, Laura and Allan Little, *The Death of Yugoslavia*, London, 1995

Siegart, Paul, *The International Law of Human Rights*, Oxford, 1983

Stalker, John, *Stalker*, New York, 1988

Starke, Joseph G., *Introduction to International Law*, 11th ed., London, 1994

Supperstone, Michael, *Brownlie's Law of Public Order and National Security*, London, 1981

Tanja, Gerard J. and Astrid J.M. Delissen (eds), *Humanitarian Law of Armed Conflict: Challenges Ahead*, Boston, 1991

Taylor, Peter, *Stalker: The Search for Truth*, London, 1987

Thurston, G., *Coronership*, London, 1980

Tolley, Howard, *The UN Commission on Human Rights*, Boulder, 1987

Urban, Mark, *Big Boys' Rules: The Secret Struggle Against the IRA*, London, 1992

Van Dijk, P. and G.J.H. Van Hoof, *The Theory and Practice of the European Convention on Human Rights*, 2nd ed., Boston, 1990

Vasak, Karel (ed.), *The International Dimensions of Human Rights*, Westport, Conn., 1982

Vattel, Emer de, *The Law of Nations*, London, 1934

Waddington, P.A.G., *Arming an Unarmed Police*, London, 1988

———— *The Strong Arm of the Law*, Oxford, 1991

Walker, Clive, *The Prevention of Terrorism in British Law*, Manchester, 1986

Walsh, Dermot P.J., *The Use and Abuse of Emergency Legislation in Northern Ireland*, London, 1983

Walzer, Michael, *Just and Unjust Wars: A Moral Argument with Historical Illustrations*, New York, 1978

Wilcox, A.F., *The Decision to Prosecute*, London, 1972

Wilkinson, Paul, *Terrorism and the Liberal State*, London, 1986

Williams, Glanville, *Textbook of Criminal Law*, 2nd ed., London, 1961

Articles

Aldrich, George H., *Guerrilla Combatants and POW Status*, 31 Am. U. L. Rev. 871 (1964)

———— *New Life for the Laws of War*, 75 Am. J. Int'l L. 764 (1981)

———— *Compliance with the Law: Problems and Prospects*, in *Effecting Compliance* (Hazel Fox and Michael A. Mayer eds) (1993)

———— *Jurisdiction of the International Criminal Tribunal for the Former Yugoslavia*, 90 Am. J. Int'l L. 64 (1996)

Alexander, George J., *The Illusory Protection of Human Rights by National Courts During Periods of Emergency*, 5 Hum. Rts L. J. 1 (1984)

Almond, Harry, *Law and Armed Conflict: Some of the Shared Politics*, 9 Case W. Res. J. Int'l L. 175 (1977)

Andrews, J.A., *The European Jurisprudence of Human Rights*, 43 Md. L. Rev. 463 (1984)

Baxter, Richard R., *So Called 'Unprivileged Belligerency': Spies, Guerillas and Saboteurs*, 28 Brit. Y. B. Int'l L. 323 (1951)

———— *Multilateral Treaties as Evidence of Customary International Law*, 41 Brit. Y. B. Int'l L. 275 (1965–6)

———— *The Privy Council on the Qualifications of Belligerents*, 63 Am. J. Int'l L. 290 (1969)

———— *The Law of War*, in *The Present State of International Law and Other Essays* 107 (Maarten Bos ed.) (1973)

———— *Humanitarian Law or Humanitarian Politics? The 1974 Diplomatic Conference on Humanitarian Law*, 16 Harv. Int'l L. J. 1 (1975)

Becket, James, *The Greek Case Before the European Human Rights Commission*, 1 Hum. Rts L. J. 91 (1970–1)

Bernhardt, Rudolf, *Reform of the Control Machinery Under the European Convention on Human Rights: Protocol No. 11*, 89 Am. J. Int'l L. 144 (1995)

Bishop, Jeanne E., *The Right to Be Arrested: British Government Summary Execution*, 11 N. Y. L. Sch. J. Int'l and Comp. L. 207 (1982)

Bond, James E., *The Protection of Non-Combatants in Guerrilla Wars*, 12 Will. and Mary L. Rev. 787 (1971)

——————*Application of the Laws of War to Internal Conflicts*, 3 Ga. J. Int'l and Comp. L. 345 (1973)

Bouchard, Edwin M., *The Local Remedies Rule*, 27 Am. J. Int'l L. 729 (1934)

Boyle, Kevin and Hurst Hannum, *The Donnelly Case*, 68 Am. J. Int'l L. 440 (1974)

Bristow, Alan, *Police Officer Shootings – A Tactical Evaluation*, 54 J. Crim. L. Criminology and Police Science 1 (1963)

Brownlie, Ian, *The Individual before Tribunals Exercising International Jurisdiction*, 11 Int'l and Comp. L. Q. 701 (1962)

——————*Interrogation in Depth: The Compton and Parker Reports*, 35 Md. L. Rev. 501 (1972)

——————*Superior Orders – Time for a New Realism*, Crim. L. Rev. 396 (1989)

Buergenthal, Thomas, *The Domestic Status of the European Convention on Human Rights*, 13 Buff. L. Rev. 354 (1964)

——————*The Revised OAS Charter and the Protection of Human Rights*, 69 Am. J. Int'l L. 828 (1975)

Chomsky, Noam, *The Rule of Force in International Affairs*, 80 Yale L. J. 1456 (1971)

Colvin, Eric, *Exculpatory Defences in Criminal Law*, 10 O. J. L. S. 381 (1990)

Comment, *Bases and Effectiveness of International Law*, 63 Am. J. Int'l L. 270 (1969)

Cotter, Cornelius P., *Emergency Detention in Wartime: The British Experience*, 6 Stan. L. Rev. 238 (1954)

Dadisman, MaryAnn, *The Irish Question: Into the Lion's Den, Britain Grilled on Human Rights Issues of Northern Ireland*, 21 (3) Hum. Rts 14 (summer 1994)

De Schutter, Bart and Christine van de Wyngaert, *Coping with Non-International Armed Conflict*, 13 Ga. J. Int'l and Comp. L. 279 (1983)

Dinstein, Yoram, *The International Law of Inter-State Wars and Human Rights*, 7 Isr. Y. B. H. Rts 139 (1977)

——————*The New Geneva Protocols: A Step Forward or Backward?*, 33 Y. B. World Aff. 265 (1979)

Doran, Sean, *The Use of Force by the Security Forces in Northern Ireland: A Legal Perspective*, 7 Legal Studies 291 (1987)

Draper, G.I.A.D., *The Relationship Between the Human Rights Regime and the Laws of Armed Conflict*, 1 Isr. Y. B. Hum. Rts 191 (1971)

——————*The Status of Combatants and the Question of Guerilla Warfare*, 45 Brit. Y. B. Int'l L. 173 (1971)

——————*The Implementation of the Modern Law of Armed Conflict*, 8 Israel L. Rev. 1 (1973)

——————*Humanitarian Law and Internal Armed Conflicts*, 13 Ga. J. Int'l and Comp. L. 261 (1983)

Edwards, J., *Capital Punishment in Northern Ireland*, Crim. L. Rev. 750 (1976)

Erickson, Richard J., *Protocol I: A Merging of the Hague and Geneva Law of Armed Conflict*, 19 Va. J. Int'l L. 557 (1979)

Farer, Tom J., *Humanitarian Law and Armed Conflict: Towards the Definition of International Armed Conflict*, 71 Colum. L. Rev. 37 (1971)

———— *The Inter-American Commission on Human Rights: Operations and Doctrine*, 9 Int'l J. L. Lib. 251 (1981)

Farer, Tom J. and Felice Gear, *The UN and Human Rights: At the End of the Beginning* in *United Nations, Divided World* 240 (Adam Roberts and Benedict Kingsbury eds, 2nd ed.) (1993)

Feingold, Cora S. *The Doctrine of Margin of Appreciation and the European Convention on Human Rights*, 53 Notre Dame L. Rev. 90 (1977)

———— *The Little Red Schoolbook and the European Convention on Human Rights*, 3 Hum. Rts Rev. 21 (1978)

Flaherty, Martin, *Human Rights Violations Against Defense Lawyers: The Case of Northern Ireland*, 7 Harv. Hum. Rts J. 87 (1994)

———— *Choice Without Delay: Interrogation Centers, Legal Advice, and International Human Rights*, 27 Colum. Hum. Rts L. Rev. 1 (1995)

Forsythe, David P., *The 1974 Diplomatic Conference on Humanitarian Law: Some Observations*, 69 Am. J. Int'l L. 77 (1975)

Fox, Donald F., *Inter-American Commission on Human Rights Finds United States in Violation*, 82 Am. J. Int'l L. 601 (1988)

Fraleigh, Arnold, *The Algerian Revolution as a Case Study in International Law*, in *The International Law of Civil War* (Richard Falk ed.) (1971)

Francioni, Francesco, *International 'Soft Law': A Contemporary Assessment*, in *Fifty Years of the International Court of Justice* (V. Lowe and M. Fitzmaurice eds.) 167 (1996)

Franck, Thomas M., *Some Observations on the ICJ's Procedural and Substantive Innovations*, 81 Am. J. Int'l L. 116 (1987)

————*Legitimacy in the International System*, 82 Am. J. Int'l L. 705 (1988)

———— *The Emerging Right to Democratic Governance*, 86 Am. J. Int'l L. 46 (1992)

Frowein, Jochen A., *The European and the American Conventions on Human Rights – A Comparison*, 1 Hum. Rts L. J. 44 (1980)

Gardner, John, *Instrumentalism and Necessity*, 6 O. J.L.S. 431 (1986)

Garro, Alejandro, *The Role of the Argentine Judiciary in Controlling Governmental Action Under a State of Siege*, 4 Hum. Rts L. J. 311 (1983)

Gasser, Hans Peter., *A Measure of Humanity in Internal Disturbances and Tensions: A Proposal for a Code of Conduct*, 28 Int'l Rev. Red Cross 38 (Jan.–Feb. 1988)

Gearty, Conor, *The European Court of Human Rights and the Protection of Civil Liberties: An Overview*, 89 Camb. L. J. 122 (1993)

Goldman, Bob, *International Humanitarian Law and the Armed Conflicts in El Salvador and Nicaragua*, 2 Am. J. Int'l L. and Pol. 539 (1987)

Golsong, Herbert I., *The European Commission of Human Rights*, 2 Conn. J. Int'l L. 285 (1987)

Gormley, W. Paul, *The Procedural Status of the Individual Before Supranational Judicial Tribunals*, 41 U. Det. L. Rev. 282 (1964)

Graham, David E., *The 1974 Diplomatic Conference in the Law of War: A Victory for Political Causes and a Return to the 'Just War' Concept of the Eleventh Century*, 32 Wash. and Lee L. Rev. 25 (1975)

Green, L.C., *Derogations of Human Rights in Emergency Situations*, 16 Can. Y. B. Int'l L. 92 (1978)

Greenspan, Maurice, *The Protection of Human Rights in Time of Warfare*, 1 Isr. Y. B. H. Rts 228 (1971)

Greenwood, Colin, *The Evil Choice*, Crim. L. Rev. 4 (1975)

Greer, D.S., *Legal Control of Military Operations – A Missed Opportunity*, 31 NILQ 15 (1980)

Greer, Stephen, *Military Intervention in Civil Disturbances: The Legal Basis Reconsidered*, Public Law 573 (1983)

Gross, Oren, *The Grave Breaches System and the Armed Conflict in the Former Yugoslavia*, 16 Mich. J. Int'l L. 783 (1995)

Grossman, Claudio, *States of Emergency: Latin America and the United States* in *Constitutionalism and Rights* 176 (Louis Henkin and Albert J. Rosenthal eds) (1990)

Guelke, Adrian, *International Legitimacy, Self-Determination and Northern Ireland*, 11 Review of Int'l Studies 37 (1985)

Hadden, Tom, *Legal Controls on the Use of Lethal Force: Options for Reform* in *Standing Advisory Commission on Human Rights*, Report 129 (1992–3)

Harris, D., *The Right to Life under the European Convention on Human Rights*, 1 Maastricht J. Euro. and Comp. L. 122 (1994)

Hartman, Joan F., *Derogation from Human Rights Treaties in Public Emergencies*, 22 Harv. Int'l L. J. 1 (1981)

———— *Working Paper for the Committee of Experts on the Article 4 Derogation Provision*, 7 Hum. Rts Q. 89 (1985)

Hatchard, John, *The Implementation of Safeguards on the Use of Emergency Powers: A Zimbabwean Perspective*, 9 O. J. L. S. 116 (1989)

Hay, Alexandre, *The ICRC and International Humanitarian Issues*, 238 Int'l Rev. Red Cross 3 (Jan.–Feb. 1984)

Heuston, R.F.V., *Liversidge v. Anderson in Retrospect*, 86 L. Q. Rev. 33 (1970)

———— *Liversidge v. Anderson: Two Footnotes*, 87 L. Q. Rev. 161 (1972)

Higgins, Rosalyn, *Aspects of the Case Concerning Barcelona Traction, Light and Power Co. Ltd.*, 11.Va. J. Int'l L. 327 (1971)

———— *Derogations Under Human Rights Treaties*, 48 Brit. Y. B. Int'l L. 281 (1976–7)

Hinsley, F.H., *The Modern Patterns of War and Peace* in *Studies in International Law*, 77 (F.A. Mann ed.) (1973)

Hollands, Denys C., *Emergency Legislation in the Commonwealth*, 13 Current Legal Problems 148 (1960)

Jackson, John, *The Northern Ireland (Emergency Provisions) Act 1987*, 39 NILQ 235 (1988)

Jennings, Anthony, *Northern Ireland: The Legal Control of the Use of Lethal Force*, 135 NLJ 921 (1985)

Jessup, Philip, *Should International Law Recognize an Intermediate Between Peace and War?*, 48 Am. J. Int'l L. 98 (1954)

Joseph, Sarah, *Denouement of the Deaths on the Rock: The Right to Life of Terrorists*, 14 Neth. Hum. Rts Q. 5 (1996)

Junod, Sylvie, *Additional Protocol II: History and Scope*, 33 Am. U. L. Rev. 29 (1983)

Kalshoven, Fritz, *Reaffirmation and Development of International Humanitarian Law Applicable in Armed Conflicts: The Diplomatic Conference, Geneva, 1974–77*, 8 Neth. Y. B. Int'l L. 107 (1977)

————— *Guerrilla and Terrorism in Internal Armed Conflict*, 33 Am. U. L. Rev. 67 (1983)

Kaufmann, Edy and Patricia Weiss Fagen, *Extrajudicial Executions: An Insight into the Global Dimensions of a Human Rights Violation*, 3 Hum. Rts Q. 81 (1981)

Kiss, Alexandre, *Commentary by the Rapporteur on the Limitation Provisions*, 7 Hum. Rts Q. 16 (1985)

Klabbers, Jan, *The Redundancy of Soft Law*, 65 Nordic J. Int'l L. 167 (1996)

Leary, Howard R., *The Role of the Police in Riotous Demonstrations*, 40 Notre Dame L. Rev. 499 (1965)

Lester, Anthony, *Fundamental Rights: The United Kingdom Isolated?*, Pub. L. 46 (1984)

Lillich, Richard B., *Two Perspectives on the Barcelona Traction Case*, 65 Am. J. Int'l L. 522 (1971)

————— *Guidelines for Bodies Monitoring Respect for Human Rights During States of Emergency*, 85 Am. J. Int'l L. 717 (1991)

Livingstone, Stephen, *A Week is a Long Time in Detention: Brogan and Others v. United Kingdom*, 49 NILQ 288 (1989)

Llewellyn, Karl, *A Realistic Jurisprudence: The Next Step* in Karl Llewellyn, *Jurisprudence: Realism in Theory and Practice*, 1962

Lockwood, Bert B., Jr. *et al, Working Paper for the Committee of Experts on Limitation Provisions*, 7 Hum. Rts Q. 35 (1985)

Lowry, David, *Ill-treatment, Brutality and Torture: Some Thoughts on the Treatment of Irish Political Prisoners*, 22 De Paul L. Rev. 553 (1973)

Lysaght, Charles, *The Scope of Protocol II and Its Relation to Common Article 3 of the Geneva Conventions of 1949 and Other Human Rights Instruments*, 33 Am. U. L. Rev. 9 (1983)

Maher, Major M., *The Right to a Fair Trial in Criminal Cases Involving Classified Information*, 120 Mil. L. Rev. 1 (1988)

Mahoney, Paul, *Judicial Activism and Judicial Self-Restraint in the European Court of Human Rights: Two Sides of the Same Coin*, 11 Hum. Rts L. J. 57 (1990)

Mangan, Brendan, *Protecting Human Rights in National Emergencies: Shortcomings in the European System and a Proposal for Reform*, 10 Hum. Rts Q. 372 (1988)

McAuley, Finbar, *Anticipating the Past: The Defence of Provocation in Irish Law*, 50 Md. L. R. 133 (1989)

McCoffin, Frank, *Judicial Balancing: The Protean Scales of Justice*, 63 N. Y. U. L. Rev. 16 (1988)

Marks, Stephen, *Principles and Norms of Human Rights Applicable in Emergency Situations: Underdevelopment, Catastrophes, and Armed Conflicts* in *The International Dimensions of Human Rights* (Karel Vasak and Philip Alston eds) (1982)

Meron, Theodor, *On the Inadequate Reach of Humanitarian Law and Human Rights Law and the Need for a New Instrument*, 77 Am. J. Int'l L. 589 (1983)

———— *Towards a Humanitarian Declaration on Internal Strife*, 78 Am. J. Int'l L. 859 (1984)

———— *On a Hierarchy of International Human Rights*, 80 Am. J. Int'l L. 1 (1986)

———— *The Geneva Conventions as Customary Law*, 81 Am. J. Int'l L. 348 (1987)

———— *International Criminalization of Internal Atrocities*, 89 Am. J. Int'l L. 554 (1995)

Montealegre, Hernan, *The Compatibility of a State Party's Derogation Under Human Rights Conventions with Its Obligations Under Protocol II and Common Article 3*, 33 Am. U. L. Rev. 41 (1993)

Morrison, Fred, *Legal Issues in the Nicaragua Opinion*, 81 Am. J. Int'l L. 160 (1987)

Morrisson, Clovis C., Jr., *Margin of Appreciation in European Human Rights Law*, 6 Hum. Rts J. 263 (1973)

Mullerson, Rein, *The Efficiency of the Individual Complaint Procedures: The Experience of the CCPR, CERD, CAT and ECHR*, in *Monitoring Human Rights in Europe* 31 (Bloed ed.) (1993)

Murphy, Thomas, *Sanctions and Enforcement of the Humanitarian Law of the Four Geneva Conventions of 1949 and Geneva Protocol I of 1977*, 103 Mil. L. Rev. 3 (1984)

Ní Aoláin, Fionnuala, *The Emergence of Diversity: Differences in Human Rights Jurisprudence*, 19 Fordham Int'l L. J. 101 (1995)

———— *The Fortification of an Emergency Regime*, 59 Albany L. Rev. 1353 (1996)

———— *Where Hope and History Rhyme – Prospects for Peace in Northern Ireland?*, 50 J. Int'l Aff. 63 (1996)

Note, *Secret Surveillance and the European Convention on Human Rights*, 33 Stan. L. Rev. 1113 (1981)

O'Boyle, Michael P., *Emergency Limitations and the Protection of Human Rights: A Model Derogation Provision for a Northern Ireland Bill of Rights*, 28 NILQ 160 (1977)

———— *Torture and Emergency Powers Under the European Convention on Human Rights: Ireland v. UK*, 71 Am. J. Int'l L. 674 (1977)

O'Donnell, Daniel, *States of Exception*, 21 ICJ Rev. 52 (1978)

O'Donnell, Thomas A., *The Margin of Appreciation Doctrine: Standards in the Jurisprudence of the European Court of Human Rights*, 4 Hum. Rts Q. 474 (1982)

———— *Commentary by the Rapporteur on Derogation*, 7 Hum. Rts Q. 23 (1985)

O'Higgins, Paul, *The Northern Ireland Act 1972*, 35 Md. L. R. 295 (1972)

Opsahl, Torkel, *The Right to Life* in *The European System for the Protection of Human Rights* 207 (R. St J. Macdonald *et al* eds) (1993)

O'Reilly, Gregory W., *Criminal Law: England Limits the Right to Silence and Moves Towards an Inquisitorial System of Justice*, 85 Nw. J. Crim. L. and Criminology 402 (1994)

Partsch, K.J., *Experiences Regarding the War and Emergency Clause (Article 15) of the European Convention on Human Rights*, 1 Isr. Y. B. Hum. Rts 327 (1971)

Paust, Jordan J., *Law in a Guerrilla Conflict: Myths, Norms and Human Rights*, 3 Isr. Y. B. Hum. Rts 39 (1973)

Pictet, Jean S., *The Need to Restore the Laws and Customs Relating to Armed Conflicts*, 1 Rev. Int'l Comm'n. Jurists 22 (1969)

Porter, Harold, Jr., *The Lawless Case: A Beachhead for Civil Rights*, 49 A. B. A. J. 79 (1961)

Przetacznik, Franciszek, *The Right to Life as a Basic Human Right*, 9 Revue des Droits de L'Homme 585 (1976)

Quigley, John, *Israel's Forty-Five-Year Emergency: Are There Time Limits to Derogations from Human Rights Obligations?*, 15 Mich. J. Int'l L. 491 (1994)

Quinn, Thomas P., Jr., *Judicial Interpretation of Silence: The Criminal Evidence Order of 1988*, 26 Case W. Res. J. Int'l L. 365 (1994)

Ramcharan, B.G., *The Role of International Bodies in the Implementation and Enforcement of Humanitarian Law and Human Rights in Non-International Armed Conflicts*, 33 Am. U. L. Rev. 99 (1983)

Reidy, Aisling, Françoise Hampson and Kevin Boyle, *Gross Violations of Human Rights: Invoking the European Convention on Human Rights in the Case of Turkey*, 15 Neth. Q. H. Rts 161 (1997)

Reisman, W. Michael, *Has the International Court Exceeded Its Jurisdiction?*, 80 Am. J. Int'l L. 128 (1986)

Robertson, A.H., *The First Case Before the European Court of Human Rights – Lawless v. Ireland*, Brit. Y. B. Int'l L. 343 (1960)

Robertson, B., *Deadly Force and Riot Control in the UK*, Public Law 13 (1988)

Schachter, Oscar, *Towards a Theory of International Obligation*, 8 Va. J. Int'l L. 300 (1968)

———— *The Twilight Existence of Non-Binding International Agreements*, 71 Am. J. Int'l L. 296 (1987)

Schindler, Dietrich, *The Different Types of Armed Conflicts According to the Geneva Conventions and Protocols*, 163 Recueil des Cours 117 (1979–II)
———*International Humanitarian Law and Internationalized Internal Armed Conflict*, 230 Int'l Rev. Red Cross 225 (Sept.–Oct. 1982)
Schwarzenberger, Georg, *Jus Pacis ac Belli?*, 37 Am. J. Int'l L. 469 (1943)
———*International Jus Cogens*, 43 Tex. L. Rev. 455 (1965)
———*Human Rights and Guerrilla Warfare*, 1 Isr. Y. B. Hum. Rts 246 (1971)
Shelton, Dinah L., *Abortion and the Right to Life in the Inter-American System: The Case of 'Baby Boy'*, 2 Hum. Rts L. J. 309 (1981)
———*The Inter-American System for the Protection of Human Rights: Emerging Law* in *International Human Rights Law* 369 (Irwin Cotler and F. Pearl Eliadis eds) (1992)
Singer, Joel, *The West Bank and Gaza Strip: Phase Two*, 7 Justice 5 (Dec. 1995)
Smith, J.C., *The Right to Life and the Right to Kill in Law Enforcement*, 144 NLJ 354 (1994)
Sohn, Louis, *The Human Rights Law of the Charter*, 12 Tex. Int'l L. J. 129 (1977)
Solf, Waldemar A., *The Status of Combatants in Non-International Armed Conflicts Under Domestic Law and Transnational Practice*, 33 Am. U. L. Rev. 53 (1983)
Solf, Waldemar A. and George Grandison, *International Humanitarian Law Applicable in Armed Conflict*, 10 J. Int'l L. and Econ. 567 (1975)
Spjut, R.J., *The 'Official' Use of Deadly Force by the Security Forces Against Suspected Terrorists*, Public Law 38 (1986)
Stannard, John, *Lethal Force in Self-Defence*, NILQ 173 (1980)
Stoddard, Ellwyn E., *The Informal 'Code' of Police Deviancy: A Group Approach to Blue Coat Crime*, 59 J. Crim. L. Criminology and Police Science 201 (1968)
Stravos, Stephanos, *The Right to a Fair Trial in Emergency Situations*, 41 Int'l and Comp. L. Q. 342 (1992)
Street, H., *The Prevention of Terrorism (Temporary Provisions) Act 1974*, Crim. L. Rev. 196 (1974)
Twining, William, *Emergency Powers and Criminal Process: The Diplock Report*, Crim. L. Rev. 406 (1973)
Uelmen, G.F., *A Study of Police Policy Regarding the Use of Deadly Force in LA County*, 6 Loy. L. A. L. Rev. 1 (1973)
Veuthy, Michel, *Implementation and Enforcement of Humanitarian and Human Rights Law in Non-International Armed Conflicts: The Role of the ICRC*, 33 Am. U. L. Rev. 83 (1983)
Waddington, P.A.G., *Overkill or Minimum Force*, Crim. L. Rev. 685 (1990)
Walkate, Jaap A., *The Human Rights Committee and Public Emergencies*, 9 Yale J. World Pub. Ord. 134 (1982)
Walker, Clive, *Shooting to Kill – Some of the Issues in Farrell*, Md. L. Rev. 591 (1980)
———*Irish Republican Prisoners – Political Detainees, Prisoners of War or Common Criminals?*, XIX Ir. Jur. 189 (1984)
Walsh, Brian, *The European Court of Human Rights*, 2 Conn. J. Int'l L. 271 (1987)

Walsh, Dermot P.J., *The Impact of the Antisubversive Laws on Police Powers and Practices in Ireland: The Silent Erosion of Individual Freedom*, 62 Temple L. Rev. 1099 (1989)

Warbrick, Colin, *The European Convention on Human Rights and the Prevention of Terrorism*, 32 Int'l and Comp. L. Q. 82 (1983)

———— *The Prevention of Terrorism (Temporary Provisions) Act 1976 and the European Convention on Human Rights: The McVeigh Case*, 32 Int'l and Comp. L. Q. 557 (1983)

Watson, Cary S., *The European Convention on Human Rights and the British Courts*, 12 Tex. Int'l L. Rev. 61 (1977)

Wehbery, Hans, *Pacta Sunt Servanda*, 53 Am. J. Int'l L. 775 (1959)

Weiner, Robert and Fionnuala Ní Aoláin, *Beyond the Laws of War: Peacekeeping in Search of Legal Framework*, 27 Colum. Hum. Rts L. Rev. 293 (1996)

Weissbrodt, David and Beth Andrus, *The Right to Life During Armed Conflict*, 29 Harv. Int'l L. J. 59 (1988)

Weston, Burns *et al*, *Regional Human Rights Regimes: A Comparison and Appraisal*, 20 Vand. J. Transnat'l L. 585 (1987)

Wiebe, Virgil, *The Prevention of Civil Wars Through the Use of the Human Rights System*, 27 Int'l L. and Politics 437 (1985)

Williams, Glanville, *Measures Short of Arrest*, Crim. L. Rev. 590 (1954)

Cases

Aloeboetoe et al (Reparations), Judgment of 10 September, 1993, 1 I.H.R.R. 208, 213 (1994)

Attorney-General for Northern Ireland's Reference, [1977] AC 105

Badder, Menis, Meinhof and Grundman v. The Federal Republic of Germany, Application no. 6166/73, D.R. 2 at 58, 18 Y.B.E.C. 132 (1975)

Barcelona Traction, Light and Power Co. Ltd, ICJ Rep. (1970)

Bautista v. Colombia, Communication no. 563/1993 reprinted in 17 Hum. Rts L. J. 19 (1996)

Brannigan and McBride v. United Kingdom, 258 Eur. Ct. H. R. (ser. A) at 31 (1993)

Brogan and Others v. United Kingdom, 145B Eur. Ct. H. R. (ser. A) at 16 (1989)

Bruggeman and Scheusten, 12 July 1977, D & R 10 (1978) 116

Caballero-Delgado v. Colombia, Inter-Am. Ct. H. R., Judgment of 8 December, 1995, reprinted in 17 Hum. Rts L. J. 24 (1996)

Carmargo de Guerro v. Colombia, Communication no. R.11/45; Report of the Human Rights Committee, UN GAOR, 37th Sess., Supp. No. 40, Annex XI, at 137, UN Doc. A/37/40 (1982)

Compulsory Membership in an Association Prescribed by Law for the Practice of Journalism (Arts. 13 and 29 American Convention on Human Rights), 5 Inter-Am. Ct. H. R. (ser. A) (1985)

Consuelo Salgar de Montejo v. Colombia, Communication no. R.15/64; Report of the Human Rights Committee, UN GAOR, 37th Sess., Supp. No. 40, Annex XV, at 168, UN Doc. A/37/40 (1982)

Cyprus Case, 1958–59 Y. B. Eur. Conv. on H. R. 174 (Eur. Comm'n on H. R.)

Cyprus v. Turkey, Application nos 6780/74 and 6950/75, report of 10 July 1976

de Jong, Baljet and van den Brink v. Netherlands, 77 Eur. Ct. H. R. (ser. A) at 22–25 (1984)

Disabled People's International, Inter-Am. Ct. H. R., OAS Doc. OEA/Ser. L/V/II.67, doc. 6 (1986) (decision on admissibility)

Donnelly v. United Kingdom, Application nos 5577/72–5533/72, Collection of Decisions 122 (1973); decision on admissibility, 5 April 1973

Dudgeon v. United Kingdom, 45 Eur Ct. H. R. (ser. A) (1980)

Egan v. Macready (1921) 1 IR 265

Ensslin, Badder and Raspe v. The Federal Republic of Germany, Application nos 7572/76, 7586/76 and 7587/76

Ex parte Briand (1991) 1 All E.R. 720

Fairen Garbi and Soris Corrales Case (ser. C) No. 6 (1989) (judgment)

Farrell v. MoD (1980) WLR 172

Farrell v. United Kingdom, No. 9013/80 (December 1982) 30 D & R 96 (1982)

Godinez Cruz Case, Inter-Am. Ct. H. R. (ser. C) No. 5 (1989) (judgment)

Golder v. United Kingdom, 18 Eur. Ct. H. R. (ser. A) at 17 (1975)

Habeas Corpus in Emergency Situations, 8 Inter-Am. Ct. H. R. (ser. A) at 33, OEA/Ser. L/V/ 111.17, doc. 13 (1987)

Handyside v. United Kingdom, 24 Eur. Ct. H. R. (ser. A) (1976)

Herrere Rubio v. Colombia, Communication no. 161/1983, Doc. A/43/40 at 190

Hughes v. Casares (1967) 111 Sol. Jo. 637

Hume v. Londonderry Justices (1972) NILR 91

Inhabitants of Alsember and Beersel, Kraainem, Antwerp and Environs, Ghent and Environs, Louvain and Environs, and Vilvorde v. Belgium, 4 Eur. Ct. H. R. (ser. A) (1967) ('Belgium Linguistic Case [No. 1]')

Ireland v. United Kingdom, 1976 Y. B. Eur. Conv. on H. R. 512, 516, 518 (Eur. Comm'n on H. R.)

Ireland v. United Kingdom, 25 Eur. Ct. H. R. (ser. A) (1978)

Jaona v. Madagascar, Communication no. 132/1982, Report of the Human Rights Committee, UN GAOR, 40th Sess., Supp. No. 40, Annex IX, at 179, UN Doc. A/40/40 (1985)

Judicial Guarantees in States of Emergency (Arts. 27[2], 25 and 8 American Convention on Human Rights), 9 Inter-Am. Ct. H. R. (ser. A) at 40, OEA/ser. L./VI/111.9, doc. 13 (1987)

Kelly v. MoD (1989) NI 341

Kelly v. United Kingdom (No. 17579/90), 74 D & R 139 (1993)

Klass v. Germany, 28 Eur. Ct. H. R. (ser. A) at 5 (1978)

Korematsu v. United States, 323 US 214 (1944)

Landinelli Silva et al v. Uruguay, Communication no. 34/1978, *in* Selected Decisions of the Human Rights Committee Under the Optional Protocol 65–66 (1985)

Lawless v. Ireland, 1 Eur. Ct. H. R. (ser. A) at 55

Legality of the Threat or Use of Nuclear Weapons, International Court of Justice, Advisory Opinion of 8 July 1996

Lynch v. MoD (1983) 2 NIJB

McCann, Farrell and Savage v. United Kingdom, Case 17/1994/464/545, Application no. 18984/91

McEldowney v. Forde (1970) NILR 11

McFeeley et al v. United Kingdom, Application no. 8317/78 (1980) 3 EHRR 161

McGlinchy v. Wren (1982) IR 154

McLaughlin v. MoD (1977) unreported

Magill v. MoD (1987) NIJB

Marbary v. Madison, 5 US (1 Cranch) 137 (1803)

Marckx v. Belgium, 29 Eur. Ct. H. R. (ser. A) (1980)

Military and Paramilitary Activities in and against Nicaragua (Nicaragua v. United States) (Merits), 1986 ICJ Rep. 14 (Judgment of 27 June)

Military Prosecutor v. Kassem, as reviewed in 65 Am. J. Int'l L. 409 (1971)

Mitchelstown Inquisition (1882) 22 LR IR 279

Mohamed Ali and Another v. Public Prosecutor (1986) 3 All E.R. 488

Mojica v. The Dominican Republic, Communication no. 449/1991, reprinted in 17 Hum. Rts L. J. 18 (1996)

Mrs W v. United Kingdom, 32 D & G 190

Neira Alegria et al v. Peru, Judgment of 19 January 1995, reported in 2 Neth. Hum. Rts Q. 224 (1996)

Paton v. United Kingdom (1980) 3 EHRR 408

Phillips v. Eyre (1870) LR 6 QB 1

Prosecutor v. Tadic, Case IT-94-1-T, Decision on Jurisdiction (10 August 1995)

Prosecutor v. Tadic, Case IT-94-1-AR72, Appeal on Jurisdiction (2 October 1995)

Quinn v. Robinson, 783 F.2d 776 (9th Cir. 1986)

Quinteros (María del Carmen Almeida de) v. Uruguay, Communication no. 107/1981, Report of the Human Rights Committee, UN GAOR, 38th Sess., Supp. No. 40, Annex XXII, at 216, UN Doc. A/38/40 (1983)

R v. Bailey and Jones, 8 September 1983 (unreported)

R v. Bohan and Temperley (1979) NIJB 1

R v. Foxford, NI 181 (1974)

R v. Timothy Hanley (unreported)

R v. Roy Alun Jones (1975) 2 NIJB 1

R v. McNaughton (1975) NI 203

Re Breslin Application (1987) 10 NIJB 16

Re Gillen Application (1988) 10 NIJB 48

Re Keenan, [1971] 3 All E.R. 883

Rees v. United Kingdom, 106 Eur. Ct. H. R. (ser. A) (1986)

Reference Under s.48A of the Criminal Appeal (Northern Ireland) Act 1968 (No. 1 1975) [1977] AC 105

Restrictions to the Death Penalty, Advisory Opinion OC-3/83, 8 September 1983, reprinted in 4 Hum. Rts L. J. 339 (1983)

Schonenberger and Durmaz v. Switzerland (1988) 11 EHRR 202

Shannon v. Fanning (1984) 8 BNIL 43

Stewart v. United Kingdom (No. 10044/82) 39 D & R 162 (1984)

The Sunday Times v. United Kingdom, 30 Eur. Ct. H. R. (ser. A) (1979)

Tellis and Others v. Bombay Municipal Corporation (1987) LRC 351

Tyrer v. United Kingdom, 26 Eur. Ct. H. R. (ser. A) (1978)

United States v. Carolene Products Co., 304 US (1938)

Valasquez Rodiguez Case, Inter-Am. Ct. H. R., Preliminary Objections (Government of Honduras), judgment of 26 June 1987 (1987) Inter-Am. Y. B. Hum. Rts at 807

Wemhoff v. The Federal Republic of Germany, 6 Eur. Ct. H. R. (ser. A) (1968)

X v. Belgium, 1961 Y. B. Eur. Conv. on H. R. (Eur. Comm'n on H. R.) 224

X v. The Federal Republic of Germany, Application 5207/71, Yearbook XIV 698 (1971)

X v. Ireland, Application 6040/73, 16 Y. B. 388 (1973)

X v. Netherlands, 1966 Y. B. Eur. Conv. on H. R. (Eur. Comm'n on H. R.) 565

X v. United Kingdom, Application 8416/79, D & R 19 (1980) 244 (249–250)

Reports and other

Americas Watch, *Chile Since the Coup: Ten Years of Repression* (1983)
———— *Human Rights in Nicaragua 1985–87* (1987)
———— *Truth and Partial Justice in Argentina* (1987)   .

Amnesty International, *Nicaragua: The Human Rights Record* (1986)
———— *Political Killings in Northern Ireland* (1994)

Committee on the Administration of Justice, *Adding Insult to Injury? Allegations of Harassment and the Use of Lethal Force by the Security Forces in Northern Ireland* (1993)

Consideration of Reports Submitted by State Parties Under Article 40 of the Covenant, UN Human Rights Committee, 4th Sess., UN Doc. CCPR/C/1/ Add. 25 (1978)

Daes, Eric-Irene, *The Individual's Duties to the Community and the Limitations on Human Rights and Freedoms under Article 29 of the Universal Declaration of Human Rights,* UN Doc. E/CN 4/Sub. 2/ 432/Rev. 2 (1983)

Despouy, L., *First Annual Report and List of States which Since 1.1.1985 Have Proclaimed, Extended or Terminated State of Emergency,* E Cn. 4/Sub. 2/1987/19 (18 August 1987)

Fourth Periodic Report by the United Kingdom of Great Britain and Northern Ireland to the Human Rights Committee Under Article 40 of the International Covenant on Civil and Political Rights, UN Human Rights Committee, 3rd Sess., UN Doc. CCPR/C/1/Add. 17 (1977)

Gormally, Brian and Kieran McEvoy, *Release and Reintegration of Politically Motivated Prisoners in Northern Ireland* (1995)

Guidelines for Bodies Monitoring Respect for Human Rights During States of Emergency, 85 Am. J. Int'l L. 717 (1991) ('Queensland Guidelines')

Helsinki Watch, *Human Rights in Northern Ireland* (1993)

IACHR, *Annual Report 1985–86,* OEA/Ser. L/V/II.68, Doc. 8, rev. 1

———— *Annual Report 1986–87,* OEA/Ser. L/V/II.71, Doc. 9, rev. 1

International Commission of Jurists, *States of Emergency: Their Impact on Human Rights* (1983)

———— *The Failed Promise: Human Rights in the Philippines Since the Revolution of 1986* (1991)

International Law Association, *Report of the 64th Conference Held at Queensland* (1990)

———— *Second Interim Report of the Committee on the Enforcement of Human Rights Law* (1988) ('Warsaw Report'), 85 Am. J. Int'l L. (1991)

Lawyers Committee for Human Rights, *Uruguay: The End of a Nightmare?* (1984)

———— *Colombia: Public Order, Private Injustice* (1994)

New Ireland Forum, *The Cost of Violence Arising from the Northern Ireland Crisis Since 1969* (1984)

Oslo Statement on Norms and Procedures in Times of Public Emergency or Internal Violence, reprinted in UN Doc. E/CN. 4/Sub. 2/1987/31 (1987)

Report of the Commission of International Jurists on the Administration of Justice in Peru (30 November 1993)

Report of the Commission to Consider Legal Procedures to Deal with Terrorist Activities in Northern Ireland, para 1, Cmnd. 5185, London, HMSO, 1972 ('Diplock Report')

Report of a Committee to Consider, in the Context of Civil Liberties and Human Rights, Measures to Deal with Terrorism in Northern Ireland (1975) ('Gardiner Report')

Report of the Committee of Inquiry into Police Interrogation Procedures in Northern Ireland, Cmnd. 7497, London, HMSO (1979) ('Bennett Report')

Report of the Human Rights Committee, General Assembly, Official Records, 34th Sess., Supp. No. 40 (A/30/40), United Nations, § 73, p. 18 (report of Chile)

Report of the Human Rights Committee, 34 UN GAOR Supp. No. 40, UN Doc. A/34/40 (1979) § 383 (Consideration of Reports)

Report of the Human Rights Committee, UN GAOR, 36th Sess., Supp. No. 40, Annex VII, at 110, UN Doc. A/36/40 (1981)

Report of the Human Rights Committee, UN GAOR, 37th Sess., Supp. No. 40, at 58, UN Doc. A/37/40 (1982)

Report of the Secretary-General on the United Nations Observer Mission in El Salvador, S/1994/375 (31 March 1994)

Report on the Situation of Human Rights in El Salvador, OEA/Ser. L./V/11.46, doc. 23 rev. 1 (1978)

Report of the Situation of Human Rights in Panama, OEA/Ser. L/V/II.44 doc. 38, rev. 1 (1978)

Report on the Situation of Human Rights in the Republic of Colombia, Inter-American Commission of Human Rights, OEA/Ser. L./V/11.53, doc. 22 (30 June 1981)

Report of the Situation of Human Rights in the Republic of Nicaragua, OEA/Ser. L/V/II.44, doc. 38, rev. 1 (1978)

Respect for Human Rights in Armed Conflict: Report of the Secretary-General, UN GAOR, 24th Sess., Agenda Item 61, at 12 ss 24, UN Doc. A17720 (1969)

Review of the Northern Ireland (Emergency Provisions) Act 1991 by J.J. Rowe QC (17 February 1995)

Review of the Operation of the Prevention of Terrorism (Temporary Provisions) Act 1976, Cmnd. 8803, London, HMSO

Review of the Operation of the Prevention of Terrorism (Temporary Provisions) Act 1984, Cmnd. 264, London, HMSO, 1987 ('Colville Report')

Siracusa Principles on the Limitation and Derogation Provisions in the International Covenant on Civil and Political Rights (1984), reprinted in 7 Hum. Rts Q. 3 (1985) ('Siracusa Principles')

Study on the Implications for Human Rights of Recent Developments Concerning Situations Known as States of Siege or Emergency, UN Commission on Human Rights, 35th Sess., Agenda Item 10, UN Doc. E/CN. 4/Sub. 2/ 15 (1982) ('Questiaux Report')

Summary Record of the 221st Meeting, UN Human Rights Committee, 10th Sess., UN Doc./ CCPR/C/1/SR.221 (1980)

Turku Abu Declaration of Minimum Humanitarian Standards, reprinted in 85 Am. J. Int'l L. 375 (1991)

Index